Ms. Sybil L. Keith
611 3rd St. #3
Traverse City, MI 49684-2262

W9-DGA-141

Cupboard Love

CUPBOARD LOVE
A Dictionary of
Culinary Curiosities

~

MARK MORTON

Bain & Cox, Publishers
Winnipeg

Cupboard Love: A Dictionary of Culinary Curiosities
first published 1996 by Bain & Cox, Publishers
an imprint of Blizzard Publishing
73 Furby Street, Winnipeg, Canada R3C 2A2
© 1996 Mark Morton

Cover art by Joseph Cannizzaro.
Printed in Canada by Friesens.

Published with the assistance of
the Canada Council and the Manitoba Arts Council.

Canadian Cataloguing in Publication Data

Morton, Mark Steven, 1963–
  Cupboard love
  ISBN 0-921368-66-6
1. Cookery – Dictionaries. I. Title.
TX349.M67 1996   641.5'03   C96-920067-6

For my parents
David and Lois Morton

"That's enough to begin with," Humpty Dumpty interrupted: "there are plenty of hard words there. 'Brillig' means four o'clock in the afternoon—the time when you begin *broiling* things for dinner."

"That'll do very well," said Alice: "and 'slithy'?"

"Well, 'slithy' means 'lithe and slimy.' 'Lithe' is the same as 'active.' You see it's like a portmanteau—there are two meanings packed up into one word."

"I see it now," Alice remarked thoughtfully: "and what are 'toves'?"

"Well, 'toves' are something like badgers—they're something like lizards—and they're something like corkscrews."

"They must be very curious creatures."

"They are that," said Humpty Dumpty: "also they make their nests under sundials—also they live on cheese."

Lewis Carroll,
Through the Looking-Glass

Acknowledgements

Special thanks go to those who have shared, encouraged, or expressed concern for my obsession with words: Charmagne Reimer, Craig Terlson, Esmé Keith, Rob Glen, Ken Stevens, Elyse Friedman, Jeff Goodes, Sue Sorensen, Kathryn Antenbring, Alison Hanks, Janet Dirks, Melanie Sherwood, Lisa Elaschuk, Laurie Barron, Dave Moulden, Sandy Thacker, Keran Sanders, Neil Besner, Farley Mowat, Randy Bangsund, and one other.

I would like to thank the Manitoba Arts Council for its support during the writing of this book. As well, several members of the Department of Classics at the University of Winnipeg—Jane Cahill, Mark Golden, Craig Cooper, and Iain McDougall—offered numerous helpful suggestions regarding Greek and Latin sources, as did Megumi Saunders regarding Japanese sources. The reference librarians of the University of Winnipeg—Linwood DeLong and Sandra Zuk—were of great assistance in helping me access reference books. Individuals who read my manuscript and made invaluable suggestions include Esmé Keith, Nicola Schaefer, Peter Atwood, Anna Synenko and Todd Scarth. Any errors or infelicities that persist in this dictionary are solely the result of my own blockheadedness.

—M.M.

Preface

~

I'm not a linguist and I don't play one on TV. I do, however, have a linguist's fascination with language, especially with where words came from. I also have an abiding preoccupation with food, having devoutly consumed that substance everyday for the last 32 years. Out of these two interests grew this book, an etymological dictionary of food words and culinary terms.

Etymologists, as you may already know, do not study bugs—that's what entomologist do. Etymologists try to trace the history of words back to their origins, noting shifts in pronunciation, spelling, and meaning. Etymologists do this not because it promotes world peace or because it gets people to the moon, but simply because it is darn fascinating. For instance, who would have thought that the word *baguette* is related to the word *bacteria*? That *soufflé* is a cousin of *flatulence*? That *canapé* derives from the Greek word for *mosquito*? That *ravioli* means *little turnip*? That *pudding prick* is an obsolete name for a kitchen utensil? Such delicious tidbits of knowledge lie ahead.

But first, let me provide some background for the entries in this dictionary.

Most of the 500,000 words in the English language evolved from a language that existed about 8000 years ago in a region north of the Black Sea. This ancient language—which I refer to as Indo-European—gave rise to several language "branches," including Celtic, Indo-Iranian, Slavic, Baltic, Greek, Italic, and

Germanic. In turn, each of these branches gave rise to numerous languages, many of which still exist but some of which are now extinct. From the Celtic branch arose Irish, Gaelic, Welsh, and Breton; from the Indo-Iranian branch arose Sanskrit, Urdu, Hindi, and Persian; from the Slavic branch arose Russian, Polish, and Czech; from the Baltic branch arose Lithuanian and Latvian; from the Hellenic branch arose Greek; from the Italic branch arose the language of ancient Rome—Latin—which in turn gave rise to French, Italian, Portuguese, Rumanian, and Spanish; and from the Germanic branch arose an East Germanic "twig" that gave rise to Gothic, a North Germanic "twig" that gave rise to Swedish, Danish, Norwegian, and Icelandic, and a West Germanic "twig" that gave rise to German, Flemish, Frisian, Dutch, and—in the middle of the fifth century A.D.—English.

The middle of the fifth century is when English emerged because it was then that several Germanic tribes left the northeastern corner of the European mainland, crossed the English Channel, and settled in what is now called England. The language of these Germanic tribes became Old English, which changed enormously over the following centuries, becoming Middle English then Modern English, thanks to its exposure to other languages from which it borrowed vocabulary. For instance, in the seventh century, English adopted a few Latin words from the Christian missionaries who had arrived from Rome. From the eighth century to the tenth century, English adopted numerous Scandinavian words from the Vikings who invaded their shores. From the eleventh century to the sixteenth century, English borrowed thousands of French words due to the conquest of England by the Normans. During the sixteenth and seventeenth centuries, English borrowed hundreds of words from Latin and Greek thanks to the revival of classical learning that occurred during the Renaissance. From the sixteenth century onward, English took hundreds of words from dozens of languages spoken in the diverse lands the British began to explore or colonize.

In each entry in this dictionary, I have attempted to accurately describe the history of a word while at the same time avoiding needless, distracting complexity. I have, for example, used the term *Indo-European* simply because the more precise and scholarly *Proto-*

Indo-European is such a mouthful. As well, when referring to words whose existence is only hypothetical—for example, to a prehistoric source whose unrecorded form has been reconstructed by experts— I have not observed the scholarly convention of marking such forms with an asterisk. Instead, I have tried to suggest the hypothetical status of such words by introducing them with a qualifying phrase such as "pronounced something like" as in "The Indo-European source of *clove* was pronounced something like *gleubh*." As well, I have generally avoided specifying precise stages in languages—such as Old French or Middle German—unless that information is particularly pertinent and cannot be inferred from the context; for example, instead of writing "In the fourteenth century Middle English borrowed the word *chich* from Old French," I have written "In the fourteenth century English borrowed the word *chich* from French." I do, however, distinguish Latin—meaning Classical Latin—from Vulgar Latin and Medieval Latin. I might also note that I use *English* to mean *the English language*, and that I use *the English* to denote the people of England. Lastly, I should add that when I refer to a word's appearance in English, I mean its earliest recorded appearance in *written* English, since records of spoken English date back only to 1877 when Thomas Edison invented the phonograph.

I selected each of the thousand entries in this dictionary for one of three reasons. First, I tried to include all food words or culinary terms that are familar to anyone who has spent time in a kitchen, words such as *cup* and *bread* and *potato*. Second, I included a wide variety of less familiar words whose origins are especially strange or delightful, such as *gyro*, *Cecils*, and *nosh*. Third, I include a smattering of words that simply sound bizarre, such as *blobsterdis*, *wow-wow*, *piccalilli*, and *bouce Jane*. Undoubtedly, many fascinating words have been overlooked, and the reader is enthusiastically invited to suggest additions to this dictionary by contacting me through the book's publisher or via email. My email address is *morton@io.uwinnipeg.ca* and my World Wide Web address is *http://www.uwinnipeg.ca/~caw/ mark.htm*.

Finally, I would like to briefly acknowledge the reference works that I found most useful and consulted most often as I researched and wrote this dictionary. For etymological information, my most important source was by far the *Oxford English Dictionary on Compact Disc*. I also made great use of John Ayto's *Dictionary of Word Origins*, Ernest Weekley's *Etymological Dictionary of Modern English*, Eric Partridge's *Origins: An Etymological Dictionary of Modern English*, Joseph Shipley's *Dictionary of Word Origins*, William and Mary Morris's *Dictionary of Word and Phrase Origins*, Mario Pei and Salvatore Ramondino's *Dictionary of Foreign Terms*, Hugh Rawson's *Devious Derivations*, Nigel Rees's *Dictionary of Word and Phrase Origins*, Wilfred Funk's *Word Origins*, Walter Skeat's *Concise Etymological Dictionary of the English Language*, Morton S. Freeman's *Hue and Cry and Humble Pie*, *Brewer's Dictionary of Names* edited by Adrian Room, *Brewer's Concise Dictionary of Phrase and Fable* edited by Betty Kirkpatrick, *The Random House Dictionary of the English Language* edited by Stuart Berg Flexner, and *The American Heritage Dictionary* edited by William Morris. For information regarding culinary matters, I returned again and again to *Larousse Gastronomique* originally written by Prosper Montagné in 1938 and recently updated by a host of food experts. Other sources that I consulted for culinary or cultural information include *A Dictionary of Cooking* by Ralph De Sola, *The Dictionary of American Food and Drink* by John F. Mariani, *The English Table in History and Literature* by Charles Cooper, *Concise Encyclopedia of Gastronomy* by André L. Simon, *Much Depends on Dinner* and *The Rituals of Dinner* by Margaret Visser, and *The New York Times Food Encyclopedia* by Craig Claibourne. For clarification or confirmation of matters further afield—such as the location of Cayenne Island—I frequently employed *The Encyclopedia Britannica Online*. Dozens of other sources, too numerous to list, were used incidentally as the need arose.

—Mark Morton, 1996

à la

À la is a two-word French phrase that can only be translated into English by using twice as many words: *in the style of*. In the late sixteenth century, English speakers and writers borrowed the French phrase and began to insert it into English sentences. By the late seventeenth century, as French cuisine grew more popular in Britain, phrases such as *à la roi*, *à la meunière*, and *à la mode* had become *de rigueur* in upper-class English cookbooks.

à la carte

See *table d'hôte*.

à la king

In the seventeenth century, English chefs borrowed the French phrase *à la roi*—*roi* being the French word for *king*—and applied it to certain fancy dishes such as *mutton à la roi*. The culinary phrase *à la king*, which did not become common until this century, might appear to be a direct translation of *à la roi*, but in fact it has another origin: it likely comes from Clark King, a New York hotelier, who around 1915 had the distinction of having the dish known as *chicken à la king* named after him.

à la meunière

Literally meaning *in the style of a miller's wife*, the French phrase *à la meunière* refers to a dish made by rolling fish in flour and then cooking it in butter. Although some people have assumed that this method of cooking was named after millers' wives because it, like them, is simple and easy, a more probable connection is that millers' wives had easy access to the freshly milled flour that their husbands produced.

à point

See *done to a turn.*

aam

Only ten of the 290,500 headwords in the Oxford English Dictionary begin with a double *a*, and *aam* is one of them. This peculiar-looking word was borrowed from Dutch in the sixteenth century not by devious Scrabble players, but by merchants who imported Rhenish wine into England: an *aam* of wine was a cask measuring thirty-seven gallons in some European cities and forty-one gallons in others. Although the four-gallon variation between one city's aam and another city's aam might seem to suggest a rather lackadaisical approach to international trade, the difference is proportionally smaller than the one that exists between the U.S. quart and the Imperial quart still used in Canada. Further back in its history, the word *aam* represented a much more approximate measure: *hama*, the Latin word from which *aam* derived, simply meant *water-bucket*, as did the ancient Greek *ame*.

abalone

Although pronounced the same, abalone and a baloney—as in "a baloney sandwich"—are completely different foods: far from being a congealed paste of ground-up livestock, an abalone is an edible mollusk found off the coast of California. English borrowed the name of this mollusk in the mid nineteenth century from Spanish Americans, who in turn had previously taken the word from the Monterey Indian language. The scientific name for this mollusk is Haliotis, a Greek compound meaning *sea-ear*, so named because the abalone shell is shaped like the human ear; *ear-shell*, in fact, is a common, alternative name for the abalone.

abat-faim

This French term literally means *hunger beater*, and refers to the first dish served to guests to allay the grumblings of their stomachs. The word is now obsolete, having been supplanted by *hors-d'oeuvre* in French and *appetizer* in English. *Abat-faim* and *appetizer* possess slightly different connotations, however, in that the former suggests beating the hunger down, whereas the latter implies raising the appetite up.

abattoir

An abattoir is the same as a slaughterhouse, a place where livestock are killed and turned into carcasses for the butcher. Both words, *abattoir* and *slaughterhouse*, have origins that reflect the brutal but effective method by which livestock were originally made into "dead-stock": they were beaten over the head with a club. With *abattoir* that grisly fate is evident in the word's Latin source, *battuere*, meaning *to beat*; in Medieval Latin, this word developed into *battere*, which Old French adopted as *abattre*, the added *a* at the beginning of the word being the French preposition meaning *to*. The verb *abattre* was then turned into the noun *abattoir* before being adopted by English in the early nineteenth century. Similarly, with *slaughterhouse*, the grisly fate of the butchered animal is evident in the Old English source of *slaughter*: *slean*, also meaning *to beat*. Words closely related to *slaughter* include *onslaught*, *slay*, and *sledge* (as in *sledge-hammer*); words related to *abattoir* include *battle*, *debate* (literally meaning *to beat down*), and *combat* (literally meaning *to battle together*).

abesse

For a very brief period in the early eighteenth century, the word *abesse* was used as a name for any thin sheet of rolled-out pastry. The English word developed from the French name for thin pastry, *abaisse*, which in turn derived from the French verb *abaisser*, meaning *to reduce*. However, whereas the French term *abaisse* continues to be used in France, its English counterpart, *abesse*,

---

died a quick death and has now been obsolete for almost three centuries. The differing fates of the two words may simply reflect a greater love among the French people for pastries. However, it is also possible that *abesse* never really caught on as an English culinary term because the upper-crust British, schooled in Latin, may have associated the pastry's name with the Latin word *abesse* that happens to be spelt the same way. Such a confusion would have been unfortunate for the pastry, because the Latin *abesse*, literally meaning *to be absent*, was sometimes construed as meaning *to be deficient in being*, which had long been a theological definition of evil. The sixteenth-century poet Edmund Spenser, for instance, gave the name *Abessa* to one of his allegorical characters in *The Faerie Queene* in order to emphasize her spiritual depravity. If the culinary *abesse* and the theological *abesse* were indeed confused with one another, then the upshot was that the English language deprived itself of a useful name for a thin sheet of rolled-out pastry.

abligurition

When you squander your money on treats, dainties, and comfort foods, you are engaging in abligurition, a word used during the eighteenth century but now obsolete. *Abligurition* derives from two Latin words: *ab*, meaning *away*, and *ligurire*, meaning *to eat delicately*. In turn, *ligurire* derives from *lingere*, an older Latin word meaning *to lick*, one that is also represented in the last half of *cunnilingus*. Literally, therefore, abligurition is the act of licking something till it is gone. See also *catillation*.

abominable things

There are many things that you might not want to eat, but in the Old Testament there is also a list of "abominable things" you are forbidden to eat. Deuteronomy, chapter fourteen, says that you may eat animals that chew the cud and also have a cloven hoof; however, you may not eat animals that chew the cud but do not have a cloven hoof; likewise, you may not eat animals that have a cloven hoof but do not chew the cud. In effect, these rules mean that you may not eat camels, hares, rock-badgers, or pigs. Other abominable and therefore forbidden menu items include teeming insects and several species of birds such as the ossifrage and the hoopoe (the ossifrage is an eagle whose name derives from the Latin *ossifragus*, meaning *bone breaker*; the hoopoe gets its name from its call). Deuteronomy also specifies—just in case you ever fancy doing this—that you may not boil the kid of a goat in the milk of its mother. The word *abominable*, by the way, comes from two Latin words: *ab*, meaning *away from*, and *omen*, meaning *a supernatural warning*: if an ancient Roman bumped into something *abominable*, it was a warning that she should gingerly sneak away from it. From the fourteenth to the seventeenth century, however, scholars mistakenly believed that *abominable* derived not from *ab* and *omen* but from *ab* and *homine*, the word *homine* being a declension of the Latin *homo*, meaning *human*. These misguided scholars assumed, in other words, that *abominable* described something *away from the nature of a human*, and for a long time they even spelt the word with an *h* as *abhominable*.

acetabulum

In the New Testament, the Gospel of John recounts how Jesus, just before he died, cried out, "I am thirsty," causing one of the spectators, perhaps a Roman soldier, to dip a sponge into a nearby jar of vinegar-water, which he then held to Jesus's mouth. To us, the soldier's offer of vinegar may seem like a cruel joke; however, the Romans themselves often drank a mixture of vinegar and water, and they even had a special name for the jar containing this bitter beverage. This name, *acetabulum*, is formed from *acetum*, the Latin word for *vinegar*, and *abulum*, a Latin suffix denoting a small vessel. Today, such a vessel is called a *cruet*, not an *acetabulum*, but the word still survives in a completely different context: physicians call the socket of your thigh bone the *acetabulum* because of its cup-like shape. Closely related to *acetabulum* are the words *acetar*, a now-defunct English name for a salad made with vinegar dressing, and *acetic*, as in *acetic acid*, the scientific name for vinegar. A more distant relative to these words is *acid*, which derived, like *acetum*, from the Latin word *acere*, meaning *to be sharp*.

Adam's ale

In Eden, the only ale that Adam had or wanted was water, so *Adam's ale* became, in the seventeenth century, a humorous name for drinking-water; in Scotland the term *Adam's wine* is used. Adam's name appears also in *Adam's apple*, a phrase bestowed upon both the human larynx and upon the sour fruit better known as the *bergamot*. According to folklore, the bump in the human throat was created when a piece of the forbidden fruit got lodged in Adam's throat; the bergamot, on the other hand, has indentations upon its surface once thought to represent the teeth marks of Adam.

agape

An agape was a frugal meal that the early Christians ate together to symbolize their ideals of charity and sharing, and to commemorate the last supper of Jesus and his disciples. Appropriately enough, *agape*, usually pronounced to rhyme with *bag a pay*, is a Greek word meaning *love*. It did not take long, however, for the agape meal to degenerate from a frugal celebration of love and sharing to an exercise in extravagance: by the fourth century, the typical agape had become such a banquet of excess that St. Augustine chastised those who celebrated it, and a Papal council was convened to forbid the feast from being celebrated in churches. The Eucharist—the Christian sacrament of eating and drinking consecrated bread and wine—is a vestige of the original agape celebration.

agnelotti

See *ravioli*.

al dente

A dentist looks after teeth, a trident is an ancient weapon with three teeth, you indent a paragraph when you take a "bite" out of the first line, and *al dente* means that you have cooked pasta or vegetables so that they are tender but still firm "to the tooth." English borrowed this Italian phrase in 1935; five years later Italy declared war on Britain.

~

alcarraza

When an athlete exercises, she sweats so that the droplets of salty water on her skin will carry away heat as they evaporate. The same principle cools water in the Arabic vessel known as the *alcarraza*, a pitcher made of porous earthenware: while suspended in a shady, draughty location, a small amount of the water in the vessel oozes through its surface and evaporates, thus cooling the remaining contents. Likewise, before the advent of refrigeration in America, a household jar of lemonade was often kept cool by swaddling it in a damp cloth. The word *alcarraza*—which in Arabic literally means *the pitcher*—was adopted into English in the early nineteenth century.

all nations

This eighteenth-century drinking term referred to the insalubrious potion which servants in public drinking houses concocted by emptying their patrons' unfinished beverages into a single large vessel. Drinking the resulting mixture of wine, beer, spirits, and phlegm after the patrons had left for the night was one of the perks of being a public-house servant. *All nations* took its name from the fact that the various liquors it contained had indeed been imported from around the world.

alliaceous

In botany, the Latin word *allium* refers to a genus of plants that includes garlic, onions, and leeks. *Alliaceous*—pronounced *alley ay shus*—is the adjective formed from this Latin word and it can be applied to anything, including food or breath, that smells of garlic or onions. In the Middle Ages in southern Europe, food tended to be alliaceous because garlic helped disguise the fact that warm temperatures had turned some of the ingredients bad.

allspice

Allspice acquired its name in the early seventeenth century when someone noticed that its flavour and scent resemble a mixture of cloves, nutmeg, and cinnamon—obviously these three do not encompass all 250 spices in existence, but close enough. Another plant whose name derives in part from the word *all* is *allbone*, an

---

herb whose spiny, jointed stalk makes it resemble a human skeleton. *Alligator*, however, does not mean *all gators*, but instead derives from a Spanish source meaning *the lizard*.

almond

Most people do not pronounce the *l* in *almond* and they are right not to do so because the *l* should not really be there. In Latin, the word was originally spelt *amygdala*, which in Late Latin became *amandula*. This Late Latin word slowly worked its way into Romance languages like French, Italian, and Spanish, but as this occurred people made the mistake of thinking that *amandula*— like *algebra*, *alchemy*, and *alcove*—was Arabic in origin. As a result, they assumed that the letter *a* at the beginning of *amandula* was actually a remnant of the Arabic definite article *al*, meaning *the*, and that the *mandula* part meant something like *nut*. Having made this assumption, Italians chose to drop what they supposed was a superfluous article and started spelling the word *mandola*. The French and Spanish made the same false assumption, but acted on it differently: they "fixed" the word by adding the supposedly missing *l* and ended up with *almande* in French and *almendra* in Spanish. Later the French changed their mind and dropped the *l*—so the French word is presently spelt *amande*—but not before the English had already borrowed the word from them. Accordingly, *almond* is still spelt with an *l* in English. See also *Jordan almond*.

amaretto

See *maraschino cherry*.

ambergris

Ambergris is a waxy substance, grey in colour, secreted in the intestines of sperm whales and skimmed from the surface of the ocean where it floats after being discharged. The fact that medieval cooks used this substance as a spice in ragouts, custards, and jams says much about their sense of adventure, if not their sense of taste. In origin, the word *ambergris* derives ultimately from the ancient Arabic name for this whale secretion, *anbar*. The ancient Romans adopted this term as *ambar*, which in turn developed into the French *amber*. For centuries, the French used the word *amber* to refer only to the edible whale secretion; eventually, however, the French also bestowed the name *amber* on the sticky resin exuded by trees, a resin that somewhat resembles the whale secretion. In time, though, it became confusing to have one word (*amber*) refer to two utterly different substances (tree resin and the intestinal discharge of whales), so the French renamed the whale secretion *ambergris*, meaning *grey amber*. It was this form, *ambergris*, that English adopted in the fifteenth century. Although it seems obvious that *ambergris* is simply French for *grey amber*, this self-evident origin was overlooked by seventeenth-century etymologists who mistakenly surmised that *ambergris* derived from *amber grease* (the substance being greasy in texture) or even from *amber Greece* (as if it were skimmed off the waters around Greece).

ambrosia

Life was much simpler for the gods of ancient Greece, who had to worry about a mere two food groups, ambrosia and nectar, when trying to satisfy their daily recommended dietary allowance. These two divine substances were not only exceedingly yummy— Ibycus, an ancient Greek poet, wrote that ambrosia was nine times sweeter than honey—they also conferred immortality on all who partook of them, even the occasional human, such as Adonis. Originally, ambrosia and nectar differed from each other in that the former was a solid food, while the latter was liquid; however, in the sixteenth century the two substances were briefly confused with one another—and they also declined in status—so that *nectar* came to be used as the name of light, refined bread served at tea-time and *ambrosia* became the name of a sugary wine served with dessert. In origin, the word *ambrosia* probably derives from the Greek prefix *a*, meaning *not*, and the Greek word *brotos*, meaning *mortal*, together suggesting the food's life-sustaining power. Similarly, *nectar* appears to have originated as a compound deriving from the Greek *nekros*, meaning *dead*, and *tar*, a suffix meaning *victorious*. The name implies, therefore, that the drink will allow the imbiber to triumph over death. See also *nectarine*.

amphora

See *nipperkin*.

anchovy

The word *anchovy* was introduced to English in 1596 by Shakespeare, who made the tiny fish a favourite of his most corpulent character, Falstaff. The word *anchovy* comes from Basque, a language spoken in parts of Spain and France but related to no other language in the world. The Basque source of *anchovy*—*anchoa*, meaning *dry*—was probably bestowed upon the fish because they are usually dried and salted before being sold: such preparations are necessary because small fish go bad more quickly than large fish.

andiron

Andirons are metal supports that sit on the floor of a fire-place and hold the logs in place so that they tumble neither forward nor backward while they burn; at one time, pairs of andirons were also used to support a spit, so that meat could be roasted above the fire. Although andirons have always been made of iron, the word *andiron* actually has nothing to do with the word *iron*: instead, *andiron* derives ultimately from *andero*, a Gaulish word meaning *young bull*, so called because the top ends of these iron supports were often moulded to look like a bull's head (just as the name *claw-foot* was bestowed on furniture legs moulded to resemble a lion's paw). This Gaulish word, *andero*, became the Old French *andier*, which English adopted as *aundyre* in the fourteenth century; shortly after, however, people began to assume that the iron the device was made of was also the source of its name, and accordingly they mistakenly changed the spelling to *andiron*. Other people went further in trying to "improve" the spelling of the word, sometimes spelling it *hand-iron* and sometimes even giving it the name of another cooking utensil, the *brandiron*, a griddle whose name really does derive from *iron*. In the sixteenth century, andirons also acquired a completely new name, *fire-dogs*, so named, no doubt, because they were no longer decorated with the head of a bull, but of a dog, the guardian of the hearth and home.

anet

See *dill*.

angels on horseback

See *spotted dick*.

antipasto

If matter and anti-matter come into contact with one another, they are annihilated in a cataclysmic explosion. The same, fortunately, is not true of *antipasto* and *pasta*: although antipasto, a cold hors d'oeuvre, is intended to be served before pasta, the two may, if need be, safely occupy the same plate. In truth, however, the *pasto* in *antipasto* has no relation to the word *pasta*; the Greek word *paste*, meaning *barley porridge*, is the source of *pasta*, while *pasto* derives from the Latin *pastus*, meaning *food*, which in turn derives from the Latin *pascere*, meaning *to feed*. Likewise, the *anti* of *antipasto* really has no relation to the *anti* of *anti-matter*: originally the hors d'oeuvre's name was spelt *antepast*, but in time the Latin prefix *ante*, meaning *before*, came to be spelt as if it were the more common Greek prefix *anti*, meaning *against*. Thus, the first part of *antipasto* is related to words like *antecedent*, meaning *something going before*, and *antediluvian*, meaning *before the flood*. On the other hand, the last part of *antipasto* is related to words that also derive from the Latin *pascere*; these include *repast* (meaning *to feed again*), *pasture* (a place where domestic animals feed), and *pastor* (a clergyman who gives spiritual food to his "flock"). Through sheer coincidence, these words are also related to the word *pasteurize*, the process of sterilizing milk invented by Louis Pasteur whose surname is the French form of *pastor*. Of these words, *repast*, *pasture*, and *pastor* are the oldest, having been adopted by English in the late fourteenth century; *antepast*, the original form of *antipasto*, appeared in the late sixteenth century, while the more Italian sounding *antipasto* did not appear in English till 1934. See also *Pablum* and *postpast*.

aperitif

An aperitif is a drink—usually alcoholic, but not always—taken before a meal. First recorded in the late nineteenth century, *aperitif* derives through French from the Latin *aperire*, meaning *to open*, the idea being that the drink "opens" the stomach, thereby stimulating the appetite. Other words that derive from the same source as *aperitif* include *aperture* (the opening through which a camera gathers light) and *pert* (a word that originally described someone with an "open" personality, but now meaning *saucy* or *bold*).

appetite

Although the feathers are the one part of a chicken that my Uncle Alan, even at his hungriest, will not eat, the word *appetite* and the word *feather* nonetheless derive from the same source. This shared source was an Indo-European word pronounced something like *pter*, meaning *wing*. In Greek, this word developed into *pteron*, meaning *wing*, which appears in *pterodactyl*, an extinct flying reptile whose name literally means *wing-finger*. Similarly, in the Germanic language family, the Indo-European *pter* developed into *fethra*, which evolved into the English *feather* in the eleventh century. In Latin, *pter* developed somewhat differently: it became the verb *petere*, meaning *to seek* or *to strive for*, the connection being that wings are used to fly toward some desired goal (in English, we also talk about *winging our way* toward something). This Latin *petere* then became attached to the preposition *ad*, meaning *toward*, so that the resulting *adpetere* literally meant *to strive toward something*. From *adpetere*, the word *appetite* evolved, which—when it appeared in English in the late fourteenth century—had become a noun meaning *a desire for something*, especially food. More recently, in the mid nineteenth century, *appetite* also gave rise to *appetizer*, the name of a savoury treat that stimulates a desire for food.

appetizer

See *appetite*.

apple

Neither of the two words that the ancient Romans had for *apple*—*malum* and *pomum*—are the source of the English name of this fruit. Instead, *apple* derives from a Germanic source, one likely related to *Avella*, the name of a famous fruit-growing region in Italy; however, whether the region was named after the fruit, or the fruit after the region, is unknown. In English, the word *apple* was first recorded in the ninth century, but at that time, and for centuries after, it was used to refer not only to apples in particular, but also to fruit in general: Aelfric, for example, the greatest prose writer of Old English, even referred to the cucumber as an apple. In the Hebrew Bible, the item which Adam and Eve are forbidden to eat is referred to only as "the fruit"; however, because *apple* could also mean *fruit*, translators of the Bible sometimes used it in place of *fruit*, causing later generations to suppose that the forbidden fruit eaten by Adam and Eve was an actual apple. Of the various sweet dishes made from apples, the one with the oldest name is *apple-mose*, an apple porridge first referred to at the beginning of the fifteenth century. *Apple pie* is not recorded in print until the end of the sixteenth century when it appears in a peculiar compliment invented by Robert Green for his prose romance, *Menaphon* : "Thy breath is like the steame of apple-pyes." Applesauce did not acquire its name till even later: the middle of the eighteenth century.

apple-pie order

A proper chef always keeps her kitchen in apple-pie order: spoons and forks do not fraternize wildly in the cutlery drawer, lids do not wander from their containers, salt shakers do not plummet into the crevice between oven and wall. Such a compulsion for culinary organization is known as *apple-pie order*, an idiom that may have grown out of how apple pies, in the good old days, were made by carefully arranging apple slices in a highly stylized, vortical pattern (which was then hidden under a crust of dough). Alternatively, the *apple-pie* part of the idiom may have originated as an English corruption of the French phrase *nappes pliees*, meaning *folded linen*, or as an English corruption of the French phrase *cap-à-pie*, meaning *head to foot* (Shakespeare uses this idiom when he has Horatio describe Hamlet's ghostly father as armed *cap-à-pie*); both French phrases—*nappes pliees* and *cap-à-pie*—are suggestive of minute attention to detail. Whatever its origin, *apple-pie order* was first recorded in English in the late eighteenth century.

apricot

Like Mozart, Edison, or Keats, apricots are precocious. The ancient Romans called this fruit *malum praecoquum—malum* meaning *fruit* and the Latin *praecoquum* literally meaning *pre-cooked* but metaphorically meaning *early ripened*. Apricots and geniuses are therefore *praecoquum*—or in English *precocious*—because they ripen before their peers. In the first century, Greeks took part of this Latin name, *praecoquum*, and adopted it as *praikokion*; by the sixth century, this name had changed in Byzantine Greek to *berikokkion*, which Arabic then borrowed as *al birquq*, the *al* being the Arabic definite article meaning *the*. Finally, this Arabic name was borrowed by the Spanish as *albaricoque*, which entered English in the mid sixteenth century as *abrecock* before being respelt as *apricot*. The original Latin *praecoquum*, incidentally, derives from *coquere*, meaning *to cook*, the source not only of *apricot* and *precocious*, but also of the words *kitchen*, *cuisine*, *culinary*, and *cook*. See also *cook*.

apron

Back in the fourteenth century, the outer garment that cooks wore to shield their clothes from spatters and dribbles was called a *napron*. By the fifteenth century, however, the *n* at the beginning of the word had shifted over to the indefinite article that often preceded the word: that is, *a napron* became *an apron* (the same thing happened with the word *umpire*: it was originally *numpire*, but eventually its *n* also drifted away). Further back in history, the original *napron* was derived from the French name for this article of clothing, *naperon*, which in turn is a diminutive form of the French word *nape*, meaning *tablecloth*; both the old *napron* and the modern *apron*, therefore, literally mean *little tablecloth*. The French *nape* is also the source of the familiar *napkin*, and of the now defunct *sanap*, the name of a strip of fabric placed over the edge of an expensive table cloth to prevent it from being soiled. In French, the original form of *sanap* was *sauve nape*, literally meaning *save the tablecloth*; after adopting the word in the early fourteenth century, however, English shortened it to *sanap*, a form it retained until it became obsolete in the mid fifteenth century. See also *serviette*.

aquavit

The yellowish alcoholic spirit known as *aquavit* derived its name in the late nineteenth century from the Norwegian *akavit*, which in turn developed from the Latin *aqua vitae*, meaning *water of life* (whiskey likewise derives its name from a Gaelic phrase also meaning *water of life*). Another beverage—one spiced with cloves, ginger, cardamom, and mace—has been known since the mid eighteenth century as *aqua mirabilis*, Latin for *wonderful water*. See also *water*.

artichoke

Anyone who has fondled her way through a boiled, buttered artichoke knows that this vegetable is made up of an edible, fleshy base called the *heart* and an inedible, hairy core called the *choke*. In fact, most people suppose that the so-called heart and choke of the plant gave the artichoke its name. Actually, the reverse is true: the word *artichoke* came first, entering English in the early sixteenth century, and only afterwards did its edible and inedible parts come to be known, in the early eighteenth century, as the *heart* and *choke*. In other words, after noticing that the word *artichoke* sounded vaguely like *heart* and *choke*, people mistakenly concluded that *heart* and *choke* must be the correct and original names for those two parts of the vegetable. This conclusion probably seemed all the more reasonable because you would indeed choke if you tried to eat an artichoke's tough, fibrous core. More ingenious explanations for the vegetable's name were also proposed, but they were equally mistaken. Some past horticulturalists, for instance, supposed that the artichoke took its name from *hortus*—the Latin word for *garden*—and *choke* because the plant was reputed to run wild and choke a garden. French etymologists, too, were once stymied by the French name for the vegetable, *artichaut*: they proposed that the *chaut* part came from *chaud*, meaning *hot*, or even from *chou*, meaning *cabbage*. The real origin of *artichoke* is much simpler than these false etymologies: the word comes from the Arabic *al kharshuf*, meaning *the thistle*, because an artichoke is actually the flower bud of a thistle picked before it blooms. This Arabic word was borrowed by Spanish as *alcachofa*, which was corrupted by Italian as *articiocco*, which was borrowed by French as *artichaut*, which was adopted by English as *artichoke*. See also *Jerusalem artichoke*.

asparagus

The word *asparagus* derives from two Greek words: *ana*, meaning *up*, and *spargan*, meaning *to swell*, a reference to the prominent shoots of the plant that "swell up" as it grows. Oddly, the word was used in English at the beginning of the eleventh century but then vanished until the middle of the sixteenth century, when it reappeared as *sperage*. By the beginning of the seventeenth century, books written by scholars and herbalists had made the Latin name of the vegetable, *asparagus*, familiar to the common people, but within another fifty years these same common folk had changed *asparagus*—which to them was an odd-sounding foreign word—into something that seemed more "English": *sparrow-grass*, a comforting but nonsensical name, especially considering that sparrows eat only seeds and insects. From the mid seventeenth to the mid nineteenth century, *sparrow-grass* remained the usual name of the plant, but eventually the Latin form *asparagus* was reintroduced and reaccepted as "proper." The proper plural of *asparagus*, given its Latin form, is *asparagi*, just as the plural of *alumnus* is *alumni*.

aspic

In France in October, an unheated swimming pool would be said to be *froid comme un aspic*, that is, *cold as an asp*, an asp being a snake whose cold-blooded metabolism makes it seem cool to the touch. Traditionally, this snake's name has been considered the source of the culinary *aspic*, a jelly containing cold meat, vegetables, or shellfish. However, even if we acknowledge the existence of the bright green dessert known as *grasshopper pie*, it still seems odd that anyone would name a jelly after a poisonous reptile, especially one that Cleopatra used to kill herself. Somewhat more likely is that aspic jelly derives its name from the other French *aspic*, the one meaning *spikenard*, an aromatic plant sometimes used to flavour aspic jelly. Even more likely, however, is that the jelly takes its name from the Greek *aspis*, meaning *shield*, which is what the original aspic jelly moulds were shaped like. The word first appeared in English in 1789, the year a crowd of Parisians stormed the Bastille and began the French Revolution.

aubergine

See *eggplant*.

avocado

Not only is the Nahuatl language, spoken by the Aztecs, the source of the words *chili*, *chocolate*, and *chicle* (the latter refers to a substance used to make chewing gum, such as Chiclets), it also gave English the word *avocado*, the fruit from which guacamole is made. Perhaps in an attempt to impress or frighten neighbouring peoples, the Aztecs transferred their word for *testicle*—*ahuacatl*—to the large, ellipsoid fruit that we now know as the avocado. When Hernando Cortés and his Spanish conquistadors encountered the Aztecs in the early sixteenth century, they took this fruit and its name back to Spain, giving the Aztecs many European diseases in return. In Spanish, *ahuacatl* became *aguacate*, a reasonable representation of the original Aztec word, but one which soon became corrupted to *avocado*, a shift in pronunciation that may have been influenced by the Spanish word *bocado*, meaning *delicacy*. (Thus, despite its green skin and oily flesh, the avocado's name has no relation to the Spanish word for lawyer, *avocado*, literally meaning *advocate*). In English, *avocado* first appeared at the end of the seventeenth century; shortly after, the fruit also became known as the *avocado pear*, thanks to the mistaken belief that the avocado was a member of the pear family; still later, *avocado pear* became *alligator pear*, the change occurring for the simple reason that *alligator* was a more familiar word than *avocado*. None of these alternative names, however, ever overtook *avocado* as the accepted form. See also *guacamole*, *limpopo*, and *subaltern's luncheon*.

azyme

The unleavened bread that Jews eat at Passover is called the *azyme*; in contrast, the leavened bread that members of the Greek Orthodox Church eat at communion is called the *enzyme*. The final syllable that these two words share derives from a Greek word meaning *leaven*, leaven being an ancient agent of fermentation. The two words differ only in their prefixes: the *a* of *azyme* is a Greek prefix that means *not*, whereas the *en* of *enzyme* is a Greek prefix that means *in*. Of these two words, *azyme* is the oldest, appearing briefly in English in the fourteenth century, and then vanishing until the sixteenth century: during those intervening years, England had banished all Jews from its shores. The other word, *enzyme*, did not appear in English until the mid nineteenth century; forty years later, near the end of the nineteenth century, biochemists gave new life to this somewhat obscure religious term when they gave the name *enzyme* to proteins that cause biochemical reactions similar to those produced by leavening agents.

baba

In the early eighteenth century the Polish king Stanislaw Leszczynski was exiled from his country, whereupon he took up residence in Lorraine, France. There he encountered a cake known as *kugelhopf*, which he enjoyed but found a bit dry, and accordingly began steeping it in rum before eating it. So delicious was the king's innovation that he decided to give rum-soaked kugelhopf a new name, one honouring his favourite hero in literature, Ali Baba, famous for speaking the magic words *Open, Sesame!* In Arabic, Ali Baba's full name—only half of which King Leszcsynski bestowed upon the rum cake—means *elevated Father*. Incidentally, the *Baba* part of this Arabic hero's name is related to the Aramaic word *abba*, which in the New Testament is used by Jesus when calling upon his Father, and which is distantly related to the English word *papa*. See also *sesame*.

backsplash

A backsplash is a panel placed behind a stove top to protect the wall from being splashed by the soup-spoon of an exuberant or gesticulating chef. The name of this panel appeared in the early 1950s in imitation of the word *dashboard*: dashboards were invented, or at least named, in the mid nineteenth century as a means of preventing the occupants of a carriage from being spattered by the mud dashed up by the horses' hooves. When automobiles were invented, *dashboard* was borrowed as the name for the surface above the steering console.

bacon

The term *back bacon* is redundant in that *bacon* derives from the Old German *bach*, meaning *back*; bacon, after all, is cut from the back of the pig, although the sides, which contain more fat, can also be used to produce this cured meat. The word *bacon* did not appear until the early fourteenth century; before this, the back cut was called a *flitch*, a word that derives from the same source as the word *flesh*. When the word *bacon* was introduced, *flitch*, rather than become obsolete, shifted its sense and came to denote a whole chunk of bacon before it is cut into slices; thus, the phrase *flitch of bacon* arose. Throughout the Middle Ages and even beyond, it was just such a flitch of bacon that could be won by any married couple in Dunmow, England who could prove that their first year of marriage had been free of arguments; from this custom the saying *bring home the bacon* developed. The English surname *Bacon*—as in Sir Francis Bacon—and the German surname *Bach*—as in Johann Sebastian Bach—both derive from the name of this part of the pig. See also *meat*.

bagel

Going back at least to the early seventeenth century in Poland, bagels were given as presents to women who had just given birth; this doughy gift nourished the exhausted mother, but the shape of the bagel—a yonic ring—may also have represented the cycle of life newly embodied by mother and child. The name of this bun did not enter English until 1932 when it was adopted from Yiddish. In turn, the Yiddish word, *beygel*, developed from the German *beugel*, a diminutive of *boug*, meaning *bracelet*.

baguette

The Greek word *bakterion*, meaning *rod* or *stick*, is the source of both *baguette*, a stick-shaped loaf of French bread, and of *bacteria*, the stick-shaped micro-organisms that surround us everywhere. The Greek *bakterion* gave rise to the Latin *baculum*, which evolved into the Italian *bacchio*, still with the sense of *stick*. The diminutive of *bacchio*—*bacchetta*, meaning *little stick*—was then borrowed by the French as *baguette*, a name they proceeded to bestow upon the bread. In English, references to this French loaf do not appear until 1958, although before this, dating back to the early eighteenth century, *baguette* had been used in English as an architectural term referring to a kind of decorated moulding.

bain-marie

A bain-marie is a pan full of water into which a vessel containing a sauce is placed; the water in the outer pan is then brought to a near boil, which heats the sauce without danger of burning it—a double boiler is therefore a kind of bain-marie. The name of this device, which appeared in English in the early nineteenth century, is a French phrase meaning *Mary's bath*; the French name, however, is itself a direct translation of the Latin *balneum Mariae*, the name of a similar vessel originally used by medieval alchemists in their quest to transmute base metals into gold. The Mary these alchemists named their utensil after was the sister of Moses, known both as Mary and Miriam: because she is called a prophetess in the Bible, alchemists came to see her as a patron of their own mysterious art. Eventually, however, as the practice of alchemy faded away, cooks began to assume that their kitchen bain-maries were the namesake of a more famous Mary, the mother of Jesus: it was the gentle warming of the bain-marie, they supposed, that led to its being named after the warm and gentle mother of God. A bain-marie may also be called a *balneum*, derived directly from the Medieval Latin name of the vessel. See also *costmary*.

bake

The most interesting facts about the word *bake* do not involve what it developed from, but what it developed into. Near the beginning of the eleventh century, the word appeared in Old English as *bacan*, having developed from a Germanic and—before that—an Indo-European source that meant simply *to bake*. The Old English *bacan* almost immediately spawned the word *baecere*, the name of a person who bakes for a living, which soon evolved into *baker*. The term *bakery* did not appear until much later—the mid sixteenth century—and even then it did not refer to the place where a baker works, but rather to a baker's work in general, just as *carpentry* refers not to a place but to an activity. In fact, the word *bakery* did not come to mean *baker's shop* until the early nineteenth century, when it became common for people to buy baked goods from a shop instead of making them at home. The Old English *bacan* also evolved, in the mid fifteenth century, into the Middle English *bache*, meaning a quantity of bread produced at one baking; this word was respelt as *batch* in the sixteenth century, and came to be applied to everything from cookies, to fudge, to beer, to poems. Finally, the Old English *bacan* also developed into the word *baecestre*, meaning *female baker*; around the end of the fourteenth century, this word was respelt as *baxter*, which became established as a surname shortly after. By the sixteenth century, however, the word *baxter* had ceased to be identified with women, so a new female form, *backstress*, was formed in its place. This odd looking word did not, however, outlive the sixteenth century.

baker's dozen

Nothing makes my teeth gnash more than slicing a loaf of bread and discovering that some accursed bubble has hollowed an end of the loaf: not only do I get jam all over my lap as it drips through the resulting sandwich-cavity, I feel cheated for having purchased bread and gotten air. Such unholy bubbles prompted the English Parliament to pass a statute in 1266 promising severe penalties for bakers whose loaves weighed less than they should. Bakers responded to this new law not by making their loaves bigger—which would have meant buying new sets of bread tins—but by adding a thirteenth loaf to every dozen that the customer bought. These thirteen loaves became known as a *baker's dozen*, a term first recorded in the sixteenth century.

Bakewell

The name of this dessert, made by lining a pastry case with jam before filling it with almond paste, did not originate as a piece of culinary advice, but from the town in Derbyshire called Bakewell, where it was invented in the early nineteenth century.

balderdash

Throughout the seventeenth century, the word *balderdash* referred to any drink made by jumbling together liquids that should not, in a sane universe, occupy the same glass, much less the same stomach: beer and butter-milk, beer and wine, wine and milk—all are forms of balderdash. This now-obsolete sense of *balderdash* is clearly connected with the one current today: namely, *a senseless jumble of words*. This "jumbled words" sense may, in fact, have been the original meaning of *balderdash*, a meaning that did not appear in written English until the late seventeenth century, probably because it was considered too vulgar for print. In spoken English, however, *balderdash* likely appeared in the sixteenth century or earlier as a slang compound made by combining *balder* (a dialect word meaning *to use coarse language*) and *dash* (a word of Norse origin meaning *to smack together*). Alternatively, *balderdash* may have derived from the Welsh *baldorddus*, meaning *idle talk*, or even from the Medieval Latin *balducta*, denoting a drink of hot milk curdled with wine.

baldmoney

See *spignel*.

balneum

See *bain-marie*.

banana

Scholars of Renaissance literature have long noted that nowhere in Shakespeare's comedies does a character slip and fall on a banana peel. This striking absence of fruit-slapstick is due to the fact that bananas, though they were described by travel writers during Shakespeare's life, were not commonly imported into England until much later. In fact, even if the young Shakespeare had encountered a banana in a London market, he likely would have called it a *muse* rather than a banana. The fruit had acquired the name *muse* by 1578 not because it was a source of poetic inspiration but because the Arabic word for *banana—mauz—*

managed to get itself introduced into English before its rival *banana* did. However, when *banana* did enter English in 1597, it quickly became the standard name: by 1602, *muse*, as a fruit name, was obsolete. The word *banana* also has a connection to Arabic, though it is one based on a misunderstanding. When Spanish and Portuguese traders travelled to the Congo in Africa in 1563, they mistook the fruit's African name for an unrelated Arabic word: *banan*, meaning *finger*. The mix-up was triggered, no doubt, by the resemblance of a banana to a human finger.

bannock

Since the eleventh century at least, round loaves of bread, made from barley or oats, have been called *bannock*, a name that the English derived from the Gaelic name for the same food, *bannach*. In turn, Gaelic probably derived the name of this loaf from the Latin *panicium*, Latin being the language of the Roman missionaries who converted the inhabitants of Britain to Christianity in the seventh century. Even further back in history, the ancient Romans formed the word *panicium* from *panis*, their word for *bread*. From this same source, the word *pantry*—a room for bread—and *companion*—a person who eats your bread—were also derived.

banquet

The word *banquet* literally means *a little bench*, and in fact a banquet was originally a small snack eaten while sitting on a low bench, a snack that escalated, over centuries, into the elaborate series of dishes that the word *banquet* now signifies. Ultimately, *banquet* traces its origin all the way back to a Germanic source pronounced something like *bangk*. In French, this Germanic source developed into *banc*, meaning *bench*, which led to the diminutive form *banquet*, adopted into English at the end of the fifteenth century. The Germanic *bangk* also took many other lines of development: for instance, it became the English word *bench*, first recorded in Old English a thousand years ago; via Old Norse, the Germanic *bangk* also became *bank*, as in *river bank*, a topographical feature that rises along a river like a bench; and via French, *bangk* even became *bank*, as in *Bank of Canada*, banks having originated as mere benches set between the borrower and the lender. *Banquet* is related to all these words, and also to one more: the term *bantling*, meaning *bratty child*, comes from the German word *bankling*, which denoted a child supposedly conceived on a bench—in other words, a bastard.

banyan day

A day on which no meat is served is called a *banyan day*, a term first used by British sailors in the mid eighteenth century to refer to those days of the week when, to conserve food supplies, they were fed only bread and gruel. Banyan days take their name from an Indian class called the Banians, whose religion teaches them to esteem all life and therefore to abstain from eating meat. For centuries, under India's system of castes, Banians could work only as merchants, and in fact the ultimate source of their name— *vaniyo*—is the Gujarati word for *merchant caste*, Gujarati being a language spoken in western India. Because many Banians moved to Arabic ports to conduct their trade, *vaniyo* was adopted by their Arabic counterparts, who modified the Gujarati word to *banian*. *Banian* was then adopted by Portuguese traders, who introduced the name of the caste to English at the end of the sixteenth century.

bar

See *tavern*.

barbecue

The Taino, a tribe of Haitian people obliterated by European explorers and pirates, called a framework of sticks used for sleeping on or cooking over a *barbacoa*. The word was borrowed by the Spanish in the mid seventeenth century, and entered English as *barbecue* at the end of the seventeenth century. Its early use in English retained the sense of *wooden framework*, and thus some American writers of that century speak of sleeping on barbecues. By the early eighteenth century, *barbecue* had come to mean only a device for roasting meat upon, and by the mid eighteenth century it had also been transferred to any food cooked in such a way. The popular claim that the word *barbeque* derives from the French *barbe à queue*—meaning *beard to tail* and supposedly referring to how animals were often barbecued whole or "head to foot"—is implausible for historical reasons: it was not till the early nineteenth century, two hundred years after the first appearance of *barbecue*, that it became fashionable for animals to grow beards.

bard

Certain joints of meat will dry out when roasted unless they are protected by a thin covering of bacon or sliced pork. These protective slices are called *bards*, a word whose history extends back thousands of years to the Persian *pardah*, meaning *covering*. The ancient Arabs adopted this Persian word, using it to mean *pack-saddle*, and then introduced it to the Italians, who spelt it *barda* and used it as a name for horse-armour, plates of metal or leather that protect a horse from sword-blows. When the French adopted the Italian term, they too initially used it to mean *horse-armour* but then transferred it from the battlefield to the kitchen, where they used it to refer to the protective slices of bacon. English then borrowed the culinary term in the late fifteenth century, changing its spelling to *bard* in the process. Incidentally, when scholars refer to Shakespeare as "The Immortal Bard," they have another *bard*—a non-bacon one—in mind: the *bard* that means *poet* derives from an Old Celtic word that meant *minstrel*.

barnbrack

See *bonny-clabber*.

basil

Basil Rathbone, star of the 1940s Sherlock Holmes movies, took his given name from the same source as basil the herb. Both names derive from the Greek name for the herb, *basiliskos*, literally meaning *the little king*, which entered Latin as *basilicus* before being adopted by French as *basile*. English borrowed the French name of this herb in the early fifteenth century, although *Basil* had been used as an English given name for hundreds of years before this, thanks to the prominence of St. Basil, a fourth-century bishop. The herb acquired its kingly name because of the plant's regal associations: in ancient times, it was often employed in royal potions and medicines. *Basil* is closely related to both *basilica*, a church designed to look like a king's palace, and *basilisk*, an ancient monster (now extinct) known for the crown-shaped mark on its head and its ability to kill with a glance.

basmati

The name of the Indian rice that exudes a sweet, delightful smell when cooked derives from the Hindi word *basmati*, meaning *fragrant*. In English the word first appeared in 1845 in a dictionary of Indian terms intended to help members of the British Raj adjust to their new and unfamiliar surroundings.

batrachivorous

See *omnivorous*.

bay leaf

The *bay* of *bay leaf* is not related to any of the other *bays* in English: not to the *bay* in *Hudson Bay*, not to the *bay* in "The hounds will bay all night," not to the *bay* in "He held the enemy at bay." The herb *bay* takes its name, through French, from the Latin *baca*, meaning *berry*; in ancient times the laurels crowning the heads of celebrated poets and victorious soldiers were made from the leaves and berries of the bay tree.

bean

Just as beans have changed little over the last ten centuries, the word *bean* itself has undergone no radical metamorphosis: *bean* was first recorded in Old English about one thousand years ago, spelt then as it is now. The word derives from a Germanic source that may be distantly related to the Latin name for beans, *faba*. Incidentally, this Latin name for beans is the source of the given name *Fabian* and also of the first half of *fava bean*, a name that therefore literally means *bean bean*. See also *bean-feast*.

bean-feast

The term *bean-feast* originated in the early nineteenth century as the name of an annual dinner given by employers to their employees, a name perhaps inspired by the mounds of baked beans that the boss generously ladled out at these festive events (perhaps, however, the boss's seeming generosity was a diabolical, white-collar prank: the day after the feast, the bean-stuffed labourers would have to work cheek to cheek in close quarters). Alternatively, the term *bean-feast* may have originated from *bene feast*, the word *bene* being an old name for a prayer spoken at the beginning or end of a meal. If this is indeed the origin of the term *bean-feast*, then the practice of serving beans at these events must have arisen later on, as people forgot the real origin of the feast's name. In the late nineteenth century the word *beano* arose as an abbreviation for *bean-feast* and came to mean any festive event that ended in curses being exchanged, chairs being thrown, and general rowdyism. Recently, *Beano* has also become a brand-name for a food additive that diminishes flatulence. See also *bean*.

beef

Along with *veal*, *mutton*, and *pork*, the word *beef* was introduced to English by the French-speaking Normans after they conquered England in 1066. Prior to the introduction of *beef*, native English words such as *ox* and *cow* had been used not only as the names of animals but also as the names of the meat those animals provided. The Old French source of *beef* was spelt *boef*, which derived from the Latin *bos*, meaning *ox*. Much further back in its history, the Latin *bos* developed from an Indo-European source, pronounced something like *gwous*, which also developed, through the Germanic language family, into the word *cow*. Accordingly, although they resemble each other no more than you and I do, the words *beef* and *cow* trace their origin back to the same distant ancestor. Once adopted by English, *beef* itself became the source of new words. The guards of the British monarch, for example, came to be known in the mid seventeenth century as *beefeaters*, a term that originated as a disparaging nickname for a servant who ate well but did little (the outlandish theory that arose more than a century ago—that *beefeater* derives from *buffetier*, supposedly the name of the guardian of the royal buffet—was proposed by Victorian philologists too pedantic to accept the more obvious meaning of the term). Of course, *beef* also gave rise to the name of the most English of all meat dishes, *beefsteak*; this development would hardly be remarkable had the French not adopted the English *beefsteak* as *bifteck*, a term that the English then reborrowed in the mid nineteenth century as a high-brow synonym for *beefsteak*. The existence of these two status-conscious synonyms means that at Tom's Roadside Café you sink your teeth into a juicy beefsteak, but at The Wellington you dine upon a succulent bifteck.

beestings

Beestings is the first milk drawn from a mammal after it has given birth. Beestings has long been known to be especially rich, and therefore was used often as an ingredient in custards and puddings. It might seem odd that this milk has a special name, but in fact it even has three others: *beest*, which is obviously a cousin of *beestings*; *colostrum*, which is a direct borrowing from Latin; and *green milk*, which doubtless derives not from the colour of beestings, but from the connotations of vitality and freshness that the word *green* possesses. Although *beestings* can refer to the first milk of any mammal, even a human, it is most commonly used to refer to the first milk of a cow. The origin of the word *beestings* can be traced back to the Old English word *bysting*, which meant the same thing. *Beestings* does not appear to be related to the word *beast* and, needless to say, is not related to *bee's sting*.

beet

The beet takes its name from the Latin name for the plant, *beta*. In English, the earliest reference to beets occurs in an eleventh-century manuscript devoted to the medicinal properties of plants; after that there are no written references to the red root-vegetable until the fifteenth century. During this four-hundred-year gap, beets were planted every spring and harvested every fall; they were eaten regularly by every person in England; their tops and leaves were fed to thousands of hungry pigs; and yet it appears that not once did the beet inspire anyone who possessed pen, paper, and the ability to write, to jot down its name, even in passing.

belly

The place where food goes after we swallow it derives its name from the Old English *belig*, meaning *bag*, which also evolved into *bellows*, a kind of silent accordion used to blow a fire higher. When *belly* was first applied to humans, it referred to the body in general, similar to how the German *madensack*, literally meaning *worm sack*, also refers to the human body. By the mid fourteenth century, however, *belly* had acquired its more specialized sense of *stomach*. Incidentally, the word *stomach* derives from the Greek word *stoma*, meaning *mouth*, which gave rise to *stomakhos*, meaning *throat*. In Greek, *stomakhos* came to be applied to the openings or "throats" into other internal organs, including that of the belly, and eventually its association with the belly made it a synonym for that organ. In English, *stomach* is first recorded in the fourteenth century; five hundred years later, in the late nineteenth century, it gave rise to a shortened form, *tummy*, originally used to ask children about their ailments.

belly-cheat

In the seventeenth and eighteenth centuries, a belly-cheat was an apron. The term developed from how aprons prevent food from falling onto the belly of the cook, thus "cheating" the belly of a treat. See also *apron*.

belly-timber

In his translation of Virgil's *Georgics*, the seventeenth-century poet John Dryden refers to fish as "finny flocks." A hundred years later, it was this sort of ornate poetic diction that William Wordsworth dismissed as "inane phraseology," and then set out to revolutionize poetry by writing verse that used the language of ordinary people. The term *belly-timber*, meaning *food*, might appear to be another phrase like "finny flocks," found only in the florid couplets of learned poets. However, *belly-timber* actually originated in the early seventeenth century as a commonplace, everyday term, although within fifty years it came to be seen as a ludicrous and affected compound; accordingly, after the mid seventeenth century, *belly-timber* was used only ironically, meaning that you could say it only while wiggling in the air two fingers of each hand. In Old English, the word *timber* originally meant *house*, having developed from an Indo-European source that meant *to build*. By the tenth century *timber* had come to mean *building material*, which was the sense from which *belly-timber* developed, food being the "building-material" of the human body. Later on, probably during the seventeenth century, *timber* gradually narrowed its meaning and came to signify wood or lumber specifically. The *timbre* that refers to the "colour" of a singer's voice is an unrelated word.

bergamot

The word *bergamot* refers to two utterly distinct fruits, one very sour and similar to an orange or lemon, and the other a very sweet variety of pear. Oddly, the two fruits acquired the name *bergamot* from utterly distinct sources. The sour fruit takes its name directly from Bergamo, a city in northern Italy where it was either once cultivated or through which it was exported to other parts of Europe; in turn, the city of Bergamo acquired its name from a Celtic or Ligurian source meaning *mountain* (thus making it a distant relative of the *berg* in *iceberg*). This *bergamot* appeared in English near the end of the seventeenth century. The other *bergamot* arose when Italians corrupted the Turkish name for a sweet fruit—*beg-armudu*, meaning *prince's pear*—to *bergamotta*, probably under the mistaken impression that this fruit was also grown in Bergamo. From Italian, *bergamotta* entered French as *bergamotte*, which English adopted as *bergamot* in the early seventeenth century. See also *Adam's ale*.

Berliner

See *bismark*.

berry

The word *berry* first appeared in English a thousand years ago in a translation of an Old Testament passage referring to the "berries" used to make wine: *berry* originally referred only to grapes and did not acquire its wider, current meaning until the Middle Ages. Further back in its history, *berry* may have evolved from a Germanic source that meant *red*, but little else is known about its ancestry. The word is not related to *Barry*, a personal name that derives from the Irish *Fionnbar*, meaning *fair-headed*; nor, for that matter, is it related to *beriberi*, the name of a paralysing disease whose name, in Sinhalese, literally means *weakness-weakness*.

biryani

One of the languages spoken in Iran is Persian, a member, like English, of the Indo-European family of languages. Throughout history, Persian has given hundreds of words to English, including *calabash*, *candy*, *carob*, *lemon*, *orange*, *pistachio*, and even—oddly, considering that Iran's hot climate makes keeping ice difficult—*sherbet*. These words were all adopted by English about four centuries ago. In contrast, the word *biryani*—Persian in origin, but introduced to English through Hindi—entered English only about four decades ago as the name of a highly spiced dish of meat, rice, and lentils. The Persian source of the word—*biryan*—means *fried* or *roasted*.

biscuit

In French the word *bis* means *twice* and the word *cuit* means cooked. Thus, *biscuit* literally means *twice-cooked*, which is how biscuits were originally made. By baking them, letting them cool, and then heating them again, the biscuits were made drier and harder and this improved their keeping qualities. The process had its disadvantages, too, as is suggested by what the French soldiers under Louis XIV sometimes called the flat little cakes: *pain de pierre*, meaning *stone bread*. In Italian the name *biscotti* parallels the origin of *biscuit*, as does the German word *zwieback*: *zwie*, meaning *two*, and *backen*, meaning *to bake*. In Spanish and Portuguese the food is called *rosca*, meaning *twisted* or *coiled*, because the dough was braided before baking. In the sixteenth century, the exotic sounding *rosca* gave rise to an English word that now seems quite plain and simple—*rusk*, a kind of a sweetened biscuit. *Biscuit*, on the other hand, is a somewhat older word, having entered English in the fourteenth century.

bismark

The jam-filled pastry known since the 1930s as the *bismark* is also known regionally by other names. For example, in eastern Canada it's called a *jelly doughnut*, in Manitoba it's called a *jam buster*, and in parts of the American Midwest it's called a *Berliner* or, if it's slightly elongated, a *long-john*. The pastry may be German in origin, as is suggested by two of its names: *Berliner* means *a native of Berlin*, while *Bismark* suggests Otto von Bismarck, the first chancellor of the modern German empire. However, it is possible that the bismark was named after the German chancellor only indirectly: the pastry may, for instance, have been invented in and named after Bismarck, North Dakota, a city given the chancellor's surname in a bid to entice him into financing the Northern Pacific Railway. Alternatively, the bismark pastry may have been named after *The Bismarck*, a famous German battleship whose name honours the chancellor and whose shape (until the British torpedoed it in 1941) resembled the pastry. In any event, one way or another the ultimate source of the bismark's name is the chancellor's surname. In turn, this German surname derives from *biscopesmark*, meaning *bishop's boundary*, a name the chancellor's ancestors acquired because they lived just on the edge of a bishop's jurisdiction.

bistro

According to one story, the small restaurants known as *bistros* acquired their name thanks to Cossacks who, during the Russian occupation of Paris, would barge into restaurants shouting *vee-stra!*, Russian for *hurry up!* The French restaurateurs assumed that *vee-stra!* meant *fast food!* and so later they bestowed this Russian word—which they spelt *bistro*—on little cafés that served quick snacks. The problem with this explanation is that it seems unlikely that the French would take a rude, foreign command and apply it to an inviting, cozy establishment; as well, the word did not appear in French until 1884, almost three generations after the Russian occupation in 1815. A more likely origin, therefore, is that *bistro* is short for *bistrouille*, a French name for a drink made of coffee and brandy. *Bistrouille* in turn derives from the French *bis*, meaning *twice*, and *touiller*, meaning *to mix*, the coffee first being mixed with milk and then with the brandy. In English, the word *bistro* did not appear until the 1920s. See also *biscuit*.

black pudding

See *pudding*.

blade

The most dangerous item in your kitchen, excluding a toaster with a bagel stuck in it, is the knife, each kitchen containing dozens of them, and each knife made hazardous by its sharp blade. Ironically, however, the name of this sharp and deadly component—the blade—derives from an Indo-European source, pronounced something like *bhlo*, that meant *flower*. This Indo-European source evolved not only into the word *blade* but also into *blossom* and even, thanks to successive sound changes, into the word *flower* itself. When *blade* appeared in English in the early eleventh century it referred only to the narrow leaf of a plant; it was not until the fourteenth century that the word was also transferred to the narrow, leaf-shaped length of a knife.

blanch

See *blancmange*.

blancmange

Next to taste, smell, texture, price, preparation time, and how easy it is to wash out of a blouse, colour is the most important attribute of food; thus, we have red peppers, purple onions, brown beans, blue cheese, black pudding, orange marmalade, and blancmange. The term *blancmange*, which literally means *white food*, was borrowed from French in the fourteenth century as the name of a dish of white meat, such as chicken, in a sauce of cream, eggs, rice, sugar, and almonds. By the seventeenth century, the meat had been omitted from the recipe, and blancmange came to be a sweet dish, usually one made with gelatin boiled in milk so that a white jelly resulted. The *blanc* of *blancmange* is of course the French word for *white*, related to the English *blank* that means *unmarked* or *empty* as in *blank slate* (the French equivalent being *carte blanche*). This French *blanc* is also the source of the culinary term *blanch*, first used in English in the fifteenth century, which can either refer to whitening food—for example, by removing the skin from almonds—or to preventing food from darkening—for example, by cooking it partially, cooling it, and then cooking it completely. The French *blanc* is also the source of *blanquette*, a dish very similar to the original blancmange in that it is white meat in a white sauce. The culinary *blanquette* appeared in English in the mid eighteenth century, but the word had also been adopted from French about four hundred years earlier as *blanket*, the original blankets being undyed, and therefore whitish, sheets of woolen cloth. The *mange* part of *blancmange* derives from the French word *manger*, meaning *to eat*. From the fourteenth to the seventeenth century, *manger* existed in English—where it rhymed with *stranger*—as a synonym for *banquet* or *feast*. Today, *manger* still exists in English as the name of a place where animals are fed, but it has a curious status: it is familiar to everyone because of Christmas carols like *Away in a Manger*, but no one uses it outside of its Bethlehem context. Finally, the skin disease known in English as *mange*—its symptoms being intolerably itchy scabs—also derives from the French *manger* thanks to the spider-like parasites that chow down on the afflicted beast or human. See also *mandible*.

blanquette

See *blancmange*.

blaundsore

The medieval dish of eels known as *blaundsore* seems to have a name that literally means *white from red*. The name of the dish goes back to that of an earlier dish, *sorré*, made by chopping up eels, seasoning them, and then adding powdered sandal-wood to dye the food a reddish-brown. It was this dye that gave the dish its name: *sorré* derives from the French *sorer*, meaning *to redden*, the source also of *sorrel*, a reddish-brown colour often used to describe horses. Once established as a dish, sorré inspired a new eel dish, one which the French called *blanch-de-sore*, meaning *white from red* (the *white* in the dish's name likely refers to the addition of milk or cream to the original sorré recipe). In the early fifteenth century, the English adopted the dish and its French name, but corrupted it in the process to *blaundsore.*

blintz

A kind of folded pancake stuffed with sweet or savoury fillings, the blintz takes its name from the Yiddish *blintseh*, which developed from the Russian name for the dish, *blinyets. Blinyets* was itself a diminutive of *blin*, which evolved from *mlin*, which arose as the noun form of the verb *molot*, a Russian word meaning *to grind* (blintzes are made, of course, from grain ground into flour). Even further back, the Russian *molot* arose from the same Indo-European source as the Latin *molere*, meaning *to grind*, which gave rise to the English *molar*, a tooth that grinds food, and to the Dutch *maelstrom*, meaning *grinding-stream,* that is, a whirlpool. Both *molar* and *maelstrom*, therefore, are distant relatives of *blintz.*

blobsterdis

Although it appears to be a court stenographer's shorthand for "big lobster dish"—as in "Th vctm wz fnd in th blobsterdis"—the medieval food known as *blobsterdis* actually has no known etymology; even worse, its recipe was lost after the word became obsolete in the fifteenth century. See also *bouce Jane.*

blood sausage

See *pudding.*

board

As a culinary term, *board* is now used only in compounds and phrases such as *cupboard, pastry board*, and *sideboard*. Throughout the thirteenth century, however, *board* was among the most common of kitchen words because it referred to the flat, raised surface upon which meals were eaten; in other words, *board* meant *table*. The importance of *board* as a culinary word remained unchallenged for a hundred years, until the fourteenth century when *table* began to take on its current sense; before this time, the word *table* had existed in English but only in the sense of a tablet used for writing upon. It was also at about this time that *board* came to mean the actual food served upon the supper board or table; this sense of the word persists in the phrase *room and board*, meaning *lodgings and meals*. Of course, *board* also continued to develop other non-culinary senses, including *panel of decision makers*, as in *School Board*, the people who gather around a table not to eat food but to digest each other's ideas. See also *cupboard* and *smorgasbord*.

boil

See *bouillabaisse*.

bollepunge

Although English has borrowed tens of thousands of words and phrases from other languages, other languages have also borrowed tens of thousands of words and phrases from English. The English phrase *bowl of punch*, for example, was borrowed in the seventeenth century by at least two other cultures: the French, who corrupted it to *bollepunge*, and the citizens of Bombay, who corrupted it to *palepuntz*. In time, these new words were taken back into English as British travellers and traders mistook the odd-sounding *bollepunge* and *palepuntz* for native French or Hindi words. As a result, in the late seventeenth century, British travel writers would occasionally remark on the popularity of a quaint Indian drink called *palepuntz*, or would note the fondness of the French for a beverage called *bollepunge*, apparently unaware that the names of these potations derived from their very own language. See also *punch* and *beef*.

bonbon

See *couscous*.

boned

Dating back to the seventeenth century, the word used to describe a substance prone to bursting into flames, such as kerosene, was *inflammable*, the prefix *in* actually being used to intensify the word *flammable*. Usually, however, the prefix *in* is used to negate the word it precedes, just as *incapable* means *not capable*. This linguistic ambiguity led to so many catastrophic fires—thanks to people doing things like throwing cigarette butts into vats marked *inflammable*—that in the 1950s industrial leaders officially changed the word *inflammable* to *flammable* to avoid any confusion. Less perilous, but more annoying, is the confusion caused by the word *boned*. Since the fifteenth century, *boned* has referred to meat that has had its bones removed, even though the word sounds as if it should mean the bones are still in. As a result, a statement such as "This fish is not boned" is so ambiguous that thinking about it carefully will result in a Zen-like annihilation of the self. Steps were taken in the 1940s to avoid this confusion by inventing the word *deboned*; many meat packagers, however, continue to use the ambiguous *boned*, and thus not a few consumers remain not disabused of their confusion.

bonfire

A wiener roast is usually held around a bonfire, an outdoor fire fuelled by dead branches, scraps of lumber, and marshmallows. Back in the fifteenth century, however, a community bonfire was held on a specific day—often Midsummer's night—and was fuelled by the bones of the many sheep and cattle that had been butchered and eaten throughout the year. From this custom, the bonfire, originally *bone-fire*, took its name.

bonny-clabber

Because the English have ruled or tried to rule Ireland since Henry VIII declared himself King of Ireland in 1541, the names of numerous Irish foods have made their way into English. One of the earliest of these Irish adoptions was *bonny-clabber*, a dish of sour, clotted milk whose name derives from the Irish words for *milk* (*bainne*) and for *mud* (*claba*). It was also in the seventeenth century that the English adopted the word *graddan*, a name given by the Irish to grain that is parched in a hot pan before being used to make graddan cake; the source of *graddan* is *gread-aim*, a Gaelic phrase literally meaning *I scorch*. In the mid eighteenth century, the English also came to enjoy an Irish cake that they called *barnbrack*; this name, however, was actually a corruption of the original Irish name, *bairghean breac*, meaning *speckled cake*, so called because of the currants dotting its surface. In the mid nineteenth century, several other Irish dishes were also embraced by the English, including *crubeen* and *stelk*. In Irish, *crubeen* means *little hoof*, the dish being so named because it contains a pig's foot. Stelk, on the other hand, is a vegetable dish made by mashing together potatoes, onions, and beans; its name derives from the Irish *stailc*, meaning *sulky* or *stubborn*, and may have been bestowed on the dish because the vegetables were not easily mashed (likewise, in English, butter-makers call cream *sulky* when churning fails to turn it into butter). An even more recent borrowing from Irish gastronomy is *drisheen*, a sausage made from sheep's blood, milk, and seasoning; this dish derives its name from the Irish word for intestine, *drisin*.

borscht

Beets are what give borscht its distinctive red colour, but in Russia, where the dish was first concocted, it was originally made with another sort of root, the parsnip. This original ingredient even gave the dish its name, for in Russian *borscht* means *cow parsnip*, a parsnip that grows wild in marshes. The word *borscht* was introduced to English in the early nineteenth century, but the soup itself did not become a popular menu item until the early 1920s when more than a million Russians emigrated to major European cities, including Paris and London, to escape their country's civil turmoil. See also *smetana*.

bottle

Although the word *bottle* now refers to vessels made of glass, it originally denoted a narrow-necked vessel made of any material, especially leather. The word *bottle*, which English borrowed from French in the late fourteenth century as *botel*, takes its origin from the Late Latin word *buticula*, meaning *small vessel*. In turn, *buticula* was formed as the diminutive of the Late Latin word *buttis*, meaning *cask* or *barrel*, and also gave rise to the Late Latin word *buticularius*, the name of a servant who tended the bottles in the household wine cellar. From *buticularius* the French word *bouteillier* developed, and from this word English derived *butler*, first recorded in the middle of the thirteenth century. More distantly related to *bottle*, having derived from the same Indo-

European source, is *bud*, the name of a plant-shoot that swells outward like a bottle. See also *butt* and *sewer*.

bouce Jane

During the first half of the fifteenth century, dozens of names of dishes emerged in English only to fall into disuse and obsolescence a few decades later. Many of these dishes had names whose origins are now inscrutable, either because they were in use so briefly that no one bothered to take note of where they came from, or because they arose out of a local dialect, or because they were strange corruptions of other words. One such dish whose name is utterly inexplicable is *bouce Jane*, a dish made by mincing a fowl and then boiling it in milk with herbs. *Consy*, another dish referred to only in the early fifteenth century, is also an etymological mystery, although its recipe is not: one medieval recipe for consy instructs the cook to "take capons and roast them and chop them into gobbets and colour it with saffron." Another meat dish, known as *burseu*, was made by taking the "numbles" of a pig—that is, its innards—and parboiling them in wine. *Potron*, a word that almost looks as if it is related to *poultry*, was in fact not a meat dish but rather an unusual method of cooking an egg: "Take a shovel of iron and heat it burning hot and then fill it full of salt; then make a pit in the salt and then cast the white and the yolk of the egg into the hole of the salt and let seethe over the fire till it be half-hard." The names of strange fish dishes also came and went in the early fifteenth century, including *figee* (a dish of fish and curds), *gyngawdry* (a dish of boiled cod or haddock liver), and *tavorsay* (a dish made from the liver and head of a cod). The names of sweet dishes and desserts seem to have been especially susceptible to obsolescence during these early decades of the fifteenth century, perhaps because those sorts of confection tended to be created for the nonce, that is, for special occasions: *malmeny*, *pocerounce*, and *prenade*, for example, were once names for desserts made from honey, wine, and various spices; the confection called *nesebek* was made of figs; *fauntempere* was made of rice flour and almond milk; and *raston* was made of butter, eggs, and cheese. In addition to having names with unknown origins, a few other dishes from the early fifteenth century have even become disembodied from their recipes and exist only as strange words lurking in historical dictionaries; these include *corat*, *bukenade*, *lorey*, and the delicious sounding *blobsterdis*. See also *funistrada*.

bouillabaisse

Although *bouillabaisse* now refers to a dish made of fish and herbs, it originally signified a method of cooking. The word derives from the French *bouillir*, meaning *to boil*, and *abaisser*, meaning *to reduce*; together, the two words described the culinary process of boiling a fish stock until it is reduced to a thick soup. *Bouillabaisse* was adopted by English in the mid nineteenth century, but long before then the French words that make up this compound had been borrowed separately: *abaisser* was borrowed in the fourteenth century as *abase*, meaning *to humiliate*, while *bouillir* was borrowed in the mid eighteenth century as *bouillon*, a kind of broth. Even earlier, in the thirteenth century, English had adopted *bouillir* as *boil*, the word having been introduced by the French ruling class that had seized control of England in 1066. The English had, of course, been capable of boiling water before the French took over, but they referred to it as *seething*, a word deriving from the same Germanic source as *suds*. The word *seething* still exists in figurative uses such as *seething with rage*, and its past tense—*sodden*—is still used to signify something soaked in water, although not necessarily boiling water. Incidentally, the source of the French *bouillir* (and therefore of the English *boil*) is the Latin *bulla*, meaning *bubble*, which is also the source of *bullet*, a projectile originally shaped like a bubble.

bouillon

See *bouillabaisse*.

bowl

The bowl you eat cereal from every morning takes its name from the same source as the words *ball*, *balloon*, and *ballot*. All four of these words derive from a Germanic source meaning *to swell*. This sense is still very evident in *balloon* and *ball*, items originally made by inflating animal skins, and is still fairly evident in *bowl*, a vessel "swollen" like half a ball. The relation of "swelling" to *ballot*, however, has been completely obscured thanks to changes in the election process: whereas we now mark an X on a slip of paper, the ancient Athenians voted by dropping little balls, called *ballotta*, into a box: a black ballotta counted for a *no*, a white ballotta for a *yes*. Much later, when this voting method was adopted in the eighteenth century by British social clubs, the term *blackballed* arose to describe a person whose application for membership had been rejected.

braise

See *brazier*.

braised trake

See *funistrada*.

bray

See *brioche*.

brazier

The word *brazier*—meaning a large, metal pan containing live coals—and the word *braise*—meaning the process of cooking food at a low temperature in a closed vessel—have the same origin. Both words derive from the French word *braise*, meaning *hot coals*, which in turn probably derives from the Old Norse word *brasa*, meaning *to expose to fire*. The word *brazier* entered English in 1690, about a century before the first appearance of the culinary *braise* in 1797. In common parlance the word *brazier* has been supplanted by *hibachi*, a Japanese word that also refers to a metal pan containing live coals. This decline of the word *brazier* may have been facilitated by the introduction, in 1911, of a word having a completely different origin and meaning: *brassière*. The difficulty that some people have in uttering the name of this female undergarment—and other "indiscreet" words like *panties*, *bowel movement*, and *Mulroney*—may have caused them to seek an alternative name for the similar sounding *brazier*. Likewise, farmers in the 1980s were persuaded to abandon the word *rape* as a name for an oil-producing grain and to use a new name, *canola*, in its place. See also *ravioli*.

bread

Until about a thousand years ago, baked lumps of dough were not known as *bread*, but rather as *hlaf*. The word *bread* did exist back then, but it simply meant *piece* or *fragment*: if you dropped a pottery jug, each piece would be called a *bread*, the plural of which was *breadru*. Gradually, however, the word *bread* came to be identified with the pieces of *hlaf* eaten at every meal, a shift that occurred simply because these pieces were the most important ones in the household, the ones that kept everyone alive. In time, this new meaning widened further and *bread* took the place of *hlaf* as the general name for any product made by baking dough; *hlaf* did not die out, however, but simply evolved into the word *loaf*, now meaning a single "unit" of bread, instead of bread in general. As a slang term for *money*, the term *bread* probably grew out of Cockney rhyming slang; this slang, which was to some extent a real code but for the most part just a verbal game, replaced certain common terms with a phrase whose final word rhymed with the word being replaced. *Bowl of water*, for example, replaced *daughter*, while *apples and pears* took the place of *stairs*. Sometimes the last half of the phrase was eventually dropped; thus, *bread and honey*, the rhyming slang for *money*, was reduced to just *bread*. This sense of *bread* is not recorded until the middle of this century, but, considering that it originated as slang, it was probably in spoken use much earlier. See also *raspberry*.

breakfast

Most nutritionists say that breakfast should be the largest meal of the day, partly because you have not eaten for the previous eight or even fourteen hours. These food-less hours are a fast, as are the longer periods of not eating undertaken by hunger-strikers or religious devotees. Accordingly, when you finally do sit down to your pancakes or Corn Flakes you are "breaking" your fast, and from this notion the word *breakfast* developed in the mid fifteenth century. The word *fast*, incidentally, is one of the strangest words in English because it is its own opposite. *Fast* can mean *moving rapidly*, as in *lightning fast*, or it can mean *fixed in place*, as in *hold fast, fastened*, or even *fast asleep*. The sense of *fixed in place* is the original meaning of *fast*, and in fact it is this sense that led to the word meaning *time of not eating*: when you decide not to eat, you must be "fixed" in your resolve, and you must "hold fast" to your decision. Similarly, if you are a hunter, you will only succeed in killing your animal if you stay close behind it—in other words, you must remain a "fixed" distance behind it almost as if you are "fastened" to it; from this sense of being "fast" with a fleeing animal, the word came to mean *swift* just as, for similar reasons, the Latin *rapere*, meaning *to seize*, developed into the English *rapid*.

bridecake

See *wedding cake.*

Brie

The French agricultural region of Brie, located east of Paris, is where the soft, creamy cheese known as *Brie* acquired its name. Brie is now made in Brie, but the cheese actually originated in the Île de France and was named *Brie* only because Charlemagne, the king of the Franks in the eighth century, was introduced to it while staying at a monastery in Brie. As a place-name, *Brie* derives from the word *briga*, which meant, in the language of the ancient Gauls, *hill* or *height*; the name *Brian*, though Celtic in origin, ultimately derives from the same source as *briga* and is thus a cousin of *Brie*. Brie, the cheese, was first referred to in English in the mid nineteenth century. See also *Camembert.*

brioche

Brioche, a cake made from yeast dough enriched with eggs, acquired its name in French in the fifteenth century, a name adopted by English in the early nineteenth century. The source of *brioche* is the Old Norman French word *brier*, meaning *to pound*, so named because brioche dough requires repeated kneading; *brier* is also the source of the culinary term *bray*, meaning *to crush into fragments*, a term first used in English cookbooks in the late fourteenth century.

broccoli

Why do we eat *carrots* but not *broccolies*? The reason is that English acquired the word *broccoli* in the late seventeenth century from Italian, and in Italian *broccoli* is already plural: the singular form is *broccolo*, which in turn is a diminutive of the word *brocco*, meaning *stalk* or *shoot*. The word *broccoli* therefore means *little shoots*, an apt description of the vegetable's appearance. Further back in history, the Italian *brocco* evolved from *brocchus*, a Latin adjective meaning *pointed*; this Latin origin means that *broccoli* is related to several other words that also derive from *brocchus*, including *brochette* (a pointed, culinary skewer) and *brochure* (so named because brochures were originally stitched together with a pointed needle).

brochette

See *broccoli*.

brown baker

See *white baker*.

brunch

Although *brunch* is now a familiar word, the name of this late breakfast, invented in the 1890s by combining the beginning of *breakfast* with the end of *lunch*, must have sounded as strange to the late Victorians as *lupper*, proposed in the 1970s as a name for a meal between lunch and supper, now sounds to us. The reason *lupper* has not caught on is that since the 1970s people have been eating their supper later in the day, not earlier, and so *lupper* has no reason to exist. A far more useful portmanteau word is *slake*, the name of a snack eaten in the middle of the night; invented about two minutes ago by combining *sleep* and *wake*, this new word will eventually become so popular that it will even spawn verb forms such as *slaked* and *slaking*.

Brussels sprouts

Brussels sprouts are small cabbages that actually belong to the mustard family. They take their name from Brussels, Belgium where horticulturalists first developed them in the fourteenth century. The vegetable itself was not imported to England until the mid nineteenth century, but fifty years earlier it had been referred to by name in English gardening books. The city of Brussels derived its name in the sixth century from the Germanic *broca sali*, meaning *marsh building*, an apt name considering that the city originated as a fortress built upon a low-lying island. The other half of the Brussels sprout's name, *sprout*, derives from a Germanic source that also gave rise to the words *spurt* (as in, "The ketchup spurted onto my shirt"), *sprit* (as in *bowsprit*, the shaft that "sprouts" from the bow of a ship) and *spritzer* (a drink of wine and soda water whose name was adopted from German in the 1960s).

bubble and squeak

See *spotted dick*.

buffet

The word *buffet* was borrowed from French at the beginning of the eighteenth century, and thus the North American pronunciation, *buff-ay*, is closer to the original French source than the British pronunciation *buff-it* (with the stress on the first syllable). Originally, the word referred to a dining-room sideboard where china is displayed, a meaning it retains to this day. However, *buffet* also came to mean, around the beginning of this century, the actual food laid out on such a side-board as guests walked by to fill their plates. The origin of the word *buffet* is unknown, but many ingenious explanations have been proposed: one suggestion is that the article of furniture took its name from the blow or *buffet*, pronounced *buffit*, that a host would inflict on the sideboard in order to fold out its hinged surface. It is probably mere coincidence, though, that the *buffet* meaning *sideboard* is spelt the same as the *buffet* meaning *blow*.

bulgur

The Turkish name for cracked wheat is *bulgur*, a word English adopted directly from Turkish in the 1930s. Many centuries before this, however, Arabic had adopted the same Turkish word as *burgul*, a term that English then borrowed in the mid eighteenth century, spelling it *burgoo* and using it to refer to a porridge made from cracked wheat and eaten by sailors; in North America, the word also came to refer to a stew or soup eaten at outdoor feasts.

bully beef

See *corned beef*.

bun

The painful swelling that makes big toes bigger is called a *bunion*, a word that may derive from the same source as the word *bun*. In the fifteenth century, this shared source—the Old French *bugne*, meaning *bump on the head*—was adopted by the East Anglian dialect of English as *bunny*, meaning *lump* or *swelling* (no relation, as far as anyone knows, to the *bunny* that appears on Easter Sunday); in the early eighteenth century, this *bunny* became *bunion* and was used by toe-doctors to refer to a swelling of the bursa mucosa. The French *bugne* may also be the source of the English *bun*, first recorded in the fourteenth century, since buns are lumps of dough that swell in size as they bake. Although this origin is uncertain, it is made more probable by the fact that the French themselves, by the fifteenth century, had formed a diminutive from *bugne*—*bugnet*—and used it to refer to fritters and small, round loaves. The word *bun* was first used as a name for a hair-style in the late nineteenth century. In Scotland, the word *bun* is not the name of a baked lump of dough but of a cake made from fruit and spice.

bung

The stopper used to seal a wine bottle is called a cork, while the one used to seal a wine-cask is called a bung. The word appeared in English in the mid fifteenth century and within a hundred years had inspired a variety of other words associated with the bung: for example, the opening into which the bung was stuffed became known as the *bung-hole*, the utensil used to cut the bung became known as the *bung-knife*, and thieves who pulled wallets from pockets—like bungs from barrels—came to be known as *bung-nippers*. Later on, in the mid eighteenth century, *bung* also came to mean *tavern keeper*, the person responsible for removing the bung from the wine cask. (The older name for this person—*tapster*, the person who controlled the tap—dates back to the eleventh century; the American equivalent, *bartender*, dates only to the early nineteenth century.) The word *bung* probably derives from the Latin word *puncta*, meaning *pin-prick*, which came to mean *hole* and then, by extension, *material used to plug a hole*.

burgoo
See *bulgur*.

burrito
See *chimichanga*.

burseu
See *bouce Jane*.

butcher
Although the French could not legally consume horseflesh until 1811 (when they realized that eating horsemeat had saved many lives during the Napoleonic campaigns), they have long eaten goat, not just because they liked the pungent flavour of its flesh but because goats were able to survive weather and blights that killed less hardy animals. In the early Middle Ages in France, people who slaughtered goats and sold their flesh were known as *bouchiers*, having derived their name from the French word *boc*, meaning *he-goat*; the original butchers, therefore, sold only goat-meat, although by the time the word was adopted into English in the late thirteenth century it had so widened its meaning that a butcher could, with impunity, whack almost any sort of animal over the head. The source of the French *boc*, likely a Celtic word, also developed through a different route into the word *buck*, applied to a male deer. The French *boc* also gave Old English its original name for the male goat, *bocca*, which was paired with the name for the female, *gat*. By the fourteenth

century, however, *gat*, which had evolved into *goat*, had come to mean both sexes of the animal, thus prompting the use of personal names, specifically *billy-goat* and *nanny-goat*, to distinguish the two sexes. The name for the young of goats, *kid*, first appeared in English at the beginning of the thirteenth century but was probably adopted from Old Norse centuries earlier when the Vikings were plundering the coastal villages of England. *Kid* was first used as a slang name for children in the seventeenth century and attained wide acceptance by the nineteenth century.

butler

See *bottle*.

butt

The Late Latin *buttis*, meaning *cask*, is the source of the English word *butt*, the name of a wine cask ranging in size from 108 to 140 gallons, large enough that Edward IV was able to execute his brother Clarence by drowning him in a butt of malmsey wine. The word first entered English in the middle of the fifteenth century. Earlier than this, in the late fourteenth century, *buttis* had already given rise to another English word: *buttery*, a storeroom whose name was modelled upon the French word *bouteillerie*, meaning *bottle*. Butteries, in fact, originally contained no butter, no milk fats whatsoever, only bottles and bottles of wine tended by the household's butler. Eventually, however, confusion with the unrelated word *butter* caused the meaning of *buttery* to expand, so that by the middle of the seventeenth century butteries had come to house almost any kind of provision. See also *bottle*.

butter

According to the Greek historian Herodotus, the ancient Scythians—a nomadic people of Asia and Eastern Europe—so loved butter that they used only blind slaves to churn it, ones who would not be distracted from their work by the outside world. The word *butter*, as befits the world's first edible oil product, can be traced back thousands of years to the Greek *bouturon*, which the Greeks either borrowed from the Scythians or invented themselves by combining *bous*, meaning *cow*, and *turos*, meaning *cheese*. *Bouturon* was then adopted by Latin as *butyrum*, which evolved directly into the French *beurre* and, via the Germanic languages, into the English *butter*, first recorded in the eleventh century. The word *butter* ousted the previous Old English name of the oily spread: *smeoru*, the ancestor of the Modern English *smear* (also related to the Old English *smeoru* is the Modern Danish *smor*, meaning *butter* and appearing in *smorgasbord*). Incidentally, one of the two Greek words that evolved into *butter*—*bous*, meaning cow—persists in English as *Bossy*, a traditional name for a milk-cow. See also *smorgasbord*.

butter-boat

Since the late seventeenth century, *boat* has been used as a name for an oval dish in which sauces are brought to the table. *Butter-boat*, used for melted butter, appeared in the late eighteenth century, and *gravy boat* in the late nineteenth.

buttered ermal

See *funistrada*.

buttery

See *butt*.

cabaret

See *tavern*.

cabbage

Considering that we buy cabbages in heads, it's hardly surprising that the word *cabbage* literally means *swollen head*: the name derives from the Old French *caboce*, which in turn may have developed from a compound formed from the Latin *caput*, meaning *head*, and the Old French *boce*, meaning *a swelling*. Words related to *cabbage* therefore include other descendants of the Latin *caput* such as *decapitate* (meaning *to remove the head*), *chapter* (a section of a book with its own "heading"), and *precipitate* (literally meaning *to fall head first*). In English, the word *cabbage* first appeared in the mid fifteenth century; prior to this, cabbage was called *cole*, a word still represented in *cauliflower* and *coleslaw*. See also *cauliflower* and *cole slaw*.

cabob

See *shish kebab*.

caboose

Since the mid eighteenth century, the kitchen of a war ship has been called the *galley*, while that of a merchant ship has been called the *caboose*. The origin of the word *galley* is unknown, but *caboose* derives from the Dutch *kabuis*, a shortened form of *kaban huis*, meaning *cabin house*. In the mid nineteenth century, *caboose* was borrowed by North American railroad workers as a name for the last car of a freight train, the car containing limited facilities for cooking a meal.

cacciatore

The German *jaeger* (the *j* is pronounced like a *y*), the French *chasseur*, and the Italian *cacciatore* all mean *hunter* and are all applied to certain dishes, usually simple in nature, either made from wild game or prepared with mushrooms and herbs, the kind of ingredients available to a hungry hunter out in the wilderness. Two of these three words, *chasseur* and *cacciatore*, derive from the Latin *capere*, meaning *to seize*, and are closely related to several other English words that derive from the same source, including *chase* and *capture*. The German *jaeger*, on the other hand, derives from the German verb *jagen*, meaning *to chase*, which derives from the same source as *yacht*, originally a speedy ship used to chase other ships, often in order to plunder them.

Caesar salad

Caesar salad takes its name from Julius Caesar, the most famous Roman emperor, but does so only indirectly. For twenty centuries after his death, the legacy of the emperor inspired thousands of Italian parents to name their sons *Caesar*. One of those sons was Caesar Cardini, an Italian who immigrated to Tijuana, Mexico where he opened a restaurant. In 1924, Cardini invented a salad made from romaine lettuce, garlic, croutons, Parmesan cheese, and Worcester sauce; the salad became popular with the Hollywood stars who frequently visited Tijuana, and soon came to be known as *Caesar's salad*, later shortened to *Caesar salad*. In a political—rather than culinary—context, the surname of the emperor is also the source of several other words eventually introduced into English: in ancient times the Roman emperors who succeeded Julius Caesar, such as Augustus Caesar, adopted his surname as a title in order to link themselves to their famous predecessor. Eventually, this title entered the Germanic family of languages where it gave rise to *kaiser*, a German title used until

1918 when Kaiser Wilhelm II abdicated his throne and fled to Holland (*kaiser*, incidentally, is the source of *kaiser roll*, the name of a crisp, puffy bun that takes its name from its resemblance to the kaiser's crown). The title of *Caesar* likewise entered the Slavic languages where it gave rise to *czar*, a Russian title used until 1918 when Czar Nicholas II was shot by the Bolsheviks. In a medical—rather than political—context, Caesar's surname is also the source of the term *caesarian section*: the legend that Caesar was born by being cut from his mother's womb prompted seventeenth century doctors to name this obstetric operation after him. This legend probably has no basis in fact, arising only because Caesar's surname happens to resemble the Latin *caesus*, meaning *cut*. Caesar's surname actually derives from *caesaries*, a Latin word meaning *full head of hair*, presumedly bestowed on an ancestor who had thick locks.

café

see *coffee*.

cafeteria

see *coffee*.

cake

From a linguistic point of view, the defining feature of cake is not its taste or its ingredients, but its shape: cakes are round but flat on top, whether they are made from bread dough (as they originally were back in the thirteenth century) or from flour and sugar (as they have been since the fifteenth century) or from ammonia (as they have been since the invention of the modern urinal). The word *cake* derives from the Old Norse *kaka*, and is therefore related to the Dutch word that gave English *cookie*, but is not related to the Latin source that gave English *cook*. The expression *That takes the cake*, meaning that something is outlandish or fantastic, and the word *cakewalk*, meaning that someone found something easy to do, developed when American slaves established the tradition of giving cakes to the best dancers at social gatherings. See also *cookie*.

calabash

See *squash*.

calorie

See *chowder*.

Camembert

Camembert cheese was invented during the French Revolution when a certain Marie Harel combined a cheese-making technique used in Normandy with one used in the Brie region. Harel's daughter began selling this new cheese in the village of Camembert, whose name was bestowed upon the dairy product when Napoleon rode through the village, tried some of the cheese, and declared it to be excellent. Centuries before this, the village of Camembert acquired its name thanks to its being located in a field owned by someone named *Manberht*. This personal name was combined with the Latin word for *field*—*campus*—and thus the compound *campus Manberht* was formed, gradually shortening to *Camembert*. Even further back, the personal name *Manberht* derived from a Germanic source meaning *brilliant man* just as *Albert* means *noble brilliant*, *Robert* means *fame brilliant*, and *Egbert* means *sword brilliant*. In a sense, therefore, *Camembert* literally means *field of the brilliant man*. See also *brie*.

canapé

As unlikely as it sounds, the word *canapé*, the name of those miniscule open-faced sandwiches you get at cocktail parties, derives from the ancient Greek word for *mosquito*. The ancient Greeks, irritated at having their philosophical debates and nude wrestling cut short by the stings of mosquitoes, decided to protect themselves with netting, which they called *konopeion* after the Greek word *konops*, meaning *mosquito*. The name of this netting entered Latin as *conopeum*, which gave rise to the English *canopy*, a kind of over-hanging curtain, and to the French *canapé*, originally a sofa with a curtain suspended over it. *Canapé* was then borrowed by French chefs, who decided that a morsel of bread covered with a tasty garnish resembles a curtain-shrouded sofa. In English, *canapé* first appeared in the late nineteenth century.

candy

The word *candy* emerged in English in the early fifteenth century, a few decades before the appearance of *sweetmeat*, another word that refers to a wide variety of sugary morsels. *Candy* and *sweetmeat* were originally distinguished in so far as *candy* tended to refer only to flavoured pieces of crystallized sugar, while *sweetmeat* could also include glazed fruit, sugary pastries, and gingerbread. By the eighteenth century, the two words had moved closer together in meaning, but had moved farther apart geographically: *sweetmeat*, or its shortened form, *sweet*, came to be the usual British name for such confections, while *candy* came to be the usual North American word. In origin, the word *candy* derives ultimately from a Sanskrit word meaning *to break*. From this word, the people of ancient India, who were the original writers of Sanskrit, formed the word *khanda*, meaning *broken piece*, which was applied to little chunks of sugar broken from a larger block of crystallized sugar. This word was adopted by Arabic as *qandah*, and was bestowed by the Arabs on pieces of sugar flavoured with ginger, almond, or fruit extracts. The Arabic *qandah* then became the Italian and French *candi*, finally adopted by English as *candy*. See also *mincemeat* and *sweet*.

canister

See *cannelloni*.

cannelloni

The slender tubes of pastry stuffed with seasoned meat or even with cream and chocolate take their name, *cannelloni*, from the Italian *canna*, meaning *reed* or *stalk*, a tube through which a plant's nutrients flow. In turn, the Italian *canna* goes back to a Latin source (also spelt *canna*), that developed via French into words for other tube-like structures including *cane*, *canal*, and *channel*; via Spanish, the Latin *canna* also developed into the English words *canyon* and *cannon*, the one a sort of "tube" for a river, the other for an artillery shell. Further back in its history, the Latin *canna* developed from a Greek source that also evolved into the Latin *canistrum*, the name of a basket made of reeds; it was this Latin word, *canistrum*, that was adopted by English in the eighteenth century as *canister*, a tube-shaped container no longer made of reeds, but of metal.

cannibal

When Columbus first visited the West Indies he encountered a nation of people who called themselves the Galibi, a name meaning *brave people*. Because the pronunciation of *Galibi* varied slightly from dialect to dialect, European explorers sometimes heard the name pronounced as *Carib* and sometimes as *Caniba*, prompting different words to arise from each variant. From *Carib*, the word *Caribbean* evolved, while from *Caniba*, the word *cannibal* developed, thanks to reports that the people of these islands ate one another (but after Columbus enslaved the Caribs and forced them to dig the gold out of their islands, it became more apparent who was devouring whom). After the word *cannibal* appeared in English in the mid sixteenth century, it soon became a familiar word: in the early seventeenth century, Shakespeare even punned on *cannibal* in *The Tempest* when he invented *Caliban*, the name of an enslaved brute who gathers wood for Prospero. A little known synonym for *cannibal* is *anthropophagus*, deriving from the Greek *anthropos*, meaning *human being*, and the Greek *phagein*, meaning *to eat*. In English, the word *anthropophagus* appeared at almost exactly the same time as *cannibal*, the mid sixteenth century.

cantaloupe

The two common names for this orange-fleshed melon, *cantaloupe* and *musk melon*, derive respectively from the most divine and most earthly of sources. When introduced to Italy from Armenia in the seventeenth century, this fruit was cultivated at the Pope's country villa, a place near Rome called *Cantalupo* to which His Holiness would occasionally withdraw. Accordingly, when the French started importing this melon from Italy, they called it *cantaloup*, a name that English borrowed in the early eighteenth century. The melon's other common name, *musk melon*, appeared in the mid sixteenth century, and originally belonged to another variety of melon with a very musky scent; the word was then transferred by mistake to the much less musky melon that currently has its name. The earthy origin of *musk melon* lies in *musk*, which evolved—through French, Latin, Greek, and Persian—from the Sanskrit word *muska*, meaning *scrotum*; the ancient people of India, where Sanskrit was spoken, evidently perceived a resemblance between the musk-producing gland of certain animals and the typical scrotum. The history of *musk* does not end there, however: the Sanskrit word for *scrotum*—*muska*— derived in turn from an older word, *mus*, meaning *mouse*; once again, the ancient people of India perceived a resemblance, this time between a scrotum and a mouse, and thus they gave that part of the male body a name that literally means *little mouse*. You therefore have a choice in considering the musk melon a *little mouse melon* or a *scrotum melon*. *Muscatel* (a French wine), *moscato* (an Italian wine), and *muskrat* (a Canadian rodent) derive from the same musky source as *musk melon*.

Cape Cod turkey

See *Welsh rabbit*.

capon

See *coupon*.

cappuccino

Served with a foamy head of milk, the dark coffee known as *cappuccino* takes its name from an order of friars known as the *Capuchins*. The beverage is so called either because its foamy head resembles the partly-sheared heads of the Capuchins or because a Brazilian order of Capuchins specialized in growing coffee beans in the eighteenth century. The Capuchins themselves derived their name from *cappuccio*, the Italian name for a peaked hood (in 1528, Pope Clement VII made such a hood the official headgear of the Capuchins). The name of this hood, *cappuccio*, was in turn an augmentative of the Italian *cappa*, meaning *cloak*, and thus *cappuccio*, *Capuchin*, and *cappuccino* all literally mean *big cloak*. These words are also, therefore, related to *chapel*: the Italian *cappella*—which became the English *chapel*—originated as the name of the shrine housing the holy cloak—or *cappa*—of St. Martin. Later on, when chapels became common, the choral music performed in them tended to be unaccompanied by musical instruments and thus such performances came to be called *a cappella*, meaning *in the chapel*.

caramel

When heated until it melts and browns, sugar is called *caramel*, a word that literally means *honey-cane*: in Medieval Latin, the sugar cane plant was called *cannamella*, a word formed by combining *canna*, meaning *cane*, and *mel*, meaning *honey*. *Cannamella* then evolved into Spanish as *caramelo*, where it became the name of a browned sugar resembling the sweet juice extracted from sugar canes. English adopted *caramelo* in the early eighteenth century as *caramel*, first using the word as a name for browned sugar, and later as a name for a small candy made from sugar, cream, and flavouring. See also *molasses*.

caraway

When a word is successively passed from one language to another, it not only may end up with a very different spelling and pronunciation, it may even refer to a different item than it originally did. For example, the Latin word for onion—*caepa*—became the English word *chive*, the name of a plant related to, but quite distinct from, the onion. Similarly, the Greek name for cumin became the English name for caraway. This Greek name—*karon*—was borrowed as *al-karawiya* by Arabic speakers, who still used it to refer to cumin; in the Middle Ages, however, European scholars adopted the Arabic form into Medieval Latin, and in the process transferred it to the similar-looking caraway seed and simplified its spelling to *carvi*. This new form then evolved into the Spanish *caravea*, which entered English as *caraway* in the mid fifteenth century.

carbonade

See *carbonara*.

carbonara

Diamonds, graphite, and coal are all made of carbon, an element whose name derives from the Latin *carbo*, meaning *coal*. The Italian word for coal, *carbone*, also derives from the Latin *carbo*, as does *carbonara*, a word that might be loosely translated as *in the manner of the charcoal pit*. Centuries ago, Italians gave the name *spaghetti alla carbonara* to a spaghetti sauce made with meat grilled over charcoal, a sauce that evolved over time into one made from minced prosciutto, egg yolks, and grated cheese. The French counterpart to the word *carbonara*—*carbonade*—likewise refers to a dish made by grilling beef over charcoal and then adding it to a stew, while the Spanish *carbonado* refers simply to a piece of grilled meat. The word *charcoal*, the name of that indispensable barbecue fuel, may also be related to this cluster of words, since the *char* of *charcoal* may have derived from the Old French word for coal, *charbon*. On the other hand, the *char* of *charcoal* may be of native English origin, possibly deriving from the Old English *cerran*, meaning *turn*: if this is the case, then the word *charcoal* arose from the fact that it is wood "turned" into coal.

carcake

See *carling*.

cardamom

Cardamom is a spice little used in North America or Europe, with the exception of Scandinavian countries where it is used in spiced wines and preserved fruit. In India and Middle Eastern nations, however, cardamom is used to flavour coffee, tea, cakes, noodles, and omelettes. The name of this spice, first recorded in English in the sixteenth century, derives from two Greek words meaning *cress-spice*, cress being a garden plant whose leaves are used in salads.

carling

In the sixteenth century, the Sunday preceding Easter Friday became known as *Care Sunday*, the word *care* being used to mean *sorrow* or *grief*. Because this Sunday was a part of Lent, certain foods—including meat—were proscribed, while others—such as parched peas—became traditional fare. The parching of the peas may have been intended to represent a desert-like aridity, appropriate since Lent is a commemoration of Jesus's forty days in the wilderness. In time, these peas came to be known as *carlings*, a word formed from the *care* of *Care Sunday* and the suffix *ling*, which also appears in words such as *gosling* and *darling*. Eventually, the noun *carling* also gave rise to the verb *carl*, meaning *to cook food by parching it*. In Scotland, another sort of food also owes its name to Care Sunday: *carcake*, a small cake made with eggs and sometimes with blood, was originally baked and eaten as a sign of sorrow and repentance, but eventually came to be associated with the merry-making of Shrove Tuesday. Likewise, shrove-cake was a cake given to children on Shrove Tuesday so that they would have something to eat while the adults celebrated God's forgiveness of their past sins, and their carte blanche to commit entirely new ones.

carnival

Although the word *carnival* is now used in a general sense to mean *festival* or even *circus*, the word originally had a much more precise application: it referred specifically to the holiday before Lent when Roman Catholics made merry and feasted, activities not permitted once the forty days of Lent began. To remind people that this was their last day to feast, this celebration was called, in Medieval Latin, the *carnelevarium*, a word formed by compounding the Latin *carnem*—a declension of *caro*, meaning *meat* or *flesh*—with *levare*, meaning *to lift away*. Literally, therefore, the *carnelevarium* was the day before the meat was taken away. In Italian, *carnelevarium* evolved into *carneleval*, which was later shortened to *carneval*, the form that English adopted as *carnival* in the mid sixteenth century. Closely associated with the Roman Catholic Carnival is Mardi gras, a festive holiday whose French name, meaning *fat Tuesday*, alludes to the custom of using up all the cooking fat in the kitchen before Lent. Other words that derive from the same Latin source as *carnival* include *carnivore* (a meat eater), *carnation* (a flesh-coloured flower), *incarnation* (meaning *in the flesh*), and *chili con carne* (meaning *chili peppers with meat*). Several other familiar words derive from the same source as the *gras* of *Mardi gras*, including *grease*, a type of melted fat, and *crass*, a word used to describe people whose behaviour is as thick and base as fat.

carrot

Although the carrot gets its name from an ancient Greek source, the ancients did not cultivate it as a kitchen vegetable, consuming the wild variety only occasionally as an aphrodisiac. Prior to the sixteenth century, carrots were also not eaten as food in England, although women did use their fern-like leaves as hair decorations. In fact, before the sixteenth century, the carrots that grew wild in England were not even called *carrots*: they were sometimes called *clapwype*, a word of unknown origin, now fortunately obsolete; and other times they were called *dauk*, a word that derived from a Latin name for some sort of plant similar to the carrot or parsnip. As they came to be cultivated in England in the early sixteenth century, carrots acquired their present name, which derives from the Greek word for the vegetable, *karoton*. In turn, *karoton* derives from the Greek word *kara*, meaning *head*, because the orange head of the vegetable pokes above the soil. The carrot was not, however, always orange: until the mid nineteenth century when horticulturalists began to cross-breed it, the root of the carrot was yellow. An even stranger fact is that the Oxford English Dictionary describes the root as now being "bright red."

carte

See *menu*.

carve

Before it came to mean the act of cutting up meat, poultry, or fish at the dinner table, the word *carve* signified the act of cutting designs or words into stone or wood. The word *carve* is, in fact, a cousin of the Greek word *graphein*, meaning *to write*, both words having derived from the same Indo-European source. *Carve* acquired its culinary sense in the early fourteenth century, but what has almost been lost to us is that it was once used as a generic term for dozens of more specific terms that varied according to the animal being dismantled. Thus, with knife in hand, a sixteenth-century host would proceed to *break* a deer, *leach* a boar, *rear* a goose, *lift* a swan, *sauce* a capon, *frush* a chicken, *spoil* a hen, *unbrace* a mallard, *dismember* a heron, *display* a crane, *disfigure* a peacock, *unjoint* a bittern, *untie* a curlew, *allay* a pheasant, *wing* a partridge, *mince* a plover, *thigh* a pigeon, *border* a meat-pie, *tire* an egg, *chine* a salmon, *string* a lamprey, *split* a pike, *splay* a bream, *tusk* a barbel, *culpon* a trout, *tranch* a sturgeon, *undertranch* a porpoise, *tame* a crab, *barb* a lobster, and *fin* a chevon. Knowing what term corresponded to what beast was a sign of an individual's sophistication and status, since only those blessed with endless hours of leisure could possibly memorize such huge lists of arcane gastronomic terminology.

cashew

Although it is native to Brazil, the cashew was introduced in the sixteenth century to other tropical countries, including India where the acrid oil from the nut is rubbed into floors to repel attacks by white ants. The name of the nut also originated in Brazil where the tree upon which it grows is called, in the Tupi language, *acaju*. This word was adopted by the Portuguese, who in the early eighteenth century introduced it to the English, who respelt it as *cashew*. *Cashew* is not related to *achoo*, a word first used in print in 1873 to represent the sound of a sneeze.

casserole

The notion of cooking an entire meal in a single dish is one of the oldest in culinary practice; it was a common technique during the Middle Ages when pot-dishes sometimes housed an ark-like variety of aerial and terrestrial animals (see, for example, the dish known as the *grenade*). In the early eighteenth century, English acquired the word *casserole*, the name of a dish that commonly serves as a complete meal for an entire family. Nonetheless, it was not until new, light-weight oven-dishes were invented in the 1950s that casseroles became, like hula-hoops, wildly popular, at least in North America. English borrowed the word *casserole* from French, which had earlier formed it from *casse*, meaning

~

pan or *ladle*. In turn, the French *casse* probably derives, via Latin, from the Greek *kuathos*, meaning *serving cup*. The term *cassolette*, literally meaning *a small casserole*, was first used as a culinary term in the early nineteenth century, although it had been used since the mid seventeenth century as a name for a vessel in which incense was burned. The same word, with a slightly different spelling, *cassoulet*, was again borrowed from French in the 1930s as the name of a ragout made of beans and duck or goose.

cate

A *cate* is a delicacy, a dainty, a treat, a choice morsel, a tid bit. Because no one in their right mind ever buys a single tid bit, *cate* is almost always used in the plural, *cates*. Like the word *caterer* to which it is related, *cate* derives from the French verb *acheter*, meaning *to purchase*. In fact, when the word *cate* first entered English in the middle of the fifteenth century it referred to any food or provision, not just dainties, that were purchased instead of being made at home. Within a hundred years of its first appearance, however, the meaning of *cate* had narrowed to include only dainties and treats. This narrowing occurred for several reasons. First, then as now, when people prepared a meal, they were more likely to buy the dessert—the cheese-cake—than to buy the main course—the meat and potatoes; as a result, cates came to be associated with dessert items. Second, the coincidence of the word *delicate* containing the word *cate* may have led people to associate cates with delicacies even though the words are not related; it is certain that *delicate cates* became a common phrase at the end of the sixteenth century. Finally, the word *cate* may have become associated with another word to which it is not related, the woman's name *Kate*; in the *Taming of the Shrew*, for instance, Shakespeare links the word and the name when Petruchio calls his fiancée Katharina his "super-daintie Kate." This association of the word *cate* with a name belonging to the so-called "delicate" sex may have also contributed to the "daintification" of cates. See also *caterer*.

caterer

Before the middle of the eighteenth century, restaurants did not exist and inns, which provided lodgings as well as food, were not considered places that respectable people patronized. Accordingly, if you were hungry and wealthy but too tired to order your servants to prepare a meal, you ordered your servants to hire someone to prepare a meal. These culinary mercenaries, who would bring a banquet to the comfort of your own home, were not called *caterers*, but *caters*. They had derived this name at the beginning of the fifteenth century from the French word *acatour*, meaning *a buyer of provisions*, which in turn had been formed from the French verb *acheter*, meaning *to purchase*. Even further back, *acheter* developed from the Vulgar Latin *accaptare*, meaning *to seize*, which arose from the Latin *capere*, the source also of *capture* and *catch*. By the seventeenth century, the English word *cater*, which until then had only been used as a noun to refer to the person who provides food, started to be used as a verb to refer to the action of providing food. As a result, the need arose to stick another *er* onto the end of *cater* in order to create a job name that sounded more like a noun and less like a verb: *caterer*, one who caters. See also *cate*.

catillation

Although the Old Testament does not explicitly say so, there is a good chance that some of Noah's naughty neighbours were punished because they had, among other things, engaged in *catillation*, that is, the unseemly licking of plates. This word, which does not apply to the bowls in which my mother makes her chocolate icing, appeared in the early seventeenth century, having been derived from the Latin *catillus*, meaning *plate*. *Catillus*, incidentally, is also the source of the word *kettle*.

catsup

See *ketchup*.

cauldron

See *chowder*.

cauliflower

If forced to wear a vegetable on your lapel, you would probably choose cauliflower because it—more than any other legume, stem, or tuber—actually resembles a flowery corsage. Not surprisingly, therefore, the name of this vegetable means *cabbage flower*, having derived from the Italian *cavoli*, meaning *cabbage*, and *fiori*, meaning *flower*. The Italian *cavoli* in turn derived, through Latin, from an Indo-European source that meant *hollow stem*, a source that also gave rise in the Germanic language family to *cole*, as in *coleslaw*, and *kale*, a kind of headless cabbage. The vegetable and its name were introduced to England in the late sixteenth century. See also *flour* and *coleslaw*.

caviar

Although the word *caviar* has existed in French since the early fifteenth century, and in English since the late sixteenth century, the actual item—sturgeon eggs—was not always considered a high-brow delicacy: in nineteenth-century American saloons, it was given away like peanuts to stimulate a thirst for beer. Later, in the 1920s, Russian princes who had been exiled to Paris complained that they could not buy *ikrá*, the Russian name for the delicacy; soon, through their political connections, the eggs of Russian sturgeon were flowing into the best restaurants in France, and then into the rest of Europe and North America. The Russian *ikrá* did not, however, replace the word *caviar* as the French or English name of the delicacy. In origin, *caviar* derives from the Turkish word *khavyar*.

cayenne pepper

Cayenne pepper is a seasoning made of powdered chili peppers and salt. It acquired the present spelling of its name from Cayenne Island, located off the northeast coast of South America, where the seasoning was once thought to have originated (in fact, the seasoning came from the South American mainland). The mistaken belief that cayenne pepper originated on Cayenne Island probably arose from a simple misunderstanding: in Tupi, a language spoken in the vicinity of Cayenne Island, the indigenous name for the seasoning was *quiynha*, a word not related to the name of the island, but happening to sound somewhat similar. As a result of the coincidental resemblance of *cayenne* and *quiynha*, the European merchants who traded with the inhabitants of that region in the seventeenth century confused the two words, gradually shifting the pronunciation and spelling of the seasoning's name from *quiynha* to *cayenne*. Further back in history, *Cayenne*, the name of the island, arose as a French spelling of *Guiana*, the name of the South American country to which Cayenne Island belongs. Even further back, the name *Guiana* probably developed from a Tupi word meaning *respectable*, a trait possessed by the original inhabitants of that region.

Cecils

In the early nineteenth century a dish named *Cecils* was often concocted by mixing minced meat with bread crumbs and seasonings, rolling the resulting thick paste into small balls, and frying those balls in oil. The fact that *Cecils* is spelt not only with a capital *C* but also with what appears to be the vestige of an apostrophe *s* suggests that the name of the dish was inspired by *Cecil's fast*, an expression dating back to the late sixteenth century. At that time, *Cecil's fast* was the colloquial name for certain fixed days when the public was forced to eat fish instead of meat. The policy was implemented by William Cecil, an influential minister in Queen Elizabeth's parliament, whose goal was to foster the nation's fishing industry. Not surprisingly, the meatless days were not popular with the common folk, who named them after their originator as a means of expressing their displeasure. Two hundred years later, distant memories of *Cecil's fast* probably led someone to bestow the name *Cecils* on a dish which, though not meatless, does attempt to "stretch" the meat by mixing it with bread crumbs. See also *banyan day*.

celery

See *parsley*.

cereal

The word *cereal* originated in the early nineteenth century as the name of any grain whose seeds are eaten by people. Wheat and rice are therefore cereal grains, while canola and flax are not. Later on, the meaning of *cereal* narrowed: by the end of the nineteenth century it referred to prepared breakfast foods made from grain and flavoured with sugar, and by the 1960s it referred to breakfast foods made from sugar and flavoured with grain. The word *cereal* derives from *Ceres*, the Roman goddess of agriculture, which may in turn derive from the same ultimate source as *creare*, a Latin word meaning *to create*. The Greek counterpart to Ceres was the goddess Demeter, whose name, meaning *earth-mother*, is the source of the Russian personal name *Dmitry*.

champagne

The sparkling wine known since the seventeenth century as *champagne* takes its name from Champagne, the region in northeast France where it is produced. In turn, the name of the French region arose as a borrowing of *Campania*, an Italian province whose name derives from the Latin *campus*, meaning *field*. In addition to *champagne*, the Latin *campus* is also the direct source of the English *campus* (the field where a university is located) and of *camp* (originally a field where soldiers stopped for the night); via French, the Latin *campus* also gave rise to the word *champion* (a person who emerges victorious from a field of battle), to the word *campaign* (originally a plan of attack intended for the battlefield, but later adopted by politicians), and to the word *scamper* (the *s* of *scamper* is a vestige of the Latin prefix *ex*, meaning *out of*, the word originally having denoted a cowardly retreat from the battlefield). The Latin *campus* also evolved into words in other languages, including the German *kampf* (meaning *battlefield struggle*, familiar around the world thanks to Hitler's autobiography, *Mein Kampf*) and the French *champignon* (meaning *field mushroom*). Similarly, *champagne* has also spawned words in other languages: in Japanese the wine is called *shampen* and in Russian it is *shampanskoye*.

charcuterie

Charcuterie sounds elegant, but the word is really just another way of referring to simple cold cuts; first used in English in the mid nineteenth century, *charcuterie* literally means *cooked flesh*, deriving from the Old French *char*, meaning *flesh*, and *cuite*, meaning *cooked*.

chard

Chard is the name of the juicy leaves of a variety of beet known variously as the white beet, the silver beet, and the sea-kale beet (botanically, chard is not related to sea-kale, but it does share its silvery-white colour). The most famous variety of chard is Swiss chard, so named because it is widely cultivated in Switzerland. The ultimate source of the word *chard* is the Latin *cardus*, meaning *thistle*; this Latin word evolved into the French *carde*, and was used by the French to refer to a variety of artichoke, a thistle-like plant. When the English adopted the word in the mid seventeenth century, spelling it *chard*, they initially used it to refer to the edible leaf-stalk of the artichoke. By the early eighteenth century, however, *chard* had also been bestowed on the variety of beet that now bears its name, the reason perhaps being that the root of the chard, like the core of the artichoke, cannot be eaten.

chasseur

See *cacciatore*.

Cheddar

When she married her cousin Prince Albert in 1840, Queen Victoria received as a wedding present a thousand pound wheel of cheese, a bizarre gift that helps shed light on why she has, in later portraits, an expression both dour and impending: she was simply fed up. The cheese Victoria was given was Cheddar, a dairy product named after the village in Somerset where it originated. The village, in turn, derives its name from the Old English *ceod*, meaning *pouch*, so called because the Cheddar Gorge is the home of numerous caves, caves that might be described as "pouches" in the earth. Cheddar cheese was invented near the end of the sixteenth century, but its name did not appear in print until the mid seventeenth century.

cheese

In the early nineteenth century, it became something of an American custom to honour the president on special occasions by presenting him with a large wheel of cheese. For instance, Thomas Jefferson was given a 1200 pound cheese on New Year's day in 1902. Even more gargantuan was the 1400 pound wheel of cheese presented to Andrew Jackson in 1837 on the occasion of his last official reception at the White House; unfortunately, the combination of the 1400 pound chunk of cheese and almost 10,000 schmoozing well-wishers resulted in about a 100,000 cheese crumbs being ground into carpets, dropped into sofas, and hidden in flower pots. When it was over, the White House had been turned upside-down, and the odour of this cheesy saturnalia lingered in the president's home for weeks. This historical association of huge wheels of cheese and presidents might suggest a plausible origin for the expression *the big cheese*, a term that emerged early this century to mean *the person in charge*. In fact, however, the *cheese* in *the big cheese* has nothing to do with the dairy product. Instead, the *cheese* in *the big cheese* derives from the Hindi word *chiz*, meaning *thing*, a usage parallel to English expressions like "She really thinks she's something." The dairy *cheese*, on the other hand, was first recorded in English about a thousand years ago and derives from the Latin name for cheese, *caseus*. This Latin name may in turn have evolved from the Sanskrit word *kvathati*, meaning *he boils*, the connection being that milk will bubble and froth before it turns into cheese.

cheesecake

Although cheesecake may seem like a very modern, chichi dish, its name dates all the way back to the mid fifteenth century; much more recent—the 1930s—is the use of *cheesecake* as a slang term for an attractive or "scrumptious" woman, as a synonym, in other words, for gender labels used throughout the 1920s: *dame, frail, skirt, Jane, wren, broad*. In the late 1940s, a surge in the number of manly chests bared on American movie screens prompted the invention of *beefcake*, a generic name for the "hunky" leading men who thwarted cinematic Nazis and hoodlums, thereby safeguarding the film's imperilled cheesecake.

chef

Chefs are literally the *chiefs* of the kitchen, as indicated by the tall hat that they alone are allowed to wear. Chefs started wearing these tall hats in the 1820s, although much earlier than then English cooks had sometimes worn thick, black caps to prevent their scalps from being burned as they carried roasts, on their heads, from the kitchen to the table. *Chef* derives, like *chief*, from the Latin *caput*, meaning *head*. Whereas the other words that derive from *caput* appeared in English in the fourteenth century—including *chief*, *captain*, *chieftain*, and *achieve* (when you *achieve* you become *a chief*)—the word *chef* was not adopted from French until the mid nineteenth century.

cherry

Although cherries and rhinoceroses differ in several respects, they may in fact derive their names from the same source. What links the two names is the Greek *keras*, meaning *horn*. For the animal, the ancient Greeks compounded *keras*—or rather its adjective form *keros*—with a form of *rhis*, meaning *nose*, to form *rhinokeros*, which entered English as *rhinoceros*, the name of the horn-nosed animal. Similarly, for the fruit, the ancient Greeks may have taken *keras* and turned it into *kerasos*, which they applied to the cherry tree, the connection being that the bark of a cherry tree is as smooth as horn. It is also possible, however, that the Greek word for cherry tree, *kerasos*, did not derive from *keras*, but rather from *Cerasus*, the name of a region near the Black Sea where cherry trees flourished. Whatever the origin of *kerasos*, the ancient Romans eventually borrowed the Greek word to create their own word for the cherry, *cerasus*. This Latin word then evolved into various ancient European languages. In Germanic, for example, it became *kirissa*, which developed into the Old English word for the cherry, *ciris* (the Germanic *kirissa* also became the Modern German *kirsch*, the name of cherry-flavoured brandy). In French, the Latin *cerasus* evolved into *cherise*, a form introduced into

English in the fourteenth century, one that eventually drove the original Old English form of the word, *ciris*, into extinction.

chervil

Chervil is a traditional pot-herb, that is, an herb used to flavour soups and sauces. The herb's name is an ancient one, extending back to the eighth century in English, and back even further in the classical languages. The ultimate source of *chervil* is the Greek *khairephullon*, meaning *rejoice-leaf*. Sometimes chervil is also called *cicely*, a name that derives from what the ancient Romans once called the plant, *seselis*. When this alternate Latin name was adopted by English in the mid sixteenth century, it was initially spelt *seseli*; before long, however, it came to be spelt *cicely* as people confounded it with the unrelated *Cicely*, a pet form of the personal name *Cecilia*. Incidentally, related to the word *chervil* is the word *phyllo*, as in *phyllo pastry*, a kind of Greek strudel: the word *phyllo*, like the last half of *khairephullon*, derives from the Greek *phullon*, meaning *leaf*, phyllo pastry being exceptionally thin and leaf-like.

chevaline

Although it was adopted more than a hundred years ago, *chevaline* remains a rather unfamiliar word in English because the meat it refers to—horse—is not tremendously popular in either North America or England; most butcher shops will not even stock chevaline for fear that customers will be so disgusted they will stop buying the other dismembered animals, the ones that it's "okay" to eat. This aversion to chevaline is puzzling because horsemeat is not proscribed by the Bible and is not reputed to have a bad flavour; horsemeat is actually leaner than beef or pork and is safer to eat, at least in so far as horses are not prone to diseases like tuberculosis and tapeworms that cows and pigs sometimes pass on to humans. However, horses also differ from cows and pigs in that they, like dogs and cats, are usually given personal names, a custom that probably arose from people using horses for sport: they ride them, jump them, and race them, activities that would somehow seem less majestic were they performed with pigs or cows. This naming of horses is perhaps what usually spares them from the dinner table, since humans are reluctant to devour anything named *Flicka*, *Rex*, or *Lady*. Nonetheless, horsemeat—or chevaline—has been consumed from time to time by some gastronomes, especially in France where the word *chevaline* originated. The French formed this name from *cheval*, meaning *horse*, a word that derives from *caballus*, the Latin name for *horse*. *Caballus* is also the source of several other familiar English words. First, it developed into the Latin word *caballarius*, meaning *horseman*, which developed in Italian into *cavaliere*. From this Italian word, English derived both *cavalry* (a troop of soldiers mounted on horses) and *cavalier* (a disdainful or flippant attitude, often demonstrated by medieval knights who had horses when no one else did). The Latin *caballarius* also evolved into the Old French *chivalerie*, which English then adopted as *chivalry*; the adjective formed from this word, *chivalrous*, came to mean *noble* thanks to the belief, occasionally proven true, that knights were not mere pirates on horses. See also *hippogastronomy*.

chick-pea

The chick-pea has nothing to do with young chickens, but it does have something to do with an old lawyer. These small, round legumes have been known as *chick-peas* or *chich-peas* since the mid sixteenth century, although before that, dating back to the late fourteenth century, they were known simply as *chich*, a name borrowed directly from French. The French in turn acquired the name *chich* from the ancient Romans, who called the nutritious legume *cicer*. It was this Latin plant-name, *cicer*, that inspired the surname *Cicero*: the Roman orator and lawyer who made that surname famous is said to have acquired his cognomen from a mole the size of a chick-pea that one of his ancestors bore. In the eighteenth century, the English mistakenly altered the *chich* of *chich-pea* to the more familiar-looking *chick*. At about the same time in the United States, an alternate name appeared, *garbanzo*, having been introduced to American English by Spanish settlers. Earlier on, the Spanish had developed the name *garbanzo* from an older Spanish word, *arvanço*, which derived from the Latin *ervum*, the name of a leguminous plant similar to the chick-pea. See also *fasels*.

chicken Tetrazzini

Luisa Tetrazzini was a famous opera diva at the beginning of this century. In the 1920s she gave her surname, which appears to mean *four teeth* in Italian, to her favourite dish: diced chicken in cream sauce, baked in a casserole with spaghetti and mushrooms.

chicken

The ubiquity of the chicken as a domestic fowl has often led to the name of this poultry being applied to humans. From the fifteenth to the nineteenth century, the word *chicken* could be used to refer to a child, much the way *kid*—a goat's offspring— still is. Since the early seventeenth century, the word has also denoted a coward, someone who's a "fraidy-cat." Throughout the eighteenth and nineteenth century *chicken* also meant a naive person, an easy target, a "pigeon," so to speak. And since the 1920s the diminutive of *chicken*—*chick*—has been bestowed on attractive women, also known as "foxes." The word *chicken* is very old: it first appeared in English about a thousand years ago, having derived from an even older Germanic source that also evolved into the Dutch *kieken*, the German *küchlien*, and the Swedish *kjukling*.

chicken à la king

See *à la king*.

chili

A short form of both *chili pepper* and *chili con carne*, the word *chili* derives from the Nahuatl language, spoken by the peoples of southern Mexico and Central America. At the end of the fifteenth century, Christopher Columbus returned to Europe after contacting these people and reported that they used the hot fruit of a native plant to season their food; however, because Columbus was still under the mistaken impression that he had indeed made it to India, these peppers were originally referred to as *Calcutta peppers*. The Spanish were the first to use the Native American name, *chili*, but by the mid seventeenth century, the real, Nahuatl origin of *chili* had been more or less forgotten, leading some experts to mistakenly suppose that the peppers were named after the South American country called Chile. (Of course, neither *chili* the pepper nor *Chile* the country are related to the English word *chilly*, but by a strange coincidence the name *Chile* may derive from a Native South American word meaning *cold*.) In English, *chili* did not appear until the mid seventeenth century, while the dish called *chili con carne*—Spanish for *chili peppers with meat*—was not referred to by name till the mid nineteenth century.

chimichanga

A chimichanga is a fried burrito; a burrito is a folded tortilla cooked on a griddle and then filled with various savoury ingredients; a tortilla is a corn-meal pancake. Of these three food items, the burrito and chimichanga have names that derive from animals. *Burrito* is a diminutive of the Spanish word *burro*, meaning *donkey* or *ass*, and therefore literally means *little ass*. The dish acquired this name because donkeys are often draped with a blanket, thus making them resemble a folded, meat-filled tortilla (agnelotti, an Italian pasta whose name means *little lamb*, acquired its name for similar reasons). *Chimichanga* was long thought to be a Spanish nonce word—that is, a word, like the English *thingamajig*, that someone playfully made up on the spur of the moment. *Chimichanga* may, however, derive partly from *changa*, the Spanish word for *monkey*; as well, the *chimi* part of *chimichanga* may derive from the Spanish *chimenea*, meaning *chimney*. If this truly is the literal meaning of *chimichanga*, then a harder question is why the dish was given a name meaning *chimney-monkey* in the first place. Perhaps, long ago, some Spanish peasant was struck by the resemblance between a folded tortilla and a monkey sitting with its arms folded around its knees; the same peasant might also have noticed that a piping-hot burrito, with steam wafting from its two ends, also resembles a smoking chimney. If such an astute observation was not the inspiration behind the name *chimichanga*, then the dish must surely have been named in honour of an indentured monkey pulled through a chimney to freedom by super-intelligent simians from another planet. See also *ravioli*.

chine

See *carving*.

chive

The Latin name for the onion—*caepa*—is not the source of the word *onion*, but it is the source of the word *chive*, a small bulb-plant related to the onion. The Latin *caepa* became the French *cive*, which was adopted into English at the beginning of the fifteenth century. Pronounced like *shive*, the word *cive* remained the English name of this bulb until the mid nineteenth century when its spelling and pronunciation changed to that of the current form, *chive*. The older spelling of the name, *cive*, is the one that appears in *civy*, the name of a medieval sauce made by stewing the entrails of a hog with spices, herbs, and especially chive. Slightly more appetizing is the sauce named *civet*, made by soaking slices of toast in water and wine, then seasoning them, again with onions or chives. Apparently invented in the early eighteenth century, civet is still served with game dishes.

chocolate

Montezuma, the King of the Aztecs when Hernando Cortés and his conquistadores first encountered them, so believed in chocolate as an aphrodisiac that he reportedly drank fifty large cups of chocolate beverage each day. If this is true, then the lusty Montezuma must have imbibed about five cups of chocolate every waking hour, a quantity that surely prevented him from doing anything with his kingly phallus except relieve his burgeoning bladder. The word *chocolate* derives from the Nahuatl language spoken in southern Mexico and Central America by Montezuma and his subjects: their name for an unsweetened beverage made from cocoa beans was *xocolatl*, meaning *bitter water*; this word was adopted by Spanish as *chocolate*, which was then borrowed by English at the beginning of the seventeenth century. Perhaps surprisingly, the word *cocoa*, the name of the bean from which chocolate is made, is not related to the word *chocolate*: like *chocolate*, however, *cocoa* does derive from a Nahuatl word: *cacahuatl*, meaning *beans of the cocoa tree*. In what was perhaps their only act of moderation, the Spanish conquistadores took only half of the word *cacahuatl*—the *caca* part—when they returned to Spain with bags and bags of the tasty beans. In the mid sixteenth century, English adopted this Spanish name, but spelt it *cacao*, a form it retained until the beginning of the eighteenth century when its vowels shifted around and it became *cocoa*. Unfortunately, this new spelling led to great confusion, because people inevitably mixed up *cocoa* with the unrelated *coco*, which appears in *coconut*, and with the unrelated *coca*, the name of a shrub whose leaves yield cocaine. See also *coconut*.

choke-priest

Perhaps in return for making gluttony a sin, gastronomes have often made men of the cloth their target when it comes to naming dishes. The Italians, for example, named a soup made with short pieces of pasta *strozzapreti*, which was translated literally and then adopted into English as *choke-priest* in the mid nineteenth century. Priests were once reputed to have little difficulty in swallowing any food put before them, and thus the name *choke-priest* may have been intended to suggest that the pasta made the soup so thick that even a corpulent priest would find it a daunting meal. In English, a similar idiom, *enough to choke a horse*, is likewise applied to an over-abundance of an item. Similarly, the port-wine known as *kill-priest* was so-named to suggest that its potency would cause any priest who partook of it to keel over, kick the bucket, and push up daisies. Other foods have names that allude to certain physical features of spiritual leaders. Since the late eighteenth century, for example, the terms *pope's nose* and *parson's nose* have been used to refer to the esculent rump of a fowl; these terms probably originated not so much as religious slurs as euphemisms for *rump*, just as *white meat* and *dark meat* originated as euphemisms for the chicken's breast and legs. Finally, the term *deaconing* derives from the name of another Church official, the deacon, the spiritual leader who serves as the priest's link to the community. In the secular world, deaconing is the merchant's practice of placing the best fruits and vegetables on top of the pile to attract the attention of the passing consumer. The term arose in the nineteenth century out of the special preparations households made when the deacon dropped by for a visit, preparations such as getting out the best china, taking the covers off the furniture, and placing a bible on top of the coffee table. Incidentally, the names of these church officials all derive from Latin sources: *priest* from the Latin *presbyter*, meaning *instructor*; *deacon* from *diaconus*, meaning *servant*; *pope* from *papa*, meaning *father*; and *parson* from *persona*, meaning *person* (the parson was originally the person who embodied or "personified" the church as a legal entity). See also *cappuccino* and *imam bayildi*.

chop-stick

The original and ancient Chinese name for chop-sticks was *tsze*, meaning *help*, since the utensils assisted in getting the food from your dish to your mouth. However, the Chinese eventually replaced this name with a term that sounded similar, but seemed to better describe the motion of the chop-sticks: *k'wai-tsze*, meaning *the quick ones*. British sailors, returning from voyages to the Orient in the late seventeenth century, rendered this unfamiliar term into English as *chop* and then combined it with *stick* to create the word *chop-stick*. More than two centuries later, the Chinese *k'wai*, meaning *quick*, was again rendered into English in the phrase *chop chop*, meaning *quick quick* or, more idiomatically, *make it snappy*. The *chop* in *chop suey*, however, derives from a completely different Chinese source: the Cantonese *shap sui*, meaning *bits and pieces*. This dish did not originate in China but rather on the west coast of the United States where it was invented by Chinese immigrants engaged in building railroads. Neither of these Chinese *chops*, of course, is related to the *chop* in *pork chop*.

chop suey

See *chop-stick*.

chow

According to the Oxford English Dictionary, the word *chow*—meaning *food*, as in *chow time*—derives from the name of a Chinese dog, the chow, once eaten as a delicacy in China. This suspicious etymology may have been inspired by an anecdote involving Charles George Gordon, the famous British General who suppressed several rebellions in China in the 1860s: according to this tale, Gordon presented a pedigreed dog to Li Hung Chang, a visiting Chinese statesman who, after returning home, sent a note to the general thanking him for his delicious gift. It is indeed true that some Asian cultures consider dogs to be a source of meat (it is also true that a visit to any wiener assembly line in North America will make a slice of real dog seem more palatable than any hot dog). However, even though dog is a menu item in some Eastern cultures, the suggestion put forward by the Oxford English Dictionary—that *chow* meaning *food* derives from *chow* meaning *dog*—is nothing more than a cultural cliché, a simplification whereby one culture reduces another culture to its most "peculiar" elements. Indeed, the word *chow* does derive from Chinese, but from the Mandarin *chao*, meaning *to fry*. The word appeared in English at the end of the eighteenth century as *chow-chow*, the repetition of the word being characteristic of the pigeon English that evolved from the attempt by British and Chinese merchants to communicate with one another. By the mid nineteenth century, the term had been shortened to *chow*, and by the early twentieth century it had been reintroduced as part of *chow mein*, a dish of noodles whose name literally means *fried flour*.

chowder

"The chowder in the cauldron was high in calories." This short sentence contains three culinary terms that derive from the Latin verb *calere*, meaning *to be hot*. This Latin verb gave rise to a Latin noun, *calidarium*, the name of a tub in which Romans took hot baths. In French *calidarium* evolved into *cauderon*, adopted by English in the early fourteenth century as *caudron*, a huge kitchen pot. The name of this pot remained *caudron* for two hundred years until, in the fifteenth century, scholars decided to make the word look more like its Latin source by adding an *l* to form *cauldron*. By developing along another path, the Latin *calidarium* also evolved into the word *chowder*: specifically, the Latin plural of *calidarium*—*calidaria*—became the French *chaudière*, meaning *kettle*. *Chaudiere* then became part of a phrase—*faire la chaudière*—spoken by French fishermen after they had spent the day dragging their nets along the coast of Newfoundland and New England. This phrase, literally meaning *to make the kettle*, referred to the communal pot into which every fishing crew would throw some of its catch. Eventually the word *chaudière* was transferred from the pot to the fish soup it contained, and it was with this sense that English finally borrowed the word in the mid eighteenth century, spelling it *chowder*. A hundred years later, in the mid nineteenth century, English derived yet another word from the Latin *calere*: *calorie*, a unit of heat used to measure how much energy a human can derive from a given food.

chow mein

See *chow*.

chutney

Since the early nineteenth century, the British have used chutney to enliven any part of a meal—excluding the conversation—that is bland or lacking in taste. The word *chutney*, like the spicy condiment itself, originated in India: the original Hindi word, *chatni*, meaning *strong spices*, may have derived from *catna*, an older Hindi word meaning *to lick*.

cicely

See *chervil*.

cinnamon

Cinnamon is referred to in the Old Testament and in even older Sanskrit texts, thus affirming that it was one of the first spices to be used in flavouring food and wine. The word *cinnamon* derives from the ancient Hebrew name of the spice, *quinnamon*. In England, however, where the cinnamon tree is not native, cinnamon was not referred to by name until the mid fifteenth century, almost five hundred years after the appearance of *pepper*. Before it is powdered, cinnamon is sold in *quills*, so called because the rolled sheets of bark look like the quills, made from feathers, once used as pens.

cipaille

See *sea-pie*.

citron

See *lemon*.

clam

The word *clam* appeared in English in the tenth century, but at that time it did not refer to the edible, bivalve mollusk that is an essential ingredient in chowder. Instead, *clam* referred to a device used to hold two things together, a device such as a chain or a clamp—the word *clamp*, in fact, derives from the same Germanic source as *clam*. At the beginning of the sixteenth century, the name *clam* was given to the shell-fish because that creature can clamp shut its shells like a vice. This *shell-fish* sense eventually became the primary meaning of *clam*, but the word was still used as a synonym for *clamp* right up to this century. Although *clam* did give rise to the expression *clam up*—meaning *to be mum*—it is related in no way to *clammy*, an adjective used to describe something cold and moist. *Clammy* actually derives from the Old English *cloeman*, meaning *to be sticky like clay*; in fact, the word *clay* also derives from this Old English source, making it a cousin of *clammy* but not of *clam*.

cleaver

Used by butchers to hack joints of meat in two, cleavers ultimately derive their name from an Indo-European source, pronounced something like *gleubh*, meaning *to cut apart* or *to carve*. This ancient source evolved into the Germanic word *kleuban*, which then developed into the English word *cleave* in the eleventh century; it was from this word that *cleaver*, the name of the butcher's tool, was formed in the late sixteenth century. Oddly, another *cleave* also exists in English, one that does not mean *to cut apart* but rather *to stick together*: during a marriage ceremony, for example, a minister might advise the bride and groom to "cleave together" in times of hardship. This *cleave*, however, is unrelated to the other *cleave*, deriving instead from an Indo-European source, pronounced something like *gloi*, that meant *to stick*; the word *glue* also derives from the same sticky source, as does the word *clay*.

clove

Although they are both names of items used to season food, the *clove* that refers to a segment of a garlic bulb is not related to the *clove* that refers to the aromatic dried spice. First recorded in the eleventh century, the garlic *clove* derives ultimately from an Indo-European word pronounced something like *gleubh* that meant *to cut* or *to carve*; through Germanic, this word developed into *clove* and was applied to the segments that make up a garlic bulb because those segments appear to have been cut or divided from one another. Close relatives of this *clove* include *cleft* (as in *cleft chin*), *cloven* (as in *cloven hoof*), and *cleavage* (as in what is revealed by a low-cut blouse or droopy pants); all these words describe body parts that appear to have been "cut" or split. A more distant relative of these words, but one that developed from the same Indo-European source, is the *glyphics* part of the word *hieroglyphics*, a word of Greek origin that literally means *sacred carvings*. The other *clove*—the aromatic spice—derives from a very different source. Its immediate predecessor was the French name of the spice, *clou de girofle*, which literally means *nail of the nut-leaf tree*, so named because the tree-bud from which the spice is derived resembles a nail or, in French, a *clou*. In the thirteenth century, English adopted this French name as *clowe gilofre*, but eventually this awkward-sounding phrase cleaved into two distinct names: *clowe*, which became *clove*, the present name of the spice; and *gillyflower*, which was originally an alternate name for the spice, but eventually came to refer to a variety of flower whose fragrance resembles that of clove. See also *cleaver*.

cock

Although *cock* is the original English name for a male fowl, this sense of the word has been almost completely overtaken by *rooster*, a shift that occurred over the last three hundred years as *cock* came more and more to mean *penis*. First recorded in the ninth century, *cock* probably arose as an imitation of a rooster's crowing, usually represented as *cockadoodledoo* (similarly, the French word for *rooster*—*coq*—reflects how the French represent the bird's crowing: *coquerico*). In the early seventeenth century, *cock* came to be used as a ribald synonym for *penis*; this meaning of the word may have developed because a male fowl's comb and wattle (the fleshy lobe hanging from his beak) engorge with blood as he struts, like the cock of the walk, through an admiring throng of hens. However, *cock* had also been used since the late fifteenth century to refer to the tap on a barrel of wine; this tap *cock* may be a completely different word from the rooster *cock*, or it may have been inspired by the fact that the handle on the tap was often shaped like a cock's comb. In any event, this tap *cock*— essentially a tube used to discharge liquids—could easily have inspired the use of *cock* for *penis*. The upshot of these semantic developments was that *cock* ceased to be considered a polite word, especially in North America, even when it was used in a barnyard context; as a result, the word *rooster* emerged in the late eighteenth century to take up the semantic slack, *rooster* deriving safely from the bird's tendency to roost. As a culinary term, *cock* continues to be used in the names of a few old dishes, including cock-a-leekie soup.

cock-a-leekie

Several dishes get their names because they contain a cock cooked with something else. Cock-a-leekie, as its name suggests, is made by boiling a cock with leeks, a dish first referred to by name in the mid eighteenth century. Likewise, cock-ale, a dish invented in the mid seventeenth century, is made by mixing beer with the minced meat of a boiled cock. A much older dish, now obsolete both in name and as a menu item, is *cockagrice*, made by boiling together a cock and a small pig, and then roasting them on a single spit. The last half of *cockagrice*—*grice*—emerged in the early thirteenth century and derives from the Old Norse *gris*, meaning *a young pig*; *gris* is actually still current in English but has been overshadowed by *suckling*, which appeared in the mid fifteenth century to describe a pig still being nursed by its mother. The word *cockagrice* closely resembles *cockatrice*, the name of a mythical serpent whose glance could kill, but the name of this mythical monster is Greek in origin and has nothing to do with either cocks or grices; nonetheless, sixteenth-century mythographers felt compelled to account for the *cock* in *cockatrice* somehow, so they reshaped the anatomy of the cockatrice, giving it the head of a cock and the tail of a serpent. It was as this fearful chicken-snake that the cockatrice subsequently appeared in the coats of arms of many British aristocrats.

cockle

Cockles are heart-shaped candies with phrases like *I Love You* and *You're Mine* embossed on their sugary surfaces. Cockles are also edible bivalve mollusks that may be eaten raw but are usually cooked like mussels. The connection between these two *cockles* is a bit circuitous. In the seventeenth century, anatomists dissecting human cadavers noticed that the ventricles of the human heart are shaped like cockle-shells. Accordingly, they termed these ventricles *cockles* and this appellation eventually gave rise to the expression, *To warm the cockles of the heart.* Through this association with the cardiovascular system, the name of the mollusk was then transferred to the heart-shaped candies. Bakers will also know that *cockles* are the bubbles and blisters that form on the crust of bread as it is baked, a name that probably derives from these bread bubbles being, like ventricles, rounded like shells. Also rounded like shells are cockboats, a small craft whose crew is led by a cock-swain or, in abbreviated form, a coxswain. The ultimate source of all these *cockles* and *cocks* is the Greek *konkhe*, meaning *conch shell.*

cocktail

For etymologists, the Holy-Grail of words is *cocktail*, a word that has enticed many bright-eyed scholars to squander their youth and research grants while seeking its origin, but has so far eluded the prying fingernail of discovery. Of the many explanations proposed for the name of this mixed drink, the most absurd is that it derives from *Xochitl*, the name of an Aztec princess who supposedly invented it; trailing this explanation in terms of implausibility is the suggestion that *cocktail* derives from *kaketal*, a West African name for the scorpion, and that it is so called because the drink, like the insect, has a "sting." Somewhat more feasible is the notion that the drink gets its name from the French *coquetier*, meaning *egg cup*: an apothecary named Antoine Peychaud served a drink of brandy and bitters in such a cup after settling in New Orleans in 1795. This origin at least accords with the first appearance of *cocktail* in print in 1806. Around the same time, the word *cocktail* was also used as the name for any race horse that is not a thoroughbred, that is, for a horse of mixed-parentage; this equine term seems to have originated from such horses having their tails cropped, so they "cocked up," whereas thoroughbreds' tails were left uncut. The name of these "mixed" horses may have been transferred to the name of the mixed drink. About fifty other theories for the origin of *cocktail* have been proposed over the last hundred years, none of them fully convincing.

cocoa

See *chocolate*.

coconut

Although often confused with *coca* (the shrub whose leaves yield cocaine) and with *cocoa* (the bean that yields chocolate), the word *coco* as in *coconut* is related to neither. Both *coca* and *cocoa* developed from words native to the Americas, the former word from South America, the latter from North America; in contrast, *coco* is European in origin, even though coconuts are a tropical fruit. The nut acquired its name when, in the late fifteenth century, Portuguese explorers fancied that the three indentations on the base of the large, hairy nut looked like a grinning face; accordingly, they named it *coconut*, the word *coco* meaning *goblin* or, more literally, *grin-face*. In the early seventeenth century, more than a hundred years after the Portuguese sailors gave the nut its ghoulish name, the word *coconut* appeared in English. Surprisingly, *copra*, the name given to coconut flesh after its oil has been extracted, appeared in English in the late sixteenth century, about thirty years before *coconut* itself. *Copra* derives from the Hindi word for coconut, *khopra*.

cod

Although a piece of cod is tasty, a cod-piece is not, a surprising difference considering that these two *cod*s derive from the same source. The word *cod* can be traced back a thousand years to the Old English *codd*, a word referring both to a sack in which items could be carried and to the seedcase of a plant. Five hundred years later, in the middle of the fourteenth century, *codd* was also extended to the fish, a semantic development that occurred either because the rumpled cod-fish has a sack-like appearance, or because it produces, like a seed-case, an astonishing number of eggs: one American biologist calculated that if all the eggs laid during the life of a single cod developed into adults, the ocean would be a solid mass of fish. Near the end of the fourteenth century, the word *cod* also came to mean *scrotum*, with both the *sack* and *seedcase* meanings being intended. Fifty years later, it became the height of fashion for men to take a good-sized gourd, split it, dry it, and then fasten it over their genitals, thus managing simultaneously to conceal and accentuate their manhood. These sartorial accessories were named, naturally enough, *cod-pieces*.

coffee

Not surprisingly, the linguistic history of the word *coffee* parallels the trade route coffee followed as it was introduced to Europe in the sixteenth century. The French, Spanish, and Portuguese word for the beverage, *café*, the German *kaffee*, the Swedish and Danish *kaffe*, the Dutch *koffie*, and the Russian *kophe* all derive from the Italian name for the beverage, *caffè*. The Italian word, in turn, comes from the Turkish word *kahveh*, which the Turks derived from *qahwah*, an Arabic word that once referred to both coffee and wine. This Arabic name may have developed from an Arabic verb meaning *to have no appetite*, the connection being that these beverages were used to stimulate a healthy hunger. Alternatively, the Arabic name may have developed from *Kaffa*, an area in Abyssinia to which coffee is indigenous. In 1615, only a few years after the introduction of the word *coffee* itself, the term *coffee-house* appeared and soon became associated with the famous literary and political figures who patronized those establishments. *Café*, which is what the French have called a coffee-house since the middle of the seventeenth century, was taken into English at the beginning of the nineteenth century, but within a hundred years had come to mean any casual restaurant. The French *café* is also the source of the word *caffeine*, which first appeared in 1830. The Spanish word, *café*, on the other hand, gave rise to the Spanish *cafeter*, meaning *coffee-seller*, the source of the word *cafeteria*. First recorded in 1839, *cafeteria* also contributed to the English language by establishing the *teria* suffix that has become a part of recent words such as *groceteria* and *fruiteria*—places that sell, respectively, groceries and fruit—and *washeteria*—another name for a laundrette. See also *bistro* and *restaurant*.

coffin

Until about two hundred years ago, it was common for cookbooks to instruct aspiring chefs to pour their stewed beef or sliced apples into a coffin. By *coffin*, however, they did not mean a burial casket but rather a pastry-crust or a pie-tin. This culinary use of *coffin* is, in fact, the original one, dating back to the early fifteenth century, whereas the *corpse-box* sense did not emerge until the early sixteenth century. Of course, as the funereal associations of *coffin* came to dominate the word, it gradually ceased to be used in relation to baking, this sense finally dying out in the mid eighteenth century. In origin, *coffin* derives from the Greek *kophinos*, meaning *basket*, which is also the source of the word *coffer*.

Colby

First produced at the end of the nineteenth century, Colby cheese takes its name from the city where it originated, Colby, Wisconsin. The city, in turn, takes is name from the surname *Colby*, which derives from an Old English source meaning *by the coal mine*.

colcannon

Colcannon is an Irish dish made by pounding together cabbage and potatoes and then stewing them in butter. The name is a compound formed by combining *cole*—an old name for cabbage that also survives in *coleslaw*—and *cannon*, the name of a weapon used to blow one's godless enemies to smithereens. The compound arose when Irish peasants turned cannon balls into kitchen implements by using them to pound vegetables into a paste; by so doing, they effected a transformation rivalling the United Nations' mandate to turn swords into ploughshares.

cole slaw

The need to change the peculiar into the familiar is powerful, as is demonstrated by the repeated attempts, since the eighteenth century, to turn *cole slaw* into *cold slaw*. The *cole* in *cole slaw*, however, has nothing to do with the word *cold*, even though this cabbage salad is indeed chilled before being served; instead, *cole* represents the Dutch *kool*, meaning *cabbage*, while the *slaw* is an English respelling of *sla*, a Dutch abbreviation of *salade*. Although *cole* may now seem like a peculiar word, it was once commonplace, that is, until *cabbage* appeared in English in the fifteenth century and gradually replaced it. In Scotland the word has persisted as *kale*, the name of a cabbage whose leaves curl outward like ears instead of inward to form a head. Kale was once such an important part of the Scottish diet that gardens were called *kale-yards* and dinner was sometimes called *kale-time*. The word *cole*, or rather its German cousin, also exists in *kohlrabi*, meaning *cabbage-turnip*, yet another variety of cabbage.

colostrum

See *beestings*.

comestible

See *eat*.

commensal

This adjective is used to describe a situation in which several people eat together. The word comes from two Latin words, the preposition *cum*, meaning *together* or *with*, and the noun *mensa*, meaning *table*. *Commensal* therefore literally means that dinner guests are brought together by their table. Introduced in the fifteenth century, the word can also be used as a noun; if you are dining with a mysterious someone tonight, you can refer to him or her as your *commensal*. See also *mensa*.

companion

From an etymological point of view, a companion is anyone who shares a loaf of bread with you: the word derives from the Latin *cum*, meaning *with* or *together*, and the Latin *panis*, meaning *bread*. *Companion* entered English at the end of the thirteenth century, about the same time that the related form *company* was introduced. The original significance of breaking bread with another person is still evident in the sacrament of the Christian Eucharist: the consecrated bread of communion establishes a holy bond among those who partake of it. A third word, now obsolete, that derives from the same source is *companage*; from the early fourteenth century to the late seventeenth century this useful word referred to anything eaten with bread, including butter, cheese, or meat but excluding wine, beer, and milk. See also *commensal* and *opsony*.

concoction

See *decoction*.

consy

See *bouce Jane*.

contradiction

In the eighteenth century, punch was sometimes referred to as *contradiction*, so called because its various ingredients contradicted one another: the rum, for instance, was opposed to the water, while the sugar was opposed to the lemon. Today we refer to such contradictory concoctions as *sweet and sour*, a phrase that also dates back to the early eighteenth century.

cony

See *rabbit*.

cook

Job names, like *teacher* or *farmer*, usually arise almost as soon as their verb forms, *teach* or *farm*, come into existence. Other times the verb form may precede the appearance of the job name by centuries, as with *weld* and *welder*, because it takes that long for the job to be recognized as a valid employment. Much more unusual, however, is for the job name to precede the appearance of the verb; this has happened with *lawyer*, which has never developed a verb form: lawyers do not "lawyer" for a living, they practice law. For hundreds of years, the same state of affairs held true for *cook*, which arose as a job name in the early eleventh century but did not become a verb until the fourteenth century, about the same time that the word *cookery* was invented. During those three intervening centuries, cooks could not claim to *cook* for a living—they could only say they worked as cooks. This late appearance of the verb form is made more strange by the fact that the job name *cook* actually developed from a verb, the Latin verb *coquere*, meaning *to cook*: *coquere* gave rise to the Latin job name *cocus*, which became, in the eleventh century, the English noun *cook*. *Cook* is not the only word to develop from the Latin *coquere*. *Coquere* also gave rise to what the Romans called a kitchen, *coquina*, which in English became the actual word *kitchen*, first recorded in the eleventh century. Taking a different route, the Latin *coquina* also evolved into the French word for kitchen, *cuisine*; this French word was then adopted by English in the late eighteenth century as a chichi name for the food produced in a kitchen. Finally, *coquina* also developed a slightly different Latin form, *culina*, that also meant *kitchen*. This word entered English twice: first in the eleventh century as the word *kiln*, a furnace for baking food or pottery, and then in the seventeenth century as the adjective *culinary*. See also *decoction* and *apricot*.

cookie

The obvious source of the word *cookie* is the wrong one: *cookie* has no relation to *cook*, which seems less surprising when you stop to consider that cookies are not cooked but baked. Whereas *cook* derives from a Latin source, *cookie* derives from a Germanic one: namely, the Dutch *koekje*—a diminutive of *koek*, meaning *cake*—which became the English *cookie* in the mid eighteenth century. Prior to this, and even still in England, cookies were called *biscuits*. Given its Dutch origin, *cookie* is closely related to the word *cake*, which developed from the Old Norse *kaka* in the thirteenth century. See also *cake*.

cordial

The fruit-flavoured liqueurs known as *cordials* take their name from the Latin *cor*, meaning *heart*, so named because cordials were thought to invigorate the heart. The Latin *cor* is also the source of *concord*, literally meaning *united heart*, and of *courage*, the heart being the seat of courage. Surprisingly, however, *cor* is not the source of *coronary*, a synonym for *heart attack*; instead, *coronary* actually derives from *corona*, a Latin word meaning *crown*, the connection being that the heart is encircled by a "crown" of arteries and blood vessels. As the name of the liqueur, *cordial* entered English in the late fourteenth century; a hundred years later, in the late fifteenth century, the word also came to describe anyone with a sincere, warm, and "hearty" personality. This sense eventually paled somewhat, so that by the late eighteenth century *cordial* had simply come to mean *pleasant* or even just *polite*.

coriander

It is difficult to say what is more surprising: that coriander belongs to the carrot family, or that its name may mean *bedbug*. *Coriander* derives from what the ancient Greeks called the spice, *koriannon*, a name they may have formed from their word for the bedbug, *koris*, because the odour emitted by such insects resembles that of coriander. Despite their similar aroma, however, chefs rarely substitute bedbugs for coriander.

corn

In North America, the grain characterized by its long, yellow cobs is called *corn*, a word of Indo-European origin; in England, the same grain is known as *maize*, a word of Caribbean origin. The different names arose in the early seventeenth century, when the Pilgrims came to their new world: the grains they brought from England and tried to grow in America withered in their new climate, but the kernels generously given to them by the Native Americans flourished. At first, the Pilgrims honoured their Native saviours by calling their new grain *Indian corn*, the word *corn* having been used since the ninth century in England as a name for seeds harvested from all grains. By the beginning of the eighteenth century, however, the Americans had dropped *Indian* from their original name for the yellow-cobbed grain and simply started calling it *corn*. Meanwhile, in Europe, the yellow-cobbed grain had been completely unknown until it was brought from the Americas in the sixteenth century. The Spanish were among the first to bring this grain back to Europe, having been introduced to it by the Caribs, a people who gave their name to the Caribbean islands where they lived. The Carib word for the grain was *marichi*, which was rendered into Spanish as *maisi* and then adopted into English at the end of the sixteenth century as *maize*. See also *corned beef*.

corned beef

Corned beef contains no corn, but it does contain salt—lots of salt, because that is how the meat is cured. Nonetheless, despite the absence of corn in corned beef, the salty meat and the yellow niblets do derive their names from the same source. In the Germanic language from which English developed, the word *kurnam*, meaning *particle*, developed in two directions: it became the Old English *kernel*, meaning *seed*, but it also became the Old English *corn*, meaning both *seed* and, more generally, *particle*. From the *seed* sense of *corn* arose words such as *peppercorn*, denoting the dried berry of the pepper plant, while from the *particle* sense of *corn* arose compounds such as *corned beef*, named after the particles of salt that permeate the beef after it is soaked in brine (a similar compound, *corn-powder*, was used up until the eighteenth century as a name for granulated gunpowder). The term *corned beef* appeared in English in the mid sixteenth century, about a hundred years before the appearance of the synonymous *bully beef*, formed as a corruption of the French *bouilli boeuf*, meaning *boiled beef*. Incidentally, the *corn* in *corned beef* and in *corn on the cob* is not related to the *corn* in *cornucopia* nor to the *corn* caused by wearing too-tight shoes; both of these latter *corns* derive from the Latin *cornu*, meaning *horn*. See also *corn* and *cornucopia*.

cornet

See *cornucopia*.

cornucopia

A cornucopia is literally a horn of plenty, deriving as it does from the Latin *cornu*, meaning *horn*, and *copia*, meaning *abundance* or *a copious amount*. Overflowing with fruits and vegetables, the cornucopia is still a common sight at Thanksgiving, although the original goat's horn, a symbol of the nanny-goat that nursed the god Zeus when he was an infant, is now usually replaced by a horn made of straw. The *corn* of *cornucopia* is in no way related to the grain *corn*, but it is related to the *corn* in *unicorn* (a one-horned beast), to the *corn* in *Capricorn* (the horned goat of astrology), to the *corn* caused by too-tight shoes (a horn-like protuberance), to the *corn* in *corner* (an angle sticking out like a horn), to the *corn* in *cornet* (a pastry shaped like a horn), and to the *corn* in *Cornish pastry* (*Cornish* comes from the English county called *Cornwall*, and *Cornwall* evolved from *Corn-Welsh*, so-called because the county sticks out into the sea like a horn).

corsned

A *corsned* was once a dreaded morsel of bread used in the Middle Ages to determine the guilt or innocence of a person accused of a crime. The accused was made to swallow an ounce of bread, known as the *corsned*, that had been exorcised and consecrated by a priest. If, after swallowing, the accused gagged or went into convulsions, he or she was pronounced guilty. However, if the corsned had no such effect, then the individual was deemed innocent. The word—which became obsolete after the practice was abandoned almost one thousand years ago—derives from the Old English word *cor*, meaning *trial*, and *snaed*, meaning *piece*.

cos

The variety of long-leafed lettuce known since the late seventeenth century as *cos*—and also known since early this century as *romaine lettuce*—takes its name from the island of Kos situated between Greece and Turkey. See also *Romano cheese*.

costmary

For hundreds of years, the British have grown costmary in their gardens and used it as an herb in salads or to give flavour to ale. Originally, the plant was simply called *cost*, a name that travelled from Sanskrit, to Arabic, to Greek, and then to Latin before entering Old English about a thousand years ago. In the fifteenth century, for unknown reasons, the herb named *cost* came to be associated with St. Mary, leading to a new name, *cost St. Mary*, soon shortened to *costmary*. The name *Mary*, incidentally, probably derives from an Egyptian source meaning *to be fat*, which would have had the extended sense of *to be pregnant*. The herb known as *rosemary* has a completely different origin, one that has nothing to do with roses or Mary: the ancient Romans called this herb *ros marinus*, meaning *dew of the sea*; this Latin name entered English in the eleventh century as *rosemarine*, but by the mid fifteenth century people were pronouncing it *rosemary*, perhaps due to the influence of *costmary*. When rosemary flowers are steeped in wine, the resulting spirit is called *Hungary water*, so named, according to legend, because a hermit gave the recipe to the Queen of Hungary, who drank it as a cordial. See also *irrorateur*.

cottabus

On any winter night, in any Canadian city, beer-soaked, toque-clad young men slump on sticky kitchen floors, flipping bottle caps in an attempt to strike a target worthy of their skill: perhaps the top of an empty bottle or the nose of an unconscious peer. This sport is called *caps* and it parallels, if not descends from, a game played thousands of years ago by young Greek men after they finished dining. Called *kottabos*, a name that derived from a Greek word meaning *cup* and then entered Latin as *cottabus*, the game demanded that each young Greek fling the dregs of his wine into a metal vessel placed some feet away. As he did so, he shouted the name of his mistress and if the wine made the vessel ring, it was a sign that she loved him. The word *cottabus* first appeared in English in the early nineteenth century.

counter

Every kitchen has a counter, a surface on which food is prepared before it is carried to the oven or the table. The name of this kitchen furnishing is not related to the identically spelt *counter* that means *contrary*, as in *counter-clockwise*; that *counter*—the contrary one—derives from the Latin preposition *contra*, meaning *against*. On the other hand, two words that do not resemble the culinary *counter*—*amputate* and *reputation*—are indeed its relatives. The common source of these three words is the Latin *putare*, meaning both *to cut away* and, by extension, *to reckon*. From the former sense arose the word *amputate*, literally a cutting away, while from the latter sense arose the word *reputation*, a reckoning of one's merit. The word *counter* also developed out of the *reckoning* sense of *putare*: the ancient Romans combined *putare* with the preposition *cum* to form *computare*, meaning *to reckon together*. *Computare* is obviously the direct source of the word *compute*, but it also developed into the French word *countour*, the name of a financial officer who collected and reckoned debts. English adopted this job name in the thirteenth century, respelling it as *counter* about fifty years later. In the seventeenth century, the word shifted its meaning from the financial officer to the desk at which he sat, and in the nineteenth century it came to denote any sort of desk-like surface, whether found in a bank, shop, or kitchen.

coupon

Although *coupon* and *capon* are similar-sounding words, and although they both derive from sources meaning *to cut*, the two words are not related to one another. The ultimate source of *coupon* is the Greek *kolaphos*, meaning *a blow* or *a punch*, which Latin adopted as *colaphus*; this Latin word then evolved into the French *coup*, also meaning *a blow* as in *coup de grâce* or *coup d'état*. From this noun, French formed the verb *couper*, meaning *to cut*, which in turn gave rise to two French words that English adopted in the early nineteenth century: *coupon*, the name of a food voucher that can be cut from a magazine or newspaper, and *coupé*, originally the name of a carriage that was a "cut-off" version of a longer one, but now—after having been Anglicized to *coupe*—the name of a two-door car. In contrast, the ultimate source of *capon*, the name of a rooster castrated to make its flesh more tasty, is the Greek *koptein*, which also happens to mean *to cut*. From this Greek word, the ancient Romans derived the word *capo*, a word they bestowed on roosters that had received, like Julius Caesar, "the most unkindest cut of all" (according to Plutarch, the ancient Greek historian, Brutus stabbed Caesar in his testicles). In the eleventh century, or perhaps even earlier, Old English adopted this Latin word as *capun*, which was respelt in the fourteenth century as *capon*. A distant relative of *capon*, but one that also derives from the Greek *koptein*, is *comma*, the name of a punctuation mark indicating where a clause or phrase is terminated or "cut off."

course

A course is a division of a meal, consisting of a single dish or of a set of dishes brought to the table all at once. From the sixteenth to the middle of the nineteenth century, most formal dinners had two or three courses plus a dessert. The name of this basic meal division, the course, derives ultimately from the Latin verb *currere*, meaning *to run*: *currere* gave rise to the Latin *cursus*, signifying *a running*, which developed into the French word *cours*, which was borrowed by English as *course* at the beginning of the fourteenth century. The word *course* originally meant *a sequence of stages*, but eventually it also came to mean *a stage in a sequence*. The culinary *course* is, of course, related to the many other English words that derive from the Latin *currere*, including *current*, *courier*, *cursor*, and *occur*. See also *hors d'oeuvre*, *entrée*, *pièce de résistance*, and *entremets*.

couscous

There are a number of entries in this dictionary that look as if the author got up to fill his coffee cup and then, upon returning to his keyboard his keyboard, accidentally retyped the words he last completed. These words include *couscous*, *jubjub*, *wow-wow*, *gîte-gîte*, *piri-piri*, *pili-pili*, *mealie-mealie*, and *bonbon*. Such words, all of them names of foods, demonstrate a linguistic anomaly called reduplication, the repetition of a syllable in a word. In the case of *couscous* (a dish made from pounded wheat), the Arabic word from which it derives, *kouskous*, is itself reduplicated, as is the older Arabic word from which *kouskous* in turn developed: *kaskasa*, meaning *to pound*; the word *kaskasa*, with its repeated *kas* syllable, may have been formed in imitation of the sound made by pounding a mallet or pestle up and down. *Couscous* first appeared in English at the beginning of the seventeenth century. *Piri-piri*, the name of a sauce made from red peppers, first appeared in English in 1964, and also derives from a source that is itself reduplicated: *pili-pili*, the name of a very hot African pepper. In turn, *pili-pili* is a corruption of the Arabic word *felfel*, meaning *strong pepper*. The source of this Arabic word is unknown, but certainly *felfel* is similar to the sound you make after you bite into a too-hot pepper. Other reduplicated food words have been formed not from a previous source but out of thin air. *Wow-wow*, for example, was invented in the early nineteenth century as a self-consciously silly name for a stewed-beef sauce; later in that century, Lewis Carroll, the author of *Alice in Wonderland* and the poem *Jabberwocky*, invented *jubjub* as the name of a chimerical, ferocious, and delicious bird. Reduplicated words may also develop from children's tendency to repeat sounds: *mama*, *dada*, and *pee pee* are reduplications, as is *bonbon*, the French name for sugar candy that literally means *good-good*. *Bonbon* was first used in English at the end of the eighteenth century. *Gîte-gîte* is also French in origin but does not derive from the jabbering of children. In French, *gîte-gîte* refers to the fleshy part of an ox's shin used in ragouts; it derives from the verb *gésir*, meaning *to lie down*, because it is this part of the animal's shin that touches the ground when it beds down for the night. Why this part of the ox became known as *gîte-gîte* and not simply *gîte* is a bit of a mystery. My own suggestion is that the doubling of *gîte* results from an ox having two pairs of shins, front and back. Finally, quasi-reduplications include *knick-knack* and *pish-pash*. *Knick-knack* appeared in the late seventeenth century as a name for trinkets but also for any light, dainty article of food; a hundred years later, *knick-knack* also came to mean a meal to which every guest brought a dish. In origin, *knick-knack* is simply a playful variation of the older *knack*, a word that meant *a trick*. Similarly, *pish-pash*—the name of a rice-soup fed to British babies in India in the nineteenth century—is likely an extension of the older *pish*, a word used since the sixteenth century to express contempt for a trivial matter.

crab

The Latin word for crab, *cancer*, was borrowed in the early seventeenth century as the name of a malignant disease that creeps like a crab through its victim. *Cancer* is not, however, the source of the English *crab*. Instead, the English name of this crustacean, first recorded about a thousand years ago, derives from an unknown Germanic source, one that is probably also the source of the word *crawl*. *Crab* the crustacean may in turn be the source of *crab* the apple: the tart flavour of that fruit may have reminded people, back in the fifteenth century when this sense of *crab* first appeared, of the "sour" and "biting" temperament of the sea-creature. Alternatively, *crab* the apple may derive from the Swedish *skrabba*, meaning *wild apple*.

crab apple

See *crab*.

cracker

The word *cracker* meant many things before it came to refer to a kind of unsweetened wafer: when the word appeared in the early sixteenth century, it meant *liar* or *boaster*; then, in the late sixteenth century, it came to refer to a noisy firework, a *firecracker*; and finally, in the early seventeenth century, it came to mean a device used to shell nuts. Not until the early eighteenth century did *cracker* come to denote a dry, unsweetened wafer, and even then the word was used almost exclusively in North America; in England, dry, soda-raised wafers continued to be known as *biscuits*, a word that North Americans now use to refer to small, moist loaves made of yeast-dough. What these various senses of *cracker* have in common is the idea of a loud, sharp noise—a "cracking": this is obvious with firecrackers and nutcrackers and even with soda crackers, which are so dry they make a cracking sound when bitten. Similarly, liars and boasters make a lot of noise, although this sense of *cracking* and *cracker* was probably also inspired by the resemblance of *crack* to *croak*, the sound a bullfrog makes when it wants to draw attention to itself. The *boasting* or *liar* sense of *cracking* and *cracker* is now almost obsolete, although a related sense still exists in idioms such as *to crack a joke* and *wisecracks*.

cran

See *nipperkin*.

crayfish

A crayfish is no more a fish than a cat-fish is a cat; the original name of this edible crustacean was *crevice* (no relation to the *crevice* that means *gap*), which was adopted from French in the fifteenth century; this French name, in turn, was a borrowing of the Old German name for crab, *krebiz*. After entering English, *crevice* remained the standard spelling of the crab-like creature's name until the fifteenth century, when its associations with the sea caused people to corrupt the pronunciation and spelling of the word, first to *crefish* and then to *crayfish*. See also *crab*.

crenellate

The top of a castle tower is usually crenellated; that is, the perimeter of its battlements forms a repeating pattern of thick stone, gap, thick stone, gap, and so on, thus affording both protection and a view of what's going on down below. The edges of most coins are also crenellated with tiny notches, a design that prevented sneaky people, back when coins were actually made of precious metals, from shaving slivers of gold or silver from their edges. Crenellation is also a culinary technique, as when a baker pinches a pie crust along the edge to form a pleasing pattern. As a word, *crenellate* has been borrowed twice by English.

Most recently, in the mid nineteenth century, *crenellate* was acquired by adapting the French *créneller*, meaning *to indent*. Long before this, however, in the early thirteenth century, the French *créneller* was borrowed as *kernel*, meaning *indentation*, a word that became obsolete in the seventeenth century (the other *kernel*, the one meaning *grain*, derives from an unrelated source). Further back in history, the French *créneller* evolved from the Vulgar Latin *crena*, meaning *notch*, which is also the source of the word *cranny*, as in *nook and cranny*. In culinary use, a common synonym for *crenellate* is *crimp*, a word that emerged in the early eighteenth century. The source of *crimp* is a Germanic word, pronounced something like *kram*, that meant *to pinch*; this Germanic *kram* is also the source of numerous other "pinching" words, including *cramp*, *cram*, *clamp*, and even *clam*. See also *clam* and *rimmer*.

Creole

Creole cooking, a cuisine employing lots of shellfish and spices, grew out of the French, East Indian, and African cultures thrown together in the West Indies in the seventeenth and eighteenth centuries. The word originally referred to the descendants of Spanish settlers who were born in the Caribbean, but later was also used to refer to the descendants of French settlers in Louisiana. In the early seventeenth century, English adopted the word *Creole* from French, which had derived it from the Spanish term, *criollo*; in turn, *criollo* probably developed from the Spanish *criado*, meaning *breed* or *off-spring*, which evolved from the Latin *creare*, meaning *to create*. The Latin *creare* is also the source of the word *creature*, and is even related to the English *crescent* (a crescent moon grows in size, just as a creature does) and to the French *croissant* (a crescent-shaped pastry). See also *croissant*.

crêpe

Just as the English language uses the apostrophe to indicate missing letters in words such as *can't* or *o'clock* (shortened forms of *cannot* and *of the clock*), the French language uses a mark called the circumflex to indicate that the word once possessed a now-absent *s*. Thus, French words such as *hôtel*, *croûton*, and *crêpe* were formerly spelt, in Old French, *hostel*, *crouston*, and *crespe*;

not surprisingly, the letter *s* is also found in the same position in the Latin words from which these three French words derive: *hospes* (meaning *stranger*), *crusta* (meaning *hard shell*), and *crispus* (meaning *curled*). In Old French, *crespe* possessed the *curled* sense of its Latin ancestor, and therefore it—or rather its later form, *crêpe*—became, in the seventeenth century, the name of a curled and crinkled fabric. In the eighteenth century, the British adopted this form of the word—*crêpe*—as a name for curled and crinkled fabric or paper, but they also invented a more "English" spelling, *crape*, and gave this name to crinkled, black strips of cloth draped over coffins or worn around the arm as a sign of mourning. A hundred years later, in the late nineteenth century, *crêpe* finally acquired its culinary sense, thanks to the invention of the crepe Suzette, a thin pancake with curled edges, served in a liqueur sauce and named by a Parisian chef after the actress Suzanne Reichenberg.

cress

Although the water-cress is the best known, there are actually over thirty different cresses, many of which have leaves that can be added to salads or soups. The name of the plant derives from *kreson*, a Germanic word meaning *to creep*, and therefore descriptive of how the plant grows. In English, *cress* dates back to the eighth century, but *water-cress* is not referred to until the fifteenth century.

crimp

See *crenellate*.

crisp

Nowadays, having crisp hair is a sign that you need to switch to a less astringent shampoo. However, when the word *crisp* entered the English language in the tenth century, it meant—like its Latin source, *crispus*—that something was curly, and it was often used to describe the curly hair of handsome knights and lovely maidens. It was not until the early sixteenth century that *crisp* developed its current sense of *brittle* or *crunchy*, a shift in meaning caused partly by the sound of the word itself—*crisp* sounds crisp—and partly because many things, like bacon, not only become curly as they cook but also crisp and crunchy. This *crunchy* sense of the word *crisp* led to its being used as a noun in the 1920s when it became, in England, the name of slivers of potatoes fried, salted, and eaten cold—in other words, what North Americans call *potato chips*. Later still, in the 1960s, *crisp* gave rise to *crisper*, a drawer in a refrigerator where vegetables are kept fresh and crunchy.

crock pot

Like the last clause in this sentence, the term *crock pot* is redundant because *crock* means *pot*, and *pot* means *crock*. This sense of *crock* is still evident in the old-fashioned phrase *crock of gold*, now heard only in conjunction with leprechauns and rainbows. The word *crock*, which in the mid eighteenth century gave rise to the word *crockery*, meaning *earthenware*, dates back in English to at least the eleventh century. In other languages, *crock* has numerous relatives—for example, the Dutch *kruik*, the Welsh *crochan*, the Greek *krossos*, and the German *krug*—but the ultimate source of all these words is unknown. One other relative of *crock*, the Old Saxon *kruka*, is notable because it was adopted by Old French as *crue*. In Anglo-Norman French, this *crue* gave rise to the diminutive *cruet*, meaning *little pot*, which English adopted in the late fourteenth century as a name for a small glass bottle used at the dinner table to dispense oil or vinegar.

croissant

One night in 1686, Turkish soldiers from the Ottoman empire attempted to gain access to Budapest, the capital of Hungary, by sneakily tunnelling under the city's fortifications. The good citizens of Budapest, snoring in their beds, heard nothing as their mole-like enemies burrowed right beneath their floor boards—nothing, that is, until the Ottomans started tunnelling under a bakery where bread-makers and pastry-cutters had gotten up early to prepare the next day's wares. Hearing the scuttling and smelling a rat, the bakers raised the alarm, thus foiling the Turks' subterranean attack; to commemorate their part in the victory, the bakers of Budapest invented the croissant, a flaky pastry shaped like the crescent moon on the defeated Ottomans' flag. This story, as much as it sounds like an episode of *Hogan's Heroes*, is the traditional explanation for the appearance of the croissant, a pastry whose name is indeed the French word for *crescent*. In origin, however, the word *croissant*, as well as the word *crescent*, derives from a Latin word that did not initially describe a shape but rather a process: that word is the Latin *crescens*, meaning *growing*. One object that has always grown and shrunk before everyone's eyes is the moon, and thus the phrase *luna crescens—growing moon*—came to describe the earth's satellite as it waxed from new to full. Eventually, the Latin *crescens* came to be so associated with the waxing moon that the word—and its English and French derivatives, *crescent* and *croissant*—came to refer to anything shaped like a lunar arc. It was this sense of the word *croissant* that led to the pastry's French name, a name that first appeared in English at the end of the nineteenth century. Other words that derive from the same Latin source include *increase* (a synonym for *grows*), *crescendo* (the climax to which a piece of music grows), and *creature* (a thing that grows to maturity).

crouton

See *crust*.

crubeen

See *bonny-clabber*.

cruet

See *crock pot*.

cruller

In 1809, American author Washington Irving published a book called *A History of New York*, ostensibly written by one Diedrich Knickerbocker, an imaginary Dutch immigrant. Nine years later, in 1818, Irving introduced the word *cruller* to the English language when he briefly mentioned the curly pastry in his *Legend of Sleepy Hollow*. That Irving both invented the name *Knickerbocker* and introduced the word *cruller* is a strange coincidence: he could not have known, when he created his Diedrich Knickerbocker persona, that forty years later *knickerbocker* would become the ethnic nickname for Dutch immigrants, the same Dutch immigrants who introduced the cruller pastry to North America (later still, Irving's *knickerbocker* was adopted as the name of the knee-length shorts often worn by Dutch men). Of course, not only is the cruller Dutch in origin, its name is too: the Dutch *crullen*, meaning *to curl*, is the source of the name of the pastry because it is twisted and curled before it is fried in oil. However, this was not the first time that English had borrowed the Dutch word *crullen*: in the fourteenth century, the adjective form of the word, *crul*, was adopted by English to describe hair curled into ringlets. For more than a hundred years, *crul* remained the usual spelling and pronunciation of this word until, in the sixteenth century, the middle vowel and consonant traded places—a process known as metathesis—thus establishing the word *curl*. Accordingly, the *curlers* you put in your hair, and the *crullers* you put in your mouth, are actually one and the same word.

crumb

In the fifteenth century, the word *crumb* meant the part of a loaf of bread that is not the crust; recipes calling for bread often instructed the cook to slice the crust from the loaf and use only the *crumb*. The word *crumb*, however, is older than this particular usage, dating back to the tenth century when it referred more generally, as it does again now, to any particle of food that has broken away from something larger. The ultimate source of *crumb* was a Germanic word, pronounced something like *kram*, that meant both *curled* and *rounded*: from the *rounded* sense, the word *crumb* developed, since a crumb is roughly round in shape; from the *curled* sense, other food words developed, including *crumpet* and *cruller*, since these foods were originally curled before being cooked or as a result of being cooked. When *crumb* first entered English a thousand years ago, it was spelt *crum*; the *b* was not added until the sixteenth century (likely to make it resemble words such as *limb* and *comb*), and even then the *crum* spelling remained the usual form until the eighteenth century. This original spelling is still present in *crummy*, meaning that something is so shoddy it is crumbling to pieces.

crumpet

Many foods made from fried dough, such as crêpes and crullers, get their name from words that mean *curled* since the action of cooking them makes them crinkle, bend, fold, and twist. The crumpet is another such food, having derived its name from a fourteenth century term, *crompid cake*, literally meaning *curled cake*. *Crompid*, in turn, derives from a much older Germanic word, pronounced something like *kram*, that gave rise to a host of other words that involve bending or curling, including *crouch* (a posture achieved by bending your knees), *crochet* (a kind of knitting done with a bent needle), *croquet* (a game originally played with curved sticks), and *crimping* (the action of bending the edge of a pastry shell to give it a fancy pattern). See also *crenellate* and *crêpe*.

crust

Five hundred years ago, the mark of a skilful baker was the ability to make a pie or loaf of bread with a hard, shell-like crust; refrigeration and plastic bags had not been invented yet, so a thick, tough crust prevented bugs from burrowing in, and kept the inside from drying out. It is not surprising, therefore, that English derived the word *crust*—perhaps via French—from the Latin word *crusta*, meaning *shell*, a sense that still exists in the name of the marine creatures known as *crustaceans*. The source of the Latin *crusta*, incidentally, was an Indo-European word meaning *hard* that also gave rise, through Greek, to the word *crystal*. The word *crust* appeared in English in the early fourteenth century and was followed a few decades later by *crustade*, the name of a pie made of meat, eggs, and milk, all enclosed with a crust. By the middle of the fifteenth century, this new word, *crustade*, underwent a peculiar change in pronunciation, the result being that the word *custard* was formed. For the next 150 years a custard continued to be a meat-pie; it was not until the beginning of the seventeenth century that its recipe changed and *custard* came to mean a dessert made by baking a mixture of eggs, milk, and sugar, often served in a pastry shell. In the Middle Ages the French also had a dish similar to the original meat-filled *crustade*; they called it a *croustade*, deriving the name from their word for crust, *crouste*. English borrowed this French *croustade* in the mid nineteenth century as the name for a dish made by scooping out the middle of a loaf of bread and then filling it with a ragout. Earlier in the nineteenth century, another French word that derived from the original Latin *crusta* was borrowed by English: *crouton*, a crust of bread used to garnish soups or salads. See also *crumb*.

cucumber

If you were to eat a two-pound cucumber, you would ingest only an ounce of actual "cuke" material; the rest of it—96%, in fact—would be water. The name of this moist fruit derives from the Greek *kukuon*, which evolved into the Latin *cucumis*. Accordingly, when English adopted this Latin word in the late fourteenth century, it was spelt *cucumer*, that is, without a *b*; it retained this form until the fifteenth century when the influence of the French name, *coucombre*, caused the English spelling to change to *cucumber*. Later on, in the sixteenth century, the French *coucombre* again affected the English word, causing the first syllable to change so that the word was spelt and pronounced *cow-cumber*. The appearance of the term *horseradish* at about the same time may also have partly inspired the *cow-cumber* spelling, even though the notion of a cow having cumber must have seemed absurd (at that time, the word *cumber*, now obsolete, meant *embarrassment*). *Cow-cumber* remained the standard spelling and pronunciation of the word until the early nineteenth century, when it became associated with the uneducated masses who grew them; as a result, snooty scholars restored the *cucumber* spelling and pronunciation to make the word look more like its original Latin form, although by the same reasoning the *b* should have been removed as well, but was not. The phrase *cool as a cucumber* is surprisingly old—its first recorded use is in 1732 in a poem by John Gay: "I, cool as a cucumber, could see the rest of womankind." The abbreviated name of the fruit, *cuke*, dates back to the beginning of this century.

cuisine

See *cook*.

culinary

See *cook*.

culpon

See *carving*.

cumin

Although it is now considered a somewhat exotic spice, one associated with Middle Eastern cookery, English writers referred to *cumin* as early as the ninth century, long before references to other spices appeared. The immediate source of *cumin* was the ancient Roman name of the spice, *cuminum*, which derived in turn from the Hebrew or Arabic name of the spice.

cup

Often the shortest words have the most complex histories, as is the case with *cup*. In origin, *cup* can be traced back to an Indo-European word pronounced something like *kaup* and meaning *round container*. In Sanskrit, *kaup* became *kupas*, meaning *hole*, while in Greek it became *kupe*, meaning *ship*, and in Latin it became *cupa*, meaning *cask*. The Indo-European *kaup* is also the ultimate source of the German word *kopf*, meaning *head*, and—thanks to a bzillion tiny shifts in pronunciation—it is even the ultimate source of the English words *head* and *hive*, both of which are round containers with things buzzing around inside. The Latin derivative, *cupa*, also gave rise to a number of linguistic offspring. First, the Latin *cupa*, meaning *cask*, became the Late Latin *cuppa*, meaning *cup*; it was this word that developed into the Old English *cuppe*, first recorded a thousand years ago, which in turn became the modern *cup*. Second, the Latin word *cupa* also developed into the Middle English word *cowpe*, meaning a basket in which chickens are kept; this Middle English *cowpe* developed into Modern English *coop*, meaning a building for chickens. Third, the Latin word *cupa* also gave rise, through German, to *cooper*, the name of the person who makes casks. And finally, the Latin *cupa* developed through Italian into a kind of grand, architectural cup: *cupola*, the dome of a building. See also *cupboard*.

cupboard

No one has pronounced the *p* in *cupboard* since the sixteenth century, which slightly obscures the fact that in origin the word is actually *cup board*, a board for cups. During the sixteenth and seventeenth centuries, this origin was in fact even harder to see, as common spellings of the word ranged from *cubberd* to *cobord* and even to *cowbard*. Rational eighteenth century scholars eventually set things right, however, by insisting that the word be spelt, if not pronounced, *cup-board*. The word first appeared in English at the beginning of the fourteenth century, when it meant a table or shelf upon which cups and plates were put for display. It was not until the early sixteenth century that the word acquired its current meaning of a closed cabinet where cups are stored out of sight and out of harm until needed. See also *board* and *cup*.

cupboard love

Cupboard love is love pretended to the cook in the hopes that a meal or snack will result. Although the strategy has been exploited since the invention of the cookie jar, the term itself did not emerge until the middle of the eighteenth century. This practice of feigning affection was also known in the eighteenth century by a less endearing name, *lump-love*, the idea again being that the true object of the pretender's desire is a lump of food.

cupcake

Although you might suppose that cupcakes take their name from being little cups of cake, this is likely not the case. When cupcakes were given their name in the early nineteenth century, they were not referred to in the plural as *cupcakes*, but rather in the singular as *cup cake*; in other words, you made a batch of *cup cake* not a dozen *cupcakes*. The *cup* in *cupcakes* probably originated from all the ingredients for the dainty being measured in cups: one recipe from the turn of the century called for three cups of flour, one cup of sugar, one cup of milk, and half a cup of butter (the poundcake likewise acquired its name in the mid eighteenth century because its recipe called for a pound of each ingredient). By the second decade of this century, however, people started to assume that the *cup* in the *cup cake* referred to the little moulds the batter was poured into, and thus the name changed to *cupcakes*.

curd

The Old English word *creodan*, meaning *to press together*, is the source of the word *crowd* (a throng of people pressing together) and also of *curd* (lumps of coagulated milk that may be made into cheese). When the word first appeared in English in the middle of the fourteenth century it was spelt and pronounced as *crud*; however, by the fifteenth century the *r* and the *u* sounds had traded places—a process known as metathesis—thus giving rise to *curd*, which in turn developed the verb form *curdle*. About fifty years ago, however, the word *crud*—meaning lumps of disgusting, foreign matter—suddenly reappeared in English, either as the result of a reverse metathesis of *curd* or as the result of someone intentionally resurrecting the original, defunct form of the word.

currant

Currants are small, round berries that are dried and used in jellies and pastries. Their name is not related to the word *current* as in *current affairs*—a word that derives from the Latin *currere*, meaning *to run*—but rather derives from *Corinth*, the name of a city in Greece. In ancient times, Corinth exported dried grapes to the rest of Europe, grapes that in France acquired the name *raisins de Corinthe*. In the early fourteenth century, this phrase was adopted into English as *raisins of Corauntz*, which by the early sixteenth century had shortened to just *corauntz*. This form of the name was then mistaken for a plural, causing people to assume that a single one of these dried grapes was a *coraunt*, a word later respelt as *currant*. Finally, in the last half of the sixteenth century, the word *currant* was applied by the English to a shrub—introduced to their island from the continent—that they falsely believed to be the source of the Greek currants. These berries, which are actually related to the gooseberry, were called *bastard currants* by those who realized that they were in no way related to real currants, but in time they too became known just as *currants*, or sometimes as *red currants* and *black currants*. Incidentally, the city of Corinth—or as the Greeks call it, *Korinthos*—takes its name from a Pelasgian word, *kar*, meaning *point*, an allusion to Corinth's location on the tip of an isthmus.

curry

In India, where it originated, recipes for curry powder vary from region to region and even from caste to caste. As a result, importers and manufacturers in Europe struggled for centuries to standardize the seasoning's recipe. They finally succeeded in obliterating variety when, at the 1889 Universal Paris Exhibition, a fixed formula was established by joint international legislation: two parts of mustard, two of pepper, two of cumin, three of fenugreek, three of turmeric, five of chili pepper, twenty of coriander, thirty-four of tamarind, and forty-four of onion. The Tamil name of the seasoning—*kari*, meaning *sauce*—is the source of its English name, which first appeared in the late sixteenth century.

cutlet

You might suspect that *cut* is to *cutlet* as *pig* is to *piglet*; however, *cutlet*, the name of a small piece of mutton or veal cut from the ribs, is not a diminutive of the word *cut*. Instead, it is a diminutive of the French word *côte*, meaning *side*, or rather it is a double diminutive of that word: from *côte* the diminutive *côtele* was formed, and then from *côtele* the diminutive *côtelete* was later formed. A *cutlet*, therefore, is literally a *little, little side*, an appropriate name for the often tiny chunk of meat that some restaurants try to pass off as an entrée. *Cutlet* did not enter English until the beginning of the eighteenth century but is closely related to two much older words: *coast*, the side of a continent, and *accost*, the action of coming up alongside someone.

dab

See *dollop*.

dainties

See *opsophagy*.

dairy

See *dough*.

dariole

Like the word *custard*, the word *dariole* was originally, back in the early fifteenth century, the name of a savoury pastry filled with meat; also like *custard*, the word *dariole* eventually shifted its sense and came to mean a sweet dessert made from milk, eggs, and sugar. Unlike *custard*, however, *dariole* shifted its sense once more as it became, in the early nineteenth century, the name of a small baking tin shaped rather like a flower pot. In origin, the word *dariole* derives from the French *daurar*, meaning *to turn golden*, a reference to the golden brown crust of the original meat-filled dariole.

dark meat

The terms *dark meat* and *white meat* came about during the 1870s in the United States as euphemisms for, respectively, the breast and legs of a cooked chicken. Rather than say such naughty words—which might cause the gentlemen at the table to start thinking about the breasts and legs of the gentlewomen, which might cause them to fornicate, which might damn them to hell and, worse, bring eternal shame upon the house—people instead used the two tones of the chicken carcass to distinguish its parts. (For similar reasons, polite company of the time referred to the four supports of the tables and chairs as *limbs* to avoid having to speak the word *l*gs*.) In the twentieth century, the terms *dark meat* and *light meat* have ceased to be euphemisms and instead have become useful ways of distinguishing the moister dark meat from the dryer white meat. *White meat* can also be used to refer more generally to meat such as chicken, veal, and rabbit as opposed to beef, mutton, and lamb; this use of the term dates back to the middle of the eighteenth century, but the corresponding term, *red meat*, did not appear until the end of the nineteenth century. Spelt as one word, the term *whitemeat* was also used from the fifteenth to the nineteenth century as a generic name for any food prepared from milk (*meat*, at that time, could be used to mean *food* in general). See also *meat*.

dashi

See *sushi*.

date

Like the banana, the long slender fruit known as the *date* derives its name from a word meaning *finger*. With *date*, this source was the Greek *daktulos*, which the ancient Romans borrowed as *dactylus*, shifting its meaning in the process: to the Romans it could denote either a poetic rhythm (one based on three beats, just as the human finger has three joints) or it could denote a long, finger-shaped grape. As the Latin *dactylus* evolved into the French *date*, its meaning shifted again and it was once more applied to the fruit of the date palm; it was with this spelling and meaning that English borrowed the name of the fruit in the late thirteenth century. About a hundred years later, English acquired its other *date*, the one that refers to a given day of a month. This unrelated *date* evolved from the Medieval Latin *data*, meaning *given*, which in turn derived from a phrase used by ancient

Romans when dating their letters: *data Romae*, meaning *given at Rome*. See also *banana*.

deaconing

See *choke-priest*.

deboned

See *boned*.

decoction

Soup is always a decoction but it may also be a concoction. The difference between the two culinary terms is that when you *decoct* something you boil it until you have extracted its flavour, ending up with a bouillon; on the other hand, when you *concoct* something, you take several ingredients and boil them together so that their flavours merge. Both words derive from the Latin *coquere*, meaning *to cook*, but they are distinguished by their prefixes: *de* means *away from*, while *con* means *together*. *Decoction* has been a culinary term since the fifteenth century; *concoction* only since the nineteenth. See also *cook* and *apricot*.

demijohn

Although *demijohn* is a good name for a washroom containing no bathtub or sink, it actually refers to a wine bottle or vinegar jug whose body is fitted with a wicker-work casing. *Demijohn*, in fact, has nothing to do with the name *John*, but instead is an English corruption of the French *dame-jeanne*, a name that literally means *Lady Jane*. The French may have jokingly bestowed the name *dame-jeanne* on such vessels because their long-necked, wide-bodied shape resembled an overweight dowager, a resemblance heightened by the wicker casing covering the body of the bottle like a skirt. *Dame-jeanne*, which emerged in French in the seventeenth century, made its way into English by the mid eighteenth century but was not converted to the more English sounding *demijohn* until the early nineteenth century. The word was also adopted by numerous other languages, including Italian (*damigianna*), Spanish (*dama-juana*), and even Arabic (*damajanah*).

dessert

The *dessert* that refers to the sweet treat that concludes a meal has no connection with the *desert* that appears in *Sahara desert*, a word that derives from the Latin word *deserere*, meaning *to abandon*. However, *dessert*—the sweet treat—does have a connection with the other *desert*, the one appearing in phrases such as "He got his just deserts." Both words take their origin from the Latin noun *servus*, meaning *slave*. From this Latin noun came the Latin verb *servire*, meaning *to serve*, which entered French as *servir* and was there combined with the negating prefix *de* to form *desservir*, meaning *to un-serve* or, by extension, *to remove*. This French *desservir* then evolved into the term *dessert*, which first referred to the act of removing the dishes and cutlery at the end of a meal, and then came to be identified with the sweet dish brought to the table after it had been cleared. The French *desservir*, incidentally, also gave rise to the English word *disservice*; this shared origin means that *dessert* (a yummy food) and *disservice* (an offensive behaviour) are essentially two faces of the same word. *Dessert* and *disservice* both appeared in English at the beginning of the seventeenth century. Long before all this, the *desert* in *just deserts* arose when the Latin *servire* was combined with the prefix *de*, used this time not to negate the verb but to intensify it; the resulting new word, *deservire*, thus did not mean *to un-serve*, but rather *to serve really well*. Via French, the Latin *deservire* entered English at the end of the thirteenth century as *desert*, meaning *well-deserved prize* or *suitable reward*. Also via French, the original Latin *servus* developed in the early thirteenth century into *servant*, a lackey who filled the cup his master emptied, and emptied the pot his master filled. See also *serviette*.

dill

Since first being recorded in Old English twelve centuries ago, the word *dill* has changed very little: it has acquired a second *l*, originally having been spelt *dil* or *dile*, but it refers to the same herb it always did. The dill plant has, however, had other names in English as well. From the thirteenth century to the nineteenth century it was also known as *anet*, a name deriving from the Latin *anethum*, which is what the ancient Romans called the plant. *Anethum* is also what the ancient Romans called *anise* because they did not realize that dill and anise are distinct plants. In the United States in the previous century, dill seeds were also known as *meetin' seeds* because they were given to children to chew during long meetings; these nineteenth century Americans believed, like the ancient Romans, that dill had revitalizing properties, and would therefore keep the children from falling asleep.

dim sum

After first appearing in English in 1948, the Chinese *dim sum*, the name of bite-sized dumplings filled with seafood and meat, went through numerous spellings—including *deem sum*, *tim-sam*, *dim sim*, and *tim sun*—before returning to its original form, *dim sum*, in the early 1980s. Translated literally, the name means *speck heart*, but more idiomatically the phrase suggests a little something that "touches" your heart and invigorates it.

dinner

No doubt many guests have arrived for a Sunday dinner much earlier or later than the host intended thanks to the ambiguous nature of the word *dinner*: a guest might understand dinner to be the meal eaten at noon (followed hours later by supper); a host might understand dinner to be the meal eaten at six o'clock or so (having been preceded at noon by lunch). Looking to the origin of the word for clarification does not help, since *dinner* literally means *breakfast*: it derives ultimately from the Vulgar Latin *disjunare*, formed by compounding *dis*, a prefix meaning *not*, and *jejunium*, meaning *a fast* or *a hungry period*. The Vulgar Latin *disjunare* therefore means *to stop being hungry* or *to break a fast*, specifically the fast undertaken when we fall asleep for eight hours every night. The Vulgar Latin *disjunare* entered Old French as two words: first as *desiuner*, the name of a morning meal that developed into the Modern French word *déjeuner*; somewhat later, the Vulgar Latin *disjunare* also became the Old French *disner*, meaning *to dine*, which became the Modern French word *dîner*. It was this Old French word, *disner*, which gave rise to the English *dine* and *dinner*, although by the time English developed these words, in the late thirteenth century, the meal they denoted had shifted from early morning to midday. The Latin *jejunium* also happens to be the source of the word *jejune*: when *jejune* entered English in the early seventeenth century, it meant *hungry* or *fasting*, but by the mid seventeenth century it had come to mean something insipid, something that provides no "mental nourishment." See also *lunch* and *postprandial*.

dish

See *plate*.

Dobos torte

Made by alternating layers of cake with layers of chocolate cream and then covering the top with caramel, the Dobos torte takes its name from its inventor, Joseph Dobos, a Hungarian pastry chef who introduced his creation to the world at an 1885 exhibition of tortes and cakes. Within thirty years, recipes for the Dobos torte were being included in English cookbooks. In contrast, the linzertorte, though also a torte, takes its name not from a person but from a place: *Linz*, a city in Austria that derives its name, like the Belgian city of Limburg, from *lindo*, an ancient Germanic word meaning *linden tree* (in Europe, the linden, a tree cultivated for the shade it provides, is sometimes called a lime tree but is not related to the tropical tree that produces that green, citrus fruit). Linzertortes were first referred to in English in the early twentieth century, about the same time as Dobos tortes.

doed-koek

When the Dutch founded New York in the seventeenth century, one of the customs they brought with them from Holland was that of the *doed-koek*. Literally meaning *dead-cake*, a *doed-koek* was a funeral biscuit, marked with the initials of the person in the coffin and given to each pall bearer. The custom is likely related to "sin-eating," the practice of hiring someone to symbolically consume the sins of a person who had recently died: first, the family of the deceased placed a morsel of bread and a piece of cheese on the chest of the corpse; then, the designated sin-eater entered the room, picked up the food, and ate it while standing before the body. Rather than thank the sin-eater for thus purging their dearly departed, the family of the deceased then concluded the ritual by hustling him out of the house and into the street, cursing him and throwing stones. No doubt this bum's rush out the door was a vestige of the custom described in the Old Testament of chasing a goat, supposedly laden with the sins of the community, out of the village and into the wilderness. This execrated animal was known as the scapegoat.

dollop

Although the volume or weight of a dollop has never been precisely established, it is roughly the amount of warm butter that you can scoop onto the end of a spatula before dropping it into your frying pan. This culinary sense of *dollop* is a fairly recent development, apparently having originated in the nineteenth century; prior to this, and as early as the mid sixteenth century, *dollop* referred to a clump of grass in a field. The origin of the word is unclear, but it is probably related somehow to the Norwegian *dolp*, meaning *lump*. Other small and indefinite measurements sometimes used by cooks include *dab* and *smidgen*. *Dab* arose as a verb in the early fourteenth century and meant *to peck*, as a bird does when it is gobbling up grubs or seeds; it then came to denote any sort of swiping motion, and finally, in the mid eighteenth century, came to refer to a clump of material, like butter, that might be smooched onto an implement, like a knife, by making a swiping motion. *Smidgen*, first recorded in the mid nineteenth century, appears to have developed from the older *smitch*, also meaning *a small amount*; in turn, *smitch* likely evolved from the now-obsolete *smit*, which denoted a small piece of something—ice, for example—struck off from a larger chunk. *Smit* arose as a noun form of the verb *smite*, meaning *to strike*, and therefore its descendant, *smidgen*, is related to *smith*, a person who hammers metal on an anvil, and to *smithereens*, meaning *tiny fragments*.

donair

See *shish kebab*.

done to a turn

The microwave oven, a culinary innovation not even as old as some extant Christmas fruit-cakes, has one thing in common with the spit, a cooking utensil dating back to the invention of the stick: both microwave ovens and spits rotate the food being cooked so that the heat is distributed evenly. With a spit, these rotations are especially crucial, for failing to turn a spit over an open fire results in the roast being charred on one side and raw on the other. Over the course of a few hours a spit might turn thousands of times, but nonetheless good cooks used to brag that they had turned the roast exactly the right number of times—neither one too many, nor one too few. Such a roast was *done to a turn*. The French counterpart for this term is *à point*, meaning *to the point*, or—more idiomatically—*done to the point between medium-rare and well-done*. The English word *appointment* has the same origin as the French culinary term: an appointment occurs at a point between an earlier time and a later time.

doner kebab

See *shish kebab*.

dormouse

See *mussel*.

dough

The Indo-European source of the word *dough* is also the ultimate source of many other words, including *dairy* and *paradise*. This ancient source, pronounced something like *dheigh*, meant *to mould clay*, but when it evolved into Germanic it came to mean *to knead bread dough*, a natural development considering that bakers and potters do essentially the same thing to different materials. This Germanic word then shifted meaning again as it came to refer not just to the action of kneading but to the actual material that is kneaded; it was this meaning that the word possessed when it emerged in Old English as *dag*, later respelt as *dough*. In some parts of northern England, the word *dough* came to be pronounced *duff* (like *enough*), a pronunciation that probably crept back into standard English in expressions such as

Get off your duff, the human duff being rather soft and doughy. The word *dairy* also derives from the same source as *dough* and *duff*: a thousand years ago, a woman whose job was to make dough for her community was called a *daege*, meaning *kneader*. Gradually, *daege* lost this very narrow sense and came to denote any female servant; a little later, however, the word narrowed in meaning again as it came to refer to a woman whose job was to milk cows, make butter, and so on. Eventually, by the late twelfth century, the shed where the *daege* did all her milk-work became known as the *deierie*, which acquired its current spelling, *dairy*, in the seventeenth century. The word *paradise* appears to have little in common with *dough* and *dairy*, but it does: the Persian ancestor of *paradise*—*pairidaeza*, meaning *enclosed garden*—was formed from *pairi*, meaning *around*, and *diz*, meaning *to mould*, the idea being that the walls of the garden are moulded around it. The latter of these two Persian words—*diz*—derives from the same Indo-European source as *dough* and *dairy*, thus making *paradise* their distant cousin. See also *plum-duff*.

doughnut

Although doughnuts no longer resemble nuts, they once did: the earliest references to doughnuts—in the early nineteenth century—reveal that the pastry was originally just a ball of sweetened dough fried in oil. Not until the mid nineteenth century did doughnuts acquire their hole, an innovation that solved a problem afflicting the original doughnuts: uncooked centres. Now a North American institution, the original doughnut was introduced by the Dutch settlers who founded New York City: they called their pastries *oliekoek*, meaning *oil-cake*, a word that became familiar to speakers of English in the nineteenth century, but never really challenged *doughnut* as the dominant name of the pastry. See also *dough* and *nut*.

dove's dung

In the Old Testament (2 Kings 6:24—29) a famine so devastates Samaria that the king encounters a woman who tells him that she and a neighbour made a bargain to eat her son one day and the neighbour's son the next; now, however, the woman is upset because they did indeed eat her own son, but the neighbour's child has gone into hiding. Children were not the only bill of fare during this famine: the same biblical passage describes how some Samarians paid through the nose for an ass's head and three pints of dove's dung, items they apparently cooked and ate. The eating of dove's dung certainly suggests the severity of the famine, but actually the Hebrew word traditionally translated as *dove's dung* may have been confused with a similarly spelt Hebrew word that means *locust pods*. In any event, the King James version of the Bible retains the *dove's dung* translation, but more modern versions, like The New Jerusalem Bible, usually substitute something less repellent, such as *wild onions*.

drisheen

See *bonny-clabber*.

drumstick

The lower legs of poultry have been called *drumsticks* since the mid eighteenth century, but the word really gained currency during the mid nineteenth century: prudish Victorians used it in place of *leg*, a word avoided at the supper table for fear its suggestive overtones would reduce the dinner guests to paroxysms of sexual frenzy. The shape of a turkey's leg was, of course, the inspiration behind *drumstick*, as it was for the French equivalent, *pilon*, meaning *pestle*.

dumpling

Gastronomically, a dumpling is a little ball of poached dough accompanying a meat dish; etymologically, a dumpling is a little dump, just as a duckling is a little duck. The *dump* in *dumpling* is not related to the *dump* in *down in the dumps* (that *dump* probably comes from the Dutch *domp*, meaning *haze*); neither is the *dump* in *dumpling* related to the *dump* in *garbage dump* (that *dump* probably comes from the Danish *dumpe*, meaning *to fall* as in "He took a bad dump and scraped his knee"); neither is the *dump* in *dumpling* related to the *dump* in *dumpoke* (the name of this East Indian dish of steamed chicken comes from the Persian *dam*, meaning *breath*, and *pukhte*, meaning *cooked*, as if the meat were "breath-cooked" by the steam). The *dump* in *dumpling* does not really seem to be related to any other *dump*, deriving all by itself at the beginning of the seventeenth century from the German *dump* that means *damp* or *moist*. See also *noodle*.

dumpoke

See *dumpling*.

eat

Foreign words have sometimes contributed more to English than their native English counterparts. For example, the Old English *etan*, meaning *to eat*, contributed a mere two words to Modern English: it evolved into *eat* and gave rise to *ort*, an almost defunct word that literally means *not eaten*. In contrast, the Latin *edere* is the direct source of *edible* but it is also—via its past participle form, *esus*, meaning *eaten*—the source of *comestible*, *semese*, and *obese*. These last three words are distinguished by their prefixes. With *comestible*, the *com* represents the Latin prefix *cum*, signifying *completely*, and thus *comestible* literally means *completely eaten*; since the early nineteenth century, however, the word has been used as a jocular synonym for *food*. With *semese*, the *sem* represents the Latin prefix *semi*, meaning *half*, and thus *semese* means *half-eaten*. With *obese*, the *ob* signifies *away* and therefore *obese* literally means *eaten away*. Surprisingly, the word *obese*—or rather its Latin source, *obesus*—was once used to describe an extremely skinny person, one "eaten away" by hunger. Eventually, however, *obesus* flipped its perspective and came to describe someone who appeared to have "eaten away" everything he could lay his hands on. As a result, the original meaning of the Latin *obesus* (*skinny*) is the opposite of what its English derivative, *obese*, now means (*fat, corpulent, having only a distant memory of one's toes*). The oldest in this cluster of words is *eat*, first recorded in the ninth century; *ort* and *comestible* followed in the mid fifteenth century, *edible* and *obese* in the mid seventeenth century, and *semese* in the mid nineteenth century. See also *ort*.

Eccles cake

The sweet, flaky, currant-filled pastry known as *Eccles cake* takes its name from Eccles, the town in northeast England where it originated. The town's name derives through Celtic from the Latin *ecclesia*, meaning *assembly* or, in ecclesiastical Latin, *church*; in turn, the Latin *ecclesia* developed from the Greek *ekkalein*, meaning *to call out*, citizens having been called to meetings by someone shouting from a roof top or street corner. In time, these town criers were often replaced by bells, such as the ones rung on Sunday morning to rouse sinners from their beds.

éclair

The frosted, cream-filled buns known as *éclairs* acquired their name, French for *lightning bolt*, not from their shape but from the speed with which they vanish from a plate: like lightning, they are gone in a flash. The word developed through Latin from an Indo-European source, pronounced something like *klar*, that meant *to shout clearly*. This *shouting* sense of the Indo-European source is not apparent in *éclair*, but it is evident in other descendants of *klar* such as *exclaim* and *clamour*. In contrast, *éclair* developed from the *clear* sense of *klar*, as did the word *clairvoyant* (one who sees clearly) and also the word *clear* itself. Still other descendants of the Indo-European *klar* seem to hang between the *shouting* sense and the *clear* sense: *clarinet* (a musical instrument with a shrill, but clear, sound) and *chaunticleer* (the traditional name for a rooster, meaning *clear singer*). English borrowed *éclair* from French in the mid nineteenth century.

Edam

Before being sold, Edam cheese is usually pressed into a ball and coated with a layer of red wax, a process inspiring its French nickname *tête de mort*, meaning *dead man's head*, the idea being that the wax-coated ball of cheese resembles the hooded head of an executed prisoner. *Edam*, however, is its real name, one that it acquired from the town in Holland where it was invented. The town, in turn, derives its name from its being founded near a dam on the river Ye: *Ye dam* became *Edam* just as *Amstel dam* and *Rotte dam* became *Amsterdam* and *Rotterdam*. As a cheese, Edam was first referred to in English in the early nineteenth century.

edible

See *eat*.

egg

Until the sixteenth century, the yolk-containing ovoid produced by a hen was commonly called an *eye*, a word in no way related to the *eye* that refers to the organ of sight. This *eye*—the one meaning *egg*—was the direct descendent of the Old English *aeg*, meaning *egg*, first recorded more than a thousand years ago. Sometime in the sixteenth century, however, this *eye* disappeared as it was gradually supplanted by the word *egg* itself, an Old Norse word introduced to English in the ninth or tenth century by Scandinavian raiders. In all probability, the Old Norse word (*egg*) managed to displace its native English cousin (*eye*) because the *eye* that meant *egg* was too confusingly similar to the *eye* that means *eye*: England was not big enough for the two *eye*s, so one of them had to go. Unrelated to either of these words is *egg* the verb, the one meaning *to urge* as in "Timmy knew better than to tease the ferret, but his friends egged him on." This *egg* derives from another Old Norse word, *eggja*, meaning *edge*, the idea being that urging someone to do something makes them "sharp" or "keen" to do it.

eggnog

Made from eggs, sugar, cream, and rum, eggnog is a traditional Christmas drink, first referred to in the early nineteenth century. Originally, however, the refreshment was made with ale instead of rum, as suggested by the *nog* part of its name, *nog* being an archaic English word meaning *strong ale* (eggnog is sometimes still made with ale in Germany, where it is called *bieresuppe*, meaning *beer-soup*). The word *nog* was first recorded in English in the late seventeenth century, but little else is known about its origin. Likely it is somehow related to *noggin*, a seventeenth century name for a small drinking cup, one that held only a quarter of a pint; in turn, this *noggin* is likely the same one that means *head*, as in "He bumped his noggin," the connection being that the head is a kind of "cup" for the brain (the word *head*, in fact, derives from an Indo-European source that meant *cup* or *bowl*). See also *cup*.

eggplant

Although my six-year-old niece will not eat eggplant, she will eat aubergine, a strange phenomenon considering that they are one and the same plant. The two names appeared in English at almost the same time in the late eighteenth century, with *aubergine* eventually becoming the usual name for the plant in Britain, while *eggplant* became the usual name in North America. Of these two names, *eggplant* has the most obvious origin: the purple fruit of the plant is shaped (somewhat) like an egg. In contrast, you probably would not guess that *aubergine* derives from a Sanskrit word meaning *the vegetable that prevents farting* or, more literally, *the vegetable that cures the wind-disorder*. This Sanskrit name, pronounced *vatinganah*, was bestowed upon the plant because it was believed to have a carminative effect upon the digestive system. *Vatinganah* was then borrowed by Persian as *badingan*, which in turn was borrowed by Arabic as *al-badinjan*, the *al* simply being the Arabic definite article meaning *the*. The Arabic name then became the Spanish *alberengena,* which French adopted as *aubergine* in the early seventeenth century. Finally, in the late eighteenth century, the French name of the plant was adopted by the English, who might have stuck with the name *eggplant* had they known the actual meaning of *aubergine*.

Emmental

Emmental, a hard Swiss cheese riddled with more holes than a phony alibi, has a name closely related to the word *dollar*. What connects the two words is the German word *taler*, meaning *valley*, a word that long ago joined up with the personal name *Emme* to form *Emmentaler*, meaning *Emme's valley*. It was in this Swiss valley, not far from Bern, that the cheese was first produced, thus inspiring its original name, *Emmentaler*, later shortened to just *Emmental*. In Czechoslovakia, the German *taler* likewise joined up with the personal name *Joachim* to form *Joachimstaler*—that is, *Joachim's valley*, the name of a valley where silver has been mined since the Middle Ages. In the sixteenth century, a large coin minted from the silver these mines produced was named, after the valley, the *Joachimstaler*, a name that in High German was later shortened to just *taler*. In Low German, *taler* became *doler*, which English adopted in the mid sixteenth century to refer to the famous German coin. Near the end of the eighteenth century, about a decade after the American Revolution, *doler*—which by then had been respelt as *dollar*—was also adopted by the United States as the official name of their currency, the intent being to distinguish their monetary system from that of England. In time, other new countries also adopted the dollar as their monetary unit: Canada in 1858, Australia in 1966, and New Zealand in 1967.

empanada

The Spanish pastry called the *empanada* has a name that literally means *in bread*: it is essentially a pastry-shell filled with meat. Although *empanada* did not appear in English until the 1930s, a closely related Spanish word, *panada*, was adopted in the late sixteenth century as the name of a dish made by boiling bread to a pulp and then flavouring it with sugar, spices, and currants. The ultimate source of the Spanish *panada* is the Latin *panis*, meaning *bread*, which is also the source of *pantry*, a place where bread is kept. See also *pantry*.

enchilada

A tortilla stuffed with meat, cheese, and sauce made from chilies is called an *enchilada*; the Spanish name of this Mexican dish might be literally translated into English as *in-chillied*, but—since no such term exists in English—it is better translated idiomatically as *filled with chili*. The word did not enter English until the end of the nineteenth century, about two hundred years after the word *tortilla* first appeared. This late appearance may be due to the enchilada not becoming a staple of Mexican cuisine until it was "discovered" in the late nineteenth century by Anglophone tourists.

engastration

The art of stuffing one animal inside another before bringing it to the dinner table is called *engastration*, a word that derives from the Greek *en*, meaning *in*, and *gaster*, meaning *belly*. Engastration may involve a mere two creatures, or dozens, so long as each is smaller than the previous. Although slaying the beasts before attempting their engastration seems prudent, Petronious, an ancient Roman satirist, wrote a fictional account of a feast where, to the astonishment of every guest, live sparrows flew out of the belly of a roast boar. Despite being an ancient practice, engastration is not referred to by name in English until the early nineteenth century.

entire

See *three-threads*.

entrée

In North America an entrée is the main dish of a meal; in Britain it is the dish served before the roast; and in France it is the third course, one usually served with a white or brown sauce. In a sense, it is the British use of the word that most nearly retains the original meaning of the word: an *entrée* is literally the *entrance* to the meal proper (which means that the hors d'oeuvre and the fish dish that appear even before the *entrée* are essentially the welcome mat and door bell of the meal). The word *entrée* was borrowed as a culinary term from French in the middle of the eighteenth century. However, four hundred years earlier, English had already taken the word from French and Anglicized it as *entry*, a high class synonym for the older and more rustic *close*, meaning *passageway*. The ultimate source of the French *entrée* is the Latin *intrare*, meaning *to go in*.

entremets

In French, the name of any dish prepared for the table is *mets*; the fish of the first course, the entrée of the second, and the roast of the third are all *mets*. Between these courses—and the French word for *between* is *entre*—are served the *entremets*, or what in English are more commonly called *side dishes*. The word *entre*, incidentally, has nothing to do with the word *entrée*, meaning *main dish*: *entre* and *entrée* both derive from Latin sources, and there may be some ancient connection between them, but that distant link was not on the minds of those who gave the entremets their name. The word *entremets* is actually more closely related to the English word *mess*, as in *mess hall*, the place where military personnel eat: both the *mets* of *entremets* and the *mess* of *mess hall* derive from the Latin word *mittere*, which strictly means *to send* but which also came to mean *to put*, especially with the sense of putting food on a table. In fact, when the word *entremets* was first taken into English in the early fourteenth century, it was spelt *entremess*; the current spelling, *entremets*, did not take hold until the late fifteenth century. In France, *entremets* could also mean a spectacular entertainment involving dwarves, elephants, and paper maché dragons that was performed between the courses of a meal; the word was never used with this sense by the English, who called the same kind of entertaining spectacles *subtleties*. See also *mess*.

enzyme

See *azyme*.

epicure

The Greek philosopher Epicurus, from whose name the word *epicure* is derived, is remembered for two doctrines. First, he asserted that the gods did not give a hoot about what humans did; and, second, he insisted that pleasure was the highest good a person could pursue, so long as that pleasure was temperate and allied to virtue, not vice. Because this latter doctrine was subject to some interpretation, the word *epicure* swung between two meanings from the middle of the sixteenth century to the middle of the eighteenth. For some authors, the ancient philosopher's emphasis was on the need for temperance when pursuing pleasure; these authors used *epicure* to mean someone who is selective and dainty about what he eats and drinks. For other authors, the ancient philosopher's real emphasis was on mere pleasure; these authors used *epicure* to mean someone who is greedy, gluttonous, and without restraint when sitting at the supper table. By the end of the eighteenth century, these two meanings had battled it out, and the former—the one characterizing the epicure as selective and temperate—had emerged as its primary sense, the one still in use today. The name Epicurus, incidentally, derives from a Greek source meaning *helper* or *ally*.

ewer

Pronounced like the first two syllables in the sentence "You were early," a ewer is a large water-jug used for washing hands before eating a meal. The word appeared in English in the early fourteenth century, and literally means *waterer*, deriving from the French *eau*, meaning *water*. In turn, the French word *eau* developed directly from the Latin *aqua*, a good example of how the French like to take words from other languages and strip them of consonants, the goal being to develop a language made up of nothing but *A*s, *E*s, *I*s, *O*s, *U*s, and sometimes *Y*s. In the mid fifteenth century, the servant who poured the water from the ewer onto the dinner guests' hands became known as the *ewerer*, pronounced like the first *three* syllables of "You were early."

expresso

The reticent nature of our ancestors is attested to by the fact that *express*—the action of putting feelings into words—literally means *to press out*, as if our fore-fathers revealed their emotions only when hard-pressed to do so. (Long before it became the name of a device for publishing the news, the press was an instrument of torture used to extract confessions.) Similarly, the coffee known as *expresso* takes its name from high-pressure steam being forced or "pressed" through the grounds, resulting in a very strong brew. The Italians, who invented the process, call this coffee *espresso*, which is the spelling the name had when it was first used in

English in the 1940s. Today, *expresso* and *espresso* are used interchangeably.

faggot

When the word *faggot* appeared in English in the fourteenth century, it simply meant *bundle*, specifically a bundle of sticks or twigs tied together for kindling. This original sense lies behind most of the later senses of *faggot*, including a culinary one: in British kitchens, a faggot is a little ball of minced pork, liver, onions, and breadcrumbs wrapped or "bundled" together with a caul, a membrane cut from a pig's bowels. For similar reasons, in the sixteenth century, the word *faggot* was used as a contemptuous name for an old woman, the idea being that such women—with their bent, bony frames wrapped in a tattered shawls or cloaks—supposedly resembled a bundle of dried-out sticks (the modern counterpart, *old bag*, is based on the same purported resemblance). This *old woman* sense of *faggot* survived until early this century when it then inspired homophobes to transfer the term to gay men: such men, as far as their homophobic enemies were concerned, were as worthless and feeble as they believed old women were. This explanation of how *faggot* came to mean *gay man* runs counter to a false one that has achieved wide circulation over the past decade or so: namely, that gay men were called *faggots* because they, like bundles of sticks, were once burned. It is certainly true that homosexuals, like other "heretics," were once burned at the stake for their supposed crimes, but considering that *faggot* came to mean *gay man* a mere eighty years ago, it is highly unlikely that a sixteenth century punishment inspired the current *gay* sense of *faggot*.

falafel

The Middle Eastern dish known as *falafel* is made by deep-frying balls of ground chick peas and hot pepper, and then serving them in a pita with tahini sauce. Its name, introduced to English in the 1950s, derives from the Arabic word for *hot pepper*—*filfil*—a word that may represent the sound a person makes after biting into a too hot or spicy food.

Fanny Adams

One of the paradoxes of human nature is that we are capable of mocking the death of someone we probably would have risked our own life to save. In 1867, an eight year old child named Fanny Adams was murdered and dismembered in England. Members of the distinguished Royal Navy, perhaps distanced from the tragedy by the sensationalised coverage it received in newspapers, subsequently dishonoured themselves by jokingly bestowing the name of Fanny Adams on the tins of meat that were their daily fare. Worse, the name *Fanny Adams* later came to be used as a mild curse, most often heard as *Sweet Fanny Adams!*, a development likely caused by the coincidence that the child's initials—*F.A.*—were also used as an abbreviation or euphemism for *fuck all*. In Australia, the name of another murder victim—Harriet Lane, killed in 1875—was bestowed by merchant-marines on the tins of preserved meat that they received as rations.

farce

Farce is a seasoned mixture of chopped ingredients that chefs stuff into other things—things like chickens, fish, or even ravioli. Farce is also known as *stuffing*, *dressing*, or *force-meat*. Etymologists once believed that *farce* was a corruption of the word *force* in *force-meat*, but in fact the opposite is true: *farce* comes from the Latin word *farcire*, meaning *to stuff*, and was corrupted to *force* on the assumption that a cook must *force* it in. *Farce*, in the sense of a brief, slap-stick comedy, also comes from the Latin *farcire*. In the fourteenth century, extra chants, known as *farsa*, were sometimes "stuffed" into the usual liturgy of the church; in the sixteenth century, this liturgical term was borrowed by dramatists, who changed the spelling to *farce*, to refer to short, zany, impromptu plays "stuffed" between the main pieces in a performance. Thus, the farce we eat and the farce we laugh at have the same linguistic origin.

farctate

When you are so full that you can eat no more, you are farctate. Like the word *farce*, *farctate* derives from the Latin *farcire*, meaning *to stuff*.

fare

Once an everyday term, the word *fare*, meaning *food provided by a host*, now seems relegated to a few old-fashioned phrases such as *bill of fare* and *daily fare*; anyone who now uses the word on its own—as in "My dear fellow, what fare do you offer today?"—instantly declares himself to be someone we will cross the street to avoid. In other contexts, the word *fare* has fared better: when our children leave for university, we pay the *air fare*, when we say goodbye to them at the airport we sob a tearful *farewell*, and when they are unable to find a job after receiving a B.A. in Philosophy, they go on *welfare*. All these *fares* derive from the same source, namely, the Old English word *faran*, meaning *to pass through* or *to travel*, which is distantly related to the Latin word *portare*, meaning *to carry*. How a word that originally meant *to travel* came to mean *food* is a roundabout process that began in the eleventh century. First, *fare* shifted from meaning *to travel* to meaning *to travel in a lavish manner*. It then shifted again as it came to mean *to entertain guests in a lavish manner*, especially with food and drink. And finally, *fare* shifted once more as it came to denote the actual food provided as part of a host's entertainment.

farrago

See *hodgepodge*.

fasels

When a word tries to do too much, it may end up doing nothing at all. That may have been the fate of the now defunct *fasels*, a word used in the sixteenth and seventeenth centuries to refer to both the chick-pea and the kidney bean. The trouble with this double-duty was that it made for ambiguity: a cook would be stymied by a recipe calling for two cups of fasels—should she use kidney beans or chick peas, or both? Perhaps because of this ambiguity, the word *fasels* became obsolete at the end of the seventeenth century, its double function being taken over and split between *kidney bean* and *chick pea* (or *garbanzo*, commonly used in the United States). Dissatisfaction with the word *fasels* was actually voiced early in its history: in 1562 the British herbalist William Turner, seeking an English equivalent for the legume's Greek name, wrote "Phasiolus may be called in English *fasels* until we can find a better name for it." Incidentally, this Greek name—*phasiolus*, or, more properly, *phaselos*—is the source not only of the English *fasels* but also of the Spanish *frijoles*, a kind of kidney bean often fried and eaten as a side dish. See also *chick-pea* and *kidney bean*.

fast

See *breakfast*.

fauntempere

See *bouce Jane*.

fava bean

See *bean*.

feast

The word *feast* is related to the word *festival*, and of these two words it is *festival* that has remained closer in meaning to the Latin source from which they both derive. This Latin source was the word *festa*, the name given by the ancient Romans to public celebrations, celebrations that did not necessarily involve food. *Festa* was borrowed by Old French as *feste*, which in turn was adopted by English at the beginning of the thirteenth century as the name of a sumptuous meal; by the fourteenth century, the word had acquired its current spelling, *feast*. English reborrowed the French *feste*—or rather its Modern French form, *fête*—in the mid eighteenth century and used it to signify a gala held to honour some worthy individual. A hundred years later, the Spanish equivalent, *fiesta*, was borrowed as a synonym for the much older *festival*, which had been current in English since the fourteenth century. Early on, feasts and festivals were associated with the many saints to whom the English once dedicated their churches. The most important of these feasts became known, in the early thirteenth century, as *double feasts*, that is, twice as "feasty" as the normal feasts; later on, in the fifteenth century, feasts were also divided into *movable feasts* (that is, the ones, like Easter, tied to the lunar cycle and whose date therefore changed from year to year) and *immovable feasts* (that is, the ones, like Christmas, tied to the solar cycle and therefore occurring on the same date every year).

fennel

From the first century A.D. to the fifth century, the people whose descendants founded the British Empire did not yet live in England (England was not even named *England* yet). These people, now called the Anglo-Saxons, lived on the northern coast of Europe and spoke a language that sounded more like German than what we now recognize as English. Thanks to occasional encounters with travelling Roman salesmen, they also had exposure to Roman spices and Latin words, including *feniculum*, the name of a plant whose leaves taste like anise. This name entered Old English as *finul*, and by the fourteenth century it had acquired its present spelling, *fennel*. Much later, in the early eighteenth century, the Italian name of this plant—*finochio*, which also derived from the Latin *feniculum*—was adopted as the name of a particularly sweet kind of fennel. Amazingly, both *fennel* and *finochio* are related to the word *female*: they all derive ultimately from an Indo-European source that meant both *to nurse* and *to produce*. This Indo-European source developed on the one hand into *femina*, meaning *she who nurses*, which later evolved into *female*; it developed on the other hand into *fenum*, meaning *hay* (the "produce" of a marsh), which later gave rise to *feniculum*, literally meaning *little hay*.

feta

Feta is made by allowing milk to curdle, pressing the curds into a mould, and then slicing the resulting mass into slabs that are soaked in brine. One of the stages in this process—the slicing— gives feta its name, deriving as it does from the Modern Greek *tyri pheta*, meaning *cheese slice*. The *pheta* part of this Greek name, which was the part adopted by English as *feta* in the 1930s, was derived by the Greeks from the Italian word *feta*, meaning *slice*. The Italians themselves employed this word when they gave fettuccine—a pasta cut into long, narrow strips—its name. See also *fettuccine*.

fettuccine

In Italian a large strip of something is called a *fetta*, a little strip of something is called a *fettucina*, and many little strips of something are called *fettuccine*. For this reason, a bowl full of little strips of pasta came to be called *fettuccine*. The particular dish known as *fettuccine Alfredo*—or technically *fettuccine all'Alfredo*—takes the last half of its name from Alfredo Di Lelio, a restaurateur in Rome during the early decades of this century. The word *fettuccine* rapidly established itself in English after Mary Pickford and Douglas Fairbanks visited Alfredo's restaurant in 1927 and dubbed the owner "The King of the Noodles."

fidgeltick

See *voip*.

fig

That fresh figs are pear-shaped is probably little known in North America, where most people are familiar only with the dried, scrunched-up version of the fruit. Usually imported from the Mediterranean, the fig takes its name from a Mediterranean language, a long-forgotten one that existed even before Indo-European emerged. From this Mediterranean language, Latin acquired its word for *fig*—*ficus*—which was adopted by Provençal, a dialect spoken in southeast France, as *figua*. This Provençal word then entered Old French as *figue*, which was adopted by English in the early thirteenth century as *fig*. The old expression, *I don't give a fig*—meaning *I don't care* or *I don't give a damn*—also owes its existence to this seed-filled fruit. The expression did not arise from figs being worthless (an imported fig was actually an expensive item in England) but rather arose in Italy where the name of the fruit was sometimes used to refer to an obscene gesture, one performed by thrusting one's thumb between one's index and middle fingers. There are at least two possible explanations that account for this gesture and its name. The least offensive is that the thumb between the fingers represents a woman's clitoris, a gesture that came to be called a *fig*—or in Italian, a *fica*—because a ripe fig, when split open, purportedly resembles the female genitalia. The other explanation, more bizarre, is that the gesture alludes to a punishment inflicted upon two Italians who dared to insult the wife of Frederick I, the King of Prussia: under threat of death, and using only their teeth, they were each forced to extract a fig that had been inserted into the anus of a donkey. If this explanation is true, then the obscene gesture arose as an imitation of this punishment—the thumb between the fingers representing the fig—and came to be known as *the fig* for obvious reasons. In any event, whatever its origin, the Italian gesture and its name were borrowed by the English in the early sixteenth century. In time, the gesture fell out of use, but *fig*, as in *I don't give a fig* continued to mean *something unwanted*. This sense of *fig* was also adopted by the French, whose expression *faire la figue* means—roughly translated—*to give him the finger*.

figee

See *bouce Jane*.

filbert

The word *hazelnut* is a native English word, dating back to at least the eighth century. In the early fifteenth century, however, hazelnuts also came to be known as *filberts*, a name introduced by the French, who called the nut *noix de Philibert* because it is usually ready to be harvested on St. Philibert's day, August 22 (incidentally, in Old German, Philibert's name means *very bright*). Ironically, after giving English the word *filbert*, the French themselves ceased to call the nut *Philibert* and instead started to refer to it either as *noisette* (a word derived from *noix*, the French word for *nut*) or as *aveline* (a word derived from *Avella*, the name of an Italian town famous for its nuts and fruit, and possibly the source of the word *apple*). Later on, the French also transferred the name *noisette* to certain cuts of beef or mutton that are small and round like a nut, and are surrounded by a layer of fat resembling a shell. English adopted *noisette* with this *cut-of-meat* sense in the late nineteenth century. See also *apple*.

filet mignon

The *mignon* part of *filet mignon*, the name of a choice cut of beef, is a French word meaning *dainty* or *delicate*. The term *filet mignon* did not appear in English until early this century, but *mignon* itself was adopted in the early sixteenth century as *minion*, the name of a dainty and delicate underling—or as John Florio defined the word in his dictionary of 1598: "*Minion*—a dilling, a minikin, a darling."

fillet

A fillet is a cut of meat: with beef it is the undercut of the sirloin, with poultry it is the underside of the breast, and with fish it is one of the two sides that pull easily away from the backbone. The name of this cut of meat (pronounced like the first two words in "Fill it up!") appeared in English in the early fifteenth century, having been borrowed from the French, who call the same cut of meat the *filet* (pronounced like the last two words of "That was Phil, eh?"). Further back in history, the French themselves acquired the word *filet* by adding a diminutive ending to the Latin *filum*, meaning *thread*; literally, therefore, *filet* and *fillet* mean *little thread*. How a word meaning *little thread* came to be applied to cuts of meat is a complicated story: back in the early fourteenth century, the French *filet* was used as a name for the string that men and women sometimes tied around their head to keep their hair in place. *Filet* continued to be used for this item when the string was replaced by a ribbon or even by a fairly wide strip of material. In time, this new *strip* sense of *filet* inspired someone to transfer the name to the "strips" of meat that are cut away from a carcass, a usage that parallels that of *band* in both *head-band* and *band of muscle*. Having thus acquired *filet*—which they respelt as *fillet*—the English acquired it again in a more direct manner several hundred years later: in the eighteenth century, the name *fillet* was given to any thick slab of meat rolled up and tied with a thread or *fillet*, thus preventing it from unrolling while cooking. Still later, in the early part of this century, English again adopted the word *filet*—this time retaining the French spelling—when *filet mignon* became a fashionable dish.

finochio

See *fennel*.

fire-dog

See *andiron*.

firkin

See *nipperkin*.

fish

Although the origins of the names of individual fish species are often uncertain, the origin of the word *fish* itself is quite clear. *Fish* ultimately derives from an Indo-European word pronounced something like *piskos*. This word entered the Germanic family of languages as *fiskaz*, which became the Old English word *fisc*, which by the thirteenth century had been respelt as *fish*. The Indo-European *piskos* also worked its way into another language family: it became the Latin word for fish, *piscis*, the plural of which is *Pisces*, the name of the twelfth sign of the zodiac. The Latin *piscis* also exists in English as part of the word *porpoise*. This large sea mammal—in the Middle Ages a popular dish among British royalty, who garnished it with tiny minnows—derives its name from the Latin *porcus piscis*, literally meaning *pig fish*.

fixin's

Fixin's are the savoury adjuncts that accompany both grub and vittles: fixin's include condiments such as ketchup and relish, but they may also extend to gravy, salad dressing, and black-eyed peas, all of which help to turn a mere heap o' food into a fine spread. In use since the early nineteenth century, the word *fixin's* is simply a contracted form of *fixings*; the verb from which this noun is formed—*fix*—derives from the Latin *figere*, meaning *to fasten*, a meaning still apparent in the word *fixin's* in so far as these items are attached or "fastened" to the main dishes. Words related to *fixin's* include *crucifix*, literally meaning *fastened to a cross*, and *fixate*, meaning *to become obsessively attached to something*.

flannel cake
See *pancake*.

flapjack
See *pancake*.

flatulence
See *soufflé*.

flavour
See *soufflé*.

flesh
See *meat*.

flesh-monger
Before they were known as *butchers*, people who sold cuts of meat were called *flesh-mongers*, a term first recorded in the eleventh century. The *monger* part of this word, still current in terms such as *fish-monger* or *war-monger*, derives from the Latin *mango*, which is what the ancient Romans called someone who traded goods for a living (this *mango* is not related to the fruit of the same name). Butchers ceased to call themselves *flesh-mongers* in the late sixteenth century when the term came to mean *pimp*, a person who deals in human flesh. For a briefer time, from the early fourteenth to the mid fifteenth century, butchers were also sometimes called *flesh-hewers*, a term so graphic that it's hardly surprising it quickly became obsolete.

fletcherize

"Nature will castigate those who don't masticate" was one of the catchy slogans invented by Horace Fletcher, a self-styled dietician who, in the late nineteenth and early twentieth centuries, convinced thousands of people to chew each mouthful of food thirty-two times, a number partly determined by most people having thirty-two teeth. This was not Fletcher's only contribution to nutrition, but it is the one that became attached to his name: *fletcherize* appeared in 1903 as a verb meaning *to chew thoroughly*. Fletcher's surname, incidentally, means *arrow-maker*, a job once held, presumably, by one of his ancestors.

flipper

See *sweller*.

flitch

See *meat*.

flour

The poet John Keats died in the flower of his youth; Sir Lancelot was the flower of chivalry; Shakespeare's plays are the flower of English drama. This use of *flower* to mean the blossom or best part of something is where flour—the best part of the grain after it has been milled and sifted—gets its name. This *ground grain* sense of *flower* arose in the mid thirteenth century and existed along side its *blossom* sense for five hundred years; it was only in the eighteenth century that people started to distinguish the milled-grain *flower* from the blossom *flower* by spelling the former word *flour*. The ultimate source of *flower*—and therefore also of *flour*—was an Indo-European word pronounced something like *bhlo*. When this word entered the Latin and Germanic language families it developed in two different directions: in Latin it became *flos*, the source of words such as *flower*, *flour*, *floral*, and *flourish*; in the Germanic language family it became *blomon*, the source of words such as *bloom*, *blossom*, and even *blade*. At your next dinner party, therefore, you may be arm's length from three very different items—the flour in the bread, the blade of your knife, and the blossoms in the centre-piece—whose names all derive from a single, ancient source.

flummery

People who are not from Wales have great difficulty reproducing certain Welsh consonants; as a result, the Welsh word *llymru* was rendered into English not only as *flummery* but also as *thlummery*, the latter most easily said after a trip to the dentist. *Flummery*, of course, prevailed over *thlummery* and from the early seventeenth to the mid eighteenth century the word referred, like the original Welsh term, to a sour jelly made by boiling oatmeal with the husks. In the mid eighteenth century, *flummery* also developed two new meanings: it became the name of a sweet dish made of milk, flour, and eggs, and simultaneously it came to mean *empty praise* or *gibberish*. In this, *flummery* underwent the reverse development of the word *trifle*, whose original sense was *idle tale* but which also came to denote a dish of sponge-cake and cream.

fondue

The fondue, a dish/punishment invented by the Swiss, is essentially a pot of molten oil, cheese or chocolate into which feckless guests are forced with spindly forks to thrust and withdraw morsels of food, morsels so tiny that you burn more calories attempting to get them out of the pot than they end up supplying you with anyway. Modelled, no doubt, on the La Brea Tar Pits in Los Angeles, the fondue takes its name, via French, from the Latin word *fundere*, meaning *to melt*. Other words that derive from this *melting* sense of *fundere* include *foundry*, a place where molten metal is cast into forms, and *confound*, literally meaning *to melt together*. The Latin *fundere* could also be used, however, to mean *to pour*, and it was this *pouring* sense of the word that gave rise to *profound*, literally meaning *to pour forth*, and *refund*, literally meaning *to pour back*. All these words are much older than their relative *fondue*, which entered English only about a hundred years ago.

force piece

See *thrive bit*.

force-meat

See *farce*.

fork

Although the word *fork* dates back to about the eleventh century as the name of an implement used to pitch hay, the table fork was not used in England until 1611. It was then that a country squire named Thomas Coryate returned from a trip to Italy, where forks had been used since at least the eleventh century, bringing back with him the newfangled eating utensil and an enthusiasm for using it. Coryate's countrymen, however, thought his zeal for eating with a fork was at best a foreign affectation and at worst an affront to God: he was mocked on the stage for his effete reluctance to touch his food with his hands, and he was castigated in churches for putting a devilish fork between himself and the food that his Lord so graciously gave him. Perhaps, however, much of this uproar was merely sour grapes, since it was evident that Coryate, unlike everyone else in England, was now able to eat a meal without smearing it all over his hands, clothes, and table cloth. In time, therefore, reason prevailed and the dinner fork did catch on in England. In origin, the word *fork* derives from the Latin *furca*, meaning *a two-pronged fork*; the diminutive of *furca*—*furcula*, meaning *little fork*—was adopted by ornithologists as the anatomical name for what everyone else calls a wishbone. See also *wishbone*.

frangipani

In the sixteenth century, the custom of the *baissemain*—that is, greeting a superior by kissing her hand—was still common in French aristocratic circles. For Muzio Frangipani, an Italian Marquis living in Paris, the one drawback of this quaint custom was that the fingers of his French acquaintances did not smell as sweetly as they might. To solve this embarrassing problem, Frangipani invented an almond-scented perfume for gloves, one that was soon odoriferizing the dainty digits of French aristocrats everywhere. So popular was this new almond-based glove-perfume that Parisian chefs borrowed its name, *frangipani*, and bestowed it on an almond-flavoured cream used in making pastries and desserts. Later on, in the mid nineteenth century, the name of this almond-flavoured cream eventually made its way into English, where it is now sometimes loosely used as a name for any pastry made with ground almonds. Incidentally, the Italian surname *Frangipani* appears to mean *broken bread*: the *frangi* half of the surname may derive, like the English *frangible*, from the Latin *frangere*, meaning *to break*; likewise, the *pani* part of the surname may derive, like the English *pantry*, from the Latin *panis*, meaning *bread*.

Frankfurter

See *hot dog*.

fricasee

See *fritter*.

fridge

The peculiar thing about the word *fridge* is that it contains a *d*, while the word it stands for, *refrigerator*, does not. The original abbreviation of *refrigerator* was *frig*, a spelling used as early as 1926 and as recently as 1960. Beginning in the 1930s, however, the alternate form *fridge* started to appear, a spelling invented likely because the original *frig* form looked too much as if it should be pronounced with a hard *g*, that is, as if it rhymed with *twig*; such a pronunciation would simply not do, since *frig*, with a hard *g*, had been used since the late sixteenth century to mean *masturbate*. This problem was surmounted by the new spelling, *fridge*, because the *idge* ending has long been employed in English to represent a *j* sound, as in *ridge* and *midge*. The switch from *frig* to *fridge* may also have been facilitated by the fact that one popular brand of refrigerator—the *Frigidaire*—did contain a *d* in its name, a *d* that could be moved to a position before the *g* without too much difficulty. The manufacturers of the *Frigidaire* were, of course, playing on the word *frigid* when they invented their brand name, *frigid* being a word that derives, like *refrigerate*, from the Latin *frigus*, a noun meaning *coldness*.

fritter

A fritter is a piece of meat, fruit, or vegetable that is battered and then fried in oil. The snack derived its name in the early fifteenth century from the Late Latin *frictura*, which in turn derives from the Latin *frigere*, meaning to fry. (The other *fritter*—the one meaning *to squander*, as in "He frittered away his inheritance"— derives from the unrelated Latin *fractura*, meaning *broken into fragments*.) The Latin *frigere* is also the source of *fry*, first recorded at the end of the thirteenth century, of *fricandeau* (a French dish of fried veal served with sauce), of *frikkadel* (a South African dish made by frying a ball minced meat), and even perhaps of *frizzy*, descriptive of hair that appears to have been washed in boiling oil. The dish known as *fricassee* derives the first part of its name, via French, from the Latin *frigere*, but the last part derives from the French *casser*, meaning to break, since the meat in the dish is broken into pieces before being fried. Further back in history, the French *casser* evolved from the Latin *quassare*, meaning *to dash into pieces*.

fruit

On one hand the expression *to enjoy the fruits of your labour* is a metaphor because what you are enjoying may not actually be fruit; on the other hand, the expression is quite literal because the word *fruit* derives from a Latin source, *frui*, meaning *to enjoy*. The ancient Romans applied this word—or rather a derivative of it, *fructus*—to cherries, oranges, apples, and so forth because nature provides those fruits for our enjoyment. Several other English words also derive from the Latin *frui*. *Fruition*, for example, appeared in the early fifteenth century as a synonym for *enjoyment*; thus, a statement such as "My hard work will soon come to fruition" means "My hard work will soon come to the point where I can enjoy it." More surprising is that the word *frugal* also derives from *frui*, even though frugal people might seem ill-disposed to enjoy anything. However, *frugal* did indeed acquire its current *thrifty* meaning thanks to a series of gradual shifts in sense: enjoyable things are profitable things, and profitable things are economical things, and economical things are thrifty things. As a result of these semantic shifts, which occurred over centuries, *frugal* shifted its meaning from *enjoyable* to *thrifty*. See also *frumenty*.

frumenty

Made by boiling wheat in milk and then seasoning it with sugar, cinnamon, and almonds, frumenty is a simple dessert invented by French peasants in the late fourteenth century and first referred to in English in the early fifteenth century. The dish derives its name from the Latin *frumentum*, meaning *grain*. In turn, *frumentum*—like *fructus*, the Latin word for *fruit*—derives from the Latin *frui*, meaning *to enjoy*, the notion being that grain and fruit are the main enjoyments offered by the earth.

frush

See *carving*.

fu yung

Fu yung, a sauce made of eggs and vegetables, was invented in the United States by Chinese immigrants; its name, which appeared in English early this century, is Cantonese for *lotus*.

fudge

The candy now known as *fudge* was invented by accident in the late nineteenth century when a toffee recipe went awry and the main ingredient—sugar—recrystallized into a semi-soft mass. The new candy received its name from students in New England women's colleges who turned fudge-making into an all-night bonding ritual, and fudge-selling into a means of funding their colleges' social events. The students likely chose the name *fudge* because the word had been used, since the middle of the eighteenth century, as a mild exclamation—*Oh, fudge!*—of surprise or disbelief. As well, since the middle of the sixteenth century *fudge* had also been used as a verb to denote the action of patching something together, especially in a sneaky manner. This verb form of the word—which derives from a much older word, *fadge*, also meaning *to patch together*—is unrelated to the exclamation; however, its sense of pulling together various pieces is germane to the fudge-making process, so it too may have inspired someone to name the new candy *fudge*.

fumet

See *fumosity*.

fumosity

Fumosity refers to the potential of a given food to induce flatulence. Currently, no standard of fumosity has been established, although one based on logarithms, like the Richter scale for earthquakes, would seem most appropriate. First used in the fifteenth century, the word derives from the Latin *fumus*, meaning *smoke* or *steam*. From the same Latin source derives *fumet*—pronounced *fyoo-mett*—which can refer either to the savoury odour given off by meat as it cooks, or to a concentrated fish stock made by steaming away excess liquid. These culinary senses of *fumet* appeared in the eighteenth century; earlier than this, dating back to the fifteenth century, the word *fumet* referred only to the excrement of a deer. This excremental *fumet* derived not from the Latin *fumus* but from the Latin *fimus*, meaning *dung*; it is possible, however, that the two Latin words developed from a single "fumy" source.

funistrada

Funistrada does not exist. It is an imaginary food name invented by the U.S. armed forces to see if the participants of written food surveys were paying attention to the questions or just answering randomly. In a 1974 survey, respondents ranked funistrada higher than eggplant, instant coffee, apricot pie, Harvard beets, canned lima beans, grilled bologna, and cranberry juice. Two other imaginary foods fared less well—buttered ermal and braised trake. Given that *funistrada* is a nonce word, it has no real etymology; we might conjecture, however, that the word is a fusion of syllables taken from the names Annette *Funi*cello—always a favourite of military personnel—and Eric E*strada*—that manly embodiment of the 1970s.

furcula

See *wishbone*.

gallimaufry

See *hodgepodge*.

gallon

See *pint*.

garbage

Five hundred years ago, it was not uncommon for a housewife to serve her family a supper of garbage, a meal they would devour with relish. The family relished such a meal because back then the word *garbage* did not mean *trash* or *rubbish* but instead referred to what we now call *organ meat* or *viscera*. These inner parts of the animal were originally highly prized, as they were thought to be sources of strength and vigour; for a time, in fact, one of the officers of the British royal kitchen—specifically the one in charge of preparing chicken carcasses—was honoured with the title of *Sergeant Garbager*. By the beginning of the sixteenth century, however, internal organs—or *garbage*—began to fall out of favour as culinary treats, reaching a nadir in 1983 when I chose to go hungry rather than eat my mother's kidney pie. As organ meats declined in popularity, the word *garbage* started to mean worse and worse things until it finally acquired its current sense of *filth*, *trash*, or *rubbish*. The ultimate origin of the word *garbage* is unknown, but likely it was adopted into English from French cookbooks in the early fifteenth century. See also *humble pie* and *offal*.

garbanzo

See *chick-pea*.

garble

Although no longer associated with the kitchen, the word *garble* was originally a culinary term. When it first appeared in English in the late sixteenth century, *garble* referred to the refuse or chaff left over after spices had been sifted: when you *garbled* something, you were separating the usable from the unusable. By the late seventeenth century, however, this sense of dividing the good from the bad had come to be associated with deception: a farmer might "garble" a sample of his grain so that it would seem to have fewer weed seeds than it really did. From here, *garble* easily shifted from meaning *to sift deceptively* to currently meaning *to mix up* or *to confuse an issue*. In origin, the word *garble* is Latin: *cribellare*, meaning *to sift*, was adopted by Arabic as *gharbala*, which then entered Italian as *garbellare* before being adopted by English as *garble*. Incidentally, the original source of *garble* (the Latin *cribellare*) derived from an even older Latin word—*cernere*, meaning *to separate*—which is the source of the English *discern*. Two words, therefore, that are now almost opposites—*garble*, meaning *to mix up*, and *discern*, meaning *to tell apart*—evolved from exactly the same source.

garlic

Plants are often named by combining a word that describes the shape of their leaves or stem with the name of a similar plant that already has a name. Thus, *spikenard* is literally *a spike of nard* while *garlic*—less obviously—is literally *a spear of leek*. With *garlic* this origin is somewhat disguised because the Old English word for *spear*—*gar*—became obsolete in the mid thirteenth century, except as part of *garlic* and as part of *garfish*, a fish with a spear-like snout. Incidentally, the Indo-European source of the Old English *gar* also gave rise to the word *goad*, the action of "prodding" someone along. Both *goad* and *garlic* appeared in English about a thousand years ago. See also *leek*.

garnish

A garnish is some sort of food accompanying another dish and complementing the flavour and appearance of that dish; a garnish can be as simple as a sprig of parsley or as elaborate as a ragout blended with sauce and poured into a pastry shell. In origin, the word *garnish* derives from the Old French word *guarnir*, meaning *to protect* or *to provide with necessities*. This was the meaning that *garnish* possessed when it first appeared in English in the fourteenth century, and it was used especially in relation to fortresses provided or "garnished" with arms and soldiers. Of course, more pleasant things can also be provided to someone, including items merely luxurious rather than necessary; accordingly, it was not long before *garnish* also came to mean *to embellish*. It was this sense of *garnish* that led to the word being used in the late seventeenth century as a name for a food item that complements or embellishes a main dish. Other words also developed from the Old French *guarnir* but stayed closer to its original sense of *to provide*; these include *garrison* (a fortress provided with a detachment of soldiers) and *garage* (a place where vehicles are provided with fuel and repairs). Incidentally, the *garnish* that refers to the action of seizing someone's assets until he repays a debt is the same word as the culinary *garnish*: originally, this legal *garnish* meant to provide someone with an official writ warning him to pay up or suffer the consequences.

gastronomy

Gastronomy is the art and science of good eating, taking its name from the Greek *gaster*, meaning *stomach*, and *nomos*, meaning *law*. Gastronomy therefore concerns the law of the stomach (just as astronomy concerns the law of the stars). The word originated as the title of a work by an unknown, ancient Greek author, a work that two thousand years later, in 1801, inspired the French poet Berchoux to write a poem entitled *Gastronomie*. About ten years later, English adopted this word as *gastronomy*, which soon gave rise to another term, *gastrophile*, a person who loves his stomach.

gazpacho

Gazpacho, a cold soup made of tomatoes, vegetables, and bread crumbs, is a Spanish dish, but the name itself—meaning *soaked bread*—is Arabic in origin. Throughout most of the Middle Ages, Arabic contributed many such words to Spanish due to the presence of the Arabic-speaking Moors who controlled Spain until El Cid undertook its reconquest at the end of the twelfth century. *Gazpacho* entered English in 1845.

gelatin

See *jelly*.

gherkin

A gherkin is a small cucumber pickled in vinegar. The name of this condiment appeared in English in the mid seventeenth century as a respelling of the Dutch name of the pickle, *gurkkijn*. In turn, *gurkkijn* was invented as a diminutive of the Dutch *gurk*, meaning *cucumber*, which evolved through Polish from the Medival Greek name of the pickle, *angourion*. Even further back, it is possible that *angourion* arose from the Greek *agouros*, meaning *youth*, since gherkins are made from unripe—and therefore "young"—cucumbers. Gherkins are also sometimes known by their French name, *cornichon*, meaning *little horn*, a word that derives, like *cornucopia*, from the Latin *cornu*, meaning *horn*. See also *cornucopia*.

giblets

Poultry are blessed with two sorts of giblets: the internal—including the gizzard, heart, liver, and kidneys—and the external—including the head, neck, wingtips, and feet. English acquired the word *giblet* in the early fourteenth century by adapting the French word *gibelet*, meaning *game stew*; such stews, made out in the wild after bagging the game, usually contained those parts of the animal thought to bestow courage and strength on the hunter (the heart, for example) as well as those parts whose removal made the bird more compact (the head, for example, and the feet). The French name of the stew was easily adapted by the English for the parts of the bird that usually went into such a stew. Further back in the history of the word, the French *gibelet* arose as a diminutive of the word *gibier*, meaning *game*; this word in turn developed from a much older Frankish word, *gabaiti*, meaning *a hunt with falcons*. See also *parties nobles*.

gin

Gin was invented in the mid seventeenth century by a Dutch doctor who claimed that his new spirit cured a variety of ailments; because it was flavoured with oil from juniper berries, the doctor called his wonder tonic *genever*, meaning *juniper*, a word that derives from the Latin name for the juniper plant, *juniperus*. When the spirit was introduced to England in 1706, its name was changed from *genever* to *geneva*, thanks to the mistaken belief that the spirit was somehow connected with Geneva, a city in Switzerland. Once in England, the new and inexpensive spirit became wildly popular among the poor, so much so that in less than ten years its name was shortened to the more English sounding *gin*. Widespread addiction to gin also caused it to lose its reputation as a cure-all, becoming instead an embodiment of social evil: whereas one author, writing in 1706, politely defined *geneva* as "a kind of strong water," another author, writing only a few years later in 1714, called it "that infamous liquor." By 1736, gin alcoholism had so decimated the lower classes of England that parliament passed laws restricting its sale. Today, gin is employed in dozens of mixed drinks, including *gin and it*, the *it* being short for *Italian vermouth*. Sloe gin, which is actually a cordial rather than a true gin, takes its name from the blackthorn berries that flavour it, berries known as *sloe* since the eighth century. See also *martini*.

ginger

Thousands of years ago, someone in India pulled a ginger root from the ground, decided that its most remarkable feature was the horn-like protrusions that grew from the main body of the root, and promptly named it *horn-body*, which in Sanskrit, an ancient language of India, was *srngam-veram*. Over time, this

Sanskrit name evolved into the Greek *zingiberis*, then into the Latin *zingiber*, then into the French *gengibre*, then into the Old English *gingiber*, and finally ended up in Modern English as *ginger*. In English, the word is about as old as *pepper*, dating back about a thousand years to the eleventh century. Somewhat more recent is *gingerbread* (first recorded at the beginning of the fourteenth century), *ginger-beer* (the beginning of the nineteenth century), and *ginger-ale* (the end of the nineteenth century).

gîte-gîte

See *couscous*.

gizzard

Lacking teeth, a chicken must grind its food in some other way, a process accomplished in its gizzard. Before reaching the gizzard, however, the chicken's lunch must pass through its *craw* or *crop*, a pouch in the bird's gullet where gastric juice begins to soften the food. (Nowadays, the word *craw* is best known in exclamations like, "That really sticks in my craw"; the word *crop* on the other hand, is related to *croup*, a throat disease in children.) Once in the gizzard, small stones previously swallowed by the chicken grind the food into a paste, which then—à la Jules Verne—completes its journey to the centre of the bird before finding its way back to the surface of the barnyard. The word *gizzard* derives, through French, from the Latin *gigeria*, the name of a delicacy made by the ancient Romans from cooked poultry intestines. When it first appeared in English in the early fifteenth century, the name of this poultry organ was spelt *giser*. The final *d* that appeared at the end of the word in the sixteenth century is what linguists call a parasite: that is, a consonant that appears when the people who speak the language decide that the word sounds incomplete without it.

globbe

See *slurp*.

glutton

Despite their enlightened attempt to become one with the universe by devouring everything it contains, gluttons are often depicted as greasy, grunting grub-grabbers, gratifying their gross appetites with whatever falls within their greedy grasp. Their name, however, has a more temperate and less alliterative origin: it derives simply from the French *gluton*, which in turn developed from the Latin *glutire*, meaning *to swallow. Glutton* did not appear in English until the early thirteenth century, surprisingly late considering the French had already been ruling England for a century and a half. The Latin *glutire* is also the source of the word *glut*—which originally denoted the condition of being too full to swallow another mouthful—and of *gullet*, another name for the throat.

gnocchi

The small, curled dumplings known as *gnocchi* take their name from the Italian *nocchio*, meaning *knot*. The word appeared in English at the end of the nineteenth century.

goat

See *butcher*.

gob

Gob was adopted in the fourteenth century from Old French, where the word was used to mean *a mouthful of food*. The word still exists in Modern French, but now refers to a food-ball used to poison packs of wild dogs, or a ball roughage sometimes found in the stomachs of sheep. In English, a gob was originally any lump or clot of an unrecognizable substance, but by the sixteenth century it had reacquired the original French sense of *a mouthful of food*, especially food that is crude, raw, or barely palatable. Surprisingly, *gob* did not become a verb, meaning *to spit out*, until the late nineteenth century, about the same time that the eating of gobs fell out of favour. A related word is *gobbet*, a diminutive of *gob* that appeared as early as the fourteenth century. Although very similar in meaning to *gob*, *gobbet* refers more specifically to a lump of raw meat or to a lump of regurgitated food. In 1900, *gob* gave rise to yet another word when author Henry Lawson combined *gob* with *blob* to form *glob* (*blob* was already a well-established word, having appeared in the early sixteenth century).

Unrelated from an etymological point of view, but almost an exact synonym for *glob*, is *lopyn*, a word of unknown origin that arose and died in the fifteenth century.

gofer

See *wafer*.

goober

See *peanut*.

goulash

The dish known as *goulash* originated around the ninth century as a kind of pemmican, at least in so far as it originally consisted of meat cooked and then dried in the sun for later consumption. In time, the meat was no longer dried after being cooked, and thus goulash became what it presently is—a thick beef soup made with onions and paprika. The word *goulash*, like the dish itself, is Hungarian in origin, deriving from *gulyas hus*, meaning *herdsman's meat*; the Hungarian name was shortened to *gulyas* before being adopted into English as *goulash* in the mid nineteenth century.

gourd

Although many people still pronounce *gourd* so that it rhymes with *moored* or *steward*, it is becoming more common to hear it pronounced so that it rhymes with *sword*. This shift in pronunciation is, naturally, a source of consternation for men who are named *Gord*, but they may take heart in knowing that their name is in no way related to that of the head-shaped, hard-shelled fruit (although the gourd is eaten like a vegetable, it really is a fruit). The ancient Romans called the gourd *cucurbita*, a word that the French mangled badly when they adopted it and turned it into their word *gourde*. English then borrowed the French term in the early fourteenth century, first using it as a name for the fruit, and later, from the seventeenth century onward, also using it as the name of a water-bottle or cup made from a gourd or even from some other material. The original Latin term, *cucurbita*, was also adopted by English as early as the fourteenth century, when it was used as the name of a vessel employed by alchemists to distill liquids. In contrast with the Latin ancestry of *gourd*, the personal name *Gord*—or rather its full form, *Gordon*—derives from a Welsh source: *gor*, meaning *large*, and *din*, meaning *fort*. The Gaelic equivalent of the Welsh *din* is *dun*, a word found in the names of many Scottish cities, such as *Dundee* and *Dunbar*, that originated as forts.

graddan

See *bonny-clabber*.

grain

See *pomegranate*.

granola

In the late nineteenth century, W.K. Kellog invented a cereal he called *Granola*, made of wheat, oats, and corn-meal. Kellog's inspiration for the name was the word *granulated*, the idea being that the cereal is made by cooking its ingredients until they become clumped, or granulated. *Granita*, the name of an Italian sorbet, likewise refers to that dessert's granular texture, as does *granite*, a crystalline rock used as a building material. In the late 1960s, *granola* came to refer more generally to any breakfast cereal made from "natural ingredients," including nuts and dried fruit.

grape

Long ago, grapes were known in England only as *wineberries*, a name that suggests that the clusters were not so much plucked and eaten as stomped on and fermented. At the end of the thirteenth century a new name, *grape*, was borrowed from the French, who had long used the word to refer not to a single grape but to a bunch of them—in other words, the Old French *grape*, like the Modern French *grappe*, meant *cluster*. However, even before the French used the word *grape* to mean *cluster*, they also used it to mean *hook*, the connection between the two meanings being that clusters of grapes were stripped from their vines by means of a grappling hook. The word *grapple*, in fact, arose as a diminutive of the French *grape* that means *hook* (however, the similar sounding *grab*, *grope*, and *grip* derive from a completely different source). See also *raisin*.

grapefruit

The grapefruit acquired its name in the early nineteenth century because its fruit grows in clusters like grapes; the word *grape*, in fact, once meant *cluster*. See also *grape*.

gravy

When *gravy* first appeared in English at the end of the fourteenth century it referred to a fancy sauce for white meat made from broth, almond milk, wine, and spices; it was not until the end of the sixteenth century that it came to mean *a sauce made from meat juices*. The source of this word is the French *grané*, which medieval English cooks—studying the much esteemed French recipe books—misread as *gravé*, which in turn soon became *gravy*. Why the French named the original sauce *grané* is unclear: perhaps the name alluded to the "grains" of spices flavouring the sauce, spices such as *grain de poivre*, meaning *peppercorn*. If this really is the origin of the French *grané*, then both it and *gravy* are related to other words that derive from the same "grainy" source, including *pomegranate*, *grenadine*, and *grenade*. See also *butter-boat*.

green milk

See *beestings*.

grenade

In the endless pantheon of strange British dishes, one of the strangest is the grenade, an eighteenth-century dish made by surrounding six pigeons and a ragout with slices of veal and bacon, and then cooking the whole thing not on top of a fire, but rather between two fires. The name of this meaty dish may have been formed directly from the Latin word *granum*, meaning *grain*, due to its being seasoned with "grains" of spice. Alternatively, the dish may have been named after the hand-held explosive known as the *grenade* because that munition's shell-like construction resembles the successive layers of meat that make up the dish. (It's even possible, though not very likely, that it was the fumosity of this meaty dish—that is, its tendency to induce flatulence—that led to its being associated with the hand grenade's explosive force.) Incidentally, the weapon known as the *grenade* acquired its name in the sixteenth century thanks to its resemblance in size and shape to the pomegranate: that fruit, in French, is called a *grenade*, a name it acquired in the Middle Ages because of the countless seeds or "grains" contained within its tough and leathery rind. See also *pomegranate* and *gravy*.

grenadine

See *pomegranate*.

griddle

Although we now use griddles and gridirons only to cook food, they were once used as instruments of torture, that is, as large, metal grates that inquisitors would set a person on and set a fire under. This may have been the original meaning of *griddle* and *gridiron*, since the words are used as names of torture devices in thirteenth-century manuscripts, but do not appear in written records as names of culinary utensils until the fourteenth century. More likely, however, is that the culinary sense was indeed the original meaning of these words, but was slow to find its way into written manuscripts simply because cooking utensils were considered less worthy of being written about than a gruesome account of torture. In origin, *griddle* and *gridiron*—as well as a host of other familiar words—derive ultimately from the Latin word *cratis*, meaning *a wicker screen*. *Cratis* gave rise to *craticulum*, a diminutive meaning *little wicker screen*, which then evolved into the Old French word *gredil*, a fire-pan whose surface was criss-crossed by ridges resembling a screen. In the late thirteenth century, the British borrowed the Old French *gredil*, but from it, for some unknown reason, they formed two words instead of just one: *griddle* and *gridire*, two names for the same culinary instrument. The second of these words would probably still be spelt *gridire* had people not mistakenly assumed that its final syllable had something to do with iron, an assumption prompted by the coincidence that gridires were indeed made of iron. Well-intentioned etymologists, acting on this false assumption, then changed the spelling of *gridire* to *gridiron*. Eventually the new form, *gridiron*, became so established that, in the nineteenth century, the first syllable broke away from the word and became *grid*, the name of any structure whose lattice-like pattern resembled the surface of a gridiron; the word *grid*, in other words, developed from the word *gridiron*, not the other way around. Other words that developed from *cratis* (the Latin source of *griddle* and *gridiron*) include *cradle*, *crate*, and *grate*. Of these three words, *cradle* has remained the closest to the original *wicker screen* sense of *cratis*: even today cradles are often made of wicker. Crates, on the other hand, originated as wicker boxes, while grates—such as those placed before a fireplace or over a sewer hole—have a lattice-like pattern resembling that of a wicker screen. See also *andiron* and *grill*.

griddlecake

See *pancake*.

gridiron

See *griddle*.

grill

Unlike English, which no longer assigns a gender to its nouns, Latin classifies all its nouns as masculine, feminine, or neuter. Some Latin nouns, however, once had two spellings, each representing a different gender, as was the case with the Vulgar Latin *craticula* and *craticulum*. These two words meant the same thing (*little wicker screen*) and they evolved from the same source (the Latin *cratis*, meaning *large wicker screen*), but they differed in that *craticula* was the feminine spelling while *craticulum* was the neuter. Over hundreds of years, these initially minor differences in spelling became amplified as the words evolved in other languages. *Craticulum*, for example, developed into the French *gredil*, which in the thirteenth century became the English *griddle*; *craticula*, on the other hand, developed into the French *grille*, which in the seventeenth century became the English *grill*. Once these words had drifted so far apart in spelling, they easily developed different, but related, meanings: *grill* came to mean a screen-like structure on which meat was broiled, while *griddle* came to mean a pan, often with a criss-crossed surface, on which batter was cooked. See also *griddle*.

grinder

See *poor boy*.

grits

Although grits have become a culinary tradition in the southern United States, both the dish and its name were familiar in England long before Europeans had even heard of the New World. The ultimate source of *grits* was an Indo-European word pronounced something like *greut*, meaning *to crush* or *to pound*; this Indo-European word made its way through the Germanic language family and ended up in English as two words: *groats*, which appeared in the twelfth century, and referred to hulled, crushed grain used for making gruel; and *grit*, which appeared in the eighth century, and referred to the chaff left over after grinding grain. In the eleventh century, *grit* also came to refer to small particles of rock, and in the sixteenth century the plural form, *grits*, became established as the name of a porridge-like dish of boiled, ground grain. In the seventeenth century in the United States, grits also came to be known as *hominy*, a word of Native American origin. The source of *hominy* is the Algonquian name for a similar dish, *appuminneonash*, a word that derives from the Algonquian *appwoon*, meaning *he bakes*, and *minneash*, meaning *grain*. In the southern United States, the European and Native American names are often combined to form *hominy grits*.

groaning

In the mid sixteenth century, the period extending from when a woman took to her bed to give birth to when she was strong enough to get back on her feet was called her *groaning*, a blunt reference to her labour pains. During this time, the food provided for the woman's attendants and visitors was laid out on the *groaning board* and the special status of each dish was emphasized by prefacing its name with the word *groaning*; thus, visitors ate *groaning cake*, *groaning bread*, *groaning cheese*, and *groaning pie*; they were also served *groaning beer* or *groaning wine* that the husband had made especially for the occasion. In some areas of England, *groaning* continues to be used to form such compounds to this day. In origin, the word *groan* derives from an Indo-European source that meant *to gape*, a source that also gave rise to the word *grin*: grinning and groaning express very different emotions, but both are characterized by an open, gaping mouth.

grocery

Whereas the word *spice* is related to the words *specialty* and *specific* (because spices were sold by merchants who specialized in specific items), the word *grocery* is related to *gross*. Many centuries ago, the Late Latin word *grossus*, meaning *large* or *bulky*, gave rise to the Medieval Latin *grossarius*, the job-name of someone who sold merchandise in large quantities. *Grossarius* then became the French *grossier*, which in the early fourteenth century became the English *grocer*, from which *grocery* developed in the fifteenth century. Also in the fifteenth century, *grossus* itself was borrowed from Latin Latin as *gross*, meaning *huge*, but more recently used to mean *repellant*. The *gross* that means *144* derives from the same source: the French called twelve dozen of something a *grosse douzaine*, meaning *a large dozen*; this term was shortened to *gross* when it entered English in the fifteenth century. In the last book of the Bible, 144,000 saints (one thousand gross) are allowed to enter the New Jerusalem; in jewelry, 144 carats equal one ounce; in five-pin bowling, 144 is a decent score. See also *spice*.

grog

Made by mixing hard liquor with water, grog owes its name to Edward Vernon, a British admiral whose men nicknamed him *Old Grog* because he always wore a grogram coat (grogram is a coarse fabric, its name deriving from the French *gros grain*, meaning *coarse grain*). In 1740, Old Grog instituted the policy of adding water to the allowance of rum that every sailor received each day; the diluted liquor, which became known as *grog*, was supposed to reduce the likelihood of sailors being involved in drunken accidents like falling overboard or forgetting to tie the anchor to the ship. That the Admiral's scheme failed to make the sailors more careful is attested to by the fact that *grog* eventually inspired the word *groggy*, meaning *half-asleep*, a condition the admiral abhorred.

grub

The word *grub* has been used as a colloquial synonym for *food* since the mid seventeenth century, but long before that, dating back to the fourteenth century, it was used as a verb meaning *to dig*. This original *dig* sense of the word probably inspired its later *food* sense: root vegetables, such as potatoes or turnips, had to be "grubbed" out of the ground, prompting people to call such vegetables *grub*, a usage later extended to any sort of food. (This "earthy" origin of *grub* also accounts for the common expression, "I'll dig up some grub".) The insect larvae known as *grubs* get their name for a similar reason: they too dig their way through the soil. The ultimate source of *grub* was an Indo-European word, pronounced something like *ghrobh*, that also evolved into the word *grave* (a burial place dug into the earth) and *groove* (a channel dug into a surface). Centuries after appearing in English, *groove* inspired people to exhort one another to "Get in the groove," an expression that led to *groovy*, the epitome of hippy slang.

guacamole

Although *avocado* has been used in English since the seventeenth century, *guacamole*, the name of a green paste made from avocados, did not appear until early this century. *Guacamole* derives from two words in the Nahuatl language: *ahuacatl*, meaning *testicle*, which is what the Aztecs thought the avocado resembled, and *molli*, meaning *sauce*. See also *avocado*.

gudge

See *slurp*.

guest

See *host*.

gumbo

Although the okra used in gumbo makes that soup extremely thick and gummy, *gummy* is not the source of *gumbo*. *Gum* and *gummy* derive from a Greek source, whereas *gumbo* comes from Bantu, an African language. The Bantu word for okra, *ochinggombo*, was brought to America, along with the plant, by slaves who modified its name to *gumbo* and bestowed it upon a soup made from its pods. The word was then adopted by English in the early nineteenth century when the soup became a popular Louisiana dish. Not surprisingly, the word *okra* is also of African origin: it derives from the Tshi *nkruman*, Tshi being a language spoken in Ghana. English adopted *okra* as the name of the plant in the early eighteenth century, but other European languages did not. In French, for example, the plant is called *gombo*, a name obviously deriving from *gumbo*.

gusto

See *ragout*.

guttle

See *slurp*.

gyngawdry

See *bouce Jane*.

gyro

A gyro is a sandwich made by roasting lamb, slicing it, and rolling it into a pita. The sandwich originated several decades ago at Greek lunch counters in the United States, and therefore derives its name, pronounced *yheero*, from Greek: *guros*, meaning *a spiral* or *a turn*, was Anglicized as *gyro* and applied to the sandwich because the meat turns on a spit as it roasts. The name *gyro* is obviously related to the English words *gyroscope* and *gyrate*, which developed from the same Greek source. However, *gyro* is also related to some surprising words in other languages including the Irish word *gúaire*, meaning *hair of the head* (curls of hair are like spirals), and the Gaelic word *guairdeam*, meaning *vertigo* or *dizziness*. Incidentally, it is also possible that *gyro* inspired *hero sandwich*, the name of a meat-filled, submarine-shaped sandwich;

admittedly, *hero sandwich* appeared in print before *gyro* (in 1955 as opposed to 1971), but "foreign" words such as *gyro* often exist in spoken English for decades before they appear in print. If so, then there is nothing "heroic" about the hero sandwich, its name being nothing more than a misinterpretation of a Greek sandwich's name. See also *poor boy* and *shish kebob*.

haddock

The name of this fish, once commonly eaten for breakfast in Britain, is first recorded in English in the early fourteenth century. Although its origin is uncertain, it may have derived from the French word for the same species of fish, *hadot*. This word in turn may have developed from the French word *adouber*, meaning *to prepare*, just as the related Italian term *adobbo* refers to a brine used to pickle and preserve fish. If this is the origin of the word, then *haddock* originally did not refer to a particular species of fish, but to a method of preparing any fish; over time, the method perhaps became so associated with one kind of fish—the haddock—that the term was transferred to that species. Almost the same thing has happened to *stockfish*, which is not really the name of a fish, but rather refers to the food made by taking cod, splitting it open, and drying it without salt on a stick—or on what in Germany is called a *stock*. In the sixteenth century, *stockfish* also came to mean an exceptionally naughty or stupid person, the connection being that such a person—like the hard, dry stockfish—had to be beaten before he was any good. Like *haddock*, the word *stockfish* first appeared in English in the early fourteenth century.

haggis

The Old French name for the magpie was *agace*, pronounced *agg-ass* and deriving from a much older word meaning *pointed*, as is the bird's beak. As Rossini's opera *The Thieving Magpie* attests, this noisy and quarrelsome bird is infamous for its larceny, filling its nest with stolen scraps of cloth and bits of shiny metal. The resulting hodgepodge of twigs, strings, and tin evidently reminded some medieval French wag of a well-known Scottish dish, one made by stuffing chopped liver, heart, lungs, onions, and oatmeal into a sheep's stomach. As a result of this perceived similarity between the bird's nest and the Scottish dish, the French began calling the dish *agace*, a name the English adopted in the fifteenth century after changing the spelling to *haggis* (the word *haggis* was even adopted by the Scots, who previously knew the dish by a Gaelic name, *taegeis*). See also *pie*.

halal

The Arabic word *halal*, meaning *lawful*, corresponds to the Hebrew word *kosher*, meaning *right*, in so far as both words refer to food that followers of those religions are permitted to eat. Derived by compounding *halal* with another Arabic word—*khurdan*, meaning *to eat*—is the Persian term *halalcor*, meaning *lawful to eat*. This term, however, refers not to classes of foods but to classes of people: in countries such as Iran and India, a halalcor is someone who may eat anything he chooses. Paradoxically, though, this power to choose belongs not to the highest but to the lowest caste of people: the assumption is that such people are so worthless that no one, not even the Almighty, cares what they eat. See also *abominable things*.

halibut

The scientific name for the halibut is *hippoglossus*, Greek for *horse tongue*, so called because of its wide, flat shape. In contrast, its more common name, *halibut*, derives not from its shape but from when the fish was usually eaten—on Church holidays, or, as they were originally called, on holy days. The halibut, therefore, is literally a *holy butt*, the word *butt* being an old name for flatfish. This *butt*—which derives from a Germanic source meaning *blunt*, a source that also gave rise to *buttocks*—appears also in *turbot*, another sort of flatfish. At one time it was believed that *turbot* took its name from the Latin *turbo*, meaning *tornado*, as if the fish somehow spun through the water as it swam. In fact, however, the first syllable of *turbot* comes from the Swedish *törn*, meaning *thorn*, the connection being that the turbot has thorn-like nodules on its back. In English, turbots were first referred to by name in the early fourteenth century, halibuts in the fifteenth.

ham

Back in the sixteenth century, when fawning courtiers complimented Queen Elizabeth for her hams, they were not praising her culinary skills, but rather her limber legs that allowed her to dance more featly and jump more lightly than any other woman in her court. One Renaissance painter even depicted the dancing Queen in the midst of a marvellous leap, her feet higher than the shoulders of the admiring courtiers, who must crane back their heads to view her manifest grace and magnificent hams. *Ham*, in fact, was commonly used to refer to the human leg up until the nineteenth century, a usage still evident in *hamstring*, the name of the tendon running behind your knees. It was not until the mid seventeenth century that *ham* also acquired the more specific sense of a particular cut of pork, one taken from the rear leg of a pig. In origin, the word *ham*, which appeared in English about a thousand years ago, derives from a Germanic source that meant *crooked* or *bent*, a leg's ability to bend being one of the things that makes walking possible (the word *elbow* likewise derives from two Germanic words meaning *arm-bend*).The *ham* that means *bad actor* may or may not derive from the culinary *ham*: it may have come from *ham fat* (a substance once used to remove theatrical makeup), or from *amateur* (pronounced by over-aspirating thespians as *hamateur*), or from *Hamlet* (a role prone to over-acting). The name *Hamlet*, incidentally, derives from a source meaning *little home*, not *little ham*.

hamburger

The word *hamburger* dates back to 1834 where it appeared on a menu from Delmonico's restaurant in New York. At that time, and even into the twentieth century, hamburgers were better known as *hamburger steak*, a kind of beefsteak ground in the style of butchers from Hamburg, a city in Germany. The name of this city derives in part from the German *burg*, a word meaning *fort* and related to the English word *borough*; the *ham* part of *Hamburg* is likely the German *ham* that means *port*, the city having long been a harbour for ships. The hamburger, therefore, takes its name from a German phrase meaning *port-fort*, just as the cheese known as *Limburger*, a name that appeared in English about the same time as *hamburger*, takes its name from a German phrase meaning *linden-tree fort*. In the 1930s, *burger* came to be used as a shortened form of *hamburger*, leading to all kinds of new burgers: *nutburger* in 1934, *chickenburger* in 1936, *cheeseburger* in 1938, and *porkburger* in 1939. The emergence of these new meat names so detached *burger* from the original word *hamburger* that restaurateurs became concerned that people would assume hamburgers contained ham; thus, in 1940 the word *beefburger* appeared as an alternate name for the hamburger. Another alternate name appeared at the end of the nineteenth century, *Salisbury steak*, named after J. H. Salisbury, an American doctor who advocated grinding food before eating it to make it easier to digest. *Salisbury steak* did not really catch on until the first World War, when some citizens of Allied countries made a concerted effort to replace "German" words with native English ones. British citizens who had German names even felt compelled to change them: in 1917, for example, the prominent Battenberg family— from whom Prince Philip descends—changed their surname to *Mountbatten*.

hare

Although they both have long ears and are prepared for the table in a similar manner, hares and rabbits are not considered by zoologists to be the same animal: hares are larger, for example, and do not live in burrows. Nonetheless, their overall resemblance has long caused people to confuse them, resulting in frequent misapplication of their names. The Belgian hare, for example, is actually a rabbit, while the American jack rabbit is actually a hare.

The hare acquired its name from a Germanic word pronounced something like *khason*, a word that may have originally meant *grey*: the word *khason* seems, for instance, to have been the source of the Old English *hasu*, meaning *grey*, and of the Modern English *hoary*, meaning *grey with age*. If *grey* was indeed the original meaning of *khason*, then the word was bestowed upon the long-eared animal because of its grey fur, just as the bear acquired its name from an Indo-European word that meant *brown*. Whatever its original meaning, once the word *khason* became the Germanic name of the animal, it evolved into the Old English *hara*, respelt as *hare* in the twelfth century. Likewise, in German, *khason* evolved into *hase*, as in *hasenpfeffer*, a dish of peppered hare. In the sixteenth century, the word *hare* also became established in many expressions and compounds. *Harelip*, for example, came to denote a medical condition in which a person's upper lip is cleft like that of a hare, while *to kiss the hare's foot* came to mean *to be late for dinner*, the idea being that the latecomer must dine on the only part of the roast hare that remains—its feet.

haricot

See *kidney bean*.

herb

The word *herb* derives from the Latin name for such plants, *herba*. When the French adopted the word in the eleventh century, they dropped the *h*, spelling it *erbe*, and it was this form that the English borrowed in the late thirteenth century. The word retained this spelling until the sixteenth century when scholars reattached its lost *h* to make it look more like its Latin ancestor. In spite of the change in spelling, however, *herb* continued to be pronounced *erb*, at least until the nineteenth century when people started to say the *h* in a host of words in which it had previously been silent, words such as *humble*, *history*, and *humour*. Today, only a few words, such as *honour*, *honest*, and *heir*, have retained their silent *h*. The word *herb* is not related to the *Herb* that is short for *Herbert*, a name of Germanic origin that means *army bright*.

hero sandwich

See *gyro*.

herring

The North Atlantic fish known as the *herring*, long an important source of food in Britain, has had its current name for over thirteen hundred years. The name may have developed from the Old English word *here*, meaning *army* or *multitude*, in reference to the huge schools of herring that swim to the coast of Europe in certain seasons to spawn. More likely, however, is the possibility that *herring* developed from the Old English *har*, meaning *grey* or *grizzled*, because the fish is grey in colour. If so, then *herring* is related to *hoarfrost*—the grey frost that covers everything after a humid, frigid night—and perhaps also to *hare*, a rabbit-like animal that may take its name from its grey fur.

hibachi

Made from two Japanese words—*hi*, meaning *fire*, and *bachi*, meaning *pot*—*hibachi* entered English in 1863 as the name for a large, clay pan in which charcoal was burnt in order to heat a living room. The word did not come to signify a culinary implement until the 1960s in America, where it also acquired the sense of being small and portable. In common parlance, the Japanese *hibachi* has replaced the English *brazier*, which means the same thing. See also *sushi*.

hiccup

The involuntary spasm of the glottis that occurs when you bolt down your food or eat something excessively spicy was not originally called a *hiccup*: it was called a *yex*, and if you suffered a series of them, you were *yexing*. The word *yex*, which first appeared in English around 1400, acquired a rival around 1540 in the form of *hickock*, a word that originated as an imitation of the sound of a hiccup. From *hickock*, the word *hiccup* developed around 1580, which then acquired an alternate spelling in 1626 as *hiccough*; this alternate spelling, based on the mistaken impression that a hiccup is a kind of cough, has never affected either the pronunciation of the word or the production of the spasm. Meanwhile, as the word *hiccup* underwent these vagaries, the word *yex* remained quietly current and stable; even in the late nineteenth century it was still used as a quaint alternate for *hiccup*.

hippogastronomy

The art of cutting, cooking, and eating horsemeat is called *hippogastronomy*, a word invented in the nineteenth century by combining the ancient Greek word for *horse—hippos—*with the word *gastronomy*. The Greek *hippos* is also represented in *hippopotamus*, a word that literally means *river horse*, and in *hippodrome*, the French name for the racetrack. The word *horse*, incidentally, derives ultimately from the Germanic name for that animal, *khorsam*; this ancient word is also the source of *Ross*, a name that literally means *horse* but which books such as *A Thousand and One Baby Names* usually translate, somewhat euphemistically, as *steed*. See also *chevaline* and *gastronomy*.

hoagie

See *poor boy*.

hockey

In rural England, the day in late autumn when the last of the crop is harvested and brought back home is called the *harvest-home*, a day of celebration and gaiety. The feast held on this day is called *the hockey*, a puzzling name because its origin is completely unknown and yet it has been commonly used, both on its own and as part of numerous phrases: *hockey cart*, for example, refers to the last cart of grain brought out of the field, *hockey cake* refers to a seed-cake eaten during the celebration, and *hockey night* refers to the nocturnal festivities that traditionally follow the harvest-home. The feast itself, however, is simply called *the hockey*, a term probably much older than its first appearance in print in the mid sixteenth century; *hockey* is still used in this sense in England, but in North America the word has been superseded by *Thanksgiving*, a celebration formalized in the early seventeenth century. The other *hockey*, the one synonymous with Wayne Gretzky, also emerged in English in the mid sixteenth century as the name of a game played in a field with sticks and a ball or, on ice, with a puck. However, this *hockey* does not appear to be related to the harvest-home *hockey*, deriving instead from the word *hook*, a reference to the players' hooked sticks.

hodgepodge

Although we now use them metaphorically to refer to a confused mess of anything, the words *hodgepodge*, *gallimaufry*, and *farrago* all originated as names of jumbled mixtures of food. The oldest of these three is *hodgepodge*, a word that, in a slightly different form, dates back in English to the fourteenth century. At that time, the word was spelt *hotch-pot*, a form closer to the original French source of the term: the *pot* is the French *pot*, meaning *a deep pan for cooking*, while the *hotch* is a corrupt form of the French verb *hocher*, meaning *to shake together*. Originally, therefore, the term *hotch-pot* referred to a simple dish of vegetables and meat, shaken together and cooked in a pot. Over time, though, the pronunciation and spelling of *hotch-pot* was corrupted as people unconsciously changed the last half of the word to rhyme with the first half: the resulting *hotch-potch* appeared in the late sixteenth century, and is still the form used by many people in England. By the early seventeenth century the word had been further corrupted to *hodgepodge*, the form that now, at least in Canada, seems to prevail. As these changes in spelling and pronunciation occurred, the word's original culinary sense faded into the background, and its metaphorical application to jumbles and mixtures of all kinds came to predominate. The word *gallimaufry*, like the word *hodgepodge*, also originated as a French cooking term: it referred to a stew made from varied ingredients, and it was formed by compounding the Middle French *galer*, meaning *to rejoice*, with the Middle French *mafrer*, meaning *to eat abundantly* (*galer* is also the source of the English *gala*, meaning *a party*). English adopted this French compound in the late sixteenth century, using it both as the name of a culinary dish and as a synonym for *zany mixture*. Adopted slightly later, in the early seventeenth century, was *farrago*, a Latin word which the ancient Romans bestowed on a blend of grains fed to cattle, but which the English borrowed to mean *ridiculous medley*. The source of *farrago* is the Latin *far*, meaning *corn*, a word that also gave rise to *farina*, an alternate name for corn flour. Incidentally, before the word *farrago* was adopted by English, such blends of grain were called *bullimong*, an odd word whose last half derives from the Old English *imong*, meaning *mixture*, and whose first half is of unknown origin. Other particularly strange words that once referred to mixtures of food include *mingle-mangle*, *powsoddy*, *jussel*, and *olio*. The first of these odd-looking terms, *mingle-mangle*, emerged in the mid sixteenth century as a name for the hodgepodge of scraps fed to pigs, and was formed by combining the verb *mingle* (meaning *to mix together*) with *mangle* (meaning *to tear to pieces*). *Powsoddy* also appeared in the sixteenth century, and was the name of a dish made from a sheep head and an assortment of other ingredients; the word likely derives from *pow*, a Scottish term meaning *head*, and *sodden*, meaning *boiled*. Somewhat older, dating back to the late fourteenth century, is *jussel*, the name of a stew-like dish made by mincing and mixing meat and herbs; the word derives through French from the Latin *jus*, meaning *broth*, which is also the source of the English *juice*. Finally, *olio* refers to a dish of Spanish origin made from beef, chicken, bacon, pumpkin, cabbage, turnip, and other ingredients; adopted by English in the mid seventeenth century, *olio* derives from the Spanish *olla*, meaning *pot*.

hoecake

See *pancake*.

hog

See *pig*.

hogo

In the mid seventeenth century, the English borrowed the French phrase *haut-goût*—literally meaning *high taste*—and applied it both to foods with a pleasantly piquant flavour and to foods that stink to high heaven. Sometimes the English spelt the term as *hogo*, representing how they actually pronounced the French term, but the new spelling never completely overtook the original. The two forms, *haut goût* and *hogo*, have existed side by side ever since.

hogshead

A hogshead is a liquid measure that varies in capacity depending on what is being measured. Thus, a hogshead of wine is 63 gallons, of beer 54 gallons, of ale 48 gallons, of molasses 100 gallons, of claret 46 gallons, of port 57 gallons, of sherry 54 gallons, and of Madeira 46 gallons. These varying capacities might seem to reflect the spectrum of sizes to which our tasty, porcine friend—the hog—may grow, but no one actually knows why this liquid measure was named after a hog's head. The name of the measure originated in England at the end of the fourteenth century, and from there was adopted into a host of other European languages. In some of those languages, though, the *hogs* part of the word was mistaken for the word *ox*, and thus Dutch ended up with *oxhooft*, German with *oxhoft*, and Danish with *oxehoved*.

hog-wash

The water you boil wieners in, the tea left over from lunch, the tops of carrots and the bottoms of celery—all these were once thrown into a bucket and hauled out daily to pigs that would actually fight for the privilege of swallowing this hog-wash. The word first appeared in the middle of the fifteenth century but encountered a competitor in the middle of the sixteenth century with the appearance of *swill*, a word deriving from the Old English *swillan*, meaning *to wash out*.

Hollandaise sauce

The egg-and-butter sauce known as *Hollandaise* takes its name from the country where it originated. In turn, the name *Holland* probably derives from a Dutch source meaning *hollow land*, so called because the topography of the country is flat and low, some areas even lying below sea-level. Similarly, Holland's other name—The Netherlands—means *lower land*, the Dutch word for *lower* being *neder*.

hollow meat

Unlike large animals such as cows or deer, small animals such as chickens, rabbits, and ducks can be cooked whole, meaning that before they go into the oven they have a "hollow" where their innards once were that can be filled with stuffing or force-meat. These small, "hollow" animals were not originally sold by butchers, who specialized only in the large animals that had to be cut into manageable sizes; accordingly, the term *hollow meat* emerged as a generic name for meats not sold in butcher shops. The term *hollow meat* was first used in the late nineteenth century, but the word *hollow* itself is much older, going back to the mid thirteenth century. *Hollow* derives from an Indo-European source that meant *to hide*; from this source also developed the words *hell* (a place where the Almighty hides the sinful from His sight), *hall* (a place where Anglo-Saxons once gathered to hide from fiends such as *Beowulf's* Grendel), *helmut* (a covering that hides your head), and of course *hole*.

honey

The first sweetener used by humans, honey has long been associated with pleasure and happiness: in the Old Testament, for example, the Promised Land of the Israelites is said to be flowing with milk and honey. The word *honey* itself is likewise of ancient origin, ultimately deriving from an Indo-European source that meant *pale yellow*, the colour of honey. The earliest reference to honey in English dates back to the ninth century, and since then the word has been used to form dozens of compounds, including *honeycomb* and *honeymoon*. With *honeycomb*, dating back to the eleventh century, the *comb* originally referred to the parallel "plates" suspended from the roof of a beehive and which, viewed from the side, line up like the teeth of a comb; later on, the word also came to describe the hexagonal cells that the bees build on the surfaces of these plates. With *honeymoon*, dating back to the mid sixteenth century, the word arose from the perception that marriage is sweet at first—as sweet as honey— but then, like the moon, wanes and grows dim; this sardonic connotation persists in the phrase *the honeymoon's over*, but for the most part the word is now used without its original, ironic overtone. As a term of endearment—a synonym, in other words, for *snookums*, *pookie*, and *sweet-baboo*—*honey* dates back to at least the mid fourteenth century.

hors d'oeuvre

This phrase does not, as my father believes, derive from *horse ovaries* but rather is French for *outside the work*, the "work" being the courses of the meal; an hors d'oeuvre, therefore, is a small dish to be served either before the main courses or between them. The *oeuvre* part of this phrase developed from the Latin *opera*, which is the plural of the Latin *opus*, meaning *work*. *Opus*, in turn, is related to *Ops*, the name of the Roman goddess of plenty whose favour ensured that one's hard work would result in opulence. The phrase *hors d'oeuvre* was first used in English in the mid eighteenth century.

horseradish

See *radish*.

host

By definition a stranger is strange, and since this strangeness may evoke fear or delight, a stranger may be seen as either an enemy or a friend. Accordingly, the Indo-European word that meant *stranger*—*ghostis* (which is not related to the English word *ghost*)—developed by different routes into words that apply to enemies and words that apply to friends. For example, in Greece the Indo-European *ghostis* evolved into the Greek word *xenos*, meaning *stranger*, from which English gets *xenophobia*, the fear of foreigners; similarly, in Italy the word *ghostis* evolved into the Latin word *hostis*, meaning *enemy*, from which English gets the word *hostile*. However, another Latin word also developed from the Indo-European *ghostis*: namely, *hospes*, a word the ancient Romans applied to someone who looks after strangers and treats them as friends. In the twelfth century this Latin word (*hospes*) developed into the French *hoste*, which, at the beginning of the fourteenth century, became the English word *host*, denoting someone who entertains guests. The Latin *hospes* also gave rise to the English words *hostel* and *hotel*—places where strangers are given food and shelter—and to *hospital*—a place where doctors nurse complete strangers back to health. *Ghostis*, the original Indo-European source of all these words, also gave rise to another line of words in the Germanic language family: it evolved into the Germanic *gastiz*, meaning *friendly stranger*, which in turn developed into the English word *guest*, first recorded about a thousand years ago. The words *host* and *guest*, therefore, derive from the same source, a fact more apparent in French where *hôte* refers to both the person who is hosting and to the person who is guesting.

hot cross buns

Hot cross buns acquired their name from being indented with a cross commemorating Good Friday, the only day they were eaten; originally known simply as *cross buns*, they became *hot cross buns* in the early eighteenth century because of a rhyme shouted by street vendors: "One a penny, two a penny, hot cross buns, butter them, and sugar them, and put them in your muns," *muns* being slang for *mouths*. The word *hot* in this rhyme not only made the baked goods more appealing, it also gave the rhyme its effective rhythm (try reading it without the word *hot* and see how bad it sounds). In time, the word *hot* became not just an adjective describing the *cross buns*, but an integral part of their name, a name they retain even when they are frozen solid.

hot dog

The basic idea behind the hot dog—injecting a variety of minced meats into a pig's intestine—is common to many cultures, and thus the hot dog has been known by many other names. *Frankfurter* and *wiener*, which appeared at the end of the nineteenth century, both derive from the European cities where they were made: *frankfurter* from *Frankfurt* (a German city whose name literally means *ford of the Franks*, so named because it marks the place where the Frankish army crossed the Main river in the first century) and *wiener* from *Vienna* (an Austrian city whose name literally means *white-river fort*). In Europe, these sausages were known as *Frankfurter wurst* and *Vienna wurst*, but the *wurst* part—which means *sausage*—was dropped soon after the introduction of the name to North America. In contrast, the origin of *hot dog* is more circuitous and perhaps more apocryphal. Apparently, German immigrants to America sometimes called wiener sausages *dachshunds*, the shape of the sausage somewhat resembling the long body of the dachshund dog. The name became popular at baseball stadiums where vendors shrieked out, "Red hot dachshunds! Red hot dachshunds!" (This cry is also the source of yet another name for the hot dog—the *red hot*.) These "dachshund" sausages became so popular that a cartoonist—Tad Dorgan, well-known at the time for his dog-like caricatures of Germans—decided to ride the wiener-craze by drawing a cartoon of a dachshund dog lying in a large bun. However, after finishing the drawing and moving on to the caption, he realized that he did not know how to spell *dachshund* and so, with his deadline approaching, he simply changed the vendor's cry to "Red hot dogs! Red hot dogs!" Dorgan's cartoon ran in 1906, two years before the next appearance of *hot dog* in print.

hot cake

See *pancake*.

humble pie

Although the expression *to eat humble pie* only dates back to the early nineteenth century, the actual dish called *humble pie* is ancient. A humble pie contained the parts of a deer known as the *umbles*: the heart, liver, and intestines. Although once prized by hunters as a revitalizing food, umbles fell in esteem as hunters lost their honoured role in society and became mere servants of the queasy aristocracy. Accordingly, food made from umbles, such as *umble pie*, came to be seen as fit only for inferior social classes, a perception that prompted people to make a connection between the word *umble* and the unrelated word *humble*. Indeed, in those British dialects that drop *h*s, the two words would have been pronounced identically. Eventually the association between *umble* and *humble* caused the name of the food to be respelt as *humble*, and the act of eating *humble pie* came to be synonymous with humiliation. The word *umble*, by the way, had undergone respelling even before it became *humble*. Before the sixteenth century, the word *umble* was actually the word *numble*; the initial *n* was likely lost because spoken phrases like *a numble pie* could easily be misinterpreted as *an umble pie*. *Numble*, in turn, was derived in the thirteenth century from the Latin word *lumbulus*, meaning *a little loin*. In fact, the words *loin* and *lumbago*—a rheumatic condition afflicting the lower back—also derive from the word *lumbulus*, making them cousins of the *humble* in *humble pie*. See also *bouce Jane*.

Hungary water

See *costmary*.

hydromel

Several beverages and culinary concoctions derive their names from *meli*, the Greek word for *honey*, including *hydromel*, *acetomel*, and *oenomel*. Hydromel, as might be guessed from the first half of the word, is a beverage made by mixing honey with water. Likewise, oenomel is a drink made by mixing honey with wine (in Greek, *oinos* means *wine*), while *acetomel* is a pickling fluid made by combining honey with vinegar (in Latin, *acetum* means *vinegar*). When the first of these concoctions, hydromel, is allowed to ferment and become alcoholic, it is called *mead*, a word that evolved from the Old English *meodu*; in turn, *meodu* developed from an Indo-European source, pronounced something like *medhu*, that meant *sweet drink*. This same Indo-European source also evolved into another Greek word for wine, *methu*, from which English formed the word *methyl* as in *methyl alcohol*. When heavily spiced, mead is called *metheglin*, a word resembling the Greek *methu*, but in no way related. Instead, English acquired the word *metheglin* from Welsh in the early sixteenth century, the Welsh having invented the word by combining their words *meddyg*, meaning *healing*, and *llyn*, meaning *liquor*; *metheglin* is therefore a compound meaning *healing liquor*. Incidentally, the first part of this Welsh compound is not really a native Welsh word; instead, *meddyg* is a Welsh adaptation of the Latin *medicus*, meaning *physician*. In contrast, the second part of the compound—the *llyn* part—really is a native Welsh word: it derives from the same source as *lynne*, meaning *pool of liquid*, a word best known in compounds such as *Dublin* and *Brooklyn*, and which also became *Lynne*, a woman's name. See also *molasses*.

ice

The word *ice* derives from a Germanic source that also evolved into the German *eis*, the Danish *is*, and the Dutch *ijs*, all meaning *ice*. In Old English, the word was spelt *is*, a form that persisted until the fourteenth century when it was respelt *ice*. Another word associated with winter and freezing temperatures was the Old English *gicel*, a word meaning *icicle* but not related to *ice*. By the fourteenth century, the spelling and pronunciation of *gicel* had shifted to *ickle*; simultaneously, people began to suppose that an ickle was not just an icicle but any sort of long projection, and they therefore felt a need to invent a new name for an "ickle" made of ice. The result was *iceickle*, a word that was tautological in so far as it literally meant *ice icicle*. In time, the word *iceickle* came to be spelt *icicle*, and the older word—*ickle*—gradually faded away, falling out of use by the seventeenth century. In 1922, however, the word *ickle* was revived, after a fashion, when Frank Epperson of Oakland, California invented a frozen treat he called the *Epsicle*, a name he changed the next year to *Popsicle*. The Popsicle then inspired numerous spin-offs, including the *Fudgsicle* and the *Creamsicle*, all exploiting *sicle* as a kind of "frozen-treat" suffix (admittedly, *sicle* does differ from the much older *ickle* in that it begins with an *s*, one representing the *s* sound produced by the first *c* in *icicle*). Another word that developed from *ice* is *icing*, a sugary glaze spread over the surface of cakes and pastry. *Icing* appeared in English in the mid eighteenth century, the same time that the synonymous *frosting* came into use.

imam bayildi

According to Turkish legend, this dish of eggplants stuffed with onions and tomatoes is so tasty that when it was served to a Muslim priest, he fainted from gastronomic delight. Thenceforth, the dish was known as *imam bayildi*, meaning *the priest fainted*, a dish first referred to in English in 1935. Further back in history, the title of *imam* derived from the Turkish word *amma*, meaning *to go before*. See also *choke-priest*.

impanation

Impanation is the Christian doctrine that the bread consecrated and eaten during communion actually becomes, or at least unites with, the body of Christ. The term is a compound formed from the Latin prefix *in*, meaning *in*, and the Latin *panis*, meaning *bread*, and was adopted from Medieval Latin in the middle of the sixteenth century.

infare cake

Today, most brides and grooms cut their wedding cake in full view of their friends and family, and then slip away to cross the threshold of their new home—or hotel room—in private. Long ago in England, however, these two events were one and the same, as wedding guests crumbled infare cake over the head of the bride as she and her husband crossed the threshold of their new abode. This shower of cake crumbs was intended to ensure fertility and bounty, and thus the original cakes were made of hearty grains such as wheat or oats. This English custom traces its origin to ancient times when Romans sometimes solemnized marriages through the rite of *confarreatio*, a word literally meaning *to unite with grain-cake* (the *far* in the middle of *confarreatio* is the Latin *far*, meaning *grain*, a word that also appears in *farina* and *farrago*). In contrast, the English *infare* literally means *to go in*, deriving as it does from the word *in* and from the Old English verb *faran*, meaning *to go* or *to travel*. Before it was applied specifically to cake, *infare* could also refer to a feast provided for guests when someone, newly married or not, took possession of a new home. See also *wedding cake*, *fare*, and *hodgepodge*.

ingredient

The name of an item called for by a recipe—an ingredient—is closely related to some surprising words, including *aggression* and *congress*. The common source of these words is the Latin verb *gradi*, meaning *to walk* or *to go*. By attaching this verb to the preposition *in*, Latin formed the word *ingredi*, meaning *to go in*, which then gave rise to a present participle form, *ingrediens*, meaning *going in*. In the mid fifteenth century, the Latin *ingrediens* became, via French, the English *ingredient*, an ingredient literally being *something going in* to a dish. The Latin *gradi* also became attached to the prefix *ad* to form *adgradi*, whose pronunciation and spelling was soon simplified to *aggredi*, meaning *to go toward in a menacing manner*. In English, the past participle of *aggredi*—*agressus*—gave rise to *aggression*, first recorded in the early seventeenth century. The word *congress*—literally meaning *a going together*—arose in a similar way at about the same time.

innards

See *trollibags*.

insipid

See *sapid*.

invitation

After spending all of May traipsing from one friend's wedding to another, you might be unwilling to attend the vernal equinox party being hosted by your sister-in-law's accountant. Your frantic search for an excuse to decline the invitation—"I'm having my hedgehog spayed"—would not surprise an ancient Roman, whose word for an invitation—*invitatio*—bears a striking resemblance to the Latin *invitus*, meaning *unwilling*. Whether or not these two Latin words are actually related to each other is uncertain, since the ultimate origins of both *invitatio* and *invitus* are unknown. However, if the two words do derive from a common source, then it suggests that invitations, in ancient times, were rather like subpoenas compelling an unwilling guest to attend some sort of ghastly formal occasion. In English, the word *invitation* appeared in the middle of the sixteenth century; prior to this, and dating back to the ninth century, an invitation was called a *lathing*, a word that likely derives from a Germanic source meaning *willing*.

irrorateur

If the stench wafting from a malodorous guest makes it difficult to appreciate the subtle fragrance of your almond chicken, you might address the problem by whipping out your irrorateur and discharging it over the dinner table. This culinary accoutrement, a kind of perfume-filled spray gun, was invented by an eighteenth-century gastronome, Jean-Anthelme Brillat-Savarin. The name of the device derives from the Latin *rorare*, meaning *to drop dew*, which in turn derives from the Latin *ros*, meaning *dew*. See also *costmary*.

isinglass

The next time you are about to throw out all your old sturgeon bladders, resist the temptation. Instead, peel the outer skin from each bladder and wash what is left in cold water. Next, remove the bladder's inner skin and squish it with a bowling ball until it becomes a nearly-clear ribbon. You can then use this substance—called *isinglass*—to thicken jellies or soups, which is what people have done with isinglass for centuries. Although the substance is semi-transparent, isinglass does not really get its name from its resemblance to either ice or glass. Instead, the word *isinglass* derives from *huysenblas*, a Middle Dutch compound formed from *huysen*, meaning *sturgeon*, and *blas*, meaning *bladder*. When the word *huysenblas* was introduced to English in the mid sixteenth century, however, the spelling was changed to *isinglass*, partly because the see-through nature of the gelatin reminded people of glass.

it

See *gin*.

jaeger

See *cacciatore*.

jalapeno

In 1912, Wilbur Scoville invented a system for measuring the "heat" of different chili peppers, that is, their ability to tantalize, tenderize, or traumatize the palate. Under this system, jalapeno peppers rate around 5000 Scoville units, thus affirming what everyone already knows: that they are hot. Still, jalapenos are as fiery as talcum powder compared to habanero peppers, which rate about 300,000 Scoville units, making them roughly sixty times as hot as jalapenos. Both these peppers take their names from places where they originated: *habanero* from *Havana*, and *jalapeno* from *Jalapa*, a city in Mexico whose name in Nahuatl means *sand by the water*. The names of both peppers were introduced to English in the 1930s.

jambalaya

According to folk etymology, the Cajun-Creole dish known as *jambalaya* acquired its name when a salesman from the northern United States stopped for a bite to eat at a New Orleans café. After telling the waitress he wanted to try the café's specialty, the waitress shouted to the cook in the kitchen: "Jean, throw something together!", a command that in Louisiana French would be spoken as "Jean, balayez!" After finishing his meal, the customer left and travelled across America with the mistaken impression that "Jean, balayez!"—or what he remembered as "Jambalaya!"—was the name of the delicious dish he had been served. Those who wish to accept this dubious explanation of the name *jambalaya* may do so with impunity, because the actual origin of the word is unknown, apart from the fact that it first appeared around 1872. However, considering that one of the main ingredients in jambalaya is ham, it may be that *jambon*—the French word for *ham*—lurks somewhere in the name's past. Although there is no *l* sound in *jambon*, the pronunciation may have been influenced by association with the word *jumble*, which is what jambalaya—containing not only ham, but also rice, pork, sausage, shrimp, and crayfish—certainly is.

java

Although *java* has become a slang name for coffee, the word originally meant *barley*: thousands of years ago, an Indonesian island famous for its barley acquired the Sanskrit name *Yavadvipa*, *yava* meaning *barley*, and *dvipa* meaning *island*. In time, the name of the island shortened to just *Yava*, which in English became *Java*. Because the island of Java was also, at one time, the world's main producer of coffee beans, coffee came to be known as *java*, a term first recorded in English in the middle of the nineteenth century. *Java* may have also inspired coffee's other nickname, *joe*, as in *cup o' joe*, an expression dating back to the early 1940s; however, as far back as the nineteenth century the name *Joe* had also been used to mean *American male* (as in *G.I. Joe*), an eponym that may have led someone to transfer the name to the beverage epitomizing American culture—coffee.

jelly

Although they hardly look the same, the word *jelly* and the word *cold* derive from the same source, an Indo-European word, pronounced something like *ghel*, that meant *to be cold*. This ancient word evolved into the Germanic word *kal*, which eventually developed into the English words *cool*, *chill*, and *cold*.

The same Indo-European source, *ghel*, also evolved into the Latin words *gelu*, meaning *frost*, and *gelare*, meaning *to freeze into a solid*. From *gelare*, Old French acquired *gelee*, meaning both *frost* and *jelly*, which English borrowed in the late fourteenth century as *gely*; the word retained this spelling until the seventeenth century when it came to be spelt *jelly*. Shortly after, in the early eighteenth century, *jelly* also shifted in meaning: when it first emerged in English, *jelly*—or *gely*—had referred to the semi-solid substance extracted from an animal's carcass by boiling it and skimming off the slumgullion that rises to the surface; in the early eighteenth century, however, the word *jelly* started to be used as a name for sweet fruit preserves whose semi-solid consistency resembled animal jelly. Eventually, the word *jelly* became so identified with this popular fruit preserve that a new word had to be found to refer to the "jelly" extracted from animal carcasses. Accordingly, the French word *gélatine*, which derives from the same Latin source as *jelly*, was adopted at the beginning of the nineteenth century as *gelatin*, which thereafter took over the original sense of *jelly*.

jerk

Beef jerky, a snack of dried beef sold in convenience stores, is a kind of jerk, a strip of meat preserved without salt by drying it in the sun. The word *jerk* derives from the Quechua language, spoken by the indigenous peoples of Peru, including those once under the rule of the Inca Empire. The Quechua called meat preserved in this manner *charqui*, a word borrowed by Spanish Americans before being adopted by English in the early eighteenth century as *jerk*.

Jerusalem artichoke

The Jordan almond is not from Jordan, but at least it is an almond. The Jerusalem artichoke, on the other hand, is not only not from Jerusalem, it is not even an artichoke. Instead, the Jerusalem artichoke is a tuber, much like a potato, and is native to North and South America. The vegetable was introduced to Europe in 1617 as *topinambour*, named after a tribe in South America; however, the Italians soon started calling it *girasole articiocco*, meaning *sunflower artichoke*, because it tasted like an artichoke and because its flower turned throughout the day to follow the path of the sun. Literally, the *girasole* part of *girosole articiocco* means *sun turner*, the *gira* part being related to our word *gyre* and the *sole* part to our word *solar*. However, this lovely origin was lost on the English who, around 1640, began mistaking the word *girasole* for *Jerusalem* and thus accidentally renamed the vegetable. See also *Jordan almond*.

Johnny-cake

See *pancake*.

Jordan almond

The Jordan almond, an especially fine and tasty variety of almond, has nothing to do with either the country called Jordan or the river Jordan running through it. Instead, the *Jordan* of *Jordan almond* is a corruption of the French word *jardin*, meaning *garden*. Such sweet garden almonds are cultivated for use in pastries, while their wilder cousins—bitter almonds, which contain poisonous hydrocyanic acid—are crushed to produce oil. In turn, after the hydrocyanic acid is removed, this almond oil is used to make flavouring extracts. See also *Jerusalem artichoke*.

kaiser roll

See *Caesar salad*.

kale

See *cole slaw*.

kebab

See *shish kebab*.

kechel

See *quiche*.

ketchup

Although squabbles still erupt over whether the spelling is *catsup* or *ketchup*, the original form of the tomato-based condiment's name was a happy blending of the two spellings—*catchup*—which appeared in 1690. Today, the *ketchup* spelling has become established in Britain and Canada, but *catsup* remains the main form in most parts of the United States. The word—or words— derive from Amoy, a dialect of southeastern China from which English has also taken *pekoe*, the name of a highly prized tea. In Amoy, the original name of the condiment was *ke tsiap*, meaning *brine of pickled fish*, a name that suggests how much the ingredients of ketchup have changed since its introduction to Europe three hundred years ago.

kickshaw

Kickshaws are tidbits of food like the cashews, cookies, and mints scattered in bowls around your grandparents' home. However, the original meaning of *kickshaw* was slightly different: from the late sixteenth to the late nineteenth century, it was a disparaging name for a dish that seemed needlessly fancy or suspiciously exotic. British food, according to the British, was hearty and substantial and put hair on your chest, but those frothy, cloying foreign foods were something else. This distaste for "something else" is, in fact, reflected in the word *kickshaw* itself, which is simply a corruption of the French *quelque chose*, meaning *something*. A similar corruption of another word led to the appearance of *sunket*, another name for a tid-bit of food or a dainty: *sunket* derives from the word *somewhat*, formerly used as a synonym for *something* as in "Give me somewhat to eat." The change in pronunciation from *somewhat* to *sunket* probably occurred in Scotland, where the *wh* of many words becomes so aspirated that it almost sounds like a *qu* or a *k*; after undergoing this Scottish change in pronunciation, *sunket* entered, or rather reentered, English at the beginning of the eighteenth century.

kid

See *butcher*.

kidney bean

The kidney bean takes its name from its resemblance in shape to the human kidney, an organ that cleanses the blood of wastes. In turn, the kidney takes its own name from something it resembles: an egg. In Middle English, *egg* was spelt and pronounced *ey*, which is exactly how it appears at the end of the word *kidney*; the other part of *kidney*—the *kidn* part—likely derives from an Old Norse word that refers to the anatomical location of the kidney: near the belly, which in Old Norse was called the *kvithr*. A kidney, therefore, is literally a *kvithr ey* or *belly egg*. The name *kidney bean* first appeared in English in the mid sixteenth century, but a hundred years later the same legume also came to be known as the *French bean* and as the *haricot bean*. *Haricot*, in fact, is the French word for beans in general, a word deriving from what the Aztecs called the bean, *ayacotl*.

kilderkin

See *nipperkin*.

kill-priest

See *choke-priest*.

kimchi

So hot that some nations have considered using it as a plutonium substitute, kimchi is a Korean pickle seasoned with garlic, horseradish, or ginger. The Koreans derived their name for this condiment from the Chinese, who called a similar pickle *chen cay*, meaning *steeped vegetables*. The Korean name was introduced to English in the late nineteenth century.

kissing-crust

When loaves of bread bake, they expand in size, sometimes causing one loaf to lean against another. This point of contact, usually soft instead of crusty, is called the *kissing-crust*, a baking term dating back to at least the early nineteenth century. Although the name sounds delightful, bakers—before the invention of plastic bags—tried to avoid kissing-crusts because their softness, compared to the rest of the loaf, made them susceptible to mould and burrowing insects. Incidentally, the word *kiss*, which probably originated as an imitation of the sound of a kiss, dates back in English more than a thousand years; since then, of course, other words have also been used to mean *kiss*, including the fourteenth century's *beslobber* and *dab*, the sixteenth century's *smack* and *buss*, the seventeenth century's *neb*, *osculate*, and *suaviate*, and the early nineteenth century's *smack*. As well, since the mid eighteenth century, *X* has been used in love letters to mean *kisses*.

kitchen

See *cook*.

kiwi fruit

In the early nineteenth century, British scientists studying the flora and fauna of New Zealand decided to name a flightless bird they found there the *apteryx*, an ugly Greek name meaning *wingless*. Luckily, however, the British settlers of New Zealand took to calling the bird by its much more mellifluous Maori name, *kiwi*, which in the early twentieth century became a slang name for the New Zealanders themselves; fifty years later, in 1963, kiwi also became the name of a fuzzy, green fruit that had flourished in New Zealand since being introduced to that island in 1906. Before acquiring the name *kiwi*, the fruit had been called the Chinese gooseberry, the Chang Kiang Valley of China being its place of origin. The name was changed to *kiwi*, however, for marketing reasons: it was thought that associating the fruit with New Zealanders and their famous bird would boost sales in North America.

knaidel

See *noodle*.

knick-knack

See *couscous*.

knife

The meaning of *knife*, unlike that of *spoon* or *fork*, has not varied since it was first recorded in English in the eleventh century. Its spelling and pronunciation, however, have changed significantly. From the eleventh to the thirteenth centuries the word was spelt *cnif*, with the initial *c* being pronounced like a *k*, and with the *i* in the middle being pronounced as a short vowel to rhyme with *sniff*. By the fourteenth century, though, the spelling had been changed to *knyf*, thanks to a modified spelling system introduced by the French after the Norman Conquest; the *k* sound of *knyf* continued to be pronounced for another century until it fell silent in the fifteenth century, about the same time it started to be regularly spelt as *knife*. Given that tape recorders were still centuries away, how can you tell when the *k* sound in words like *knife*, *knight*, *knee*, and *knuckle* were dropped? You can tell by the appearance of literary puns that had never before been made. Chaucer, for example, writing in the late fourteenth century, never makes a pun out of *knight/night* because he pronounced the two words differently; Shakespeare, however, writing in the late sixteenth century, does pun on *knight/night* because for him, like us, the words were homonyms.

kosher

See *halal*.

kugel

Made from noodles or potatoes and sometimes sweetened with raisins, the Jewish pudding known as *kugel* derives its name from the German *kugel*, meaning *ball*, so called because of its shape. This *kugel* is also present in *kugelhopf*, an Austrian yeast cake made with raisins; the *hopf* part of the name may represent the Old German word for *hoop* (the cake is often made in a ring-shaped mould) but could also represent the German *hopfen*, meaning *to jump*, an allusion to how this yeast cake rises as it bakes. See also *baba*.

kumquat

See *loquat*.

langet

See *spatula*.

lasagne

Although highly advanced as law-makers, administrators, and civic engineers, the ancient Romans had no flush toilets. They were forced, therefore, like the vast majority of people who have lived and died on this planet, to use a chamber pot if they wanted to relieve themselves without venturing outside. This pot was called a *lasanum*, a word the ancient Romans derived from the Greek name for a three-legged stand used to support such a pot. In later Latin, this word became *lasania*, meaning *cooking pot*, a name eventually given to the long, wide strips of pasta frequently cooked in these pots. In Italian, the Latin *lasania* evolved into *lasagna*, the plural of which, *lasagne*, was borrowed by English in the mid nineteenth century.

lax

More than twelve hundred years ago, the fish we now know as the salmon was called, in Old English, *lax*. Relatives of this Old English word exist in other languages to this day, including the German *lachs*, the Yiddish *laks*, the Swedish, Danish, and Dutch *lax*, and the Russian *losos*. After the Norman Conquest in 1066, *lax* developed a rival due to the introduction of the French name of the fish, *samoun*. By the seventeenth century, the word *lax* had been so overtaken by *samoun*—which had by then acquired the spelling *salmon*—that no one really remembered what *lax* had once referred to; one writer in 1656 knew that the lax was some sort of fish, but he had a monstrously exaggerated impression of its size, claiming that the lax grew to twenty-four feet in length. Eventually, in the eighteenth century, *lax* dropped out of English altogether. Ironically, however, the death of *lax* permitted its eventual resurrection in the late nineteenth century: it was then that English cooks borrowed the long-forgotten *lax* from Norwegian and applied it to a specific kind of northern salmon, a name it still possesses. Yet another form of the word appeared in 1941 when English took the Yiddish word for salmon, *laks*, respelt it as *lox*, and bestowed it upon a kind of smoked salmon usually served with a bagel. See also *salmon*.

lazy Susan

The revolving platforms that sit in the centre of a dinner table and confer on guests the god-like power of spinning distant dainties into an orbit closer to their own plates have been known as *lazy Susans* since about 1917. The name is whimsical in origin, alluding to how the device obviates the need for indolent guests to go to the trouble of asking one another to pass a desired item. The words that make up the name *lazy Susan* do, however, have real etymologies: *Susan* derives from the Hebrew word for *lily* and was introduced to English through the Old Testament; *lazy* probably derives from the German *lasich*, meaning *lazy* or *loose*, and was not adopted by English until the middle of the sixteenth century. Before that time, you could be slack, slothful, and idle, but not lazy.

leek

Because the ancient Romans believed that eating leeks gave a person a clear, strong voice, the emperor Nero, famous for fiddling while Rome burned, is said to have consumed leek soup everyday so that his speeches could be heard far and wide. However, whereas Nero would have called this onion-like plant a *porrum*, the English have used the name *leek* for more than a thousand years. The ultimate source of the English name for this vegetable was an Indo-European word pronounced something like *leug*, a word meaning *to bend* that was likely bestowed on the plant because of its pliable stem. The same Indo-European word also evolved into the word *lock*, a lock of hair being a curled or "bent" cluster of strands (but the *lock* that means *door fastener* derives from an unrelated source). The word *leek* is also a part of several English words that originated as compounds, including *garlic*. *Gar*, an Old English word meaning *spear*, was combined with *leek* because garlic, a member of the same plant family as the leek, has pointed, spear-like shoots. Another compound involving *leek* is *leighton*, formed from *leek* and from the Old English *tun*, meaning *enclosure*; a leighton is therefore a *leek enclosure* or, more broadly, a garden. First recorded in the tenth century, this synonym for *garden* became obsolete in the late eighteenth century except as a surname (as in Frederick Leighton, the Victorian painter) and as a place name (as in Leighton Buzzard, a town north of London). See also *garlic* and *purée*.

leftovers

Before leftovers were called *leftovers* they were called *relics*, and before they were called *relics* they were called *relief*. Historically, these words overlapped very little: *relief* appeared around the beginning of the fourteenth century and is last recorded, as a culinary term, in 1589; *relic* is first recorded in 1576 and became rare, as a culinary term, in the nineteenth century; *leftovers* was not used as a culinary term until late in the nineteenth century, 1891 to be precise. Of these three words, *relief* has the most straightforward origin: it derives ultimately from an Indo-European source—pronounced something like *lengw*—that meant *to make something lighter*. This Indo-European source became the Latin word *levare*, meaning *to lift up*, which became the Latin *relevare*, meaning *to lift up again*. The Latin *relevare* then became the French *relever*, also meaning *to lift up again*, which became the French word *relief*, meaning both *leftovers* (food you lift up again from the table) and *assistance* (you often have to lift up someone who needs assistance). The French *relief*—with both these senses—was borrowed by English, but, as mentioned, the *leftovers* sense was lost in the late sixteenth century. The word *relic* has a slightly more complex history. It too derives ultimately from an Indo-European word, one pronounced something like *leikw* and meaning *to leave*. This Indo-European word became the Latin *linquere*, meaning *to abandon*, which then became *relinquere*. The Latin verb *relinquere* then became the Latin noun *reliquum*, meaning *something left behind*, and it was this word that became the French *relique*. English adopted this French word as *relic* and first used it to refer to legendary chunks of Christian history such as the bones of St. George; the word then acquired, in the late sixteenth century, its sense of *leftovers* or food left behind at the table. Amazingly, the word *eleven* derives in part from the same Indo-European source as *relic*: *eleven* literally means *one left over*, this being a shortened way of saying *ten and one left over*. See also *relevé*.

legume

Considering that life is essentially a "gathering in" of things we need for survival, it's not surprising that nearly thirty English words have derived from *legere*, a Latin verb originally meaning *to gather*. Some of the descendants of *legere* include *legend*, *lecture*, *intelligent*, *neglect*, and *legume*. With *legume* it is fairly easy to see the semantic connection: legumes are plants such as beans or peas whose pods may be picked or "gathered" by hand; this, at least, is how the ancient Romans defined such plants, and accordingly they used *legere* to form the vegetable name *legumen*. This Latin word was then adopted by French as *legume*, which was subsequently adopted by English in the late seventeenth century. The idea of *gathering* is also fairly close to the surface of the word *intelligent*, intelligence being the ability to "gather in" data from the outside world. One way of gathering such data is by reading, and in fact *to read* eventually displaced *to gather* as the primary meaning of the Latin *legere*. Thus, the word *legend* literally means *something to be read*, the word *lecture* literally means *about to read*, and the word *neglect* literally means *something unread* or, more broadly, *something not gathered in.*

lemon

Closely related to each other as species, the lemon and the lime also derive their names from the same source: the Arabic *limah*, meaning *lime*. This Arabic word entered French as *lime*, which was then adopted by English in the early seventeenth century. *Limah* also, however, gave rise to another Arabic word, *limun*, which the Arabs invented as a name for a slightly different citrus fruit. *Limun* was borrowed by Medieval French as *limon*, which English adopted in the early fifteenth century as *lemon*. In French, the word *limon* persists in *limonade*, a beverage made from lemons, but for the most part the French have replaced the word *limon* with the word *citron*. The French derived this *citron* by taking *citrus*—the Latin name of another sort of sour fruit—and changing its spelling to *citron* to make its ending resemble that of *limon*. In the early sixteenth century, English borrowed the French *citron* as the name for a fruit that resembles, but is distinct from, both the lemon and the lime. To complicate things further, the French refer to this same fruit—the English *citron*—as the *cedrat*. All these sour fruits are high in vitamin C and thus British sailors once ate them on long voyages to avoid getting scurvy; when these British sailors voyaged to North America or Australia, they were called *lime-eaters*, which became, in the late nineteenth century, the derogatory term *limey*.

lemonade

The *ade* in *lemonade* is not there because the drink comes to your "aid" when you are parched. Rather, it is a suffix meaning *produced from*, and was first used to form the name of a beverage in the late fourteenth century when *pomade* appeared, a drink made from "pommes," or what we now call *apples*. The name *pomade* did not, however, outlive the fourteenth century due to the greater popularity of the word *cider*. *Lemonade* appeared three hundred years later, an adoption of the French *limonade*. After another two hundred years, the popularity of lemonade led to the appearance between 1882 and 1892 of *limeade*, *cherryade*, and *gingerade*, none of which ever achieved the currency of *lemonade*.

lentil

If you have less than perfect eyesight, you probably have, at this very moment, two lentils perched on either side of your nose—at least you do in so far as the English word *lens* is a direct adoption of the Latin word *lens*, meaning *lentil*. *Lens* was adopted by seventeenth century opticians because the convex shape of the lentil resembled that of the pieces of glass they cut to make telescopes and microscopes. The Latin *lens* is also, of course, the source of the English word *lentil*: in Late Latin the name of the leguminous plant was turned into a diminutive—*lenticula*, meaning *little lentil*—which was subsequently adopted by French as *lentille*. English then adopted this French word in the mid thirteenth century, changing the spelling to *lentil* in the process.

lettuce

When lettuce is cut it exudes a milky juice, which is why the ancient Romans called the plant *lactuca*, a name derived from the Latin *lac*, meaning *milk*. The word was introduced to English in the late thirteenth century, but the English did not commonly cultivate it in their gardens until the fifteenth century. Words related to *lettuce* include *lactic acid*, a substance that forms in milk when it sours, and *galaxy*, so called because the distant regions of our own galaxy—the Milky Way—stretch across the night sky like a creamy band.

licorice

Although not often used in gastronomy, the juice of the licorice root has been widely used to make candies and throat lozenges since at least the Middle Ages. The name of this plant looks as if it might be related to the word *liquor*, a resemblance even more striking in Britain where *licorice* is usually spelt *liquorice*. However, the resemblance between these two words—*licorice* and *liquor*—is only superficial, based merely on a misapprehension of the plant's original Greek name, *glukurrhiza*, meaning *sweet root*. When the ancient Romans borrowed this Greek name, they would have normally rendered it into Latin by spelling it something like *glycyrrhiza*, which in fact was the spelling suggested by Pliny the Elder, an ancient Roman historian. Other Roman authors, however, made the mistake of thinking that the name of the plant had something to do with the extract or "liquor" derived from its root, and therefore they altered the spelling of its name from *glycyrrhiza* to *liquiritia*. It was this "reformed" spelling that caught on in Latin, and that later evolved into the Old French *licorece*. In the thirteenth century, English adopted the word from French, spelling it *licorice*, and then later, in the sixteenth century, respelt it as *liquorice*, again on the mistaken assumption that the word was related to *liquor*. The two forms, *licorice* and *liquorice*, have competed with each other ever since. Incidentally, the Old French name of the plant, *licorece*, underwent a further strange change as it continued to develop in French: the *l* at the beginning of the word and the *r* in the middle traded places, a phonological process known as metathesis. The result of the switch was *recolisse*, which developed into the Modern French word for *licorice*—*réglisse*.

liebesknochen

Centuries ago, a woman who wanted to have a child might munch on a liebesknochen, a cream-filled, German pastry whose name literally means *bone of love* (the German *liebe* is related to the English *love* and to the Latin *libido*; the German *knochen*, meaning *bone*, is related to the English *knuckle*). Unlike edible underwear, a mere novelty item in our culture, liebesknochen originated as a genuine fertility remedy for childless couples. If, however, this creamy pastry did not do the trick, a barren Fraulein might also try vielliebchen, a cake whose appearance left little to the imagination: long and tube-like with two almonds ornamenting one end. The cake's name derives from the German *viel liebchen*, literally meaning *many darlings*. The ancient Romans had similar fertility foods: *coliphila*, meaning *love food*, and *siligone*, meaning *bread seed*, were both breads shaped like genitalia.

Lima bean

Lima beans take their name from the city in Peru where, hundreds of years ago, they were first cultivated. In turn, the city of Lima acquired its name when Spanish explorers mispronounced the name *Rimak*, which is what the Quechua, the native people of the region, originally called their city. Further back in history, *Rimak* derived its name from *rima*, a Quechua word meaning *to speak*, so named because the city was the site of a temple where Quechuan priests spoke to their gods. In a sense, therefore, *Lima bean* literally means *speaking bean*.

limburger

See *hamburger*.

limpopo

The Limpopo is a river in Africa that flows east to the Indian Ocean. Rudyard Kipling's description of it in *The Jungle Book* as "the great, grey, green, greasy Limpopo" was also thought, by some of his friends, to be an accurate description of the avocado, a fruit that Kipling despised. Accordingly, *limpopo* became a nickname for the avocado.

lingel

See *spatula*.

linguine

Linguine in Italian means *little tongues*, which the strands of the thin, flat pasta resemble. Accordingly, *linguine* is related to the words *linguist*, *language*, and *cunnilingus* whose connections with the human tongue are even more apparent. The word *linguine* entered English in 1948.

linzertorte

See *Dobos torte*.

liquor

From the Latin verb *liquere*, meaning *to be fluid*, two other Latin words arose: *liquor*, a noun, and *liquidus*, an adjective. In the early thirteenth century, English borrowed the Latin noun, *liquor*, initially using the word to refer to any liquid substance, be it vinegar, honey, blood, or wine. By the fourteenth century, however, the now dominant sense of liquor—namely, *alcoholic beverage*—began to emerge. Near the end of the fourteenth century, English also borrowed the related Latin adjective, *liquidus*, changing the spelling to *liquid* in the process. For the next three hundred years, until the early eighteenth century, *liquid* was used in English only as an adjective, that is, only in phrases such as *liquid food* or *liquid honey*; in fact, using the word *liquid* as a noun—as in "He drank the liquid"—would have been as meaningless to a fifteenth century Englishman as "She drank the hot" is to us.

litre

All the linear measurements in the metric system are ultimately based upon the distance from the equator to the north pole: one ten-millionth of that distance is a metre, one ten-thousandth is a kilometer. These linear measurements even became the basis of liquid measurements: a litre is the volume represented by a cube whose edges measure one-tenth of a metre—in other words, a cube whose edges are one hundred-millionth the distance from the equator to the north pole. The ancient Greeks certainly did not have this volume in mind when they developed the word *litra*—the basis of our word *litre*—as the name of a Sicilian monetary unit. The name of this unit was borrowed by Classical Latin as *libra*, which evolved into the Medieval Latin *litra*; in 1793, the French borrowed the latter of these two forms—spelling it *litre*—as the name of a liquid measure in their newly invented metric system, a measure whose name was introduced to English in 1797. The other and older form of the Latin term—*libra*—also emerged in English, although in an unusual form. Whereas *litra* referred first to a monetary unit and later to a liquid measure, *libra* was used by the ancient Romans as the name of a measure of weight: it was a short form of *libra pondo*, a Latin phrase literally meaning *measurement by weight*. In the ninth century, the last half of this phrase, *pondo*, became the name of an English measurement of weight, the pound; the word *libra* was not forgotten, however, as it became in the fourteenth century the standard abbreviation for *pound—lb*. In the fourteenth century, *libra* was also adopted by English as the name of the seventh sign of the zodiac, a sign represented by a balance, a device used to measure weight.

liver

The liver, an organ that sometimes purifies the blood and sometimes is eaten fried with onions, is related to the word *live*, but only distantly: the words share a common Indo-European ancestor, a word pronounced something like *leip* and meaning *to be sticky*. *Liver* developed from this Indo-European source fairly directly: the bile secreted by the liver is thick and sticky, a fact that inspired the name of the organ. *Live*, on the other hand, developed from the same Indo-European source more circuitously. First, the word came to mean, in Germanic, *to remain*, the connection being that sticky things remain in place; next, the word shifted to mean *to live*, the connection this time being that "living" is a kind of "remaining" (just as "dying" is a "passing away"). It was this sense that the word possessed when it appeared in Old English as *libban*, a form that came to be respelt as *live* by the fourteenth century. Incidentally, the word *liver* is also the direct source of the name *Liverpool*, the famous city on the river Mersey. The name of the city literally means *livered pool*, the adjective *livered* meaning *clotted and sticky like a liver*, and likely referring to the weeds clotting the river when the city was founded.

loaf

The most amazing fact about the history of the word *loaf* is not where it came from, but where it went: it became part of two Old English compounds that eventually evolved into the words *lord* and *lady*. The word *loaf* was first recorded in the tenth century, when it was spelt and pronounced *hlaf*. Back then, loaves of bread were what made the world go round: if you had none, you died, and so the powerful person who supplied you with your loaves came to be known as your *hlaf-weard*, an Old English compound meaning *loaf-ward* or *guardian of the loaves*. *Hlaf-weard* became *hlaford*, and then in the fourteenth century was further shortened to *lord*. The aristocratic counterpart to *lord*—*lady*—developed in a similar manner: it began as *hlaf-dige*, the *dige* part being an Old English word that meant *to knead*. The *hlaf-dige* or *loaf-kneader* was as important as her husband in so far as she was responsible for making the household's loaves. *Hlaf-dige* then became *laefdi*, before shortening further to *lady* in the fourteenth century. Other languages have developed titles of respect in similar ways. In Denmark and Sweden, for example, a servant would not call her employer her *mistress* but rather her *madmoder*, a term that literally means *meat mother*. Further back in its history, the Old English *hlaf* developed from an even older word that meant *to rise high*, the connection being that a loaf rises while it bakes. *Hlaf* acquired its modern spelling, *loaf*, in the fifteenth century.

lobster

Until the eighteenth century when Swedish scientist Carolus Linnaeus established the modern system of classifying animals, philosophers and scientists used a zoological system devised in the fourth century B.C. by Aristotle, who began by dividing animals into those with red blood and those with not-red blood. This rough and ready approach to classification explains why the ancient Romans had no compunctions about giving the locust and the lobster the same name: *locusta*. It did not matter to the Romans that locusts live on land and lobsters in the sea, nor did it matter that lobsters weigh hundreds of times more than locusts—as far as they were concerned, the shape and greenish blood of the two creatures made them similar enough to share a single name. In English, the Latin *locusta* has given rise to both the word *locust* and the word *lobster*. The older of these two words is *lobster*, which appeared in the tenth century as the Old English *lopystre*; this odd spelling may have arisen as people conflated *locusta* (the Latin name of the ten-legged shellfish) with *loppe* (the Old English name of the eight-legged spider), and ended up with *lopystre*. By the fifteenth century, further changes in spelling and pronunciation led to the current form of the word, *lobster*. In contrast, *locust* has undergone very few changes in form and pronunciation: when the word was adopted in the thirteenth century, the *a* was dropped from the original Latin *locusta* and the word has remained unchanged ever since.

long-john

See *bismark.*

long pig

The culinary term *long pig* arose as an English translation of a Maori name for human flesh prepared for the dinner table. It is unclear whether the Maoris thought humans resembled pigs because of their delicious flavour or because of their beastly behaviour. The eighteenth-century satirist Jonathon Swift, however, asserted in *A Modest Proposal* that pigs "are no way comparable in taste or magnificence to a well-grown, fat, yearling child, which roasted whole will make a considerable figure at a lord mayor's feast or any other public entertainment."

loquat

The pear-shaped fruit known as the *loquat* takes its name from the Cantonese *luh kwat,* meaning *rush orange,* so named because it grows best in marshy soil among rushes. One of the Cantonese words represented in *loquat* also appears in *kumquat,* a small citron fruit whose name means *gold orange. Kumquat* appeared in English at the end of the seventeenth century, *loquat* in the early nineteenth.

love apple

See *tomato.*

lox

See *lax.*

lukewarm

Water can exist at many different temperatures, but only three of those temperatures have specific names: *freezing, boiling,* and *lukewarm.* Further, while *freezing* and *boiling* are determined by the molecular structure of the water itself (becoming a solid at 0° Celsius and a vapour at 100° Celsius), *lukewarm* is uniquely determined by the body temperature of the human who is dipping his or her toe into the water—about 38° Celsius. The word *lukewarm* first appeared in English at the end of the fourteenth century; before that, dating back to the early thirteenth century, the word *luke* was used by itself to signify the same temperature. In origin, the word *luke* derives from the Old English word *hleow*, meaning *warm* or *tepid*, which dates back at least to the tenth century. Beyond that, the origin of *hleow* is unknown, apart from its being related to the word *lee*, meaning *shelter*: mountains, for example, always have a *lee side*, a side sheltered from the wind and therefore warmer. Unrelated to the *luke* in *lukewarm* is the *Luke* in *Matthew, Mark, Luke, and John*; that biblical name derives from the Greek *loukas*, meaning *man from Lucania*, Lucania being a coastal region of southern Italy.

lunch

From the mid fourteenth to the late sixteenth century, the repast we now call *lunch* was known not as *luncheon* but as *nuncheon*. The word *nuncheon* developed from *noon schenche*, the word *schenche* having derived from an Old English word meaning *drink*. A *noon schenche*, therefore, was literally a drink taken at noon, though naturally a bit of food came to be eaten with it as well. (Incidentally, the Old English *schenche* is related to the word *shin*, probably because the shinbones of animals were once used as pipes to draw drinks from barrels; likewise, the Latin word for *shinbone*—*tibia*—was sometimes used by the ancient Romans to denote a musical pipe or flute.) In the late sixteenth century, two synonyms for *nuncheon* appeared at almost the same time, *lunch* and *luncheon*. The fact that *luncheon* seems to have been formed by combining *lunch* and *nuncheon* suggests that *lunch* is the source of *luncheon* and not the other way around. *Lunch*, in fact, seems to have developed from the word *lump* in the same way that *hunch*, as in *hunchback*, derived from *hump*; a lunch was therefore originally a *lump* of food or—as the eighteenth-century lexicographer, Samuel Johnson, more precisely defined it—as much food as one hand can hold. At the same time, the development of *lunch* from *lump* may have been helped along by the existence of a Spanish word, *lonja*, meaning *slice*: the first recorded use of *lunch* in English, in fact, is as a direct translation of *lonja* in the Spanish phrase *lonja de tocino*, which we would now translate as *slice of bacon*. See also *taco*.

lurcate

See *slurp*.

macaroni

The pasta called *macaroni* derives its name from the Italian word *maccaroni*, originally the name of a food made from a paste of groats, a coarsely ground grain. This Italian word developed from *makaria*, a Late Greek name for a broth made from barley groats, the Greeks in turn having formed this name from an older word meaning *blessedness*. Why the Greeks associated this food with blessedness is puzzling, but no doubt they would be equally mystified by some of our modern food names, such as *angel food cake*. The Italian *maccaroni*—or rather its singular form, *maccarone*—also gave the macaroon its name; like macaroni pasta, the macaroon—a small, crunchy cake—is made from a paste, albeit a paste of ground almonds, not groats. Both *macaroni* and *macaroon* appeared in English at the beginning of the seventeenth century, but even a hundred and fifty years later macaroni remained an uncommon food in England. Accordingly, when a troop of young men decided, around 1750, that they were too sophisticated to eat native English food, they founded the *Macaroni Club* to manifest their ardent preference for foreign foods and manners. The affected tendencies of the members of this club—exemplified by their penchant for wearing two watches on the same arm—were so renowned that *macaroni* soon became a term of contempt, a synonym for *fop* or *affected behaviour*. This sense of the word is immortalized in *Yankee Doodle*, a song in which a certain Mr. Doodle puts a feather in his cap and "calls it macaroni."

macaroon

See *macaroni*.

mace

Just as the singular form of *pea* was once *pease*, the singular of the spice now known as *mace* was once *maces*—a medieval kitchen would therefore have bottles of pepper, garlic, and *maces*. In the sixteenth century, people began to mistakenly think that *maces* was plural, as if it were a seasoning made up of several kinds of *mace*, and so they created a singular form that had never before existed—*mace*, the form it has retained to this day. The word *mace*—or rather *maces*—appeared in English in the mid fourteenth century, but its ulterior history is unknown.

mackerel

In the fourteenth century, and for many centuries after, the word *mackerel* meant two things: it referred to a North Atlantic fish, an important food source for the northern European nations; and it referred to someone who was a pimp or, as he would be called back then, a pander. One explanation that accounts for the two senses of the word is this: the Dutch word *makelaar*, meaning *broker* or *pedlar*, was adopted by Old French as *maquerel* and was used to mean *pimp*, a person who peddles flesh. This word was then adopted into Middle English as *mackerel*, still meaning *pimp*, but then also became the name of the fish because of the popular but unfounded belief that every spring mackerels guide female herring through the ocean to their mates. Although this explanation is tidy, it is not necessarily correct; it is possible, for instance, that the belief about mackerels leading female herrings to their mates arose as an explanation for why the fish had a name that meant *pander*; in other words, the name may have led to the belief, instead of the other way around. If so, then *mackerel* the fish and *mackerel* the pimp may simply be distinct, unrelated words, in which case the origin of *mackerel* the fish remains unknown. What is known, however, is that the expression *Holy mackerel!* arose as a euphemism for *Holy Mary!*, a blasphemous exclamation of incredulity; similarly, *Dog gone it!* arose as a substitute for *God damn it!*

made dish

A made dish is one composed of several ingredients, as opposed to just one. Thus, a bowl of steamed peas is not a made dish, but cannelloni stuffed with cheese and served with sauce is. The term was first used at the beginning of the seventeenth century; although most chefs respect the skill required to prepare a good made dish, seventeenth century authors generally used the term as a dismissive metaphor, a synonym for *hodgepodge* or *farrago*.

Madeira

Although Madeira is a white wine, it has an amber tint because it is heated in its cask before being bottled. The wine takes its name from the Portuguese island where it is produced, and the island in turn was named Madeira—the Portuguese word for *timber*—because it was covered with thick forests. Ultimately, the Portuguese *Madeira* descends from a word the ancient Romans used to denote timber and other building materials, the Latin *materia*; in English, *materia* evolved into *material* and *matter*, both of which emerged in the mid fourteenth century, about two hundred years before the name of the wine was adopted in the sixteenth century. In French, *Madeira* also gave rise to a term used by wine connoisseurs, *madérisé*, applied to a white wine that has passed its prime and has started to take on the amber tint of Madeira. About fifty years ago, this bit of wine terminology was adopted by English as *maderize*.

maize

See *corn*.

malmeny

See *bouce Jane*.

mandible

A marshmallow is a highly mandible food; the hard candy called the jaw-breaker is not. The word *mandible*, meaning *chewable*, derives from the Latin *mandere*, meaning *to chew*; the word developed this meaning in the mid seventeenth century, although a hundred years earlier it had been adopted by anatomists as the name for the lower jaw. A related Latin word, *manducare*, is the source of the English word *manducate*, meaning *to chew food*, and is also the source of the French word *manger*, meaning *to eat*. *Masticate*, meaning *to chew food to a pulp* developed from a different source, namely, the Latin *masticha*, a word denoting a chewable tree resin.

manger

See *blancmange* and *mandible*.

manna

According to the Book of Exodus, manna, the food miraculously provided for the Israelites after they left Egypt, takes its name from the question the Israelites asked each other when they discovered it upon the ground: "Man hu?"—which, translated from Aramaic, means something like "What is this?" However, the Arabic word *mann*—the name of a sweet, edible sap exuded by the tamarisk plant—may also be the source of the Hebrew *man*, which is what *manna* was originally called in the early Greek and Latin versions of the Bible (the Hebrew *man* is, of course, no relation to the English word that means *male adult*). In its present form, as *manna*, the word first appeared at the end of the ninth century when Alfred, King of the West Saxons, translated a Latin work by Pope Gregory into Old English.

maraschino cherry

Although commercially produced maraschino cherries are one of the sweetest, most cloying foods ever invented, their name actually derives from an Italian word meaning *bitter*. From this word—*amaro*—the Italians derived the name *amarasca*, which they gave to a kind of sour, black cherry. In time, *amarasca* was shortened to *marasca*, which also became the name of a liqueur made from the fermented juice of the marasca cherry. English acquired the name of this liqueur in the late eighteenth century, and then used it at the beginning of this century in *maraschino cherry*, the name of a cherry marinated in the Italian liqueur. In the 1920s American manufacturers of maraschino cherries invented a process that used a solution of corn syrup and fructose, instead of real maraschino liqueur: the result was the modern, sweet, maraschino cherry. Incidentally, *amaretto*—the name of a liqueur made from almonds and apricot pits—also derives from the same Italian source as *maraschino*: *amaretto* is a diminutive of *amaro* and therefore literally means *a little bitter*. The almond-flavoured liqueur probably also gave its name to an almond cookie now known as the *amaretti*. The story that these cookies get their name from a similar sounding Italian word meaning *little loves—amoretti*—is unfounded.

marchpane

see *marzipan*.

Mardi gras

See *carnival*.

margarine

Margarine exists today thanks to Napoleon III (nephew of the more famous Napoleon Bonaparte) who offered a prize in the early 1860s to anyone who could create a butter substitute, a cattle plague having made all dairy products in France scarce and expensive. The eventual perfector of the product named it *oleomargarine*, from *oléine*, the French name for a common natural fat, and from *margarique*, a pearl-coloured fatty acid whose name had earlier been developed from the Greek *margaron*, meaning *pearl*. It was with this cumbersome name, *oleomargarine*, that the bread-spread first became known in England in the 1870s. Within a few years, however, the name *butterine* had also become familiar, a change effected by the margarine producers, who wanted to associate their product with real butter. In response, butter-makers succeeded in 1887 in forcing their competitors by law to change their product's name to something that did not allude to the word *butter* at all: *margarine*.

Margarita

At least a dozen men have laid claim to having invented and given their girlfriend's name—*Margarita*—to the cocktail made from tequila, Triple Sec, and lime juice; not wanting to disbelieve any of them, I assume they all had girlfriends name Margarita and that they all invented the drink's recipe independently. Although people remember drinking this cocktail as far back as the 1930s, its name did not appear in print until 1965. Since the 1920s, however, *Margarita* has also been used as the name of a Spanish wine. Like the word *margarine*, the name *Margarita* and its English counterpart *Margaret* derive from the Greek *margaron*, meaning *pearl*. See also *margarine*.

marinade

A marinade is a seasoned liquid in which meat, fish, or vegetables are steeped until they acquire a desired flavour. Nowadays, marinades are usually made from oil or vinegar, but the original marinades, dating back thousands of years, were simply salted water, often, in fact, mere sea water, which helped to preserve whatever was being marinated. This sea water was the inspiration for the word *marinade*, which derives, through French and Spanish, from the Latin *marina*, meaning *of the sea*. *Marina*, in turn, derives from the Latin word for *sea*—*mare*—which is also the source of the English *maritime* and *mermaid* (meaning *sea-maid*). The word *marinade* did not appear in English until the early eighteenth century, but its verb form, *marinate*, was in use in the early seventeenth century.

marjoram

See *oregano*.

marmalade

The jam known as *marmalade* in English is known as *marmelada* in Spanish, *marmelade* in French, *marmellata* in Italian, *marmelad* in Swedish, and *marmelade* in German, Dutch, and Danish. These words all derive from the Portuguese name for the jam, *marmelada*, which took its name from the Portuguese word *marmelo*, meaning *quince*, the fruit originally used in marmalade. This Portuguese fruit-name had earlier been derived from the Latin word *melimelum*, literally meaning *honey apple*, a name the ancient Romans borrowed from the ancient Greeks, who had bestowed it upon the fruit produced by grafting apple and quince. Another popular, but mistaken, explanation of the word's origin is that it derives from *Marie malade*, meaning *sick Mary*. According to this folk etymology, Mary Queen of Scots could only eat one thing when feeling under the weather: a conserve made of oranges, which was subsequently named after her. Unfortunately for this folk etymology, however, the word *marmalade* appeared in English in 1524, eighteen years before Mary was born.

marshmallow

After a hard day of waging war with sword and battle axe, the ancient kings of England—Ethelred or Arthur, for example—no doubt comforted themselves with marshmallows. To them, however, marshmallows were not bite-size snacks of sugar and starch; rather, they were swamp plants whose sweet roots yielded a medicinal extract. For about eighteen centuries this plant was the only thing that the word *marshmallow* referred to; then, in the late nineteenth century, someone used the extract from the marshmallow root to make a sweet, spongy confection, and thus the modern marshmallow was born. The word *marshmallow* literally means *a mallow found in a marsh*, a mallow being a wild plant with a hairy stem and purple flowers. Beyond this, *marsh* derives from an Indo-European source meaning *sea*, a source that also developed into the Latin word for sea, *mare*, from which English derives *marine* and *maritime*; the word *mallow*, on the other hand, derives from the Latin name of the plant, *malva*.

martini

The gin and vermouth cocktail known as the *martini* may simply take its name from Martini and Rossi, an Italian winery producing vermouth since 1829. However, other explanations for the cocktail's name abound, including that it was invented in 1910 by Martini di Taggia di Arma, a bartender at the Knickerbocker

Hotel in New York, or that it was invented by Julio Richelieu in Martinez, California. Whatever its immediate source, however, the name *Martini* means *war-like*, at least in so far as it is a derivative of *Mars*, the Roman god of war. First referred to by name at the end of the nineteenth century, the original martini recipe called for a gin to vermouth ratio of two to one; beginning in the 1920s, this ratio became even more disproportionate, the typical modern martini now having a gin to vermouth ratio of about six to one.

marzipan

The almond flavoured confection now known as *marzipan* was originally known in English as *marchpane*, a name that probably traces its origin back to an Arabic term meaning *seated king*. This Arabic term—*mawthaban*—was originally applied by the Arabs to an Italian coin depicting Christ sitting on a throne. The Italians themselves then borrowed this name, spelling it *marzapane*, and also used it to refer to the coin. Later on, they came to apply the coin's name to fancy boxes of candy, the connection perhaps being that such boxes were often decorated, like the coin, with cameos or depictions of classical figures. The Italians eventually transferred the word *marzapane* from the box to the confections it contained, and it was at this point, around the fifteenth century, that English adopted the word, spelling it *marchpane*. This spelling persisted in English until the nineteenth century when marzipan started to be commonly imported from Germany; as a result, the German word for the confection—*marzipan*, which of course developed from the same source as *marchpane*—eventually became the standard English name.

mason jar

Used by millions to preserve fruit, vegetables, and even meat, mason jars take their name from their inventor, John Mason, who patented the air-tight jar in 1858. Mason's own surname likely came from one of his ancestors being a mason, that is, as a stone-cutter. The term *freemason* arose in the fourteenth century to describe a mason who was legally permitted to travel to other districts to work on a building under construction; other masons, and other artisans in general, were allowed to work only in their own local district.

matrimonial cake

See *wedding cake*.

mayonnaise

Although mayonnaise is fairly easy to make—simply blend egg yolks, oil, vinegar, and seasonings—etymologists have had great difficulty ascertaining the origin of its name. Some have suggested the name originated as a corruption of *Bayonnaise*, a sauce named after the town of Bayonne in France; others have suggested it derives from the Old French word for egg yolk, *moyeu*; and still others have proposed that it arose from the French verb *manier*, meaning *to stir*. More likely than any of these three, however, is that the sauce was named after Mahon, a port on the island of Minorca that the Duke of Richelieu captured in 1756. To commemorate the Duke's victory, but no doubt also to benefit from association with it, French chefs named their new sauce *mahonnaise*; later on, having forgotten about the Duke's immortal triumph, the French respelt the word as *mayonnaise*, the form English adopted in the mid nineteenth century. The port of Mahon, incidentally, takes its name from Magon, a Carthaginian general who helped his brother Hannibal wage war against the Roman Empire.

mead

See *hydromel*.

meal

The *meal* in *three course meal* and the *meal* in *oatmeal* have no linguistic connection to each other. Like the word *meat*, the *meal* that refers to breakfast, lunch, and dinner derives ultimately from an Indo-European source meaning *measure*. Because people have long eaten at appointed or "measured" times—such as noon—this ancient word for *measure* developed into the Old English word *mael*, meaning *appointed eating time*. First recorded in the ninth century, the Old English *mael* became our modern *meal* and even today its original sense of *appointed time* persists so strongly that most people hesitate to call food eaten at an unconventional hour—such as three in the afternoon—a *meal*. Closely related to the culinary *meal* is the *meal* in *piecemeal*, literally meaning *to measure out piece by piece*. In contrast, the *meal* in *oatmeal* and *cornmeal* derives from a completely different source, namely, an Indo-European word meaning *to grind*, since foods such as oatmeal are produced by grinding grain. Also from this Indo-European source developed words such as *mill*, the place where grain is ground, and, via Latin, *molar*, the name of the teeth that grind food to smithereens. Because grain meal is soft and utterly inoffensive, *meal* may in turn have given rise to the word *mellow* (which, surprisingly, has no connection to the equally soft and inoffensive *marshmallow*). See also *meat* and *noon*.

mealie-mealie

At the beginning of the nineteenth century, Dutch settlers in what is now South Africa borrowed the Portuguese word *milje*—meaning *millet*, a kind of grain—and from it formed the word *mielie*, which they first bestowed upon the grain known in North America as *corn* and later bestowed upon a cake made from this corn. Eventually, because the grain and cake now had the same name—*mielie*—the corn-meal required to make the cake became known as *mielie-mielie*, literally meaning *corn for corn cake*. This word was respelt as *mealie-mealie* in the middle of the nineteenth century. *Mieli* also was combined with the word *pap*, meaning *gruel*, to form *mielipap*, a corn porridge that became a staple in the diet of millions of impoverished South Africans. See also *pap* and *couscous*.

meat

The essential difference between the words *meat* and *flesh* is that we eat the former and are the latter; in other words, although the two words denote more or less the same thing, we prefer to think of the pork chop on our plate as meat, not flesh, and we prefer to think of ourselves as flesh and blood, not meat and blood. However, the two words have shifted and shared meanings many times over the centuries. The word *flesh*, first recorded in the ninth century, originally referred specifically to the part of an animal eaten as food; it was not until the eleventh century that its meaning widened and it came to signify animal tissue in general, whether prepared for the table or left on the animal. On the other hand, *meat*, which is first recorded in the tenth century, originally referred to a portion of food of any kind, whether it was made from animals or vegetables or fish or fowl; a thousand years ago, therefore, the only things you swallowed were meat and drink. It was not for another four hundred years, in the fourteenth century, that *meat* narrowed its meaning and came to signify, as it still does, flesh used for culinary purposes. Etymologically, the two words are unrelated. *Flesh* developed from an Indo-European word, pronounced something like *pel*, that meant *split*, the slaughtering of an animal for its flesh necessitating that you split it open. The word *flitch*, meaning *a side of bacon*, derives from the same Indo-European source as *flesh*. The word *meat*, on the other hand, developed from another Indo-European word, pronounced something like *mat*, that meant *measure*, the connection being that *meat* originally signified a portion—or measure—of food. This Indo-European word is also the source of *meat's* many relatives, including *menstruation* and *moon* (both of which undergo measurable cycles), *month* (a unit of time measured by the cycle of the moon), and *meal* (food eaten at a *measured* or set time). The word *meat* is also closely related to the word *mate*, meaning *friend*: *mate* derives from the Old English word *gemetta*, meaning *together with meat*—in other words, a mate is someone with whom you share meat. See also *meal* and *dark meat*.

Melba toast

Not one, but two, dishes have been named after the turn-of-the-century opera diva, Dame Nellie Melba. The first dish to acquire her name, Melba toast, dates back to 1897 when Melba stopped in at the London's Savoy Hotel and ordered several slices of toast which, by mistake, were served to her without butter; Melba so enjoyed the dry, crunchy slices that the owner of the hotel, César Ritz, bestowed her name on them and made them a standard item on his menu. Somewhat strangely, however, Melba never refers to Melba toast in her 1925 autobiography, even though it was well-established in restaurants around the world by then. In that autobiography she does, however, recount how her name became attached to the dessert item known as *peach Melba*, made by poaching peaches in vanilla syrup and serving them with ice cream and raspberry sauce. According to Dame Melba, the chef at the Savoy Hotel—the same one who had previously served her dry toast—invented the dish and named it *peach Melba* after she dined at the Savoy in 1904; the chef himself, however, insisted that he had stopped working at the Savoy in 1898, and that he added the dish to the menu at another hotel, the Ritz Carlton, simply because the diva was constantly demanding peaches and ice cream for dessert. The origin of Melba's own name is clearer: born in Australia as Helen Mitchell, she invented her stage name as a short form of *Melbourne*. In turn, Australia's Melbourne was named after Melbourne, England, a place whose original name—*mill burn*—means *mill river*.

melon

Alexandre Dumas, the nineteenth-century author of *The Three Musketeers*, so loved melons that he offered to give all his published manuscripts to the French municipality of Cavaillon in exchange for supplying him with twelve melons a year for the rest of his life. This love of the melon was perhaps shared by the Greeks, who cultivated the fruit and called it *melopepon*, a name they derived from their word *melon*, meaning *apple*, and *pepon*, a word denoting a variety of gourd eaten only when fully ripe; the ancient Greeks, therefore, considered the melon an *apple-gourd*. In Latin, the Greek name of this fruit was borrowed in an abbreviated form, *melo*, which evolved into the French *melon* before entering English at the end of the fourteenth century. The *pepon* part of the Greek *melopepon* was not utterly lost, however. It was adopted into English, also at the end of the fourteenth century, as a name for the large fruit we now know as *pumpkin*. Later, in the mid sixteenth century, *pepon* acquired a rival when English borrowed the word *pompion* from French, *pompion* itself having evolved from the Latin *pepon*. By the mid seventeenth century, *pompion* had not only driven *pepon* out of existence, it had also undergone a transformation of spelling and pronunciation of its own, ending up as the familiar *pumpkin*. Finally, in the mid nineteenth century, *pumpkin* gave rise to *pumpkinification*, a word meaning *extreme and uncritical glorification*. The term originated as a translation of the Latin *apocolocyntosis*, used by Seneca, a Roman philosopher and dramatist who parodied the apotheosis of the emperor Claudius Caesar as a transformation into a pumpkin.

mensa

In 1962, a group of smart people, tired of each other's company, decided to form a club for people with IQ's above 148 so that they could meet other smart people of whom they were not yet tired. Certain that the name *Smart People's Club* would alienate the general public (whom they feared) they chose the name *Mensa*, which is Latin for *table*. The name was not intended to suggest their penchant for dinner parties, but rather to demonstrate that they all knew what the Latin word for *table* was.

menu

From the Latin word *minuere*, meaning *to lessen*, a whole family of English words has developed: in addition to *menu* they include *diminish*, *minute*, *minor*, *minus*, *mince*, *minuet*, and even, through a misunderstanding, *minnow*. The Latin adjective *minutus*, meaning *small*, was formed from *minuere*, and it was this word that directly gave rise to *minute*—meaning a small part of time— and *minutes*—meaning the small, detailed notes taken during a meeting. *Minutus* also developed into the French word *menu*, which restaurateurs applied to a small list of set meals as opposed to the complete list of individual dishes represented on the *carte* or *card*. Naturally, the paired terms *menu* and *carte* entered English at about the same time, early in the nineteenth century. The French, incidentally, also used the word *menu* to mean *small fish* and this sense of the word may have influenced the pronunciation of the unrelated Middle English word *menawe*, the name of the tiny fish we now call the minnow. Finally, the French *menu*, not in its sense of *list of food* or *tiny fish* but in its earlier sense of *small and detailed*, gave rise to a dance known as the *menuet* characterized by short, dainty steps. The dance and its name, respelt as *minuet*, were introduced to England in the late eighteenth century. See also *mincemeat* and *table d'hôte*.

meringue

The sweet foam made by whisking together egg whites and sugar takes its name, *meringue*, from its place of origin, Mehrinyghen, formerly in Switzerland but now part of Germany. The name was adopted into French as *meringue*, which English subsequently borrowed in the early eighteenth century. Recipes for lemon meringue pie date back at least to the beginning of this century.

merry thought

See *wishbone*.

mess

As a culinary term, the word *mess* persists only in biblical usage, as in the "mess of potage" for which Esau sold his birthright, and in military usage, as in *mess hall*. The word originally referred simply to a portion of food, enough to fill one's belly, and derived ultimately from the Latin word *mittere*, meaning *to send*. From this word the Vulgar Latin *missum* was formed, meaning *something sent*, especially food sent to the table. *Missum* entered French as *mes* before being adopted by English as *mess* at the beginning of the fourteenth century. Because the word *mess* referred indiscriminately to any sort of food—literally anything, good or bad, "sent" to the table—it began to decline in status, and by the early eighteenth century had developed the sense of *animal fodder*. Those who have fed slop to pigs or who remember what a "dog's breakfast" looked like before the invention of Puppy Chow will know that domestic animals have often been fed a farrago of jumbled leftovers; as a result of this association with mixed-up animal food, *mess* developed its now primary sense of *jumble* or *confusion*. Culinary words such as *stew*—as in "We're in a real stew now"—and *hodgepodge*—originally a dish of mixed meat and vegetables—underwent a similar shift or expansion in meaning. Another word that also developed from the Latin *mittere* is the Catholic term *mass*. In the fifth and sixth centuries, the priest concluded the Eucharistic service by saying "Ite, missa est," meaning "Go, it is the sending-away." Eventually, worshippers who understood Latin poorly began to assume that *missa*, which evolved into the English *mass* before the tenth century, was the actual name of the service. See also *balderdash* and *hodgepodge*.

meunière

See *à la meunière*.

mezzaluna

This crescent-shaped chopping knife takes its name from the Italian *mezza luna*, meaning *half-moon*. The Italian *mezza*—or its masculine counterpart, *mezzo*—are more familiar as musical terms as in *mezzo soprano* (a voice half-way between a soprano and a contralto) and *mezza orchestra* (a musical composition requiring only half the orchestra). *Luna* derives from the same Latin source that gave English *lunar* and *lunatic* (originally, a person made mad by the moon).

milk

In 1818, Abraham Lincoln's mother died of "the slows," a disease caused by contaminated milk; four years later, Louis Pasteur was born, a French chemist who invented pasteurization, a process that made milk much safer to drink. As a result of pasteurization, milk ceased, in the nineteenth century, to be treated with suspicion and instead enjoyed an immense surge in popularity, a popularity ensured by the invention of the refrigerator. These two developments also led, in the 1880s, to the invention of an icy refreshment known as the *milkshake*. Several thousand years before this, the word *milk* began to evolve from an Indo-European word, pronounced something like *melg*, that meant *to stroke*. This word was first applied to the action of milking a cow or similar animal, since the teats of the animal's udder are stroked downward to extract its milk. In time, this ancient word was applied to the nourishing liquid itself, at which point it entered various members of the Indo-European family of languages: in Old English, it became *meolc*, which evolved into *milk* by the thirteenth century; in Latin, it became the verb *mulgere*, meaning *to milk*, which eventually evolved into the word *emulsify*, meaning *to turn into a milky substance*.

milksop

See *soup*.

mim

See *pingle*.

mince

See *mincemeat*.

mincemeat

Apart from a bit of suet, there is about as much meat in mincemeat as there is in sweetmeat: none. Mincemeat (a mixture of fruits steeped in rum) and sweetmeats (sugared cakes and candies) acquired their apparently incongruous names in different ways. The word *mincemeat*, first used in English in the middle of the nineteenth century, developed from the earlier *minced meat*, first recorded in the last quarter of the sixteenth century. These original minced meats were actually made of meat, and lots of it: one early recipe called for a hare, a pheasant, two partridges, two pigeons, and two rabbits. The meat from these various species had to be chopped into small pieces—minced, in other words—before being mixed, spiced, and baked in a pastry shell. Over the next hundred years, however, what went into mincemeat changed dramatically: fruits and liquor replaced the mammals and fowl until finally, by the middle of the seventeenth century, the dish known as *mincemeat* had nothing in common with its progenitor except for the mincing of its ingredients. The word *mince*, incidentally, derives from the Latin word *minutus*, meaning *made small*, as does the word *menu*. Sweetmeats, on the other hand, never contained any meat in the first place. They acquired their name at the end of the fifteenth century when the word *meat* could mean not only *flesh* but also food in general. It is this now defunct sense of *meat* that is represented in the obsolete word *hardmeat* (animal fodder that is hard, like corn, instead of soft like grass) and in the obsolete word *spoon-meat* (liquefied food given to infants or invalids). See also *menu*, *sweetbread*, *candy*, and *meat*.

minestrone

Rather like Goldilocks, an Italian sitting down to dinner in a bear's house or a restaurant may choose from three versions of the same vegetable soup: a light, thin version called *minestrina*; a heavy, thick version called *minestrone*; and a middle, "just right" version called *minestra*. Of these three soups, the original is minestra, whose name simply means *something served*, deriving as it does from the Italian verb *ministrare*, meaning *to serve*. Likewise, *minestrone*, with its augmentative suffix, means *a big something served*, while *minestrina*, with its diminutive suffix, means *a little something served*. The first of these words to enter English was *minestra*, dating back to the mid eighteenth century; *minestrone* followed in the late nineteenth century, while *minestrina* appeared only in the last few decades. The Italian verb that is the source of these soups' names—*ministrare*—derives from a Latin verb spelt the same way and also meaning *to serve*; in turn, the Latin *ministrare* was formed from a Latin noun, *minister*, meaning *servant*, which was formed from a Latin adjective, *minus*, meaning *less*. This adjective became associated with servitude simply because less important people tended to serve more important people. Other English words that derive from the same Latin source as *minestrone* include *minister*, *administrator*, and *minstrel*, all of which once referred to people whose job was to serve someone else.

mint

Although mint—as in *Doublemint*, *Spearmint*, and *Peppermint*—has become the most popular flavour of chewing gum, Alexander the Great forbade his soldiers to chew mint leaves because his mentor, Aristotle, believed that the herb sexually excited the young men and thus diminished their desire to fight. Aristotle's notion may have had something to do with the ancient myth of Minthe, a beautiful nymph who so excited Pluto, god of the underworld, that his jealous wife, Proserpine, transformed her into the herb. This, at least according to ancient Greek etymology, is how the mint plant got its name. The Greek name, *minthe*, entered Latin as *mentha*, which evolved into the English *mint* in the tenth century, and was adopted again in the late nineteenth century as *menthol*, the name of a camphor-like substance added to various products. In the mid sixteenth century, another name for the common mint plant emerged—*spearmint*, so called because of its spear-shaped leaves. Incidentally, the other mint, the one that produces coins, derives its name from a completely different source: the Latin *Moneta*, an alternate name for the goddess Juno in whose temple money was coined (in turn, *Moneta* may derive from the Latin *monere*, meaning *to warn*).

miso

See *sushi*.

mocha

The strong Arabian coffee known as *mocha*, often used to flavour cakes and ice cream, takes its name from *Mocha*, the port on the Red Sea through which it was exported. Mocha was first referred to in English in the mid eighteenth century.

mochi

See *sushi*.

molasses

Throughout the eighteenth and nineteenth centuries, molasses was the most commonly used sweetener in North America because it was cheaper than sugar and was readily imported from the West Indies. Even in the early twentieth century, molasses remained popular until sugar prices dropped after World War I, about the same time that Boston suffered its "Great Molasses Flood." This flood occurred January 15, 1919 when a huge boiler of molasses exploded at the Purity Distilling Company: two million gallons of hot molasses poured into the streets of Boston, killing twenty-one people and—needless to say—slowing traffic to a near-standstill. This catastrophe belies the sweet origin of the word *molasses*, deriving as it does from the Latin *mel*, meaning *honey*. This Latin word gave rise to another—*mellaceum*, a name given to certain new wines because of their sweetness—which was borrowed by Portuguese as *melaço*. English then adopted this Portuguese word in the late sixteenth century as *molasses*, and bestowed it upon the syrup drained from raw sugar during refining. In the late seventeenth century, this word was more or less abandoned by the British, who started calling the same syrupy substance *treacle*; in North America, however, *molasses* has continued to be the usual name of the product. Deriving in part from the same Latin source as *molasses* is the word *mellifluous*, literally meaning *honey-flowing* and often applied to people with sweet, fluid voices. A more distant relative is the word *mildew*, a compound formed from *dew* and from *melith*, the Germanic cousin of the Latin *mel*. *Mildew* therefore means *honey-dew* and originated in the eleventh century as the name of the sticky resin secreted onto plant leaves by aphids. By the fourteenth century *mildew* shifted sense and came to refer, as it still does, to a fungus that grows on damp surfaces. See also *treacle* and *caramel*.

mortadella

Now seasoned with parsley, the lightly smoked, Italian sausage known as *mortadella* was originally seasoned with myrtle, a Mediterranean shrub whose pungent leaves taste somewhat like rosemary. Myrtle, in fact, is the source of the sausage's name, which derives from the Latin word for myrtle, *myrtus* (further back, the Latin *myrtus* derived from a Semitic source meaning *bitter*, a source that also gave rise to the word *myrrh*). From *myrtus* the ancient Romans formed the adjective *myrtatus*, meaning *seasoned with myrtle*, which was then used elliptically as a name for sausages seasoned in this manner. In Italian, the Latin name of the sausage was combined with the diminutive suffix *ella* to form *murtatella*, which evolved into *mortadella* before being adopted by English in the early seventeenth century. The earlier history of the word *myrtle*—or rather of the Latin *myrtus*—is unknown, but the shrub itself has been incorporated into many myths and superstitions. For instance, the ancient Romans believed that the tiny spots evident on myrtle leaves were the result of Phaedra wistfully puncturing a leaf with her hairpin while waiting under a myrtle tree for her tantalizing stepson. Less erotic and more pragmatic was the ancient Jewish belief that eating myrtle leaves confers the power to detect witches, a belief not so different from our modern conviction that carrots bestow good eye sight, and that fish are "brain food."

moscato

See *cantaloupe*.

mosy

Before applesauce acquired its current name, it was known as *moyse*, *moy*, *mose*, and *mosy*. These words, all of which derived from the Old English word *mos*, meaning *porridge*, ceased to be used at the end of the sixteenth century.

mousse

See *mushroom*.

mozzarella

Buffaloes are usually identified with the North American plains, but for centuries they have also roamed Italy, the birthplace of mozzarella, a cheese originally made from buffaloes' milk. The name of the cheese is also Italian in origin, deriving from *mozzare*, meaning *to cut off*, and the diminutive suffix *ella*. The cheese therefore takes its name from how it was usually sold: a little piece was cut off from a larger wheel of cheese (although it is unclear why this action was associated specifically with mozzarella but not with the dozens of other cheeses also sold in "cuts"). Mozzarella was first referred to in English early this century.

muesli

Early this century, Swiss nutritionists perfected a mixture of dried fruit, fresh fruit, and grains intended to serve as the ideal breakfast. They called the food *muesli*, a German word meaning *mixture* that found its way into English by 1939.

muffin

The word *muffin*—which in Great Britain refers to a flat, light roll raised with yeast and in North America to a globular quick-bread raised with baking powder—derives ultimately from the Medieval Latin *muffula*, meaning *fur-lined glove*; this word may have developed in turn from *mufro*, a Vulgar Latin name for a species of sheep lined not with fur, but wool. Whatever its own source, the Latin *muffula* developed into the French *moufle*, meaning mitten, which gave English its *muff*, a fur cylinder into which both hands are thrust for warmth. The softness and shape of these English muffs seems to have led someone, at the beginning of the eighteenth century, to bestow the diminutive *muffin* on the baking item. For similar reasons, the word *moufflet*—a word that refers to the softness of bread, as in *pain moufflet*—arose in French because of the softness of the warm, furry *moufles*.

muffineer

No home is complete without a muffineer, a small vessel with a perforated top from which sugar is sprinkled onto muffins. The word, first recorded in the early nineteenth century, was modelled after words such as *musketeer*, *auctioneer*, and *engineer* (but not *ginger beer*), the *eer* suffix meaning *to be associated with*.

muid

See *nipperkin*.

mulligan stew

See *mulligatawny*.

mulligatawny

This spicy soup, native to India but adopted by the English and then especially by the Australians, takes its name from *milagu-tannir*, a Tamil phrase meaning *pepper-water*. *Mulligatawny* appeared in English in the late eighteenth century, which is why some etymologists have proposed that *mulligan stew*, which appeared early this century as the name of another thick soup made from odds and ends, may have originated as a corruption of *mulligatawny*. However, *mulligan* may just as easily be a corruption or a humorous scrambling of *slumgullion*, a name once used by gold-miners and hoboes for a similar sort of ad hoc stew.

Alternatively, mulligan stew may simply take its name from some unknown individual, *Mulligan* being a common Irish name.

munch

Like the word *manger* (the name of a place where animals eat, especially at Christmas), and like the word *mange* (the name of a disease caused by parasites eating an animal's skin), the word *munch* probably derives from the French *manger*, meaning *to eat*. The word appeared in English in the late fourteenth century, followed about five hundred years later—in the early part of this century—by *munchies*, a snack eaten for lack of anything better to do. Somewhat similar in form and sense to *munch* is *scranch*, a word that appeared in the early seventeenth century meaning *to chew noisily*. However, *scranch* is not related to *munch*, deriving instead from the Dutch *schranzen*, meaning *to eat voraciously*. Although *scranch* itself is no longer commonly used, several of the words it gave rise to are still current, including *scrunch* (as in "He scrunched up his face") and *crunch* (as in *Captain Crunch*).

muscatel

See *cantaloupe*.

mushroom

Before its current name was adopted by English in the fifteenth century, the mushroom was known either as a *funge*, a word deriving from the Latin *fungus*, or as a *toadstool*, a word of fanciful English origin. When the word *mushroom* was finally adopted from French in the fifteenth century, these three words were used more or less interchangeably. By the eighteenth century, however, most people were distinguishing them: *mushroom* referred to an edible umbrella-shaped fungus; *toadstool* referred to a poisonous umbrella-shaped fungus; and *funge*—or rather *fungus*, which had been readopted from Latin in the early sixteenth century—referred generally to all mushrooms, toadstools, and mould. It was also not until the eighteenth century that *mushroom* acquired its current spelling: when originally adopted from French, the word was spelt *mousseron*, but the influence of the unrelated but familiar words *mush* and *room* caused the form of the word to change. The French themselves, incidentally, abandoned the name *mousseron* in favour of the current *champignon*, a word that derives from the Latin *campus*, meaning field. Further back in its history, *mushroom*—or rather *mousseron*—was formed by the French from *mousse*, meaning *moss*, because mushrooms commonly grow out of that velvety plant. Later on, *mousse* was also bestowed, by the French themselves, on a creamy dish whose frothiness resembles the spongy texture of moss; English borrowed the name of this dish in the late nineteenth century when mousses became popular.

musk melon

See *cantaloupe*.

mussel

The mussels you cook in a wine sauce and the muscles you use to lift the pot from the stove derive their names from the same source: the Latin *musculus*, which literally means *little mouse*. The ancient Romans bestowed this word on the small, grey shellfish because its size and colour resembles that of a mouse; they likewise bestowed the word upon the fibrous tissue that allows us to lift things because some muscles, such as the biceps, resemble a scurrying mouse as they move back and forth under the skin when successively flexed and relaxed. Both mussels and muscles have long been eaten as food, but so has the mouse: the ancient Romans bred a specific kind of mouse—the dormouse— so that they could stew them and eat them with sauce made of honey and poppy-seeds; even in the seventeenth century, dormouse pie was still eaten in France. The *dor* of *dormouse* probably derives from the Latin *dormire*, meaning *to sleep*, the animal having achieved an almost proverbial reputation as a sound slumberer; for a similar reason, the Dutch once called another sort of rodent the *slaep-ratte*, a name needing no translation. Of these words, *mouse* is the oldest, first being recorded in the ninth century; *mussel* appeared in the eleventh century, *dormouse* in the fifteenth, and *muscle* in the sixteenth. See also *cantaloupe*.

mustard

Although the mustard you put on a hamburger is made from the mustard plant, it was the condiment, not the plant, that was originally named *mustard*. The condiment acquired its name because it was made by grinding seeds—seeds harvested from what was once called the senvy plant—into a paste that was then mixed with must, *must* being an old name for new wine. This must-based paste came to be known in French as *moustarde*, which English adopted as *mustard* when the British became fond of the condiment in the late thirteenth century. By the mid fourteenth century, the senvy plant had become so associated with the condiment made from its seeds that the plant itself came to be newly-known as *mustard*, and by the seventeenth century almost everyone had forgotten that the mustard plant had ever been called *senvy*. Incidentally, the *must* that gave rise to the word *mustard* derives from a Latin phrase, *mustum vinum*, meaning *fresh wine*. In English, this phrase was adopted in the ninth century as *must*, also meaning *fresh wine*, which in the fifteenth century briefly gave rise to the adjective *musty*, meaning *fresh*. This *musty* is now obsolete, having vanished in the sixteenth century thanks to the appearance of another *musty*, one meaning *stale* or *mouldy*. This second *musty*, which derives from the same source as the word *moist*, was so opposed in meaning to the first *musty* that it drove the older term out of existence.

mutton

When alive and flouncing through your dreams, sheep are called *sheep*, but when brought to your table in a mushroom sauce the same creature is called *mutton*, a word that English derived in the late thirteenth century from the Old French *moton*, meaning *sheep*. French in turn acquired this word from a Celtic source such as the Old Irish *molt*, the Breton *mols*, or the Welsh *mollt*. It is also possible, though not certain, that even further back in history the common source of these Celtic names for sheep was the Latin *mutilare*, meaning *to cut off*: after all, mutton is not the meat of any old sheep, but specifically of those that have been castrated. If *mutilare* is the source of *mutton,* then the name of the meat literally means *mutilated*, since that word is the direct descendent of the Latin *mutilare*.

napery

See *serviette*.

napkin

See *serviette*.

Neapolitan

See *tutti-frutti*.

nectar

See *ambrosia*.

nectarine

Nectarines are essentially a kind of peach—in fact, nectarines can develop from peach seeds just as peaches can develop from nectarine seeds. The two fruits are so similar that botanists do not know which one originated first. Despite these botanical affinities, however, the word *nectarine* is a much more recent addition to English than the word *peach*: whereas *nectarine* is first recorded in a popular gardening guide published in 1664, *peach* appeared three centuries earlier in Geoffrey Chaucer's *Romaunt of the Rose*, written about 1366. The late appearance of *nectarine* is due to the late appearance of *nectar*, the word from which it is derived. *Nectar*, the name of a substance drunk by the gods of ancient Greece, did not enter English until the sixteenth century because it was not until then that Renaissance scholars began immersing themselves in the culture of ancient Greece and Rome. See also *ambrosia*.

neep

See *turnip*.

nesebek

See *bouce Jane*.

nipperkin

If any category of words is especially prone to extinction, it is those relating to measures. Words that relate to things, like *sky* or *egg*, tend to persist because the things themselves usually continue to exist; likewise, words that relate to ideas, like *freedom* or *evil*, persist because people continue to debate them. Measures, however,—whether of liquids, solids, length, or area—are neither "things" nor "ideas," and the moment they cease to serve a purpose they become mere nuisances and are duly forgotten. The word *nipperkin*, for example, is now almost unknown, but there was a period of several hundred years, after it first appeared in English in the late seventeenth century, when *nipperkin* was probably spoken tens of thousands of times each day in London alone. The word referred to a standard measure of liquor: about half a pint, the amount that you could drink if you were to "nip in" for a quick one on the way home. Both this *nip*—the one in the phrase *to nip in*—and the one in *a nip of whiskey* are the only remaining vestiges of *nipperkin*. The word derived from the Dutch word *nypelkin*, the *kin* being a diminutive meaning *little*, but no one is sure what a *nypel* was or why you would want a little one. The same diminutive ending appears in *firkin*, a cask containing about eight gallons, and in *kilderkin*, a cask containing about eighteen gallons. With these two words, the first half of the name represents a fraction: the *fir* of *firkin*, for example, derives from an old Dutch word that meant *a fourth* because a firkin was one fourth of a barrel; likewise, the *kilder* of *kilderkin* derives from an old Dutch word that meant *a fifth* because the kilderkin was one fifth of a tun, a tun being a barrel of about 250 gallons. A firkin, incidentally, tended to be used only for measuring butter; today selling butter by the firkin would be impractical: a single one would cost about $167.00 and would take up the entire refrigerator. The fifteenth-century measure known as the *tierce* also derives its name from a fraction—the Latin *tertius*, meaning *a third*—because it was one third of a pipe, which is equal to one half of a tun, two hogsheads, four barrels, or 105 gallons. The much older measure called the *sester*, dating back to the eleventh century, derives its name from being a *sixth* of a congius (a congius, as you know, being one eighth of an amphora). Other measures, such as the amphora, have taken their name from their shape: *amphora* derives from the Greek *amphoreos*, meaning *two-handles*. Similarly, *runlet*, the name of a medieval wine cask containing about eighteen gallons, originated as the diminutive of the French *ronde*, meaning *round* (although it is unclear why the roundness of the runlet was more remarkable than that of any other cask or barrel). Sometimes, instead of becoming defunct, the name of a measure came to mean something new: a muid—which takes its name from the Latin *modius*, meaning *measure*—was originally a cask of about sixty gallons, but eventually came to mean the area of land that could be sowed with a muid of seed. Finally, some measures seem to have been doomed to obsolescence by their very specificity: the cran, whose name comes from a Gaelic source meaning *a share*, was used only to measure fresh herring; in 1816 the Commissioners for the Herring Fishery fixed a cran at 42 gallons but this was raised in 1832 to 45 gallons, the equivalent of about 750 fresh herring.

no cake

See *pancake*.

noisette

See *filbert*.

noodle

According to my grade six teacher, the expression "use your noodle" came about because the brain resembles a big bowl of noodles (especially those thick, steaming noodles that the Japanese call *udon*). I was disabused of this comforting notion twenty-five years later upon discovering that *noodle*, meaning *head*, derives from *noddle*, a word that emerged in the fifteenth century, three hundred years before the appearance of the culinary *noodle*. (This *noddle*, incidentally, is probably related to *nod*, meaning *to tilt the head forward*.) The culinary *noodle*, on the other hand, which appeared in the late eighteenth century, derives from the German *nudel*, a word that has nothing to do with running around naked. Other words to which *noodle* and *nudel* are probably related include the German *knödel*, a small dumpling whose name was borrowed in the early nineteenth century, and the Yiddish *knaidel*, another kind of small dumpling whose name was borrowed in the 1950s. The ultimate source of this cluster of words may be the German *knode*, meaning *knot*.

noon

In the working world, the established time for lunch is noon, currently fixed at twelve o'clock, but formerly the ninth hour of the day, the ninth hour being three o'clock in the afternoon. The convoluted history of *noon* extends back two thousand years to when the ancient Romans reckoned the hours of the day not from midnight but from sunrise, which in southern latitudes typically occurs at what we would now call six in the morning. Accordingly, under this Roman system, the *nona hora* or *ninth hour* occurred nine hours after dawn, making it, under our current system, three o'clock in the afternoon. What then happened was that *nona*— or *noon* as it was later pronounced—became associated with lunch time; the term *noonmeat* even arose in the eleventh century as the name for this meal, a term used as late as the nineteenth century, although by then it had been corrupted to *nummet*. As eating habits changed, lunch came to be eaten earlier and earlier, and thus by the fourteenth century the meal known as *noonmeat* or *noon* had shifted from three o'clock to its current hour, twelve o'clock. This shift was assisted by the demise of the Roman system for telling time, and by the appearance in the sixteenth century of the word *lunch*, which, along with *dinner*, became the main term for the midday meal. *Noon* therefore lost its specific *meal* sense and became merely a fixed-hour in the day, as it originally had been. In phrases such as *high noon* and *solar noon*, the word *noon* is also used as a synonym for *midday*, the moment—slightly different each day of the year—when the sun reaches its zenith. See also *lunch*.

nori

See *sushi*.

nosh

The word *nosh* and the word *snoop* originally denoted the same thing: the act of eating something in secret. Both words derive from Germanic sources: the German *naschen*, meaning *to eat surreptitiously*, is the source of the Yiddish *nosh*, which English adopted in the 1960s; the Dutch *snoepen*, meaning *to appropriate and consume dainties in a clandestine manner*, is the source of *snoop*, which appeared in English in the mid nineteenth century. Of these two words, *nosh* has retained a meaning fairly close to that of its German source: it now means *to snack*, whether in public or private. *Snoop*, on the other hand, has lost its associations with food, and now simply means *to pry into other people's affairs*.

numbles

See *humble pie*.

nummet

See *noon*.

nuncheon

See *lunch*.

nut

The homely word *nut* is the country cousin of some fancy, city-slicker words, including, *nucleus*, *nuclear* and *nougat*. All these words ultimately derive from an Indo-European source that meant *lump*. This Indo-European source eventually gave rise to the Latin word *nux*, meaning *nut*, which later developed a diminutive form, *nuculeus*, meaning *little nut* or *kernel*. This diminutive form lost a syllable and entered English as *nucleus* in the early eighteenth century as the name of the head of a comet. The Latin *nuculeus* also gave rise to the French *nougat*, denoting a confection of nuts and sugar, which entered English at the beginning of the nineteenth century. The Indo-European source that led to *nucleus* and *nougat* through Latin and French also entered the Germanic family of languages and gave rise in the ninth century to the Old English word *hnutu*, which eventually became the word *nut*. In the mid nineteenth century, the astonishing resemblance of the typical human head to the typical nut prompted the expression, *He's off his nut*, which in turn led to the more familiar idiom *He's nuts!* and to the compound *nutcase*, first recorded in 1959.

nutmeg

When the word *nutmeg* entered English at the end of the fourteenth century, about the time that Chaucer was writing *The Canterbury Tales*, it was spelt *notemugge*. The medieval form of this spice's name had been derived from the French *nois muguede*, which had in turn developed from the Late Latin *nuce muscata*, meaning *musky nut*, in reference to its smell. In English, the "nutty" origin of the word is still evident in its modern form, *nutmeg*, but its "musky" ancestry has been obscured beyond recognition; the opposite occurred in French, where the "musky" origin of the word is still evident in the modern form, *muscade*, but the "nutty" component has been lopped off.

nym

If you glance through a fourteenth-century cookbook, you will see many strange words, but one will appear more than almost any other. That word is *nym*, meaning *take*, and it was used in Middle English sentences like this—"Nym a pond of ris, seth hem fort it berste"—a sentence that actually means this—"Take a pound of rice and boil it till it swells." Because *nym* was used so often, essentially every time the cook was instructed to take a new ingredient, fourteenth-century recipes came to be known as *nyms*. By the end of the fifteenth century, however, the culinary *nym* had all but vanished, having been replaced by the current idiom, *take*. At the beginning of the seventeenth century *nym* did manage a comeback, but not as term within cookbooks;

instead, *nym*—which was now spelt *nim*—came to mean *take* in the sense of *steal*; the word was even used as a noun to mean *a pickpocket*. *Nim* itself is now defunct, but a related form lives on: *nimble*, which originally referred to a person's ability to take or apprehend something quickly. See also *recipe*.

offal

When you set about to butcher a chicken, the first thing you do is chop off its legs and head; these severed items are as unimportant to you as they were important to the bird, and thus you sweep them to the edge of the table where they fall onto the floor. It is this action that lies behind the word *offal*: the word refers to the scraps of the animal that literally *fall off* the butcher's table. The reason that these scraps are called *offal* instead of *fall-off* is that the term was borrowed in the fourteenth century from Middle Dutch, which had a different way of ordering the words in such compounds. In the fifteenth century, the meaning of the word shifted slightly in English as it came to mean the innards of a butchered animal, including those innards, like the liver and heart, sometimes used for food.

oil

See *olive*.

okra

See *gumbo*.

olive

Before the word *olive* was adopted from French in the thirteenth century, the olive was known in England as the *eleberge*, literally meaning *oil-berry*. For the ancient Greeks, the olive, which they called *elaia*, was likewise a kind of oil-berry, so much so that they derived their word for *oil* from its name, calling it *elaion*. Both these Greek words were borrowed by Latin: *elaia* became the Latin *oliva*, while *elaion* became the Latin *oleum*. These words then passed through French as *olive* and *oile* before being adopted by English in the twelfth century. By that time, *oil* had come to mean any fluid pressed from a nut or seed, but the word was not applied to the thick, black fluid pumped out of the earth until about the nineteenth century. Prior to that, and as far back as the mid fourteenth century, mineral oils were called *petroleum*, a word that combines the Latin *oleum* with the Latin *petra*, meaning *rock*. Petroleum, therefore, is literally *rock-oil*.

ombrellino

See *swizzle stick*.

omelette

Strange as it might seem, the word *omelette* is related to both the word *laminate* and the word *enamel*, but is not related to the similar sounding *amulet*, a charm that wards off evil spirits. *Omelette* ultimately goes back to the Latin word *lamina*, meaning *a plate of metal*. *Lamina* gave rise to a diminutive Latin form, *lamella*, meaning *a small or thin plate of metal*, which in turn was taken into Old French as *lemelle*, meaning *blade of a knife*. The word *lemelle* was then bestowed upon the breakfast entrée because omelettes are flat and thin like a knife blade. Subsequently, the name *lemelle* underwent a number of linguistic changes, beginning with the addition of an *a* to the beginning of the word as French speakers mistook *la lemelle* as *l'alemelle*. Next, the *l* sound at the end of *alemele* was change to a *t* sound—as in *alemette*—because *ette* is the more usual diminutive suffix in French. Finally, the remaining *l* and the *m* traded places due to a common linguistic process called metathesis, giving rise to *amelette*, which was then changed to *omelette* to make it look more like the Latin word for egg, *ovum*, to which it has absolutely no linguistic connection. It was this form of the word, *omelette*, which entered English in 1611. Perhaps because of the complex history of the word *omelette*, many easier, but false, explanations of its origin have been proposed. In spite of the enticing simplicity of these suggestions, however, the word does not derive from the ancient Roman dish called *ova mellita*, Latin for *eggs with honey*, nor does it derive from *oeufs melés*, French for *mixed eggs*.

omnivorous

The Latin word *vorare*, meaning *to devour*, has been compounded with other Latin words to form *omnivorous* (*all-devouring*), *carnivorous* (*flesh-devouring*), and *herbivorous* (*plant-devouring*). All these words entered English in the mid sixteenth century as zoological terms; much more recently *batrachivorous* was adopted for application to people in nations such as France who eat *grenouille*, in England known euphemistically as *nymphe aurore*, meaning *nymph of the dawn*, or—less romantically—*frog*. See also *opsophagy*.

one-arm

One-arm refers not to a careless sausage maker, but to a kind of cheap restaurant, in vogue earlier this century, where a patron ate his meal from a seat that had one arm wide enough to support his tray.

onion

A labour union brings together many different individuals; a garden onion has many tightly bound layers. This connection explains why both words—*union* and *onion*—derive from the Late Latin *unio*, meaning *oneness* or *unity*, which in turn arose from the Latin *unus*, meaning *one*. The earliest English spellings of the bulb's name—*unyonn* back in the fourteenth century—suggest that medieval authors were more aware of the connection between *onion* and *union* than we usually are. In fact, had the connection between *onions* and *oneness* not been lost in the intervening centuries, we might be tossing onions, instead of rice, when the bride and groom descend, newly united, from the church steps.

Incidentally, the ancient Romans also used the Latin *unio* to mean *pearl*, because pearls, like onions, are made up of many layers united into a single sphere. The term *pearl onion*, therefore, is in one sense redundant.

opsony

Opsony is an exact synonym for *companage*, the name given to anything eaten with bread to give it greater savour. The word derives from the Latin *opsonium*, meaning *provisions*, but was used for only a short time in the seventeenth century. See also *companion*.

opsophagy

Holidays such as Christmas or Thanksgiving, with their endless plates of cookies, cakes, pickles, nuts, and chocolate, are an extreme form of opsophagy, the eating of dainties. The word derives from the Greek *opson*, meaning *rich fare* (especially fish), and *phagein*, meaning *to eat*. When the desire to eat such goodies becomes overwhelming, the rotund victim suffers from *opsomania*, literally meaning *crazy for dainties*. These words, like a host of other words based on the Greek *phagein*, appeared in English in the mid nineteenth century. Among the more interesting of these are *mycophagy* (the eating of mushrooms), *hippophagy* (the eating of horses), *saprophagy* (the eating of rotten food, common in college dormitories), *onychophagy* (the eating of finger nails), *lotophagy* (the eating of lotus fruit, supposed by the ancient Greeks to cause blissful forgetfulness), *galactophagy* (the drinking of milk or what the Greeks called *gala*, a word that also gave rise to *galaxy*, our own galaxy being the Milky Way), *theophagy* (the eating of God, as when Christians swallow the Eucharist), and *poltophagy* (the habit of chewing food until it is a liquid).

orange

Although you might expect oranges to have taken their name from their colour, the opposite is true: the name of the colour was borrowed from the name of the fruit. The ultimate source of the orange's name is the Sanskrit *naranga*, which made its way through Persian and Arabic before arriving in Spanish as *naranj*. The French then borrowed this Spanish name, but changed its spelling: they inadvertently dropped its initial *n* because in Old French *une naranj* sounded just like *une aranj*. Once this initial *n* was lost, the French then changed the rest of the word to *orenge*, which became the English *orange* in the fourteenth century; in the mid sixteenth century this fruit name was then borrowed as the name of a colour. Of course, all this raises a puzzling question: what did the English call the colour orange before they adopted the word *orange*? To some extent, other colours did double duty: fire, for example, was described as being red. However, not much of this double-dutying was actually necessary because in rainy, grey, medieval England orange was simply not a colour that commonly appeared in nature; even carrots were yellow until nineteenth-century horticulturalists bred them to their present hue. Considering that it was to this rather drab environment that oranges were imported, it's little wonder that their vibrant appearance gave rise to a new colour name. Incidentally, about a hundred years after *orange* became a colour, William of Orange became king of England. It was not his love of fruit or his colourful personality, however, that gave him his title; rather, he acquired it from the name of his official principality, a town in France known to the ancient Romans as *Arausio*, meaning *mountainous*, but which the French corrupted to *Orange*.

oregano

Oregano and *marjoram* are two names for the same herb, one name having a known origin, the other being a mystery. The known origin, that of *oregano*, extends back to ancient Greek where the herb was called *origanon*, a compound name made from *oros*, meaning *mountain*, and *ganos*, meaning *brightness*—the name of the oregano plant therefore means *mountain brightness*. This Greek name entered Latin as *origanum*, which became the English name of the herb in the mid thirteenth century and remained so until the late eighteenth century when the Spanish version of the name, *oregano*, was introduced and popularized. The herb's other name, *marjoram*, was once thought by medieval herbalists to be related to *amaracus*, an aromatic plant whose name means *bitter*; marjoram, however, is a sweet herb, not a bitter one, so the etymological connection seems doubtful. See also *pennyroyal*.

ort

An ort was originally a scrap of food or leftover fodder not eaten by cattle or pigs. The word then came to be applied to leftovers from the kitchen table, leftovers that were also known as *relief* or *relics*. *Ort* appeared in the mid fifteenth century as a compound of the prefix *oor*, meaning *not*, and *etan*, meaning *to eat*; quite literally, therefore, orts are the uneaten scraps of a meal. See also *leftovers*.

ortanique

See *pomato*.

oshibori

See *sushi*.

ounce

In one sense, an ounce is an inch, at least in so far as the names of both units derive from a Latin source meaning *one twelfth*, an inch being a twelfth of a foot, and a troy ounce being a twelfth of a pound. This Latin source—*uncia*—developed differently as it made its way though Old French and Germanic: in Old French *uncia* became *unce*, which English adopted as *ounce* in the fourteenth century; in Germanic *uncia* became *ungkja*, which evolved into the Old English *ynce* before being respelt as *inch* in the sixteenth century. The usual abbreviation of *ounce*—*oz.*—is unusual in so far as *ounce* is not spelt with a *z*; however, the Italian counterpart to *ounce*—*ouza*—is spelt with a *z* and it may be that this word is the source of the abbreviation. Alternatively, the *z* of *oz.* may originally have been what is called a terminal mark, that is, a symbol used by early printers to indicate that a word had been shortened. Thus, the original abbreviation for *ounce* may simply have been an *o* followed by the terminal mark *z*; in time, the function of the *z* was forgotten, but the abbreviation *oz.* persisted. The same process is responsible for the abbreviation *viz*, a short form of *videlicet*, literally meaning *one is permitted to see* but used by some authors to mean *in other words*. The original abbreviation of *videlicet* was *vi*, but with the addition of the terminal mark it became *viz*.

oven

The ultimate source of the word *oven* is an Indo-European word meaning *fire-pot* and pronounced something like *ukwnos*. This Indo-European word evolved into the Germanic *uhwnaz*, which developed into the Old English *ofn*, first recorded in the tenth century and respelt as *oven* by the fourteenth century. The Indo-European *ukwnos* also developed along a different path into the Latin word *aula*, meaning *pot*; in Spanish, the Latin *aula* evolved into *olla*, which originally meant *pot* but also came to be used as the name of a dish of stewed meat. It was with this *stewed meat* sense that English adopted *olla* in the early seventeenth century, although in the mid nineteenth century the word was readopted from American Spanish as the name of an earthenware jar used to keep water cool. See also *pot-pourri*.

oyster

Although *ostracism* and *Osterizer* both resemble the word *oyster*, only one of them is actually related to the name of that tasty mollusk. The ancient Greek word for *oyster* was *ostreon*, a word that derived from an Indo-European source meaning *bone*. From the same Indo-European source developed the Greek word *os*, meaning *bone* (as in *osteopath*), and the Greek word *ostrakon*, a word denoting shell-like fragments of broken pottery. Far from being trash, such pottery fragments were useful because they could be written on, as they were when the members of the Greek assembly cast their votes on whether some trouble-maker should be sent into exile; if, after counting, enough of the pottery shards had been inscribed with the unpopular fellow's name, he was banished from the state for ten years. This process became known as the *ostrakismos*, which became the English *ostracism* in the sixteenth century, about two hundred years after the word *oyster* was adopted in the mid fourteenth century. The food processor known as the *Osterizer*, on the other hand, takes its name from the man who patented it, John Oster; Oster's ancestors acquired their surname not because they were mollusks, but because they were hostlers, people who looked after the horses belonging to a hotel's guests.

Pablum

Pablum is the trademark name of a gruel fed to infants and other individuals too weak to defend themselves. The brand name was first registered in the United States in 1932 and derives from *pabulum*, a word meaning *nourishment* or *food*, which was borrowed directly from Latin in the early eighteenth century. Much further back, the Latin word *pabulum* developed from an Indo-European word meaning *to nourish*. This Indo-European word is the ancestor not only of *pabulum*, but also of the words *pastor*—a person who *feeds* his flock—and *pasture*—a place where a flock is nourished. In fact, this lost Indo-European word is even the ultimate source of the word *food* itself. The lack of outward resemblance between the word *pabulum* and the word *food* demonstrates how thousands of years of sound changes and spelling changes can disguise linguistic relationships.

pancake

In England, the original pancake was called a *froise*, a fried cake of dough that often contained bacon. *Froise* appeared in the early fourteenth century, and may have derived, through French, from the Latin *frigere*, meaning *to fry*. *Pancake* itself appeared in the early fifteenth century, an obvious compound of *pan* and *cake*.

Although usually considered rather plain fare, pancakes acquired a special, allegorical significance on Pancake Day, also called Shrove Tuesday, the merry-making holiday preceding Lent: the eggs that went into them symbolized creation; the flour, the staff of life; the milk, purity; and the salt, wholesomeness. Later, pancakes came to be known by dozens of other names. *Flapjack* appeared early in the seventeenth century, *flap* being a variant of *flip*, and *jack* being a word that meant *food* in some British dialects. Most of the new words for pancake appeared in the United States: *Indian cake* appeared in the early seventeenth century for pancakes made from corn meal; at about the same time, the Algonquian word *nokehick*, meaning *it is soft*, gave rise to *pancake's* most peculiar synonym, *no cake*. *Hot cakes* appeared a little later in the seventeenth century, but the phrase *to sell like hot cakes* can only be traced to the early nineteenth century. Another Native American word, *joniken*, may be the source of *johnnycake*, first recorded in the mid eighteenth century. Alternatively, *johnnycake* may have developed from *Shawnee cake*, the Shawnee being a tribe of Native Americans in what is now Tennessee, or *johnnycake* may have developed from the term *journey cake*, a food prepared in advance and taken along on a long trip. *Griddlecake*, appearing in the late-eighteenth century, clearly takes its name from the implement it was cooked upon, as might also be the case with the slightly older *hoecake*, the thin blade of a cotton hoe being a handy cooking surface when a griddle was not available out in the field; however, *hoecake* might also have evolved from the previously mentioned *nokehick* as people heard, and then mistook, "a nokehick" for "an hoecake." *Flannel cake*, a name that probably derives, like the term *flan* itself, from the Old French *flawn*, meaning *flat cake*, emerged in the late eighteenth century, followed by *buckwheat cake* in the early nineteenth century. The most recent aliases for the pancake are *flat car*, which originated among railway workers this century, and *silver dollar*, which seems to have been coined by chain restaurants hoping to sell pancakes that are numerous but tiny. See also *cake*, *griddle*, and *crêpe*.

pantry

Although pantries now contain almost any manner of foodstuff, they originally contained only bread, as is suggested by the origin of the word: the Latin *panis*, meaning *bread*. Other words in English, such as *companion*, *impanation*, and *pannier* (originally a bread basket) also derive from the Latin *panis*, although *pan* itself, as in *frying pan*, does not. The word *pantry* entered English at the beginning of the fourteenth century, having trickled down into everyday speech from the French nobles who had ruled England since the Norman Conquest in 1066. By the sixteenth century *pantry's* original sense of *bread room* had given way to its current sense.

pap

Pap is any semi-liquid food, such as bread soaked in milk or even the name-brand Pablum, that infants employ to reduce the coefficient of friction that obtains between their palms and the surface of their highchairs. The word apparently originated in the early fifteenth century as a representation of the sound babies make when they are nursing their mothers' breasts. The other *pap*—the one meaning *breast* that appeared in the thirteenth century—likely arose in the same way, as did the much older Latin word *pabulum*, meaning *nourishment*. See also *Pablum*.

papillote

Since the mid eighteenth century *papillote* has referred to a colourful paper frill tied as a decoration to the bone end of a drumstick, lamb chop, or pork chop. The word derives from the French *papillon*, meaning *butterfly*, so called because the colourful frills resemble the wings of that insect. In turn, the French *papillon* derives from the Latin *papilio*, which is also the source of the word *pavilion*, originally the name of a large tent whose door flaps were shaped like butterfly wings. In the early nineteenth century, English also acquired the French term *en papillote*, used to describe foods wrapped in greased paper (or tin foil) before being placed in the oven; potatoes are often cooked *en papillote*, as are fish.

paprika

See *pepper*.

parsley

The ancient Greeks called parsley *selinon*, a word that became—via Latin, Italian, and then French—the English word *celery*. This Greek name for the parsley plant may have shifted to the celery plant because—in dim light, from a great distance—the two plants are not dissimilar; scientists, at least, have seen fit to place both celery and parsley in the Umbelliferae family of plants, a family distinguished by the parasol shape of its species' flowers. The word *parsley*, on the other hand, developed from the Greek name for a specific variety of parsley called *petroselinon*, literally meaning *rock parsley*. The Greek *petros*, incidentally, is also the source of *Peter*, a name whose stony associations have led to its being used in the word *saltpeter* and also as a nickname for the male erection. *Parsley* appeared in English almost a thousand years ago, but *celery* did not appear until the mid seventeenth century, shortly after it began to be cultivated for culinary purposes. Prior to this, the same plant, known since the thirteenth century as *smallage*, was harvested from the wild. This earlier name, *smallage*, literally means *small parsley*, the *age* part of the word having developed from the Greek *apion*, another word for *parsley*.

parsnip

The ancient Romans either had bad-tasting carrots or good-tasting parsnips because their name for the two vegetables was the same: *pastinaca*. This name derived from an older Latin word, *pastinum*, the name of a two-pronged garden fork that in turn derived from *pastinare*, meaning *to dig*. The similarity between the prongs of the garden fork and the body of the typical parsnip or carrot—which often forks into two or more limbs—led to the name *pastinaca* being bestowed on these vegetables. In French this name evolved into *pasnaie*, which became *parsnip* when it was adopted into English in the late fourteenth century. The changing of the final syllable to *nip* was likely due to the influence of the word *nep*, which is what the turnip (another root vegetable) was called until the sixteenth century. Parsnips became fully differentiated from carrots when the word *carrot* was adopted from French in the early sixteenth century.

parties nobles

This French term, pronounced *par-tee nobleh* and meaning *noble parts*, refers to the parts of an animal eaten by a hunter immediately after a successful kill. The noble parts of the animal were those thought to embody its courage and vital essence: the brain, the sexual organs, the heart, the liver, and other delectable items that we now consider offal. Most of these organs were among those most difficult to keep fresh, so apart from whatever spiritual benefit they provided, it also made good sense to eat these bits of the creature before transporting the rest back home.

pasta

From the Greek verb *passein*, meaning *to sprinkle* or *to strew*, the ancient Greeks derived their word *paste*, meaning *barley porridge*—the connection, presumably, was that the porridge was made by sprinkling barley meal, or nowadays oatmeal, into a pot of boiling water. When the ancient Romans borrowed the Greek *paste*, they spelt it *pasta* and used it to mean *dough*, a paste made from milled grains such as barley. This Latin word gave rise to two different Italian words, *pasticcio*, the name of a pie made with many ingredients, and *pasta*, the name of small tubes or shells of cooked dough served with a sauce. *Pasticcio* was never really adopted by English, but the hodgepodge nature of that Italian pie did give rise to the French word *pastiche*, meaning *a jumble*. This French word, *pastiche*, entered English in the late nineteenth century, about the same time that *pasta* appeared. Of course, even before English acquired the word *pasta* from Italian, the British were eating pasta-like foods; however, they referred to any such food as a *paste*, a word that developed, via French, from the same Latin source as *pasta*. When *paste* entered English in the late fourteenth century it was used exclusively as a culinary term: not for another seventy-five years did it come to mean other things, such as *glue*. Other words that developed directly from either the French or English word *paste* include *pastry*, *pâté*, and *patty*. *Pastry* is the oldest of these, appearing first in the mid sixteenth century; *pâté* and *patty* did not appear till the early eighteenth century. Over the last few decades, *patty* has come to be used in connection with items that contain no dough at all—such as *hamburger patty*—although its earlier pastry sense is still heard in the children's rhyme that begins, "Patty-cake, patty-cake, baker's man."

paste

See *pasta*.

pasteurize

See *antipasto*.

pasticcio

See *pasta*.

pastrami

Via Yiddish, *pastrami* derives from the Romanian *pastra*, meaning *to preserve*, an apt name considering the meat is prepared for the marketplace by soaking beef in brine for several weeks, smoking it over sawdust for half a day, and finally steaming it for several hours. The word was introduced to English in the mid 1930s thanks to the growing popularity of Jewish-American delicatessens.

pastry

See *pasta*.

pea

Four hundred years ago, if you had a single pea in your hand, you would have called it a *pease*. That old form of the word can still be heard in a children's rhyme: "Pease porridge hot, pease porridge cold, pease porridge in the pot, nine days old." The reason that *pease* used to be the singular form of the word—and also the plural form—goes back to the word's origin. In Latin, the singular of *pea* is *pisum* and the plural is *pisa*; both forms contain the letter *s*. When English borrowed the word from Latin more than a thousand years ago, it took only the first part of this Latin word, changed the spelling to *pease*, and used that form to refer to one pea or to many peas. In the seventeenth century, though, people started to assume that the *s* near the end of *pease* was the *s* that English uses to make nouns plural. As a result, they made the well-intentioned, but erroneous, inference that the proper singular for *pease* must be the shortened form, *pea*. From then on, this new singular form, *pea*, existed alongside *pease*, which in turn came to be used only as a plural. Later, the final *e* of *pease* was dropped from the spelling, leaving us with the plural *peas* to go along with the singular *pea*.

peach Melba

See *Melba toast*.

peach

In 334 B.C., Alexander the Great did two things: he conquered Persia and he sent back to Greece the pits of a few peaches, a fruit that neither he nor anyone else in Europe had seen before. The pits were planted, the trees thrived, and soon Alexander's peaches were being introduced all over Europe. Alexander's conquest of Persia was responsible not only for the spread of the fruit but also for its name: because he first came upon it in Persia, Alexander named the peach *Persikos melon*, Greek for *Persian apple*. The ancient Romans adopted this name as *Persicum malum*, later shortened to just *persicum*, then adopted by French as *pesche*. This French name then made its way into English when, in the mid fourteenth century, it was adopted as *peach*. The one constant in the history of the word *peach* is that in almost every culture to which it has been introduced it has become associated with sex. The ancient Chinese, for example, used their word for *peach* to refer to a young bride; in French the fruit was nicknamed *téton de Venus*, meaning *breast of Venus*; and in English, beautiful young women have been called *peaches* since the mid eighteenth century. Such erotic associations may have been inspired by the resemblance of the peach's cleft, running from its stem to its posterior end, to that of the human buttocks. Ironically, however, the actual meaning of *peach*—or more accurately of its ancestor, *Persia*—is *pure*, a self-proclaimed attribute of the ancient Persians.

peanut

Originating in Brazil and subsequently introduced to the rest of the world, the peanut has been known in English by a variety of names. First it was called *pinda*, a word dating back to the late seventeenth century and deriving from the Congolese *mpinda*, the name of an African legume resembling the peanut. Next, beginning in the mid eighteenth century, the peanut came to be known as *ground-pea* and *ground-nut*, so called because it grows, like all legumes, close to the earth. In the early nineteenth century, the word *peanut* itself emerged, but it soon acquired a rival in the form of *goober*, a word that derives from *nguba*, a name given to the plant by West Africans after it was brought to their continent by Portuguese slave traders. Today, *goober* continues to be commonly used in the United States, and remains one of the few words of African origin retained by English. *Peanut*, however, has become the usual name in the rest of the English-speaking world even though it is only half accurate: the peanut is a kind of pea but not a nut—in fact, the "shell" encasing the edible seeds more closely resembles the pod of a pea than the shell of a nut.

pear

To the ancient Romans, a pear was a *pirum*, a name that Old English adopted as *peru* in the eleventh century (about six hundred years later, *Peru* was also introduced to English as the name of a South American country, a name that derives not from Latin but from the Guarani word *piru*, meaning *water*). Throughout the Middle Ages and Renaissance, the spelling of the fruit's name shifted, moving from *peru* to *peore* to *pere* to *pyre* to *peer* before finally settling on *pear* in the sixteenth century. One of these alternate spellings, *pyre*, arose due to the misconception that the fruit's name was somehow related to *pyre*, a fire in which a body is cremated; so persistent was this misconception that Carolus Linnaeus, who in the eighteenth century invented the modern system of classifying flora and fauna, mistakenly chose *pyrus* as the scientific name for the pear tree, a name employed by botanists to this day.

pecan

The pecan is native to North America and thus its name derives from a Proto-Algonquian source, one that evolved into the Cree, *pakan*, the Ojibwa *pagan*, and the Abenaki *pagann*. From these various but similar names, British settlers derived their name for the nut, *pecan*, as did the French, who call it *pacane*, and the Spanish, who call it *pacana*. The word first appeared in English in the mid eighteenth century, while the earliest recipes for pecan pie date back to the beginning of this century.

peckish

See *pickle*.

pemmican

The aboriginal people of North America made pemmican by drying strips of buffalo meat or venison, pounding them with some berries into a powder, mixing the powder with melted fat, and then storing the resulting lump in a little bag made from the skin of the animal. Although early pioneers did not like the taste of pemmican, they recognized its nutritional value. First recorded in English in the early eighteenth century, *pemmican* derives from the Cree name for the food, *pimihkaxn*; this word in turn derives from two Proto-Algonquian words—*pemy*, meaning *grease*, and *hkexw*, meaning *make*.

pennyroyal

Pennyroyal was once a folk-name for *marjoram*, much like *spuds* is still a folk-name for *potatoes*. Far from having anything to do with pennies, the herb's name essentially means *royal flea-killer*. Its original Latin name was *pulegium*, meaning *flea-bane*, because its minty leaves were used to repel the hopping pests. *Pulegium* evolved into the French plant name, *pouliol*, which became attached, for some reason, to the French word *real*, meaning *royal*. In the sixteenth century, the French *pouliol real* entered English and soon became *pennyroyal*, perhaps due to the influence of the older *pennywort*, a plant with penny-shaped leaves. See also *oregano*.

pepper

The green, red, and bell peppers you grow in your garden are not really peppers; they acquired their name by mistake when Columbus, who came upon them in the Caribbean islands, assumed them to be a variety of the real pepper plant, the one that gives us peppercorns. The real pepper plant, which is actually a vine, derived its name more than a thousand years ago from the Latin name for pepper, *piper*, which in turn evolved from the Sanskrit *pippali*, meaning *berry*. Other European languages derived their word for pepper from the same source, including German's *pfeiffer*, now a surname of people whose ancestors sold pepper for a living. The German *pfeiffer*, or rather its modern form *pfeffer*, also became part of *pfefferkuchen*, a German ginger bread whose name literally means *pepper-cake*. The Old French word for pepper—*peivre*—is the source of the English *peverade*, a medieval sauce made from pepper, whose name was modernized at the end of the seventeenth century as *poivrade*. Finally, the Hungarian word for pepper—or rather for the red peppers that Columbus misnamed—is the source of *paprika*, a seasoning made by drying and grinding sweet red peppers. Paprika has been known in Europe since Columbus returned with red peppers, but the word itself did not enter English until a hundred years ago.

petticoat tails

See *spotted dick*.

pettitoe

A cooked pig's foot is called a *pettitoe*, a word English acquired from French more than four hundred years ago. Originally, however, the term *pettitoe* referred not to the foot of a pig but to the innards of a goose, a peculiar shift in meaning that occurred partly because the English people misapprehended a French word. The original form of *pettitoe* was the French *petite oye*, meaning *little goose*; this name was given by the French to the little parts of a goose—such as the heart, liver, and gizzard—that are removed before it is cooked. When the English adopted this French term in the mid sixteenth century, they misspelt it as *pettitoe*, which obscured the word's original application to geese; accordingly, the English soon began using the word to refer to the innards of any animal, not just those of a goose. Later on, the meaning of the word shifted further, once again thanks to the English spelling of the word: *pettitoe* happens to end with *toe*, so people gradually began to associate the word not with the innards of an animal but with its feet. A final development occurred when *pettitoe* came to refer not just to any animal but to pigs in particular; this last shift in meaning may have occurred partly because *pig* and *pettitoe* both begin with *p*—a coincidence that helps to link the words— and partly because pigs, unlike cows or goats, actually do have toes (four on each foot, each ending in a little hoof).

phyllo

See *chervil*.

pica

The Latin word *pica*—meaning *magpie*, a bird infamous for eating almost anything—was adopted by doctors in the mid sixteenth century as the name for a pathological desire to eat items like chalk or dirt that are unfit as food. Even today, a doctor might still diagnose someone suffering from extreme and unusual food cravings—a pregnant woman, perhaps—as suffering from pica. See also *pie*.

piccalilli

The name of this pickle, made by preserving minced vegetables in mustard and vinegar sauce, seems to have originated in India in the mid eighteenth century when the British East India Company gained control of the nation. The word, however, does not originate from Hindi or any of India's 180 other languages but rather is a playful diminutive of the English *pickle*. The formation of the word may also have been influenced by the Spanish *picadillo*, the name of a minced meat dish.

pickle

The word *pickle* derives from the Dutch word *pekel*, meaning *sharp-tasting*, which in turn probably traces its origin back to an Indo-European source, pronounced something like *piko*, that meant *sharp* or *pointed*. The same Indo-European source also gave rise to a host of other words, many of them food-related. For example, it became the Latin *pica*, meaning *magpie*, a bird with a sharp and pointed beak; through a strange route, this Latin *pica* eventually gave rise to the English word *pie* as in *apple pie*. The Indo-European *piko* also became the Latin *picus*, meaning *woodpecker*, which seems to have evolved into the French word *pique*, originally the name of a sharp weapon; in the thirteenth century, English adopted this French *pique* as *pike* and used it both as the name of a medieval weapon and of a fish with a pointy, pike-like head. The diminutive of *pike*—*pickerel*—became the name of a smaller and more tasty fish in the mid fourteenth century. The French *pique* also developed into the French verb *piquer*, which had many shades of meaning: it could mean *to sting*, which gave rise to the word *piquant*, meaning *sharp-tasting*; it could mean *to stick in*, which prompted the culinary term *piquer*, the action of inserting bacon into another food before cooking it; and it could even mean *to pick*—after all, we "point" at what we are "picking"—which inspired *piquenique*, an outdoor dinner for which everyone "picked" a favourite food to bring. *Piquenique* was adopted by English as *picnic* in the mid eighteenth century, but within a hundred years it lost its original sense of "picking" a favourite dish and came to signify any outdoor, informal repast. Finally, the French *piquer* also seems to be the source of *peck*— something magpies and woodpeckers do—which developed in the late eighteenth century into *peckish*, the condition of being so hungry that you want to "peck" at a bit of food. See also *pie* and *pica*.

picnic

See *pickle*.

piddle

See *pingle*.

pie

From the mid thirteenth to the early seventeenth century, the bird now known as the *magpie* was simply called the *pie*. English borrowed this ornithological name, *pie*, from the French, who derived it from the Latin name for the bird, *pica*, which in turn developed from an Indo-European source meaning *pointed*, as is the bird's beak. At the beginning of the fourteenth century, someone in England hit upon the idea of transferring the bird's name to a dish that had a certain resemblance to a magpie's nest: just as the bird, a notorious thief, filled its nest with bits of string and tin, so did cooks fill their pastry shells with bits of meat or fruit. The close connection between these two *pies* was obscured somewhat in the early seventeenth century when the bird's name was expanded from *pie* to *magpie*: *mag*—a pet form of *Margaret* that in the fifteenth century had become associated with idle talk—was added to emphasize the chattering nature of the bird. See also *pica* and *haggis*.

pièce de résistance

Today, almost any excellent thing can be a pièce de résistance, whether the context is art, architecture, fashion, or literature. Originally, however, this French phrase applied only to the chief dish in a multi-course meal, the one that, along with the roast, defined the third course of the dinner. The phrase literally means *piece of resistance*, suggesting either that the dish was so colossal it would resist the diners' attempts to subdue it with their knives and forks, or that the guests had to resist eating too much of the earlier dishes to save room for this one. The phrase was first used in English in the mid nineteenth century and within a generation had developed its larger sense of any object, gastronomic or otherwise, that inspired admiration.

pig

As far as most people are concerned, *pig*, *hog*, *boar*, *sow*, and *swine* are different words for the same porky animal; however, to those versed in the niceties of the sty, *hog* denotes a castrated pig, *boar* denotes an uncastrated pig, *sow* denotes a female pig, and *swine* denotes any pig-like creature, whether wild or domesticated, castrated or uncastrated, married or divorced. Of these five words, *swine* and *sow* are the oldest, first recorded in the early eighth century. The fact that these two words appeared at the same time is perhaps not surprising, given that they derive from a single

Indo-European source (the word *hyena* also derives, through Greek, from the same Indo-European source as *swine* and *sow*, the Greeks having considered the hyena the "swine" of the dog family). *Boar* is first recorded in English in the eleventh century, although it must have been in use earlier as the male counterpart for the much older *sow*. The word *hog*, which is not recorded until the fourteenth century, must also have been in use much earlier because a word derived from it—*hoggaster*, a three-year-old hog—is recorded in the twelfth century. Interestingly, it is possible that the word *hog* did not originally refer to pigs, nor to any particular species of animal; instead, *hog* may have been applied to any domesticated animal of a certain young age: even today, and dating back to the fourteenth century, *hog* is used in England and Scotland as the name for a one-year-old sheep. If *hog* did indeed arise as a term indicating age, then the word may have derived from the Old English *hag*, meaning *to hack*, a graphic reference to the castration hogs underwent in their first year. See also *pork*.

pig-iron

A pig-iron is an iron plate suspended between a fire and the meat cooking over it to prevent the meat from burning. This plate acquired the name *pig-iron* in the mid eighteenth century, but the term itself goes back to the mid seventeenth century when *pig-iron* referred to an iron ingot—that is, an iron lump—of a particular size, one smaller than a sow-iron. *Sow-iron*, in fact, is the older term, dating back to the fifteenth century, and may have been bestowed upon the large ingot because its shape and weight, about three hundred pounds, resembled that of a sow.

pili-pili

See *couscous*.

pimento

As Classical Latin, the language of ancient Rome, evolved into Medieval Latin, the language of Europe's scholars during the Middle Ages, it changed in both pronunciation and vocabulary. For example, in Classical Latin the word *pigmentum* meant *paint*, and it was with this meaning that English adopted the word as *pigment* near the end of the fourteenth century. In contrast, in Medieval Latin *pigmentum* had become the name of a spiced drink, a name inspired by the resemblance of the reddish drink to a pot of paint. In time, this Medieval Latin word shifted even further as it came to refer to the spice that flavoured such drinks, a sense that eventually led to the Spanish word *pimienta*, meaning *pepper*. *Pimienta* entered English in the late seventeenth century as *pimento*, the name of a sweet red pepper stuffed into olives and also the name of the dried berries of the allspice tree. See also *pint*.

pingle

There are many reasons why you might accept an invitation to go out for dinner but not eat your food: you might have the flu; you might have just discovered that ox-tail soup is not just a fanciful name; or you might have recognized the chef from a case-study photo in a recent dermatological journal. In any of these situations, you are entitled to pingle, the act of picking and poking at your food but actually getting little of it past your lips. The word *pingle* appeared in the late sixteenth century, apparently a borrowing of the Swedish *pyngla*, meaning *to toil with little effect*. The word *piddle*, as in "He piddled around the office," seems to derive from a different source, although it too has been used since the early seventeenth century to refer to the act of poking vapidly at your food. With a slightly different shade of meaning is *mim*, denoting the action of toying with your food in an affected, prissy, and "daintier-than-thou" manner; arising as an imitation of the *hmph* sound made by fastidious aunts with pursed lips and tense buttocks, *mim* first appeared in the late seventeenth century. Similarly, *harumph*, an exclamation of contempt, developed in the nineteenth century as an imitation of the dismissive snort frequently emitted by gruff uncles in leather chairs. See also *slurp*.

pint

The name of the liquid measure known as the *pint* derives from the same source as *pinto*, as in *pinto bean* or *pinto horse*. Both words, *pint* and *pinto*, derive from the Latin *pictus*, meaning *painted*: the bean and the horse acquired their name because they are both characterized by their dappled colour. The liquid measure, however, acquired the name *pint* at the end of the fourteenth century thanks to the mark painted on large containers, such as a quart or gallon, to gauge what amount within them constituted a pint. The origin of *quart*—from Latin *quartus*, meaning one quarter—is more readily apparent, given that a quart is one fourth of a gallon; more surprising is that *quart* is related to the word *quarantine*, a word that originally referred to the forty days that a widow could remain in her house without being evicted by creditors (the Latin *quadraginta*, meaning forty, became the Italian *quaranta*, the source of *quarantine*). *Quart* is first recorded in the early fourteenth century, about sixty years before the appearance of *pint*. *Gallon*, however, is older than both of these; first recorded at the very beginning of the fourteenth century, *gallon* derives from the French *jalon*, which in turn developed from the Latin *galleta*, meaning *vessel for wine*. See also *pimento*.

piquant

See *pickle*.

piquer

See *pickle*.

piri-piri

See *couscous*.

pish-pash

See *couscous*.

pita

The importance of a given food to a culture can sometimes be gauged by its name. The whimsically named trifle, for example, is a delicious but ultimately trivial dessert. The flat, round bread known as *pita*, on the other hand, is a food staple in many Mediterranean and Middle Eastern cultures, as is suggested by the origin of its name: it derives from the Greek word *peptos*, simply meaning *something cooked*. The source of *peptone* was the

Greek verb *peptein*, which not only meant *to cook* but also *to digest*; this word inspired the name *Pepsi-Cola*, a soft-drink originally marketed, at the beginning of this century, as an aid to digestion. (*Pepsi-Cola* has nothing to do with *Pensacola*, a city in Florida whose name derives from a Choctaw phrase meaning *long-haired people*.)

pizza

The word *pizza* is often said to mean *pie* in Italian, probably because a pizza is pie-shaped and because its name happens to begin with the same two letters as *pie*. However, the Italian word for *pie* is *torta*, while the word *pizza* simply means *pizza*. In origin, the word *pizza* seems to have developed from an Old Italian word meaning *sharp point*, the connection being that pizzas are usually made with piquant or "sharp" sauces. From the same source as *pizza*, the Italian phrase *à la pizzaiola* also developed, a phrase attached to any dish served with a tart sauce made from tomatoes, peppers, herbs, and garlic. One more Italian word that developed from the same source as *pizza* is the Italian verb *pizzicare*, meaning *to pluck* or *to pinch sharply*; the past participle of this verb is *pizzicato*, a musical direction that tells the string players to pluck their instruments rather than bow them. This musical term was adopted by English in the 1880s, fifty years before the appearance in English of *pizza*.

plate

When I was a child, I was amazed that what my parents usually called *plates* suddenly transformed into *dishes* if company came to dinner (and, just as magically, our cutlery became *silverware*, even though they were the same spoons, forks, and knives as always). The reason why *dish*, at least in my family, has a slightly greater cachet than *plate* is unclear: perhaps it is because *plate* has application to so many other items—such as *home plate*, *name plate*, and *armour plate*—while *dish*—with the exception of the recent *satellite dish*—is used almost exclusively in culinary contexts. Alternatively, the higher status of *dish* may arise from the fact that it, unlike *plate*, has been used since the sixteenth century to describe an attractive woman: even Shakespeare, in

Anthony and Cleopatra, calls Cleopatra an "Egyptian dish." *Dish* and *plate* are at least alike in that both derive from Greek sources. With *dish*, that source is the Greek *diskos*, the name of a plate of metal thrown great distances during athletic competitions; in fact, further back in history the Greek *diskos* actually developed from the verb *dikein*, meaning *to throw*. In Latin, the Greek *diskos* evolved into *discus*, a word that the ancient Romans originally employed to refer to the metal disk thrown by athletes, but that later came to refer to a disk on which food is served, and also to a large disk, supported by legs, at which a person sat to write. English adopted all three of these meanings but gave each its own spelling: *discus*, *dish*, and *desk*. With the word *plate*, the Greek source is *platus*, meaning *broad* or *flat*. In Vulgar Latin, the Greek *platus* became *plattus*, a word that English acquired in the thirteenth century as *plate*, meaning *sheet of metal*; not until the mid fifteenth century did the word develop its current culinary sense, by which time *dish* had been in use for more than seven centuries. The number and variety of other English words that derive from the same source as plate is astonishing. They include *platter*, *plane*, *plain*, *plateau*, *plaza*, *plan*, and even *platypus* and *splat*. In one way or another, all these words originally referred to something characterized by flatness. See also *catillation*.

platter

See *plate*.

plonk

Cheap, bad-tasting wines are called *plonk*, a name that might seem to echo the sound of an empty wine bottle toppling over onto the half-eaten pizza it accompanied the night before. In fact, though, *plonk* has more highbrow origins: it appears to be a corruption of *vin blanc*, French for *white wine*. The transformation of *vin blanc* into *plonk* arose in Australia early this century and spread from there to North America and Britain.

plum

Not only are plums and prunes succulent and desiccated versions of the same fruit, their names are versions of the same word:

they both derive from the Greek word for the fruit, *proumnon*, which became the Latin *prunum* before splitting into the Old English *plume* and into the Old French *prune*. When it emerged in the eighth century, the Old English *plume* was pronounced to rhyme with *broom*; in the fifteenth century, however, the word lost its final *e* and shortened its middle vowel, thus establishing the modern spelling and pronunciation of *plum*. In contrast, the Old French *prune*, which English adopted in the mid fourteenth century, never lost its final *e* and never shortened its middle vowel. As a result of these divergent developments, the close connection of *plum* and *prune* has been somewhat obscured. Incidentally, *plum* is not related to the *plumb* in expressions such as "I'm plumb tuckered out." That *plumb* derives from the plumb line, a lead weight attached to a string and used by engineers to ensure that walls are perfectly vertical (the Latin word for *lead* is *plumbum*). Because a plumb line is so utterly straight, the name of the tool came to be used as a synonym for *utterly* or *completely*.

plum-duff

Plum-duff, also known as *spotted dick*, is a plum-free dessert, as is plum-pudding. These dishes have such incongruous names probably because plums were originally included in their recipes, but were eventually replaced by currants and raisins. Although it may seem strange that the dishes were not renamed to reflect their changed ingredients, a long-established name will often persist even when the thing it refers to undergoes a radical transformation: we still speak of "dialing" the phone, for example, even though the rotating disk that served as the original phone dial has been replaced by a keypad. The *duff* of *plum duff*, incidentally, originated in northern England as a dialect pronunciation of *dough*, a rather sensible pronunciation considering the existence of words like *enough*, *tough*, and *rough*. See also *spotted dick* and *plum*.

poach

Although poached eggs and chicken-pox are not connected causally, they are related etymologically: they both derive part of their name from a Germanic word, pronounced something like *puk*, that meant *to swell*. This Germanic source developed quite straightforwardly into *pox*, an old name for the small pustules that swell and erupt on the skin of someone who is afflicted with chicken-pox, small-pox, cow-pox, or even what the English used to call the French pox. The evolution of *puk* into the culinary term *poach* is more circuitous. First it developed into the Frankish word *pokka*, meaning *bag*, a small sack that "swells" in size when filled with grain, or potatoes, or cats. *Pokka* then was adopted by French as *poche*, meaning *pocket*, which gave rise to the French verb *pocher*, meaning *to put in a pocket*. The French then came up with the idea of using *pocher* as a culinary term because if you simmer eggs in stock, a pocket of white forms around the yolk; the English borrowed this French culinary term in the early fifteenth century, respelling it as *poach*. Other words that derive from the French *poche* include *pouch*, *pocket*, and *poke*. This last word now exists only in the phrase *to buy a pig in a poke*, meaning *to buy something without first examining it*. The expression arose out of the old trick—perhaps more often remembered than performed—of selling someone a suckling pig safely tied up in a bag; upon returning home, the hoodwinked customer would discover that his poke contained not a tasty pig but a groggy cat, one soon let out of the bag.

pocerounce
See *bouce Jane.*

poivrade
See *pepper.*

polenta
See *pulse.*

pomace
See *pomme de terre.*

pomander
See *pomme de terre.*

pomato

Unlike the other "pom" words listed above and below, *pomato* has nothing to do with the French word *pomme*, meaning *apple*. Rather, a pomato is hybrid potato that resembles a tomato, and thus its name is compounded from the *p* of *potato* and the *omato* of *tomato*; both the name and the hybrid were invented at the beginning of this century by Luther Burbank, an American horticulturalist, who apparently never considered calling the plant a *totato*. Other plant hybrids have also been given names formed by grafting part of one name onto part of another. The ortanique appeared in the 1930s, its name having been compounded partly from the names of the fruits of which it is a hybrid—the *or* of *orange* and the *tan* of *tangerine*—and partly from the *ique* of the word *unique*. Actually, however, the ortanique was hardly unique because the tangelo, a genetic and linguistic hybrid of the tangerine and the pomelo, had been produced thirty years before. The pomelo, incidentally, despite the similarity of its name to *pomato*, is not a hybrid; it is a species of grapefruit that took its name in the mid nineteenth century from the Latin *pomum* or French *pomme*, meaning *apple*. Other hybrid words have not been limited to the names of new fruits: in 1970 the Van Brode Milling Company patented the *spork*, an eating utensil combining the prongs of a fork with the bowl of a spoon.

pome-dorry

See *pomme de terre*.

pomegranate

The only edible part of the pomegranate is the red globule surrounding each of the seemingly innumerable seeds contained by the pulp and rind of the fruit. These seeds give the fruit its name, for *pomegranate* means *apple filled with seeds*, a name bestowed upon it by the ancient Romans, who originally called it, in Latin, *malum granatum*. *Granatum* developed from the Latin *granum*, meaning *seed*, which is also the source of *grain*, of *gravy* (a sauce spiced with grains of pepper), and of *granite* (a rock with a grainy texture). *Malum* developed from the Greek *melon*, meaning *apple*, which is of course also the source of *melon* as in *watermelon*. Had the Romans persisted in calling the pomegranate a *malum granatum* we might today know it as a *malumgranate*; instead, however, those fickle ancients changed the name to *pomum granatum*, perhaps because the *malum* that meant *apple* sounded like the unrelated *malum*, meaning *evil*. The Latin *pomum*—like the word *malum* before it—also meant *apple*, and in fact it developed into *pomme*, the French word for *apple*. Likewise, *pomum granatum* developed into the French *pome granate*, which became the English *pomegranate* in the early fourteenth century. In French, however, the original *pome granate* evolved very differently over the succeeding centuries: the *pomme* was dropped, and the first vowel and last consonant in *granate* shifted, resulting in a new French name for pomegranate, *grenade*. The resemblance of the pomegranate to seventeenth century hand-held explosives led to the name *grenade* being bestowed upon the munition. The French name of the fruit is also the source of *grenadine*, a syrup made from pomegranates, and even, thanks to a reversal of letters in the word, of *garnet*, a precious stone coloured red like the pomegranate. See also *pomme de terre*.

pomme de terre

Many people who know the French name for the *potato*—*pomme de terre*, meaning *apple of the earth*—might not know that several English words have also derived from the French *pomme*. For example, the French *pomme* is the source of *pomade*, a drink made of pressed apples; the word *pomade* appeared at the end of the fourteenth century but did not survive into the fifteenth century thanks to the success of its slightly older rival, *cider*. The French *pomme* was also the source in the late fourteenth century of *pome-dorry*, a medieval dish made by coating a meat ball with the yolk of an egg; it was the resulting yellow sphere that prompted the second half of the name *pome-dorry*, a borrowing of the French *doré*, meaning *gilded*, which in turn derives from the Latin *aurora*, meaning *dawn*, a time of golden light. In the sixteenth century, *pomme* also gave rise to *pomace*, the name of the pulp remaining after apples have their juice extracted for cider. *Pomme* is even the source of several words not related to food or drink: the word *pomander*, a small box of dried fruits and petals that gives fragrance to clothes, literally means *apple amber*, while the word *pummel*, the action of striking someone or something repeatedly, arose from the resemblance in size and shape of a fist to an apple. See also *pomegranate* and *lemonade*.

pompelmoose

See *shaddock*.

poor boy

The year 1952 is a momentous one in sandwich history. It was in that year the name *poor boy* was first bestowed upon a food product created by inserting meat and mixed pickles between two slices of bread. The result, a substantial sandwich that even "poor boys" could afford, caught on like hot cakes and quickly spread across the lunch counters of North America. The name of this sandwich changed, however, as it migrated from region to region. *Poor boy* was restricted to the Deep South, especially New Orleans where it originated. In New England, in 1954, the name *grinder* was also given to the sandwich, supposedly because its size demanded a lot of "grinding" or chewing. One year later, in Connecticut, the sandwich, now made with a long bun, also became well-known as a *submarine*, the change in design and name having been prompted by the frequent sightings of submarines at the naval base in Groton, Connecticut. The year 1955 also saw the appearance of the name *hero sandwich*, originally used in New York City, and *hoagie*, which became associated with Philadelphia and New Jersey. The hero sandwich may simply have acquired its name from the supposedly herculean effort needed to consume it; it is more probable, however, that the name has some connection with the Greek pita sandwich known as a *gyro* (the Greek pronunciation of *gyro* is *yheero*). The origin of *hoagie* is less certain. There is no evidence to suggest that it has any connection with the song writer, Hoagy Carmichael. As well, supposed links to Hog Island, Delaware, or to an ice-cream treat known as the *hokey pokey*, seem far-fetched. It may be possible, however, that the name is a corruption of the French term *haut goût*, meaning *high taste* or *strongly flavoured*.

Pronounced *ho go* as it sometimes was by Americans, the French *haut goût* may have been bestowed on a particularly spicy version of the original poor boy sandwich. See also *gyro*.

pope's nose

See *choke-priest*.

poppy seed

The red petals of the poppy were once used as a food-colouring, but it is the seeds of the plant that are now used in cooking, especially sprinkled on bagels or mixed in with pastry fillings. The poppy takes its name from the Latin name for the plant, *papaver*, which English borrowed as *popei* in the eighth century and then respelt as *poppy* in the fifteenth century. The *poppy* in *poppycock*, an expression meaning *utter nonsense* that emerged in the United States in the mid nineteenth century, is not related to the *poppy* in *poppy seed*. Rather, it derives from the Dutch *pappekak*, meaning *soft dung*, which in turn goes back to the Latin *pappa*, meaning *soft food*, and *cacare*, meaning *to defecate*.

porcelain

See *pork*.

pork

After the French came from Normandy in 1066 and conquered England, they decided that they would be the ones who ate the animals, while the defeated English would be the ones who raised the animals. Accordingly, most of the original English animal names—such as *pig, cow, calf, sheep,* and *deer*—continued to be used in the barnyard, but French names—such as *pork, beef, veal, mutton,* and *venison*—were given to meats once they appeared on the table. The French *porc* was borrowed as *pork* at the beginning of the fifteenth century; the French in turn had developed the word from the Latin *porcus*, meaning *hog*. This Latin word is also the source of several other English animal names, including *porcupine*, literally meaning *thorny pig*, and *porpoise*, literally meaning *fish pig*. Porcelain, the fine china brought out for special meals, also derives its name from the Latin word for *pig*: the Latin *porcus* gave rise to the Italian *porca* whose diminutive, meaning *little pig*, is *porcella*. This word, *porcella*, was given by the Italians to a seashell because its shape and contours resembled, in their minds, the external genitalia of female pigs. The name of this seashell was then borrowed by the French as *porcelaine*, which they bestowed upon the fine china because its sheen and colour resembled that of the shell. It was this word that English borrowed, without the final *e*, at the beginning of the sixteenth century.

porridge

Bland and formless, as devoid of life as a crumpled sock, porridge had nothing to take its name from except the pot in which it was made. The original name of the substance was therefore *pottage*, first recorded in English in the early thirteenth century; by the early sixteenth century, the pronunciation, and therefore the spelling as well, had shifted to what it currently is, no doubt because people who were frequently forced to eat porridge were too disheartened and malnourished to articulate all the consonants in the name. The original word, *pottage*, did not vanish, however; having lost its negative association with gruel, it was readopted from French in the mid sixteenth century as the name of a soup, especially a soup made in a French style. *Porringer*, the name of a bowl from which foods such as soup and porridge are eaten, developed in a manner similar to *porridge*: in the mid fifteenth century, the word was adopted from French as *pottinger*, but by the early sixteenth century its pronunciation had shifted to *porringer*. See also *potable*.

porringer

See *porridge*.

port

Usually drunk at the end of a meal, the strong, sweet wine known as *port* takes its name from Oporto, a coastal city in Portugal through which it is exported. In Portuguese, *Oporto* literally means *the port*, and was bestowed upon the city because of its important harbour, one never made inaccessible by ice (the same harbour eventually inspired the name *Portugal* itself). Further back, the Portuguese *porto*—the *O* of *Oporto* simply being a definite article meaning *the*—developed from the Latin *portus*, meaning *passage*. This *portus* also gave rise to a corresponding Latin verb, *portare*, which originally meant *to take through a passage*, but later came to mean *to carry*; from this verb, English derived a cluster of words relating to carrying things, including *export*, *transport*, *portage*, and *portable*. The tray used to carry items from the kitchen to the table—called a *portative*—also derives from this Latin source. Even further back, the Latin *portus* derived from an Indo-European source, one that also entered the Germanic language family and gave rise to *ford*, *fiord*, and *ferry*. English first adopted the word *port* in the ninth century, using it as a synonym for *harbour*, and readopted it eight hundred years later, when the British began to import the sweet Spanish wine.

porterhouse steak

In the late fourteenth century, labourers who specialized in carrying heavy things from place to place came to be known as *porters*, a word that derives from the Latin *portare*, meaning *to carry*. Porters, not surprisingly, tended to be large men with small wages who could only afford to quench their thirst with a cheap drink called *entire*, so named because it was supposed to be flavoured like three different kinds of beer and therefore had a "whole" or "entire" taste. In time, *entire* came to be so associated with porters that it acquired the nickname *porter's beer*, first recorded in the early eighteenth century and later shortened to *porter*. By the mid eighteenth century, taverns selling porter were called *porterhouses*, and by the late eighteenth century porterhouses had acquired a reputation for serving hearty fare such as pork chops and steaks. One such porterhouse—Morrison's Porterhouse, located in New York—popularized a cut of beef located next to the sirloin, and it was this steak that came to be known as *porterhouse steak* in the early nineteenth century. See also *three-threads*.

postpast

Just as English now uses the word *antipasto* to refer to an hors d'oeuvre served before an Italian meal, it once used the word *postpast* to refer to a little snack following a meal. *Postpast*, which derives from the Latin *post*, meaning *after*, and *pastus*, meaning *food*, was current in English only during the seventeenth century, but the custom of the postpast persists to this day: in France a morsel of cheese is often served as the postpast, while in North America it commonly takes the form of a delicious, minty toothpick. See also *antipasto*.

postprandial

The ancient Romans did not have dinner, they had *prandium*, from which English derives the term *postprandial*, literally meaning *after-dinner*—you might, for instance, indulge in a postprandial snooze. On the other hand, the Latin word for *hungry*—*jejunus*—appears in English as part of the term *ante-jentacular*, meaning *before breakfast*; typical ante-jentacular behaviour is characterized by blurred vision, a shuffling gait, and an intolerance for children and pets.

pot

See *potable*.

pot luck

See *pot-pourri*.

pot-pourri

Although it is now the name of a fragrant mixture of flower petals used to perfume a room or a closet, pot-pourri was originally a dish of many meats stewed together but then removed and served separately. The name of this dish is French for *rotten pot*, the French *pourri* deriving from the same Latin source as the English *putrid*. It was not the French, however, who originally gave the dish this bizarre name, since *pot-pourri* is a direct translation of the Spanish *olla podrida*, also meaning *rotten pot*. The Spanish called this stew *rotten* not because it tasted badly, but because the meats it contained were cooked until they fell off the bone— in other words, the dish was rotten in so far as its ingredients were falling to pieces. The Spanish name for the dish, *olla podrida*, first appeared in English in the late sixteenth century; the French name appeared a decade later at the beginning of the seventeenth.

A French dish similar to the pot-pourri in both name and substance is *pot-au-feu*, literally meaning *pot in the fire*. Long ago, such a fire-pot might be kept simmering over the hearth for days, scraps of meats and vegetables being added as they became available from other meals. A guest who dropped by unannounced would be served from this simmering pot and, depending on what had gone into it, would receive either a hearty, thick stew or a thin, watery broth; such a meal was called *pot luck* and, after first appearing in English in the late sixteenth century, came to be applied to any meal in which the quality of the fare was determined by chance. See also *oven*.

potable

Although the word *edible*, meaning *fit for eating*, is a familiar term, its counterpart—*potable*, meaning *fit for drinking*—is not. Many words that derive from the same source as *potable*, however, are very familiar, including *pot*, *potion*, and *poison*. The ultimate source of these words is the Latin *potare*, meaning *to drink*, which actually gave rise to two other Latin words: *potio* and *potus*, both meaning *a drink*. From *potus*, English derived in the thirteenth century the word *pot*, meaning *a cooking kettle* (the other *pot*, the one that means *marijuana*, appeared in the 1930s as an abbreviated form of the Mexican Spanish name, *potiguaya*). From *potio*, the other Latin word meaning *a drink*, English derived in the late fourteenth century both *potion* and *poison*, originally synonyms that referred to any liquid mixture, whether intended to heal or harm. Gradually, however, the words differentiated from one another as *poison* came to be associated with toxins, and *potion* with fairly benign beverages that, at worst, might make you fall in love with an evil prince. From the same source as *potion* and *poison*, the word *potation* also arose in the fourteenth century as a name for any alcoholic beverage; two hundred years later, in the sixteenth century, *potation* also inspired *compotation*, a drinking party characterized by loud carousing. Similarly, the word *pot* also became part of many sayings and idioms: *pot-shot*, for example, originated in the nineteenth century as a name for an unsporting shot fired at an ailing or out of season animal with the intention of merely filling the stove pot at home. The expression *gone to pot* arose from practice of taking the bones and scraps of a roast and throwing them into a pot to make soup (a fate slightly better than "going to the dogs"). See also *pot-pourri* and *potwaller*.

potato

When the word *potato* first appeared in English in the mid sixteenth century, it did not refer to what we now call potatoes—that is, it was not a synonym for *spud*—but rather denoted what we now call sweet potatoes. The word *potato* derives via Spanish from the Taino word for the tuber, *batata*, Taino being a language spoken by the indigenous people of the West Indies. After encountering these people in 1493, Columbus returned to Spain with several "batatas," which European horticulturalists began to cultivate. About a hundred years later, the other tuber—the white potato or spud—was introduced to England from South America, probably by Sir Francis Drake. This plant, little esteemed at first, became known as the *bastard potato* or *Virginia potato* due to its superficial resemblance to the other (sweet) potato. (The white potato was not actually grown in Virginia or anywhere in North America at this time, but because Drake—sailing from Columbia to England—briefly visited Virginia on his way home, the geographical origin of the tuber became muddled.) In time, the white potato became a more important food for Europeans than the sweet potato, so the qualifying adjectives—*bastard* and *Virginia*—were dropped from its name; likewise, the adjective *sweet* had to be added to the name of the other plant to distinguish it from the upstart tuber that was now bore the name *potato*. The popularity of the white potato also accounts for its many nicknames: *tater*, a shortened form of *potato*, appeared in the mid eighteenth century; *murphy*, inspired by a surname belonging to one of the many Irish immigrants who introduced the potato to North Americans, appeared in the early nineteenth century; *spud*, a word of unknown origin, arose in the nineteenth century; and *earth-apple* arose this century as a direct translation of the French name for the potato, *pomme de terre*. See also *yam*.

potron

See *bouce Jane*.

pottage

See *porridge*.

pottinger

See *porridge*.

potwaller

Throughout the eighteenth century, in some parts of England, a man was allowed to vote in the parliamentary elections so long as he was the head of his own household, and not simply a member of another man's household. Householder eligibility was determined in turn by whether the man had his own fireplace where he could boil soup in his own pot. The name *potwaller* arose to describe such eligible householders, a term derived by compounding *pot* with the Old English verb *wall*, meaning *to boil* (this Old English *wall* is not related to the *wall* in *wallpaper*, but it is related to the word *wallow*). The advantage of being recognized as a "pot-boiler" was not so much that you got to vote, as that you were given money by candidates who wanted your vote. Accordingly, scurrilous men who headed no household would sometimes get themselves declared potwallers by setting up a little fire-pit in the street and boiling a pot of soup in the presence of witnesses; the Reform Act of 1832 put an end to this flagrant abuse of kitchen utensils. See also *potable*.

pound

See *litre*.

poundcake

See *cupcake*.

prairie oyster

Whereas the ancient Aztecs referred to the avocado as *ahuacatl*, meaning *testicle*, many North Americans call a cooked calf's testicle an *oyster*, more specifically a *prairie oyster*. For the Aztecs the connection between avocado and testicle was probably based upon shape, although the Aztecs themselves might claim that size was another factor; for us, the oyster's reputation as an aphrodisiac is probably what provides the seminal link to that bovine, ellipsoid organ. This testicular sense of *prairie oyster* emerged around 1941, but the term had also been used since the late nineteenth century as the name for a cocktail made with a raw egg. See also *avocado* and *oyster*.

praline

Although pralines are a remarkably simple confection—nothing more than almonds coated with caramelized sugar—they caused a sensation when they were invented at the beginning of the seventeenth century in France: their flavour was extolled in poems, and they are even reputed to have facilitated several diplomatic ventures undertaken by the Marshall Plessis-Praslin, a minister to both Louis XIII and Louis XIV. It was Plessis-Praslin's cook, in fact, who invented pralines, and it was Plessis-Praslin himself who selflessly gave the last half of his surname to the confection. In time, however, the French changed the spelling of *praslin* to *praline*, and it was in this form that English borrowed the name in the early eighteenth century.

prenade

See *bouce Jane*.

pretzel

The shape of the pretzel has been a greater source of speculation than the origin of its name. Some experts in pretzel lore have suggested its shape originated among a cult of sun worshippers who patterned the dough to resemble a cross encircled by a ring, a pattern that evolved over time into its present shape. Others have proposed that the pretzel's shape represents arms folded across the chest like someone in prayer, the idea being that pretzels were to be given to children who had memorized their prayers. Of these two explanations, the origin of the word *pretzel* supports the "folded-arms" theory: *pretzel* appears to derive from the German name of the snack, *bretzel*, which in turn developed from the Latin *bracchium*, meaning *arm* (the word *broccoli* derives from the same source). Of course, it is also possible that the shape of the pretzel arose before its name: some pretzels, after all, are quite brittle, and a "folded-arm" shape is less prone to breaking than a mere circle or stick of baked dough. If this is the case, then it was the shape of the pretzel that inspired its name, not the other way around. The word *pretzel* first appeared in English in the mid nineteenth century. See also *broccoli*.

primordial soup

All soups—whether chicken or vegetable, vichyssoise or gazpacho, alphabet or mulligatawny—owe their existence to that first and original soup, the primordial soup that once bubbled over the steaming earth (recently, however, a break-away faction of maverick scientists has argued that the primordial soup was in fact a primordial broth; French bio-chemists, on the other hand, have long maintained that it was a primordial bouillon). Although the primordial soup was first concocted a billion years ago, scientists did not posit its existence until 1956, deriving its name from the Latin *primus*, meaning *first*, and *ordiri*, meaning *to begin*.

prix fixe

See *table d'hôte*.

prune

See *plum*.

pub

See *tavern*.

pudding

The original puddings were not made by mixing milk and sugar with rice, tapioca, or chocolate; instead, they were made by stuffing minced meat and oatmeal into a pig's intestine and then boiling it till it was cooked. Puddings, in other words, were originally the same thing as sausages, and that is also where they derive their name: the Latin word for *sausage* was *botellus*, which evolved into the French *boudin*, which English then borrowed and respelt in the fourteenth century as *pudding*. The word *pudding* continued to be used to mean *sausage* into the early nineteenth century, but this sense of the word now survives only in *black pudding*, also known as *blood sausage*. *Pudding* started to acquire a new sense in the mid fifteenth century when it became a synonym for *guts*, *entrails*, and *bowels*—the casings, in other words, in which the original *puddings* were boiled; as a slang term, this intestinal sense of *pudding* has survived to the present in phrases such as "He punched me right in the puddings." The last meaning of *pudding* to develop was the one now most familiar to us, namely, *a sweet dessert*. This meaning of *pudding* emerged in the mid sixteenth century because dessert puddings were once made by pouring milk, sugar, and flavourings into a cloth bag that was boiled until its contents solidified; this culinary process resembled the way sausage "puddings" were made, and thus *pudding* was transferred to the dessert items.

pudding-prick

Although it might be mistaken for a derisive insult aimed at men, the term *pudding-prick* actually refers to a thin skewer once used to fasten shut a bag of pudding before dropping it into boiling water to cook. This sense of *pudding-prick* arose in the early sixteenth century, almost a hundred years before the word *prick* came to be used as a coarse synonym for *penis*. In fact, before its current obscene sense began to overwhelm it in the late sixteenth century, the word *prick* had several entirely innocent applications. It could, as mentioned, refer to a kitchen skewer, but it was also used by young women as a term of endearment for their suitors. "Mother," a young lady might say, "I'd like you to meet Lord Frederick, my prick." This sense of the word *prick* probably arose from the pangs of love that "pricked" the hearts of these young women as they succumbed to their sweeties' wooing. A similar use of the word occurs in the King James translation of the Bible (Acts 9:15) where God tells Saul not to "kick against the pricks"—in other words, don't fight the pangs of conscience. See also *cock*.

pulse

Although the cardiovascular sense of *pulse* is now its most familiar, the word can also be used to refer to the edible seeds of legumes—peas, beans, lentils, and so forth. This culinary sense of *pulse* is the original one, dating back to the late thirteenth century when the word was adopted from Old French. In turn, Old French derived the word from the Latin *puls*, meaning *porridge*: peas, beans, and lentils were so often made into porridge that they eventually acquired a name that meant just that. Even further back in history, the Latin *puls* derived from an Indo-European source, pronounced something like *pel* and meaning *dust*: before being made into porridge, the peas, beans, and lentils were usually split or ground into a dust-like powder. The Indo-European *pel* also developed into several other Latin words that eventually made their way into English: the Latin *polenta*, meaning *barley meal*, was adopted in the eleventh century as a name for a porridge made from barley and chestnuts; the Latin *pulvis*, meaning *dust*, gave rise in the late sixteenth century to *pulverize*, meaning *to pound into dust*; and the Latin *pollen*, meaning *grain meal*, was adopted by English in the mid eighteenth century as a name for the yellowish powder produced in a flower's stamen. The other *pulse*—the one that refers to the rhythmic throb in your arteries— is related to none of these words, deriving instead from the Latin *pellere*, meaning *to beat*.

pumpernickel

Before it became known as *pumpernickel*, this dark, coarse bread was known in Germany as *crank broat*, literally meaning *sick bread*, a name suggesting it was once fed to the infirm. In the mid seventeenth century, the bread lost this name and came to be known as *pumpernickel*, a word that has long been a source of etymological consternation. According to one theory, the name arose when Napoleon, rejecting a poor peasant's offer of bread, said, "C'est du pain pour Nicole," French for "That's bread for Nicole" (Nicole being Napoleon's horse). The poor peasant, never having studied at the Sorbonne, assumed that *pain pour Nicole*— which he mistakenly remembered as *pumpernickel*—was a fancy name for the bread, and soon the word spread across Europe, even to countries the peasant had never heard of. The trouble with this explanation is that *pumpernickel* had been used in Germany as a synonym for *fool* for about a hundred years before

Napoleon was born. A more likely derivation of *pumpernickel* is that it originally meant *devil's fart*: the word *pumpern* had developed earlier in German as an imitation of the sound heralding that odoriferous, gastro-intestinal phenomenon (just as, in English, *burp* arose as an imitation of another noisy eructation); the word *nickel*, on the other hand, had long been a German word for *demon* (just as, in English, we sometimes refer to Satan as *Old Nick*). A German fool would therefore be called a *pumpernickel* (or *devil's fart*), just as an English fool might be called *a horse's ass*. The word was then transferred to one of the "dullest" sorts of German bread, the pumpernickel, after which, in the mid eighteenth century, it was adopted by English.

pumpkin

See *melon*.

punch

The province of India known as *Punjab* derives its name from two Persian words, *panj*, meaning *five*, and *ab*, meaning *water*, a name that alludes to the five tributaries of the Indus river that flow though that territory: the Jhelum, the Chenab, the Ravi, the Beas, and the Sutlej. Likewise, the beverage named *punch*, first referred to in the early seventeenth century, probably derives its name from the Persian word *panj* because it was traditionally made with five ingredients: rum, water, lemon, sugar, and spice. It is also possible, however, that punch takes its name from *puncheon*, the name of a large barrel used on ships to store necessities such as rum. British sailors—whose lives consisted of drinking rum, receiving the lash, and swabbing the poop deck—may have transferred the name *puncheon* from the barrel to the rum concoction it contained (sea captains regularly diluted their sailors' rum with other substances). *Puncheon* may then have been shortened to *punch*, perhaps on the analogy that drinking enough of it will, like a boxer's punch, knock you silly. In fact, however, this other *punch*—the one boxers throw—is not related to the beverage *punch*; instead, the pugilist's *punch* derives from the Latin *pungere*, meaning *to pierce*, which is also the source of the word *puncture*. Another unrelated *punch* is the one in *Punch and Judy*, a violent puppet whose name is short for the Italian *Punchinello*; in turn, *Punchinello* is a corruption of the Neapolitan word *polecenella*, meaning *little turkey*, and was applied to the puppet because of his beak-like nose. Incidentally, it was the triumph of Punch over all his opponents that inspired the saying *pleased as Punch*. See also *grog* and *bollepunge*.

puncheon

See *punch*.

purée

Before blenders and food processors were invented, purées were made by repeatedly pressing cooked vegetables through a sieve until they acquired a texture like that of mashed potatoes. Although this process does indeed reduce carrots or peas or parsnips to a kind of "pure" state—one in which the vegetable's essence is released, like a soul, from the physical constraints of shape and form—the word *purée* actually has no relation to the word *pure*. Instead, *purée* probably derives from *porrum*, a Latin word meaning *leek*, an onion-like vegetable. In Late Latin, *porrum* gave rise to *porrata*, meaning *made with leeks*, a word that evolved into the Old French name for a mashed-leek dish, *porée*. In the fourteenth century, *porée* was adopted by English as *porray* and its meaning widened to include dishes made from any strained vegetable, not just leeks; in Scotland, for example, porray—or as it is called there, *purry*—is made from chopped cabbage and oatmeal. Meanwhile, in Old French, *porée* also developed a variant spelling, *purée*, first used as the name of a dish of mashed leeks and almond-milk, and later used to denote any sort of mashed and strained food; English adopted this form of the word—*purée*—in the early eighteenth century.

quart

See *pint*.

quesadilla

In Spanish, the word *queso* means cheese, and the endings *illa* and *illo* are suffixes used to form the feminine or masculine diminutives of a word, just as French and English often use the diminutive *ette*, as in *kitchenette*. Thus, *quesadilla*, the name of a turnover filled with cheese, means *little cheese*. The *illa* diminutive is also found on Spanish words such as *tortilla*, *vanilla*, and *sarsaparilla* (also spelt *sassparilla*), all of which are little versions of something bigger. The word *quesadilla* first appeared in English in 1944. See also *tart*, *sarsaparilla*, and *vanilla*.

quiche

The word *quiche* derives from the German *kuchen*, meaning *little cake*. Had English acquired the name of this savoury custard directly from German, its present spelling and pronunciation would be much closer to the original *kuchen*. However, the German word entered English through French, which altered the spelling to suit its phonetic system, and thus *quiche* looks very little like its immediate ancestor, *kuchen*. In fact, more similar to the German *kuchen* is a word that appeared in English more than twelve hundred years ago, *kechel*, which derived from the same source as the German *kuchen*, and became the name of another sort of little cake; when made for the purpose of feeding the poor, it was known as *God's kechel*. *Kechel* did not survive the fourteenth century, but a related form, *kichel*, was used until the late nineteenth century as the name of a little cake strewn with currants.

quignon

To my chagrin, using the term *bread-bum* to refer to the end-slice of a loaf of bread is not appropriate at most formal dinner parties. Fortunately, another word exists for this crusty and much sought after part of the loaf: *quignon*. This useful word derives through French from the Latin *cuneolus*, meaning *little coin*, the connection being that the end-piece of a loaf is small and round.

quince

The quince, a relative of the apple and pear but too bitter to be eaten uncooked, derives its name from *Cydonia*, a port on the coast of Crete now known as Khaniá. Because the fruit was exported from Cydonia, the ancient Greeks called it *melon Kudonion*, meaning *Cydonian apple*. This name entered Latin as *cydoneum*, which later became *cotoneum* and was then adopted by French as *cooin*. In the late fourteenth century, English borrowed this French name, spelling it *quine* and creating a plural form spelt *quince*. Before long, however, people forgot that *quince* was supposed to be the plural form and began using it as a singular.

rabbit

Just as there were no rabbits in Australia until they were taken there by British settlers in 1859, there were no rabbits in England or in northern Europe till they were introduced from southern Europe in the twelfth century. Accordingly, most of the languages of northern Europe—including English, Celtic, German, Dutch, Norwegian, and Finnish—had to borrow their words for *rabbit* from one of the Romance languages, that is, from one of the languages that developed from Latin like French, Spanish, and Italian. English, for example, derived its original name for the rabbit—*cony*—from the French *conis*, which in turn developed from the Latin name for the long-eared creature, *cuniculus*. *Cony* first appeared in English at the beginning of the thirteenth century, but at that time the word referred only to the pelt or fur of the rabbit: it did not come to mean the living, breathing animal until the fourteenth century. The fourteenth century is also when the now more familiar name, *rabbit*, was first introduced. *Rabbit* initially meant *the young of a cony*, and did not really begin to replace *cony* itself until the eighteenth century. To some extent, the demise of *cony* was caused by its pronunciation: when first adopted, the word was pronounced so that it rhymed with *money* or *honey*, as demonstrated by poems in which it is used as part of a rhyme; this pronunciation apparently troubled no one until about three hundred years ago when a moral minority complained that the pronunciation of *coney* was too similar to that of *cunny*, a word that had emerged in the early eighteenth century as a diminutive of *cunt*. Benjamin Smart, for example, who published a pronunciation dictionary in 1836, declared that in solemn places, such as a church, the pronunciation of the creature's name should be changed so that it rhymed with words like *pony* (for a long time, saying *coney* in church could not be avoided because it was used in older translations of the Bible). Eventually, however, the controversy over the pronunciation of *coney* faded away as the word itself vanished: *rabbit* was increasingly used in its place, both in everyday speech and in biblical translations. Today, *coney* is only heard in *Coney Island*, a place where Dutch immigrants once bred rabbits. The word *rabbit*, incidentally, derives from the Walloon *rabotte*, Walloon being a form of French spoken in Belgium.

radish

The colour of the radish—reddish—is not where this hot root takes its name; rather, it derives, through Italian and then French, from the Latin word *radix*, meaning *root*. Other words that derive from the same source include *eradicate*, meaning *to uproot*, and *radical*, which originally denoted a person championing a return to the "grassroots" of society. The word *radish* dates back a thousand years in English, long before the appearance in 1968 of *radicchio*, the name of another salad vegetable whose name also derives, through Italian, from the Latin *radix*. *Radish* also appears in *horseradish*, a plant whose hot root is made into a condiment. The *horse* of *horseradish* does not mean it is eaten by that animal; rather, *horse* has been frequently prefixed to the names of fruits and vegetables to indicate a particularly common or coarse species. At least forty such compounds exist, including *horse-parsley*, *horse-cucumber*, and *horse-mushroom*. The word *horseradish* appeared at the end of the sixteenth century.

ragout

A ragout is a highly spiced dish of meat and vegetables. Originally, ragouts were given their strong seasoning because they were intended to excite or revive the appetite. In the middle of the seventeenth century, this function gave the dish its name, as *ragout* derives from the French *ragoûter*, a word compounded from the prefix *re*, meaning *back* or *again*, and *goûter*, meaning *to taste*. The history of the French verb *goûter* can also be traced further back: it developed from the Latin *gustare*, also meaning *to taste*, which derived in turn from an Indo-European source that also gave us, through another line of development, the word *choose*. The link in meaning between *taste* and *choose* is still evident when we say something like, "He has good taste"—in other words, "He's choosey." The word *ragout* is closely related to a culinary phrase used in English since the middle of the seventeenth century, but which has never lost its French associations: *haut-goût*, meaning *high taste* or, more idiomatically, *strong flavour*. Two other words adopted by English are also cousins to *ragout*. The first, *gusto*, entered English from Italian after shifting its meaning from *taste* to *zeal*; the second, *disgust*, originally meant *to ruin the taste* before developing its broader, current sense. Both words, like *ragout* and *haut-goût*, appeared in English in the middle of the seventeenth century. See also *poor boy*.

raisin

From *racemus*, a Latin word meaning *a cluster of grapes*, French derived the word *raisin*, meaning *a single grape*. English adopted this French word in the fourteenth century, first using it as a synonym for *grape* (which had been adopted a hundred years earlier) and then shifting its application to a special kind of grape, one dried in the sun until it resembles a wizened Winston Churchill. A single word, therefore, has shifted its meaning over the centuries from *a cluster of grapes* (the Latin *racemus*), to *one grape* (the French *raisin*), to *one dried grape* (the English *raisin*). It should be duly noted that *raisin* is in no way related to *raison d'etre* or *raisin' hell*. See also *grape*.

ramp

See *slurp*.

rape

See *ravioli*.

raspberry

Until the early seventeenth century, the raspberry was known simply as *raspis*, a word of unknown origin that suddenly appeared in English in the early sixteenth century. Before this time, the raspberry was known as the *hindberry*, so called because it was thought to be eaten in the wild by hinds, or what we now call deer. As a name for the derisive sound produced by placing the tongue firmly between one's lips and blowing—a synonym, in other words, for *Bronx cheer*—*raspberry* dates back about a hundred years. This sense of *raspberry* developed from Cockney rhyming slang, a code invented by London Cockneys in the nineteenth century in order to baffle outsiders and entertain each other. In Cockney rhyming slang, certain common terms are replaced by a phrase whose final word rhymes with the word being replaced. *Rosy Lea*, for example, takes the place of *you and me*, and *butcher's hook* is used in place of *look*. Likewise, *raspberry tart* arose as a substitute for *fart*, and was so used until it was shortened to just *raspberry*. In time, *raspberry* came to refer not only to genuine venting of flatulence, but also to any imitation of the noise associated with that event. See also *bread*.

ravenous

See *slurp*.

ravioli

Tiny turnips and little lambs—that is what you are metaphorically eating when you sit down to a meal of ravioli and agnelotti. The two pastas—ravioli stuffed with cheese and agnelotti stuffed with meat—both derive their names from Italian sources that describe their plump shape: *raviolo*, meaning *little turnip*, is the diminutive of the Italian *ravi*, which developed from the Latin name for turnip, *rapa*. This Latin source also gave rise in the fourteenth century to *rape*, the original English name for the turnip; after the introduction of the word *turnip* in the sixteenth century, *rape* shifted its meaning and became the name of a plant whose seeds yield an edible oil. Although unrelated to the word *rape* that means *sexual assault* (a word that derives from the Latin *rapere*, meaning *to seize*), the apparent resemblance of the two words has recently prompted farmers to rename *rape* as *canola*. The Italian name of the other pasta, *agnelotti*, meaning *little lamb*, is the diminutive of *agnello*, which developed from the Latin name for lamb, *agnus*. In English, the oldest of these two words is *ravioli*: it appeared briefly in the fifteenth century as *rafiol*, the name of a kind of meatball, and then was forgotten for many centuries until readopted with its current sense and spelling in the mid nineteenth century. *Agnelotti* is an even more recent adoption into English, probably within the last twenty years.

recipe

When the word *recipe* appeared in English in the fifteenth century, it referred only to directions for making medicines; not for another three hundred years, in the early eighteenth century, did *recipe* also come to denote directions for preparing a dish of food. Before this modern sense of *recipe* developed, instructions for making food were called *receipts*, a usage dating all the way back to the fourteenth century. The difference between calling such culinary instructions *receipts* or *recipes* is slight, at least in so far as both words derive from the same source, the Latin *recipere*, meaning *to receive* (the words are spelt differently because *recipe* developed from the present tense of *recipere* while *receipt* developed from a past tense); these two words became associated with cooking because when you make a dish you "receive" into your hand the various ingredients required by the dish. Going even further back in history, the Latin *recipere* was formed from the prefix *re*, meaning *again*, and the verb *capere*, meaning *to take*. The ancient Romans also combined *capere*, or forms deriving from it, with other words to create numerous compounds, many of which were later adopted by English. These include *participate* (from the Latin *participare*, meaning *to take part*), *prince* (from the Latin *princeps*, literally meaning *first taker*), and even *forceps* (a direct adoption of the Latin *forceps*, meaning *hot-taker*, forceps having originated as a blacksmith's tool). Incidentally, the pharmaceutical symbol ℞ (sometimes represented as Rx) stands for *recipe*; the cross-bar represents the staff of Jove, the patron of doctors, under whose auspices the medical recipe was to be prepared. See also *nym*.

reeked meat

See *smoked meat*.

relevé

In a formal, French-style dinner, a dish that follows and replaces another dish is called a *relevé*. The word literally means *lifted away*, a reference to the previous dish having been removed from the table. These dishes are also sometimes known as *removes*, and in fact *remove* is the older of the two terms, coming into use in the last quarter of the eighteenth century. *Relevé* did not appear in English until the second quarter of the nineteenth century, apparently intended as a genteel synonym for the rather blunt *remove*. See also *leftovers*.

relic

See *leftovers*.

relief

See *leftovers*.

relish

The chopped pickle you put on a hamburger, the relish, derives its name from the same source as the words *release* and *relax*. All these words evolved from the Latin verb *relaxare*, meaning *to loosen*, which in turn is a compound formed from the prefix *re*, meaning *back*, and the verb *laxare*, also meaning *to loosen*. This "loosening" sense is still at the heart of *relax* (a loosening of one's muscles) and *release* (a loosening of one's grip), but it now seems very distant from *relish*. Originally, however, the word *relish* referred to the flavour that was "loosened" or "released" from food as it was chewed and swallowed: a well-seasoned beef stew released a good relish, while a bowl of oatmeal porridge released very little. *Relish* entered English somewhat circuitously: the Latin *relaxare* was adopted by Old French as *relaisser* (which is the direct source of *release*); from *relaisser*, the French then formed *relais*, meaning *the released part*, which English adopted in the early thirteenth century as *reles*. By the early sixteenth century, *reles* had been respelt as *relish* because the *ish* ending was considered more "English," thanks to dozens of words like *selfish*, *devilish*, and *British*. At this time, *relish* still meant *flavour*: not for another three hundred years, around the end of the eighteenth century, did it come to refer specifically to a pickled side-dish or piquant sauce. Incidentally, two non-culinary words are also closely related to *relish*: *laxative* and *languish*, words that developed from the Latin *laxare* without the assistance of the *re* prefix. These two words remain fairly close to the "loosening" sense of their source, at least in so far as a laxative loosens the bowels, while a person who is languishing lies loosely on the ground.

repast

See *antipasto*.

restaurant

The word *restaurant* first appeared in French in the sixteenth century as a name for highly flavoured soups that supposedly gave strength to someone exhausted by physical exertion; the name for these soups was modelled after the French *restaurer*, meaning *to restore*, which in turn derives from the Latin *restaurare*, meaning *to give back*. In 1765, the popularity of these nutritious "restaurants" prompted a Parisian soup-seller named Boulanger to open a shop specializing in them; by the 1780s the success of Boulanger's shop had spawned many imitators, prompting the word *restaurant* to be transferred from the soups to the establishments that sold them. English borrowed the word in 1827, by which time these eating establishments sold much more than just soup. The word *café* had been borrowed from French about twenty-five years earlier, but it was not until the late nineteenth century that it lost its sense of *coffee-house* and came to denote a casual restaurant. See also *coffee* and *tavern*.

Reuben

The Reuben—a fried sandwich made with rye bread, corned beef, Swiss cheese, and sauerkraut—takes its name from its inventor, Arnold Reuben, the owner of a New York restaurant. According to his daughter, Reuben created the sandwich in 1914, but it did not become popular until 1956 when it won an American sandwich contest sponsored by the National Kraut Packers Association (by *kraut*, these packers mean *sauerkraut*). Reuben's own name is biblical in origin, his namesake being the Old Testament Reuben whose brother, Joseph, became a counsellor to the Egyptian pharaoh. In Hebrew, Reuben's name means *Behold, a son*, a name he received because his mother prayed for a son so her husband would love her.

rhubarb

When rhubarb was introduced to Europe from Mongolia, it was grown along the river banks of what was then called the Rha but is now called the Volga. From northern Europe, rhubarb was taken south to Italy, where the ancient Romans referred to the stalky plant as *rha*, since that was where it came from. Later, this name was expanded to *rha barbarum*—*barbarum* meaning *barbarian*—because the Romans tended to consider anything originating beyond the borders of their empire as barbaric. In time, this Latin name was shortened to *rheubarbum*, which was then adopted by French as *rubarb* before English borrowed it in the fifteenth century. In the sixteenth century, the *h* was reinserted in the name due to the influence of *rheum*, an alternate Latin name for the rhubarb plant, one used today as its scientific name. This *rheum* is not related to the *rheum* that means *watery discharge*, or to *rheumatism*, once thought to be caused by an excess of watery discharge in the body.

ricotta

The white, creamy, bland cheese known as *ricotta* acquired its name, which in Italian means *recooked*, from its being made from leftover whey, the liquid remaining after making other cheeses such as pecorino or mozzarella. This leftover whey must be put through a second curdling or "cooking" before it can be turned into ricotta. English adopted the word *ricotta* in the mid nineteenth century, although in the sixteenth century the word *ricoct*, derived from *ricotta*, was briefly used as a synonym for *curds*.

rigatoni

The small furrows that run up and down the tube-shaped pasta known as *rigatoni* are designed to catch the sauce and make it stick; these furrows also give rigatoni its name, deriving as it does from the Italian *rigare*, meaning *to make a channel*. This Italian word derives in turn from a Latin word, spelt the same way, which is also the source of the word *irrigate*, the action of channelling water to a field. Further back in history, the Latin *rigare* derived from the same Indo-European source as the Old English *regnian*, which eventually evolved into the word *rain*. Rigatoni was first referred to in English in the 1930s.

rimmer

According to my mother, the crimped or crenellated edge of pies is not just decorative: the little indentations allow the pastry to "give," so that the edge does not crack and crumble while it bakes. To create such a crenellated edge, a rimmer is often used, a device that clearly derives its name from its being pressed around the rim of the pie tin. Further back in history, the word *rim* evolved from the Old English *rima*, a word meaning *ridge* or *raised edge*, though the edge in question did not have to be a circular one. *Tooth-rima*, for example, was an Old English compound meaning *gums*, that is, the raised edge of flesh that holds your teeth in your head. In time, however, *rima* came to mean *circular edge*, a shift in meaning that probably occurred because of the frequent application of *rima* to the horizon of the earth: *daeg-rima*, meaning *day-rim*, was used to refer to the horizon on land, while *sae-rima*, meaning *sea-rim*, was used to refer to the horizon while at sea. These natural "rims" or horizons extend around us like circles, a fact not lost on the speakers of Old English, who began to reserve the use of *rima* or *rim* for other sorts of circular edges, especially those of plates, cups, and bowls. See also *crenellate*.

Romano cheese

The strong-tasting, hard cheese known as *Romano* and the long-leafed lettuce known as *romaine* both originated in Italy, both came to be known in English early this century, and both have names that mean *Roman*; the words differ slightly in spelling, however, because *Romano* is Italian (and masculine in gender) while *romaine* is French (and feminine in gender). According to legend, the city of Rome took its name from one of its mythical founders, Romulus, but in truth it was Romulus who was named after the city. The actual source of the city's name is likely *Ruma*, an earlier name for the Tiber river that runs through Rome; the Ruma, in turn, may have derived its name from the Greek word *rhein*, meaning *to flow*. The Greek *rhein* is also the source of the last half of *diarrhoea* but is unrelated to *Rhine*, the name of a river running through central and western Europe.

Roquefort

This cheese takes its name from the place it is made, Roquefort, in southwest France. As the name of a cheese, the word first appears in English in the early nineteenth century, but of course the name of the village is much older: the place takes its name from two Old French words literally meaning *strong rock*.

rosemary

See *costmary*.

rowtch

See *voip*.

rubbaboo

Although you will not find a recipe for pemmican in *The Joy of Cooking*, generations of grade seven history texts, recounting how this Native American food kept the early explorers alive, have made the word *pemmican* familiar to all Canadians. In contrast, rubbaboo, a stew made by boiling pemmican in water with a little flour, has been all but forgotten, even though it was reputed by the early explorers to be much more palatable than mere pemmican. Like *pemmican*, the word *rubbaboo* is Algonquian in origin and first appeared in English in the early nineteenth century. See also *pemmican*.

rudicle

See *spatula*.

rue

Although the culinary use of this bitter herb is banned in France because of the unfounded belief that it can induce abortions, rue is employed in eastern Europe to flavour cream cheeses and marinades. The herb's name is not related to the *rue* that means *to be sorrowful*, a word that is also the source of *ruthless*. Instead, the herb *rue* takes its name, via French and Latin, from a Greek name for the plant, *rhute*. The herb was first referred to in English in the late fourteenth century.

rum

Before it was known as *rum*, the alcoholic spirit made from sugar cane was called *kill-devil*, so named because the crude rum made by English colonists in the Caribbean was, according to one seventeenth-century author, a "hot, hellish, and terrible liquor." *Kill-devil*, which dates back to at least 1639, was joined a few years later by *rum*, a word whose origin remains something of a puzzle. On the one hand, *rum* may be a shortened form of *saccharum*, a Medieval Latin name for sugar produced, like rum, from sugar cane. On the other hand, *rum* may be a shortened form of *rumbullion*, which was also used as a name for the liquor. If *rum* is short for *rumbullion*, then the *bullion* part of the name is likely a corruption of *bouillon*, a French word meaning *broth*, and the *rum* part is likely the *rum* that originated in the sixteenth century as a slang term meaning *excellent*. *Rumbullion* would therefore mean *excellent broth*, a name that must have been facetious, considering the vile taste of the early rums,. However, undermining this explanation for the origin of *rum* is the possibility that *rum* is the original term and that *rumbullion* emerged only as a humorous lengthening of the name, just as *thingamajig* and *superduper* are playful extensions of *thing* and *super*. The mystery may never be solved because *rum* and *rumbullion* appeared in print at almost exactly the same time, making it impossible to know which one was in use first.

rumaki

See *sushi*.

runcible spoon

In 1871, Edward Lear, a Victorian artist and author, wrote a book of nonsense verse that included this passage from a poem called "The Owl and the Pussy-Cat": "They dined on mince, and slices of quince, which they ate with a runcible spoon." Over the next twenty years, other runcible items appeared in Lear's poetry, including a runcible goose, a runcible cat, a runcible hat, a runcible wall, and one more runcible spoon. In all these poems, the meaning of the word *runcible* is unknown: Lear invented it out of thin air simply because he liked the sound of it. In the early twentieth century, however, someone bestowed the word upon an actual piece of cutlery used to serve appetizers—a spoon whose bowl ends in three curved prongs, the last of which has a cutting edge.

runlet

See *nipperkin*.

rusk

See *biscuit*.

sabayon

See *zabaglione*.

sack

Although the word *sack* ceased to be used in the eighteenth century as the name of a Spanish wine, its frequent use by Shakespeare—who made the wine the favourite beverage of his greatest comic character, Sir John Falstaff—has prevented the word from being entirely forgotten. (The same cannot be said for the now utterly defunct names of other wines such as *aristippus*, *caprike*, *charneco*, *camplete*, and *sheranino*.) For a long time, the word *sack* was thought to have been derived from the French *sec*, meaning *dry*, the assumption being that sack was a dry wine. However, a few sixteenth century references to sack describe it as sweet, not dry, causing some etymologists to doubt its derivation from *sec*. Accordingly, it has been suggested that the real source of *sack* is the Spanish word *saca*, meaning *export*, a plausible suggestion considering the wine was indeed exported from Spain. Whatever the origin of this *sack*, it is almost certainly not related to the *sack* that means *large bag*, a word that derives, through Latin, from the Greek *sakkos*, meaning *coarse cloth*.

saffron

Used in dishes such as paella and bouillabaisse, saffron is a spice made from the dried stigmas of the saffron crocus. Since the stigma is but a tiny part of the flower, about 4000 of them are needed to make one ounce of the spice, which is why saffron is extremely expensive. Originating in the Middle East, saffron was introduced to Europe through the crusades, and thus its name is Arabic in origin: *zafaran*, which entered French as *safran* before being adopted by English in the thirteenth century as *saffron*.

sage

See *salver*.

sake

See *sushi*.

salad

See *salt*.

salami

Deriving ultimately from *sal*, a Latin word meaning *salt*, the word *salami* was borrowed from Italian in 1852 when it was used in an English translation of a German travelogue about a visit to Iceland. Exactly one hundred years later, *salami* developed a political life when, in 1952, it became part of the phrase *salami tactics*, signifying a relentless but piecemeal attack on one's opponents. The word may have been thought an appropriate name for such tactics because the opponents, like a salami, are gradually sliced to pieces. The fact that *salami* sounds somewhat like *slimy* may have also made it an appropriate name for such political manoeuvres. See also *salt* and *salmagundi*.

salep

Like tapioca, salep is a starch derived from a root and used as a thickener for soups and puddings. Salep derives its name from the Arabic *tha leb*, a shortened form of an Arabic phrase that means *fox's testicles*. The resemblance of the salep's tubers to canine testes must indeed be striking considering that the English variety of the same plant was independently named *dogstones*, the word *stone* having been used since the twelfth century to mean *testicle*. The older of these two names, *dogstones*, appeared in English in the early seventeenth century, followed a hundred years later by *salep*. See also *avocado* and *prairie oyster*.

salmagundi

To the French, a *salmigondis* is an elaborate dish made by mincing, shredding, and slicing a variety of meats, vegetables, and pickles and then arranging them in concentric circles of contrasting colours on a large, flat plate. To the English, a *salmagundi*, which derives from the French *salmigondis*, is often an ad hoc hodgepodge of whatever odds and ends are left over in the refrigerator—a dog's breakfast, so to speak, for humans. Although it is tempting to see the difference between the French and English meanings of the word as a kind of cultural allegory, more intriguing is the ambiguity around the origin of the word, which appeared in French in the sixteenth century in a work by François Rabelais. Some scholars have suggested that Rabelais, a satirist, simply invented the word *salmigondis*, as he did with over five hundred words now part of the French language. If so, Rabelais might still have had in the back of his mind the Late Latin *salimuria*, meaning *sea-salt*, the connection being that the dish often contains salty pickles and salted meat. Others have suggested that *salmigondis* derives from the French phrase *selon mon goût*, meaning *according to my taste* and alluding to how the ingredients in the dish varied according to who made it. It has even been suggested that the dish takes its name from a Madame Salmigondis, an attendant of Marie de Medici, the wife of France's King Henri IV; if so, it is still unclear why she had the honour of giving her name to a plate of pickles and salted meat. More likely than any of these explanations, however, is that the French *salmigondis*, and therefore the English *salmagundi*, derives from the Italian phrase *salame conditi*. The *salame* part of this phrase simply means *salami*, an Italian meat name that comes from the Latin word for *salt*. The *conditi* part of this phrase means *preserved*, coming from a Latin word that also gives English *condiment*. Accordingly, *salame conditi* literally means *preserved salted meat*, and with changes in pronunciation and the addition of a few more ingredients, the phrase and dish became *salmagundi*.

salmi

A salmi is a ragout made by partially roasting game such as pheasant or partridge, cooking it in a saucepan with mushrooms, and then serving it in a sauce made from its juices and wine. It has long been assumed that *salmi* is simply an abbreviation of the dish named *salmagundi*. However, as a ragout, salmi has less in common with salmagundi—originally a salad of sliced meat and vegetables—than it does with a much older dish known as *salomene*, also made by taking game and roasting it, cooking it, and serving it in a wine sauce. The difficulty in deriving *salmi* from *salomene*, however, is that the name *salomene* does not appear in print after the fifteenth century (suggesting that around then it died as a word), and yet the name *salmi* did not appear in print until the middle of the eighteenth century, three hundred years later. Although sperm banks have now made it commonplace for dead men to father children, it is unusual for an apparently long-defunct word to suddenly spawn a scion. If *salmi* does derive from *salomene*, then either *salomene* remained current in spoken language until at least the eighteenth century, all the while avoiding being recorded in print, or else *salmi* was consciously adapted from *salomene* by some eighteenth century chef who was perusing dusty, old cookbooks that had been forgotten in an attic for three hundred years. Either way, the ultimate origin of the older word, *salomene*, is also unknown. See also *salmagundi*.

salmon

Salmon acquired their name in the fourteenth century from the French name for the fish, *samoun*. The French, in turn, derived their word from what the ancient Romans named them, *salmo*, which is probably based on the Latin word *salire*, meaning *to jump*. The fish earned their name from their ability to jump up to ten feet through the air as they swim upstream to spawn. Before they acquired their current name, salmon were known as *lax*. See also *lax*.

Salmonella

The Salmonella bacterium that causes salmonellosis food poisoning has nothing to do with salmon; rather, it took its name in 1900 from the man who identified it, Dr. Daniel Elmer Salmon. Dr. Salmon's own name also has nothing to do with salmon; it is simply a variation of the Hebrew name *Solomon*, meaning *peaceful*.

salsa

See *salt*.

salt

Humans need salt to live and, more important, they need it to cook. For this reason, there are numerous words in English that derive from an Indo-European source that meant *salt*. For example, this Indo-European source evolved into the Old English *sealt*, first recorded about a thousand years ago, which eventually developed into the modern *salt*. The same Indo-European source also gave rise to the ancient Romans' word for *salt*, the Latin *sal*. From *sal* the Vulgar Latin form *salata* developed, meaning *salted*, and then became part of the name *herba salata*, meaning *salted vegetables*. The abbreviated form, *salata*, gave rise to the French word *salade*, which was adopted into English at the end of the fifteenth century as *salad*. The Latin word *sal* also gave rise to *salsa*, a Medieval Latin word that meant *salty seasoning*. This *salsa* became the French word *sauce*—so named because sauces usually contain much salt—which English borrowed in the middle of the fourteenth century. At about the same time, English also took from French the word *saussier*, denoting a dish for sauce, which eventually became the word *saucer*. The Latin *sal* followed yet another line of development when it gave rise to the French *saucisse*, applied to meat preserved with salt, which became the English word *sausage* in the middle of the sixteenth century. Most recently, in 1935, English took from Spanish the word *salsa*, the name of a spicy tomato sauce that Spanish had much earlier derived from Latin. All these *salt* words are related, incidentally, to two other non-culinary words: *silt* and *salary*. The fine soil known since the early sixteenth century as *silt* originally referred to the salty deposits found near beaches; a *salary*, on the other hand, was originally a stipend paid to sweaty Roman soldiers so that they could buy salt for themselves. Perhaps even more surprising, though, is that none of these words are related to the words *salient* or *salacious*; those words may sound like *saline*—another *salt* word—but they were actually formed from *salire*, a Latin word meaning *to leap* that is also the basis of *summersault*. See also *salmagundi* and *salt-cellar*.

salt-cellar

Wine is kept in a wine-cellar and salt in a salt-cellar, the latter being an ornamented container from which the grains are scooped with a small spoon. These two *cellars*, however, are related only by accident, not etymology. About one thousand years ago, French developed the word *saliere* from the Latin word *sal*, meaning *salt*, and applied the word first to hollowed-out lumps of bread that were filled with salt, and later to covered, silver boxes containing the same substance. This French word was adopted into English in the fourteenth century as *saler*, simply meaning *salt box*, but within a hundred years the English had lost sight of *saler*'s salty origin. As a result, the English started to call the container a *salt saler*—literally a *salt salt-box*—to emphasize what the vessel was supposed to contain. Eventually the original connection of *saler* and *salt* was entirely forgotten, allowing the English to make the mistake of respelling *salt saler* as *salt-cellar*, the word *cellar* being unrelated but similar sounding. Salt-cellars, incidentally, were formerly more than just boxes for keeping salt dry and clean: centuries ago the salt-cellar's place on a lord's dining table marked the seating division between his intimate friends and his mere attendants.

saltimbocca

Saltimbocca, an Italian dish that is a specialty of Rome, is made by browning slices of veal and ham and then cooking them in an anchovy sauce. Despite its spelling, saltimbocca does not derive its name from being especially salty. Rather, it comes from three Italian words—*saltare*, *in*, and *bocca*—which, strung together, literally mean *to leap in the mouth*. The name whimsically suggests the lively taste of the dish, but—like the slogan "finger lickin' good"—retains its charm only if the dinner guest does not visualize the image too vividly. Close relatives of *saltimbocca* included two non-culinary words: *assault* and *somersault*. Like the Italian *saltare*, these words derive from the Latin *saltare*, meaning *to jump repeatedly*. A mugger assaults a victim by jumping out of nowhere, and a gymnast performs a somersault by jumping into the air. See also *sauté* and *salmon*.

salver

A salver is a tray for serving refreshments, sage is an herb used to season food, a safe is a storage-place for valuables, and a salve is an ointment for healing burns. These items seem to have little in common, but their names derive from the same source, the Latin *salvus*, meaning *uninjured* or *healthy*. The tray known as the *salver* first began to develop its name when the Latin *salvus* evolved into the Spanish *salvar*, meaning *to save*; somewhat later, this Spanish word developed a specialized meaning of *to save a leader by pre-tasting the food*, since it used to be common to assassinate monarchs by poisoning their victuals. Once the royal food had been pre-tasted by an underling, it was then—assuming that the pre-taster's eyes had not rolled into the back of his head— placed on a special tray to indicate that the monarch could safely partake of it at his or her leisure. This "safe tray" came to be known in Spanish as the *salva*, which entered English in the late seventeenth century as *salver*. (The dining room sideboard once known as the *credenza*—from the Medieval Latin *credentia*, meaning *trusting*—acquired its name in the fifteenth century for similar reasons.) The herb known as *sage* also developed its name from the Latin *salvus*: because the plant was traditionally seen as an herb that restored health, the Romans named it *salvia*, which entered French as *sauge*, giving rise to the English *sage* in the early fourteenth century. The word *salve* likewise developed from *salvus* because a salve restores health, while the metal boxes known as *safes*—or as they were called until the seventeenth century, *saves*—acquired their name because they protect their valuable contents from harm.

samovar

Traditionally given as a wedding gift in Russia, the two-handled tea kettle known as the *samovar* has a name that literally means *self-boiler*, deriving as it does from the Russian *samo*, meaning *self*, and *varit*, meaning *to boil*. The word first appeared in English in 1830.

sandwich

The usual story behind the naming of the sandwich dates back to 1762 when John Montagu, the fourth earl of Sandwich, refused to leave his gambling table to eat, despite having been playing cards for over twenty-four hours. Instead, Montagu asked that a piece of beef between two slices of bread be brought to him at the card table, a meal that subsequently came to be known as the *sandwich*. This story prompts two obvious questions. First, why did the earl's name become attached to the sandwich? After all, Montagu did not actually *invent* the sandwich: people had been wrapping slices of bread around bits of food for thousands of years before the earl came along. Many of those earlier sandwich makers must have even eaten their meal while engaging in actions far more memorable or bizarre than the earl's compulsive gambling, yet their names were not bestowed on this commonplace food. No answer is forthcoming for this question, which leads us instead to the second question: what was the sandwich called before it acquired the earl's name? This time the answer is easy—it had no name, a fact confirmed by a computer search of the Oxford English Dictionary. In other words, it appears that for many centuries, until the earl sat down on that fateful day to gamble, a person in England could order a sandwich only by saying something as roundabout as this: "Bring me two slices of bread with roast beef laid between them." By acquiring the word *sandwich*, English therefore gained an essential word, one that several other languages later borrowed, including French and Spanish (*sandwich*), and Portuguese (*sanduíche*). Incidentally, the name *Sandwich* itself, still the name of a town in England, derives from *sand* and *wich*, the latter being an Old English term meaning *salt-pit*. Etymologically, therefore, a sandwich is a *sandy salt-pit*.

sangria

The French term *sang-froid* literally means *cold blooded*, but these two idioms have different connotations: murderers and snakes are cold-blooded, but pool hustlers display *sang-froid*. Different yet again is someone of a *sanguine* temperament—someone who "takes heart" when faced with a challenge, someone who is optimistic and even amorous. All these *sang* words derive from the Latin *sanguis*, meaning *blood*, as does the Spanish *sangría*, the name of a beverage made from, among other things, wine as red as blood. English adopted the word *sangria* about thirty years ago, although since the early eighteenth century the word *sangaree*, which derives from the same Spanish source, has been used in English as the name of a slightly different beverage made from red wine, spices, and sweetener.

sapid

In Latin, the verb *sapere* means both *to taste* and *to know*, the notion being that metaphorically "tasting" something allows you to gain knowledge about it. Similarly, in English, the word *taste* itself also has this double sense: usually it refers to the flavour of food, but having good taste can also mean knowing what is excellent and what is not. From *sapere*, Latin derived the adjective *sapidus*, meaning both *tasty* and *wise*, a word that English adopted in the early seventeenth century as *sapid*, meaning *savoury*, and as *insipid*, meaning *bland*. *Sapid* continues to be used to describe savoury food, but for the most part *insipid* has shifted its application and now refers to people—especially dinner guests— who are bland, dull, foolish, or jejune. See also *savoury*.

sardine

Although sardines were eaten fresh for thousands of years, this changed in the 1820s when the French began to can them in oil. In England, so popular did these canned sardines become that the expression *to be packed in like sardines* emerged in the first decade of this century as a metaphor for a crowded situation.

The word *sardine*, however, has been current in English for much longer, since at least the early fifteenth century. Via French, the word derives from the Latin name of the fish, *sardina*, which may have been named after Sardinia, a Mediterranean island whose coastal waters were once abundant with sardines. In turn, Sardinia was probably named after the Sards, a people who emigrated to the island from North Africa thousands of years ago. The name *Sardinia* is not related to the word *sardonic*, an adjective that describes bitter laughter, but nonetheless the island's name did indirectly affect the development of that adjective: the original Greek word for *sardonic* was *sardanios*, but in Late Greek this was changed to *sardonios* due to the influence of the Latin *herba sardonia*, a plant that took its name from the island of Sardinia where it grew. The two words—the Greek *sardanios* and the Latin *sardonia*—were associated with each other not just because they sounded similar but because the plant was reputed to cause painful convulsions and facial contortions in those who ate it, contortions resembling those caused by laughter. Accordingly, the later Greeks respelt *sardanios* as *sardonios* because they assumed, wrongly, that their word was somehow related to the Latin name of the plant, *sardonia*. Had they not made this mistake, we might now spell the word *sardonic* as *sardanic*.

sarsaparilla

Sarsaparilla, a carbonated beverage and acclaimed medicinal tonic, takes its name from the plant from which it is made. In turn, the sarsaparilla plant likely derives its name from two Spanish words: *zarza*, meaning *bramble*, and *parilla*, which is the diminutive form of the Spanish *parra*, meaning *vine*. Further back, the Spanish word *zarza* derived from the Arabic word *xarac*, also meaning *bramble* or *prickly plant*. As a plant name, *sarsaparilla* first appeared in English in the late sixteenth century, but it was not until the 1840s, when it became the name of a soft drink, that the word achieved wide currency. The popular belief that *sarsaparilla* takes its name from a Dr. Parilla may have arisen on the analogy that *Dr. Pepper*, the name of another American soft drink, actually does take its name from a Dr. Charles Pepper.

sashimi

See *sushi*.

saskatoon

The Western Canadian berry known as the *saskatoon* derives its name from the Cree *misaskwatomin*. In turn, this Cree name is made up of *misaskwat*, the name of the bush that produces the berry, and *min*, meaning *berry*. Further back, *misaskwat* derives from *misa skwat*, meaning *that which is solid wood*, so called because the saskatoon bush is thick with branches, and the branches themselves are hard and dense. Roughly translated, therefore, *saskatoon* means *the berry from the bush whose many branches are solid wood*. In 1882, the berry's name was borrowed by John H. Lake when he founded the city of Saskatoon as a temperance colony for teetotalling Methodists from Ontario. The province in which Saskatoon is located, Saskatchewan, takes its similar-sounding name from an entirely different Cree source: *Saskatchewan* derives from *kisiskatchewani sipi*, meaning *rapid-flowing river*.

satay

A satay is a Malaysian dish made by grilling pieces of meat on a skewer, and then serving them with a spicy sauce. According to the travel writer who introduced the word to English in 1934, the source of the dish's name is the Chinese word *satae*, denoting three pieces of meat.

sauce

See *salt*.

saucer

See *salt*.

saucisson

The French word *saucisse*, which entered English as *sausage*, also gave rise to the word *saucisson*, which literally means *big sausage*. Since appearing in English in the late eighteenth century, however, *saucisson* has developed a perhaps more useful meaning: it now designates a sausage that does not need to be cooked before it is eaten. Somewhat bizarrely, this new sense means that the humble hot dog, which may be rendered edible simply by thawing it on a hot car hood, is technically a *saucisson*. See also *salt*.

sauerkraut

See *sorrel*.

sausage

See *salt*.

sauté

When you sauté meat or vegetables, you shake the frying pan vigorously so the morsels of food jostle up and down and cook on all sides. This motion gives the *sauté* its name, which derives from the French *sauter*, meaning *to jump*. Further back, the French *sauter* developed from the Latin *saltare*, meaning *to jump repeatedly*, which in turn derived from the Latin *salire*, meaning *to jump*. Many other words also developed from the Latin *salire*, including *salient* and *salacious*. *Salient*, which now means *prominent*, appeared in the sixteenth century to describe animals, on heraldic coats of arms, depicted as leaping upwards. By the eighteenth century, the word had shifted its application slightly as it came to describe points or ideas that seem to "leap" into prominence. *Salacious*, meaning *lecherous*, also derives from the Latin *salire*, which was sometimes used with the more specific meaning of *to jump on a female in order to have sex*. From this sense of the word arose the Latin adjective *salax*, meaning *lustful*, from which the English *salacious* was formed in the mid seventeenth century. See also *salmon* and *saltimbocca*.

savory

The minty herb called *savory* acquired its name not because it makes dishes savoury. The herb's name, in fact, is not related to the word *savoury* at all, but rather derives from the Latin *satureia*, meaning *satyr's herb*. This Latin name was bestowed on the herb because satyrs, the mythical beasts who were half-goat and half-human, were infamous for being lecherous, and savory was a reputed aphrodisiac.

savoury

In the Old Testament, eating is used as a metaphor for learning when Adam and Eve taste the fruit of the forbidden tree of knowledge and become aware of alarming new facts—they realize, for example, that they are naked, a condition so distressing that they make themselves clothes. The same association of eating and knowledge is evident in the origin of the word *savoury*, a word that English uses to describe dishes flavoured with herbs and spices rather than sweetening agents. In origin, *savoury* derives from the Latin word *sapere*, meaning both *to taste* and *to know*; similarly, the English word *taste* can also refer to food ("That was a tasty dinner") or to knowledge ("She has good taste"). In Latin, the two senses of *sapere* allowed the word to split into distinct pairs of words as it evolved through other languages. In French, for example, the *taste* sense of *sapere* evolved into the Old French *savor*, meaning *flavour* (from which English derived *savour* in the thirteenth century), while the *know* sense of *sapere* evolved into the Old French *savoir*, meaning *to know* (as in *savoir-faire*, meaning *know-how*). Other words deriving from *sapere*—and which are therefore cousins of *savoury*—include *sage* (as in *sage advice*, advice that is wise), *savvy* (which originated as a West African corruption of the Spanish word *saber*, meaning *to know*), and *sapiens* (as in *homo sapiens*, meaning *thinking man*, a creature now threatened with extinction by *homo negotians*, business man). See also *sapid*.

scarf

See *slurp*.

schmaltz

Although *schmaltz* originated as a German culinary term, it achieved wide currency in English thanks to American jazz musicians. In German, where it is spelt *schmalz*, the word refers to animal fat, especially chicken fat rendered so that it may be more easily used in cooking. First borrowed by Yiddish, the word *schmalz* was brought to North America by Jewish immigrants, and was then picked up in the 1930s by jazz hip-cats, who used it to describe music that was mainstream and cloying instead of cool and edgy. By the 1960s the word had moved beyond the realm of jazz and was being used to describe almost anything—novels, movies, salesmen—that was maudlin and unctuous in nature. Although this metaphorical sense now dominates the word, *schmaltz* can still be used in English in its original *fat* sense, as in *schmalz herring*, a kind of oily, pickled herring. In English, *schmaltz's* closest cousin is *smelt*, the action of melting ore in order to extract the metal.

schnapps

The word *schnapps* derives from the same source as the word *snap*: both originate from the Middle Dutch *snappen*, meaning *to snatch at something with the beak* (or, if you lack a beak, with the teeth). When English derived *snap* from *snappen* in the early sixteenth century, it retained the meaning of the original Middle Dutch word. In contrast, when German derived *schnapps* from *snappen*, it shifted to mean *gulp* or *mouthful*. Later on, the meaning of the German *schnapps* shifted further when it was given to a gin-like drink that, evidently, was gulped rather than sipped. *Schnapps* was then adopted by English in the early nineteenth century when the drink was introduced to Britain.

schnitzel

German tailors, dried apple slices, and veal cutlets have one thing in common: they are all known by names that derive from *schneiden*, a German verb meaning *to cut*. From *schneiden*, German derived its word for *tailor*: *schneider*, literally meaning *cutter*, a word that also became, in the Middle Ages, a surname for many people in Germany who made and sold clothes for a living (similarly, the English word *tailor* also means *cutter*, deriving as it does from the Late Latin *taliare*, meaning *to cut*, which in turn developed from the Latin *talea*, meaning *a cutting*). From *schneiden*, German also derived the word *schnitzel*, meaning *a slice*, a name bestowed on the slices of veal used to make, among other things, *wiener schnitzel*, a cutlet coated with egg and bread crumbs; in English, schnitzel was first referred to by name in the mid nineteenth century. Closely related to *schnitzel* is *schnitz*, applied in German to the dried slices of apples used to make certain pastries and ham dishes. When it was introduced to English early this century, *schnitz*, which in German is singular, was spelt *snits*, which in English sounds and looks plural; as a result, English speakers eventually created a new singular form, *snit*, to refer to just one apple slice. Of course, another *snit* exists in English, the one that means *foul mood*, as in, "He got himself into a real snit." The origin of this foul-mood *snit* is unknown, apart from the fact that it emerged in the 1930s; however, it is possible that this *snit* was somehow inspired by the apple-slice *snit*, just as *pickle* for some reason came to mean *quandary*, as in "He got himself into a real pickle."

scone

Although the small round cake of raised dough known as the *scone* appears to have originated in Scotland, its name is probably Dutch in origin: *schoonbrot*—compounded from *schoon*, meaning *beautiful* or *white*, and *brot*, meaning *bread*—was what the Dutch called a particularly light, fine bread. This name was likely introduced into Scotland and then shortened to *scone*. *Scone*, therefore, literally means *beautiful* and is related to the English *sheen*, which developed from the same source as the Dutch *schoon*.

scranch

See *munch*.

scrumptious

When it first appeared in English, the word *scrumptious* meant *close-fisted*. It owes this original meaning to its derivation from the word *scrimp*, meaning *to be stingy*, which in turn derives from a Germanic source meaning *to shrivel up*. In the mid nineteenth century, this original meaning faded away as *scrumptious* shifted its application for no apparent reason from the person being stingy to the things he is being stingy with, things like money or tasty food. As a result, *scrumptious* ceased to mean *close-fisted* and came to mean *delicious*. This sort of semantic shifting is not uncommon, having also occurred with the words *fantastic* and *nice*: *fantastic* originally described someone with a deluded imagination but eventually came to describe a wondrous event or situation, the sort of thing a person with a deluded imagination might envision. *Nice* originally described someone who was ignorant but eventually, after centuries of gradual shifts in meaning, came to describe things that are pleasant (perhaps because ignorance is bliss). With *scrumptious*, the shift in meaning may have been facilitated by its resemblance to *sumptuous*, a word used since the fifteenth century to describe food that is extravagant and therefore, presumably, delicious.

sea-pie

Made by alternating layers of meat, fish, and vegetables with layers of broken biscuits, the dish known as *sea-pie* does not really have anything to do with the sea or with pie. Rather, the name originated in the mid eighteenth century when the English heard, and then attempted to spell, the French word *cipaille*, a word pronounced like *sea-pie* and referring to a similar layered dish. In turn, this French dish may have derived its name from the Latin *caepa*, meaning *onion*, because, like an onion, it is made of many layers; alternatively, the French name may have originated as *six-pâtes*, pronounced *see-pat* and meaning *six-pastry*, a name suggesting the number of layers in the dish.

seethe

See *bouillabaisse*.

semese

See *eat*.

servant

See *dessert*.

serviette

Like *dessert* and *servant*, the word *serviette* ultimately derives from the Latin *servus*, meaning *slave*. When English borrowed *serviette* from French in the late fifteenth century, the word denoted a small cloth placed before each dinner guest, a meaning *serviette* may have acquired because its function—to mop up spills or wipe off fingers—was once performed by Roman slaves and British servants. If so, then *serviette's* diminutive *ette* ending was intended to suggest that a serviette is like a "little servant": equally helpful in wiping applesauce from your husband's chin, but much less likely to impregnate the neighbour's milkmaid. Since the late nineteenth century, however, the word *serviette* has fallen into disrepute. In England, calling your napkin a *serviette* is tantamount to calling your host's dinner her *vittles* or her pure-bred shiatsu a *critter*; in Canada, *napkin* tends to be used when the item is made of linen, while *serviette* tends to refer to the rough rectangles of paper—seemingly made of recycled toothpicks—that are dispensed from metal boxes on restaurant tables. Why *napkin* overtook *serviette* in status is unclear. In origin, *napkin* goes back to the Latin word *mappa*, which referred to the napkin a Roman emperor might throw into a stadium to signal the beginning of the games, just as today a manager might end a boxing bout by throwing in the towel. The Latin *mappa* then developed in two directions: it became part of the Medieval Latin term *mappa mundi*, meaning *cloth of the world*, which became the English word *map*, the first maps being sketched upon sheets of cloth; *mappa* also entered French as *nape*, meaning *table cloth*, which gave rise to *naperie*—the generic term for all table linen—which entered English as *napery* in the late fourteenth century. The French *nape* also developed the diminutive form *napkin*, meaning *little table cloth*, which English borrowed at the beginning of the fifteenth century. Before *napkin* and *napery* were borrowed by English, however, the French *nape* had already developed the form *naperon*, referring to a cloth that cooks wore while in the kitchen. This *naperon* was borrowed by English as *napron* in the early fourteenth century, but by the end of the sixteenth century the initial *n* had drifted over to the preceding indefinite article; in other words, *a napron* became *an apron*. The same shift happened to *an umpire*, which used to be *a numpire*, while the reverse happened to *a newt*, which used to be *an ewt*. See also *apron*.

sesame

Before 1785, English authors spelt the word *sesame* in a variety of ways, ranging from *sysane*, to *sesama*, to *sesamo*, to *sesamy*;

after 1785, every English author spelt the word as we do, *sesame*. The almost instantaneous agreement on the spelling of the word was caused by the publication, in that year, of a translation of *The Arabian Nights*, a collection of two hundred Middle Eastern tales. The best known of those tales, *Ali Baba and the Forty Thieves*, is the one in which Ali Baba discovers the thieves' magic password, *Open sesame*. So popular was this translation of the tale that it settled once and for all the English spelling of the tiny seed's name. In origin, the word *sesame*, which first appeared in English in the mid fifteenth century, derives from the Greek name of the seed, *sesamon*.

sester
See *nipperkin*.

sewer
During the Middle Ages, guests were brought to the dinner table by the sewer, and they would have been offended had they not been accorded that honour. The sewer was not, however, a stinking, underground channel of slow-moving sludge, but rather was a man, as fragrant as a man could be back then, whose job was to arrange the table, seat the guests, and check the dishes for evidence of poison. His job name, which first appeared in the fourteenth century, was derived from the French *asseoir*, meaning *to cause to sit*, a word that developed from a Latin compound formed from the preposition *ad*, meaning *toward*, and *sedere*, meaning *to sit*. The other sewer—the one that sends steam billowing through manhole covers on cold, winter nights—takes its name from a completely different source: it derives from the Old French *essever*, which developed from the Vulgar Latin *exaquare*, meaning *to remove water*. In turn, *exaquare* was formed from the Latin *ex*, meaning *out*, and *aqua*, meaning *water*.

shabu-shabu
See *sushi*.

shaddock
Resembling an orange, but much bigger in size, the shaddock is the ancestor of the grapefruit, which was developed from the

shaddock in the early nineteenth century in the West Indies. Before settling on its current name, the shaddock was known by several others: the first was the rather whimsical *Adam's apple*, first used in the late sixteenth century. Later, at the end of the seventeenth century, it also came to be known as *pompelmoose*, a name that reflects the fusion of cultures found in Malaysia, where the fruit was also grown: the *pompe* is the Dutch *pompoen*, meaning *pumpkin*, while the *lmoose* represents the Portuguese *limoes*, meaning *lemons*. *Pompelmoose*, therefore, literally means *pumpkin-lemons*, as does *pamplemousse*, which is what the French call grapefruit. In English, *shaddock* became the predominant name of the fruit in the late seventeenth century after a Captain Shaddock sailed to Barbados with some seeds and established the tree there. Appropriately for a sailor, the captain's surname means *little herring*, the shad being a herring-like fish.

sherbet

Until ice-cream was invented in the eighteenth century, the only frozen confection available in Europe was sherbet, also known as *sorbet*. These mixtures of fruit syrup and granular ice were introduced to the rest of Europe by the Italians, who had been taught how to make them by the Turks, who had learned from the Arabs, who in turn had learned from the Chinese. The name of the refreshment does not go back quite that far, however, as it takes its origin from Arabic, but not Chinese. The ancient Arabic equivalent of the English verb *slurp* was *shariba*, equivalent because both words probably developed as imitations of the lip-smacking sounds made by someone eagerly drinking or lapping up a delicious refreshment. This Arabic verb led to the noun form *sharbah*, meaning *a drink*, which Turkish borrowed as *sherbet*; it was this Turkish form of the word that English borrowed at the beginning of the seventeenth century. A few decades before this, however, another form of the word had already been adopted: *sorbetto*, which the Italians had derived from the Turkish *sherbet*, entered French as *sorbet* and was then adopted by English. Today, both words continue to be used, but *sorbet* is considered the more exotic. A third word, far more familiar than either *sherbet* or *sorbet*, also developed from the Arabic *shariba*. This word is *syrup*, which developed from the Arabic *shariba* via the Medieval Latin *siropus*. Of *sherbet*, *sorbetto*, and *syrup*, the word *syrup* is by far the oldest, appearing for the first time in English at the end of the fourteenth century.

sherry

The fortified Spanish wine known as *sherry* has nothing to with the personal name *Sherry*. Whereas *Sherry*, the woman's name, originated as a pet form of *Charlotte* (which in turn is a feminine form of *Charles*, a Germanic name meaning *free man*), the alcoholic *sherry* derives ultimately from the name *Caesar*. Two thousand years ago, Julius Caesar gave his name to a city in Spain, a city known in Latin as *Urbs Caesaris*, meaning *City of Caesar*. After many centuries, the *Urbs* was dropped and *Caesaris* came to be spelt and pronounced, by the native population of Spain, as *Xeres* (which later became *Jerez*, the modern name of the city). It was here, in Xeres, that a certain white wine was produced, one thought to have been introduced to England in 1587 when Sir Francis Drake destroyed the Spanish Port of Cadiz and made his way back to England with 2500 barrels of the wine that he took from neighbouring Xeres. In England, this wine came to be known by the name of the city from which it was plundered (and from which it was later imported); however, the British aversion to words that begin with the letter *x* caused the English to respell the name as *sherris*. A few decades later, in the early sixteenth century, a final development took place when people mistakenly began to assume that *sherris*, which ends with an *s*, was a plural; accordingly, out of thin air they created what they believed to be the proper singular form, *sherry*, the name the wine has possessed ever since.

shish kebab

Made by sliding chunks of mutton onto a skewer and then grilling them over embers, the shish kebab takes its name from the Turkish *shish*, meaning *skewer*, and *kebap*, meaning *roast meat*. When the mutton is sliced and then wrapped with herbs around a rotating, vertical skewer it is called a *doner kebab*, the word *doner* being

Turkish for *turning*. Of these two terms, *shish kebab* is older, first appearing in English in the second decade of this century, about forty years before the appearance of *doner kebab* in the late 1950s (*doner kebab* is often shortened to *doner*, which in turn is sometimes respelt as *donair*). Adopted much earlier was the word *kebab* itself, used in English since the late seventeenth century but until the end of the nineteenth century usually spelt *cabob*.

shoulder

Because a shoulder of beef or mutton is less esteemed than other parts of the carcass, that cut of meat was once reserved for house guests whose presence had become tiresome. If the guests did not get the hint and leave, the same shoulder—this time served cold—would be presented to them the next day at dinner as a way of saying, "Here's your hat, thanks for coming." Out of this practice arose the expression *to give someone the cold shoulder*, first recorded in the early nineteenth century. The word *shoulder* itself derives from a Germanic source that may also have given rise to the word *shield*, the connection being that the shoulder blades of many mammals, including humans, are broad, flat, and therefore shield-like.

shoyu

See *sushi*.

shrab

See *sherbet*.

shrimp

Although you might think that the word *shrimp* originally referred to the small, tasty shellfish and that it was only later used as a contemptuous epithet for diminutive people, probably the reverse is true: when *shrimp* appeared in English in the fourteenth century, it referred to small creatures and items of all sorts, including people, and its specific application to the tiny shellfish probably grew out of this wider, original usage. English seems to have acquired *shrimp* by adapting the Middle High German word *schrimpfen*, meaning *to shrink*. *Schrimpfen* probably evolved from the same Germanic source as *scrincan*, an Old English word that developed into the Modern English *shrink* (which came to mean *psychiatrist* in the early 1960s, the earlier term *head-shrinker* having been used since 1950). Other words that developed from the same Germanic source as *shrimp* and *shrink* include *scrimp* (a verb meaning *to give someone less than enough*), *skimpy* (an adjective meaning *less than enough*), and even *crimp* (a verb meaning *to create a pattern by squishing something down*). Incidentally, all the other European languages derive their words for *shrimp* from entirely different sources than English. The French, for example, refer to shrimp as *crevette*, a Picardy word meaning *little goat*, so called because the swimming motion of the shrimp resembles the bounding leaps of a goat. See also *scrumptious*.

shrove-cake

See *carling*.

siligone

See *liebesknochen*.

sin-eater

See *doed-koek*.

sippet

See *soup*.

sirloin

Henry VIII, James I, and Charles II have all been credited at various times with drawing a sword in the midst of a meal in order to dub a particularly tasty cut of beef *Sir Loin*; the king's joke—whichever king it was—supposedly sent such a titter round the room that soon all England was clamouring for *sirloin*. This three hundred year old etymology of *sirloin* is as untrue as the claim that Sir Lancelot received his name because he liked his lance a lot. In actual fact, *sirloin* was derived in the mid sixteenth century from the Old French *surloigne*, the *sur* part of the word being a preposition meaning *above*; the sirloin, therefore, is literally the cut of meat above the loin. So established was the false etymology of *sirloin*, however, that it inspired someone in the mid eighteenth century to give the name *Baron of Beef* to two sirloins roasted together instead of being cut asunder. Even the French adopted the English title of *Baron* as their name for this cut of meat; however, in 1953 the Académie Française, a government agency whose mandate is to keep French unsullied by foreign borrowings, attempted to replace the English-derived *baron* with the French *bas-rond*. Restaurateurs protested, and *baron* remained.

sitophobia

Sitophobia is a psychological condition in which a person is terrified or repelled by all food or else by certain foods that most others deem edible, if not downright delicious. Sitophobia is therefore culturally specific: in Canada, my Lear-like histrionics upon finding half a beetle in my salad are considered most apropos; in other cultures, where a dearth of mammalian or piscatorial protein sources have made insects an accepted food, the same behaviour would seem sitophobic. The word *sitophobia*, first used in English about a century ago, derives from the Greek *sitos*, meaning *bread*, and *phobos*, meaning *fear*.

skillet

A skillet differs from a frying pan in that it has an especially long handle, and may even have legs that hold the bottom of the pan slightly above the heat source. The name of this utensil derives from a Latin word that has undergone double diminution: the Latin *scutra*, meaning *tray*, gave rise to the diminutive *scutella*, meaning *little tray*. *Scutella* then developed into the French word *escuele*, meaning *pan*, which gave rise to another diminutive: *escuelette*, meaning *little pan*. It was this French word that entered English at the beginning of the fifteenth century as *skelet* before developing the current spelling *skillet*.

slake

See *brunch*.

slaughterhouse

See *abattoir*.

slumgullion

First recorded in the late nineteenth century, *slumgullion* refers generally to the innards of a gutted fish and more specifically to the watery crud, mixed with oil and blood, that drains from whale blubber as it is rendered. In what now appears, with the benefit of hindsight, to be a dubious marketing strategy, *slumgullion* was borrowed by cooks during the American gold rush as a name for a kind of hash or stew.

slummock

See *slurp*.

slurp

For some reason, perhaps not too hard to guess, English has far more words to describe noisy, gluttonous eating than dainty, well-mannered eating. Of these dozen or so gluttonous words, *slurp*, first recorded in the mid seventeenth century, is the best known and the least offensive; you can safely chide your spouse for slurping his soup, and you can even refresh yourself afterwards with a *Slurpee*, a well-known drink of flavoured ice-crystals. In contrast, observe the reaction you elicit if you chide your spouse for *globbing* his soup, or try selling a drink named *Globbee*. The ugly *glob* and its equally ugly cousin, *glop*, both mean *to swallow greedily*; these two words are among the oldest of the "gluttony words," having appeared in the mid fourteenth century. *Glob* and *glop*, like many gluttony words, developed from onomatopoeia: they sound like the action they describe. *Ramp*, *gudge*, *yaffle*, *slummock*—these four verbs also arose as imitations of loud chewing and swallowing sounds; if you say them out loud in succession, someone is sure to ask you what you are eating. Two of these words, *gudge* and *yaffle*, originated in the mid seventeenth century, a time when political upheaval prompted a laissez-faire attitude toward chewing with a closed mouth; *ramp* arose about a century before this, and *slummock* about a century after. Other "gluttony" words developed not from onomatopoeia but from older words. *Guttle*, first recorded in the mid seventeenth century, derives from a conscious fusion of *gut* and *guzzle*. *Scarf*, which appeared in the middle of this century, developed from *scoff*, which appeared in the middle of the nineteenth century; in turn, *scoff* developed from *scaff*, a word dating back to the early sixteenth century when it meant *to beg for food in a contemptible manner*. Still other "gluttony" words developed from classical sources: *ravenous* derives from the Late Latin *rapinare*, meaning *to plunder*, which in turn derived from the Latin *rapere*, meaning *to seize*, which also gave rise to the English words *ravish*, *rape*, and *rapid*. Perhaps surprisingly, *ravenous* is not related to *raven*, the name of a large, black bird, but confusion of the two words may have contributed to the bird's reputation as a thief. Finally, *lurcate*, meaning *to eat ravenously*, also derives from a Latin source: *lurcare*, meaning *to eat like a glutton*. See also *pingle* and *glutton*.

smetana

The sour cream often served with borscht is called *smetana*, a word that derives from the Russian *smetat*, meaning *to sweep together*. The name alludes to cream's tendency, as it sours, to coagulate into lumps and ripples, almost as if the curds had been swept or raked onto the surface. A distant relative of *smetana* may be *smegma*, a word of Latin and, even earlier, Greek origin that denotes the sebaceous secretion that accumulates under the prepuce. See also *suet*.

smidgen

See *dollop*.

smoked meat

The word *smoke* dates back in English to the eleventh century, but it was not until the beginning of the seventeenth century that it came to refer to the process of preserving meat by hanging it in a smoke-filled room. Before the seventeenth century, this ancient culinary technique was called *reeking*, and the final product was called *reeked meet*. This now obsolete culinary term seems odd to us because *reek* now means *to emit a foul odour*. Back then, however, *reek* simply meant *to emit smoke*: its smelly sense did not emerge until the early seventeenth century when its culinary sense was usurped by *smoke*. One reason why *smoke* replaced *reek* as a culinary term may be related to the introduction of tobacco to England at the end of the sixteenth century. Tobacco smoke was then thought to be of great benefit to one's health, warding off all kinds of illness and plagues; accordingly, the word *smoke* acquired a positive connotation it never before enjoyed, and suppliers of reeked meat may have started to apply it to their wares in an attempt to benefit from the word's new cachet. In origin, the word *smoke* derives from an Indo-European source that has given rise to "smoke" words in dozens of languages, including the German *schmauch*, the Dutch *smook*, and the Welsh *mwg*. Relatives of the word *reek* also exist in most northern European languages, including Icelandic where the name of the country's capital, Reykjavik, literally means *smoky bay*.

smørbrød

This Norwegian name for an open-sandwich might be translated as *smear-bread* since the Norwegian *smor*, meaning *butter*, derives from the same source as the English *smear*. The word is first recorded in English in 1933.

smorgasbord

For many decades, the smorgasbord—or, for those too hungry to say the whole word, the smorg—has dominated the social scene of middle-class America: the success of any celebration is directly proportional to the length of the smorgasbord table and the number of hors d'oeuvres displayed upon it. Indeed, those hosts forced to make do with only a puny card table and few cold-cuts often suffer acutely from "smorg envy" or, worse, "smorg shame." The politics of the smorgasbord no doubt emerged shortly after English borrowed the word from Swedish in the late nineteenth century; the word had arisen much earlier in that language as a compound of *smorgas*, meaning *open-sandwich*, and *bord*, meaning *table*. *Smorgas*, in turn, is a compound apparently formed from the Swedish names of two common ingredients in Scandinavian open-sandwiches: butter and goose, or what the Swedes call *smor* and *gas*. See also *board*.

snack

Back in the fourteenth century, you did not refer to the teeth marks you left in your brother's leg as a *bite* but rather as a *snack*: the word *bite*, in fact, did not come to be used as a noun until the fifteenth century. *Snack*, on the other hand, meant *animal bite* when it first appeared in English but gradually lost this literal meaning as it came to signify various kinds of metaphorical bites. In the mid sixteenth century, for example, it came to denote a verbal retort, as in "Her witty snack made him blush"; even now we describe such retorts as "biting," and we might even refer to their effect as having "taken a piece out of him." The next shift in the meaning of *snack* occurred in the late seventeenth century when it came to signify a small "bit" of something, especially of liquor (a close relative of *snack*, the German *schnapps*, became the actual name of a liquor, one that English adopted in the early nineteenth century). Finally, in the mid eighteenth century, *snack* acquired the sense now most familiar to us, *a morsel of food*; here too the original *bite* sense of *snack* lingers in the background, since a *snack* is the same thing as a *bite to eat*. In origin, *snack* probably developed from the Middle English *snatchen*, which became the Modern English *snatch*. The ultimate source of *snatchen* is not known, but it is probably the same source that gave rise to *snap*, a word unlike *snatch* and *snack* in that it has never strayed far from its original sense of *bite*. See also *nosh*.

snit

See *schnitzel*.

snoop

See *nosh*.

soba

See *sushi*.

sole

Sole was the fish of choice in the kitchens of ancient Rome, as is suggested by its Latin name: *solea Jovi*, meaning *sandal of Jove*, Jove being the supreme deity in the Olympic pantheon. The specific identification of this fish with a variety of footwear was inspired by its perfectly oval form, reminiscent of the sole of a Roman sandal, a symmetry of shape marred only by the unsettling fact that both the creature's eyes are on the right side of its head. The source of this Latin word for sandal—*solea*—was *solum*, meaning both *ground* and *bottom of the foot. Solum*, of course, is not only the ultimate source of the marine *sole* but also of the terrestrial *sole*, the part of the human body that usually touches the ground. On the other hand, the *sole* that means *alone* derives from a different source, as does the homophonic *soul* referring to our divine essence: that *soul* derives from a Germanic source that means *fleeting*, suggesting that, compared with eternity, the time a soul spends in a body is a mere twinkling of an eye. Some species of the marine sole are called *lemon sole*, but the name has nothing to do with lemons; rather, the *lemon* is a corruption of the French word for sole, *limande*, and thus *lemon sole* is a tautology literally meaning *sole sole*. The term *lemon sole* dates back only to the mid nineteenth century, whereas the name *sole* itself appeared in the mid fourteenth century.

sop

See *soup*.

sorbet

See *sherbet*.

sorrel

Long used as an herb for flavouring soup, sorrel takes its name, via French, from an ancient Germanic word, pronounced something like *suraz*, meaning *sour*. This Germanic word is also the source of the word *sour* itself, and also of the Modern German *sauer*, as in *sauerkraut*, literally meaning *sour cabbage* (during World War I, the association of Germany and sauerkraut led to German soldiers being nicknamed *krauts*). The first of these three words to appear in English was *sour*, dating back to the eleventh century; *sorrel* appeared in the mid fifteenth century, and *sauerkraut* was adopted in the early seventeenth century.

soufflé

Somewhat disturbingly, the word *soufflé*, the name of a light, egg-based dish heated in an oven until it puffs up, derives from the same Latin source as the word *flatulence*, the name of a windy eructation that proceeds from the nether end of the alimentary canal. The source of both words is the Latin *flare*, meaning *to puff* (the Latin *flare* happens to be spelt like the English *flare*, meaning *to burn with a sudden, blazing light*, but the two words are not related). By taking the verb *flare* and combining it with the prefix *sub*, the ancient Romans created a new verb, *subflare*, meaning *to puff from below*, which soon had its pronunciation simplified to *sufflare*. In French, the Latin *sufflare* became *souffler*, a word whose past participle—*soufflé*, meaning *puffed up*—was fittingly bestowed on the airy egg dish. English borrowed this French term in the early nineteenth century when recipes for soufflés began to appear in British cookbooks. In contrast, *flatulence* is a much older word, first appearing in English at the beginning of the seventeenth century. English borrowed the word *flatulence*—or actually its adjective form *flatulent*—from the French, who had created the word from *flatus*, the past participle of the Latin *flare*. *Flatus* is also the source of a host of other English words, including *flavour*: in Vulgar Latin—that is, the Latin once spoken by the common people of Rome—*flatus* apparently gave rise to *flator*, meaning *smell*; this word was adopted by Old French as *flaour*, which English changed to *flavour* when it adopted the term from French in the fourteenth century. For the next three hundred years, the English used *flavour* to refer only to smells, and not just food smells: flowers, incense, skunks, and smoke all had "flavours." Beginning in the late seventeenth century, however, *flavour* came to mean *taste*, a change in meaning that may have been inspired by the simple fact that *flavour* rhymes with *savour*. One more word distantly related to *soufflé* and *flatulence* is *surf*. This name for the tall, rushing waves of the sea first appeared in English in the late sixteenth century as *suff*, apparently a shortened form of the Latin *sufflare* or the French *souffler*; the inspiration behind the name was probably the highly visible foam that "puffs up" on the waves as they surge toward the shore. The change in spelling from *suff* to *surf* began to occur in the late seventeenth century, the *r* perhaps being added as people unwittingly conflated the word *suff* with the word *surge*. Today, *surf* has become a culinary word, at least in *surf and turf*, a phrase that arose in the 1960s to describe a restaurant meal comprising both seafood and beef.

soup

Queen Elizabeth I could never have eaten soup: the word did not enter English until the mid seventeenth century, fifty years after her death. She did, however, eat soup-like foods with names such as *pottage* and *broth*, and no doubt she also dined occasionally on something called a *sop*, a piece of bread soaked in broth. In fact, the word *soup* derives from the same source as *sop*, and even originally meant the same thing—a soaked piece of bread. The common source that *soup* and *sop* developed from, although by different routes, was the Germanic word *sup*, meaning *juice* or *sap*. This Germanic word evolved more or less directly into the Old English *sop*, the soaked-bread dish whose name was first recorded in the twelfth century; although sops are no longer commonly eaten, the word itself persists in phrases like *sopping wet* and in words like *milksop*, a bread-slice soaked in milk whose name became synonymous in the thirteenth century with effeminate men. Taking a different and less direct path, the Germanic *sup* also entered Late Latin as *suppa*, which evolved into the French *soupe*, originally denoting the soaked bread-slice itself, but eventually coming to mean the broth in which the bread was soaked. English borrowed this *soupe* from French and bestowed it upon a liquid food thicker than a broth but thinner than a pottage. Still other English words also developed from the Germanic *sup*, including *sob*—a tearful and therefore watery cry of anguish—and *sip*—the action of drinking small amounts at a time. Perhaps the most familiar descendent, however, is *supper*: from the Germanic *sup*, French developed *super*, a word meaning *to eat the evening meal* (this *super* is no relation to the *super* in *superman*); English borrowed the French *super* at the end of the thirteenth century, using it as the name of the day's last meal and adding another *p* to the word in the process.

souvlaki

The Greek dish known as *souvlaki*, made by grilling pieces of lamb on a skewer, takes its name from a shoemaker's tool, the awl, a pointed rod used to poke holes into leather. The Latin name for this tool—*subula*, which derives from the older *suere*, meaning *to sew*—was adopted by Greek as *soublion*. In Modern Greek, *soublion* became *soubla* and was combined with a diminutive suffix to form *soublaki*, meaning *small awl*, a kind of kitchen skewer used to grill meat. In time, the name of the implement was transferred to the grilled meat itself, which is the sense the word possessed when English adopted it as *souvlaki* in the middle of this century. Another word that developed from the same Latin source as *souvlaki* is *suture*, a stitch used to sew together the edges of a wound.

soy

See *sushi*.

spaghetti

While spaghetti has achieved complete acceptance at the North American supper table and vermicelli has not, the word *vermicelli* entered English long before *spaghetti*. The English, in fact, were writing about the joys of eating vermicelli as early as the mid seventeenth century; in contrast, no one writing in English mentions spaghetti until the mid nineteenth century, and even then it was initially referred to as *Naples' vermicelli*. Not surprisingly, both pastas take their names from what they resemble: in Italian, *spaghetti* means *little strings*, the name being a diminutive of *spago*, meaning *string*. Vermicelli has a name even harder to swallow: in Italian the word literally means *little worms*, deriving from the same Latin source as the English words *vermin* and *varmint*. The colour known as *vermilion* also developed from the Latin word for *worm*: the ancient Romans ground up a particular kind of worm, known as the *kermes*, to make a red dye.

spam

Despite the success of Wrigley's, a gum whose brand name makes me think of worms in a rain storm, most marketing experts concur that a product cannot succeed with a bad name. A good name should be short and evocative, and should contain strong, explosive sounds like *b* and *p*. *Spam* has all these qualities: it is certainly short, it contains a *p*, and it evokes—perhaps unconsciously—its origin as an abbreviation of *spiced ham*. *Spam* began as a brand name in 1937, but by the 1940s it had also become attached to other items intended for a mass market: *spam medal*, for instance, became slang for a medal given indiscriminately to all members of a military unit. More recently, *spam* has become a cyberspace verb: if an unscrupulous business flouts Internet etiquette by indiscriminately posting unsolicited advertisments to hundreds of newsgroups, it has engaged in "spamming."

spatch cock

A spatch cock is a chicken served for dinner after skinning it, splitting it in two, and roasting it on a grill. The name of this Irish dish was originally *dispatch cock*, so named because it was easily dispatched: in fact, because it could be prepared with such ease and speed, the spatch cock became the usual dish to serve guests who dropped by with little warning. The name *spatch cock* emerged in English in the late eighteenth century, but—strangely—there are references three hundred years earlier to another dish called *spitchcock*. It does not seem possible that the name *spatch cock* could have derived from this earlier *spitchcock* because the *a* in *spatch* is part of the original *dispatch*; as well, the ingredients of the two dishes have nothing in common: far from being a grilled cock, spitchcock was a dish of fried eels dressed with bread crumbs and herbs. Accordingly, the real mystery, as yet unsolved, is how a dish of eels acquired the name *spitchcock*.

spatula

The word *spatula* was adopted directly from Latin in the early sixteenth century as a name for a medical instrument used to stir ointments and potions. This medical sense remained the primary meaning of *spatula* until this century, when the utensil gradually came to be associated with the kitchen. The Latin word from which *spatula* was derived was *spathula*, itself a diminutive of the Latin *spatha*, denoting a broad blade used to stir mixtures. This *spatha* also evolved into the Italian *spada*, the name of a broad sword, which English adopted as *spade*, the name of one of the four suits in a deck of cards. The Latin *spatha* also evolved into the Old French *espee*, which in turn developed into the Modern French *épée* (a kind of sword) and into the English *spay* (an operation, originally performed with a sword, that removes an animal's ovaries). Much further back in history, the Latin *spatha* derived from an Indo-European source, pronounced something like *spee*, that evolved through the Germanic language family into the word *spade*, the name of a gardening tool, and into *spoon*, the name of an eating tool. Incidentally, long before *spatula* came to be used as the name of a kitchen utensil, the same tool could be called a *lingel*, a *langet*, or a *rudicle*. *Lingel* and *langet*, which date back to the mid sixteenth century, both derive from the Latin *lingua*, meaning *tongue*; *rudicle*, on the other hand, dates back to the mid seventeenth century, and derives from the same Germanic source as the word *rudder*. Of course, what swords, tongues, rudders, and spatulas all have in common is their broad, flat shape. See also *linguine* and *spick and span*.

spice

In an attempt to take Jerusalem out of the hands of the Moslems, Christian leaders of western Europe launched the crusades in the eleventh century; the crusades failed, but the crusaders did bring back dozens of new spices from the East; Europeans were overjoyed with being able to season their food with something besides garlic, and by the fifteenth century the city of Venice was booming as the portal of the spice trade between East and West; when the Venetians began to exploit their spice monopoly by charging exorbitant prices, entrepreneurs such as Christopher Columbus set out to find a new route to get spices, bumping into the West Indies and the Americas along the way; my ancestors—and perhaps yours—eventually followed Columbus and here we are today. Out of all this, the word *spice* developed for the simple reason that after the failed crusades people had all "sorts" of spices to choose from. This abundance of choice prompted the Latin word *species*, meaning *sort* or *type*, to be adopted as the generic name for all these new kinds of spices. In French, *species* became *espice*, which in turn was adopted into English as *spice* in the early thirteenth century. Much later, in the early seventeenth century, the word *species* was again adopted into English, this time directly from Latin, as the scientific name for classes or "sorts" of animals and plants. Incidentally, further back in history, the Latin *species*, and therefore the English *spice* as well, derives from the Latin *specere*, meaning *to look*, because a species is identified by its appearance; the word *spectacle* developed from the same Latin source, as did the restaurant term *specialty*, literally meaning a particular "sort" or "species" of dish. See also *grocery*.

spick and span

Although it makes no sense to say that a kitchen is *spick* or that a cupboard is *span*, everyone knows what it means for either of these to be *spick and span*. This expression has changed greatly over the last seven hundred years. It first appeared in the mid seventeenth century as a shortened form of *spick and span new*, an expression dating back to the late sixteenth century. This expression in turn was an elaboration of the even older *span-new*, first recorded in the fourteenth century, which was derived from the Old Norse *span-nyr*. In Old Norse, *span* meant *a chip of wood*, and thus the expression *span-nyr* literally meant *as new as a chip of wood*, a new wood-chip being moist, clean, and fragrant. The *spick* was later added to the English translation of *span-nyr* thanks to the influence of the Dutch idiom *spiksplinter nieuw*, the *spiksplinter* part of the expression meaning *nail splinter*. The upshot of all this is that *spick and span new* is an English expression, derived from Dutch and Norse, that literally means *nail and chip new*. Incidentally, the Dutch *spik* that is represented in *spick and span* is the source of the English word *spike*; less obvious, perhaps, is that the Old Norse *span* derives from the same Germanic source as the English *spoon*: in fact, for six hundred years after its first appearance in the early eighth century, the word *spoon* denoted only a chip of wood. It was not until the early fourteenth century that *spoon* came to mean *eating utensil*, an inevitable development considering that the first spoons were indeed mere wood-chips.

spignel

Spignel, spigurnel, and baldmoney are not partners in a downtown law firm but rather are alternative names for a plant whose root, during the sixteenth and seventeenth century, was dried, ground, and used as a spice. The oldest of these names, *baldmoney*, dates back to the late fourteenth century but has nothing to do with medieval barbers or bankers; instead, it likely derives from a long-lost French source. *Spignel*, which first appears in the early sixteenth century, is probably just a shortened form of the somewhat older *spigurnel*, first recorded in the early fifteenth century. The Medieval Latin plant-name, *spigurnella*, is the source of the English *spigurnel*, although where *spigurnella* came from is unknown.

spikenard

Spikenard is a bitter extract obtained from the plant of the same name; in ancient and medieval times, spikenard was commonly used to flavour sauces and meat-dishes, but fell out of favour as new spices were introduced from the Far East. The plant's name literally means *spike of nard*, *spike* being an old word for *thorn*, and *nard* being the name of an aromatic plant. *Spike*, in turn, derived from an Indo-European word meaning *something pointed*, which also gave rise to the English word *spine* (as in *cactus spine* and *spinal column*), and to the Latin word *spica*, meaning *ear of corn* (*spica* then evolved into the English *spigot*, a tap shaped like an ear of corn). *Nard*, on the other hand, derives from a Sanskrit word meaning *reed*, a word that made its way from Sanskrit, to Persian, to Hebrew, to Greek, and to Latin before appearing in English as part of *spikenard* in the mid fourteenth century. See also *garlic* and *aspic*.

spinach

The spinach plant is native to Persia, but because it was introduced to most of Europe from Spain (where it had been brought by Arabs), it was sometimes referred to by sixteenth-century scholars as *Hispanicum holus*, Latin for *Spanish herb*. It is tempting to assume that the first part of this Latin name—*Hispanicum*—was simply corrupted into the English *spinach*, into the French *espinache*, into the Italian *spinace*, and into a dozen other names in various European languages; however, the existence of similar sounding names in Middle Eastern languages suggests that the name, as well as the plant, is Persian in origin. In all likelihood, the Persian name of the plant, *isfanakh*, was adopted by Arabic as *isbanakh*, which in turn was adopted by Spanish as *espinaca*. This Spanish name was then adopted by Old French as *espinache*, which English borrowed as *spinach* in the sixteenth century. Four hundred years later, in 1919, Elzie Crisler Segar made spinach the favourite food of Popeye, a cartoon sailor who supposedly derived his strength from the plant. In fact, however, Popeye likely consumed such large quantities of canned spinach because the minerals contained in spinach leaves alleviated his thyroid condition. This medical disorder is never explicitly acknowledged in the cartoon, but it may be inferred from Popeye's bulging eye. Popeye's name, in fact, is a close translation of the ocular condition caused by an enlarged thyroid, *exophthalmos*, literally meaning *out-eye*.

splay

See *carving*.

spoil pudding

The term *spoil pudding* refers not to a pudding, but to a person, or rather a parson, one whose sermons are so long that the congregation's Sunday puddings are left too long in the oven, thus spoiling them. The term appeared in the late eighteenth century.

spoom

See *spumante*.

spoon

See *spick and span*.

spork

See *pomato*.

spotted dick

Although you might expect spotted dick—a kind of suet pudding—to have been given its name by a man prone to whimsy or hypochondria, the name of the dish actually has a very sober origin. Since the early nineteenth century, *dick* referred to a cheese made in Suffolk, one of England's many counties; the name of this cheese was originally spelt with a capital *D*, suggesting that it may have been derived from some now-forgotten *Dick*. Shortly after, the name of the cheese was borrowed as a synonym for *pudding*, and was often used in conjunction with other words that indicated the type of pudding. Thus, *treacle dick* was pudding served with a treacle sauce, while *spotted dick* was pudding made with currants that "spotted" the surface of the dessert. (*Dick*, incidentally, did not become a slang term for *penis* until the late nineteenth century, well after *dick* the pudding had established itself.) Another dish that appears to have a whimsical name is petticoat tails, a kind of butter-cake first referred to at the beginning of the nineteenth century. Like *spotted dick*, however, the name *petticoat tails* originated from what was once a straightforward name: the French *petit gâteau*, meaning *little cake*, was simply corrupted by the English to the more familiar-sounding *petticoat tails*. Other dishes, however, have names intended from the start to be whimsical. Bubble and squeak, for example, a dish of meat and cabbage fried together, received its name in the mid eighteenth century from the sounds it emits as it cooks. Around the same time, a dish made by cooking sausages in batter came to be known as *toad in the hole* because of its resemblance to that zoological phenomenon. In the late nineteenth century, a more poetic resemblance led to the name *angels on horseback*, denoting a canapé made by rolling oysters in bacon and then serving them on crisp toast. However, the name that best manages to be both whimsical and literal belongs not to a dish, but to a beverage: *merry go down*, a strong ale popular in the sixteenth century.

spritzer

See *Brussels sprouts*.

sprout

See *Brussels sprouts*.

spumante

The sparkling wine called *spumante* takes its name from the Italian *spuma*, meaning *foam*, as does the ice-cream dessert known as *spumoni*. Both words appeared early this century, although the related word *spume* has been used since the fifteenth century to describe froth that results from beating an egg.

spumoni

See *spumante*.

square meal

The term *square meal*, denoting a satisfying, hearty meal, dates back to at least the late nineteenth century and probably arose from the association of *square* with *right*: a square's angles are right angles, so if something is *square* it is *right*, and things that are done right—like a meal—are usually satisfying. In the early twentieth century, *square meal* gave rise to *three square meals*, an expression that subsequently became so familiar that the Message Bible—a recent attempt to render the Bible into modern, colloquial English—replaced "Give us this day our daily bread" with "Keep us alive with three square meals." The term *square drink* also arose in the nineteenth century, but unlike *square meal* it derives from the actual shape of the beverage: any drink poured until it is as high in the glass as the glass is wide is a square drink.

squash

The *squash* that means *edible gourd* is a completely different word than the *squash* that means *painful racquet sport*. Squash, the sport, gets its name from the small, hollow ball being squashed into a little disk each time it hits a wall of the court or a shoulder blade of an opponent. In turn, the verb *squash* derives from the Vulgar Latin *exquassare*, meaning *to squeeze out* (the base of this verb—the Latin *quassare*, meaning *to shake to pieces*—is also the source of the English word *quash*, meaning *to annul*). In contrast, the edible *squash* derives from Narraganset, a Native American tongue belonging to the Algonquian family of languages. The Narraganset word for *squash* was *asquutasquash*, meaning *something eaten raw*, a word that English initially adopted as *squanter-squash* in 1634. The name *squanter-squash* continued to be used in English until the early eighteenth century when it was superseded by the abbreviated form, *squash*. Incidentally, the *ash* that appears at the end of the original Narraganset word—*asquutasquash*—is actually a suffix that indicates the word is plural (English likewise refers to certain foods only in the plural—*oats*, for example, and *grits*). The same plural ending is also found on *succotash*, the name of a native American dish made by boiling green corn with beans. *Succotash* is also of Narraganset origin, deriving from *misickquatash*, meaning *ear of corn*. However, the word *calabash*—the name of a large, hard-shelled gourd—is not of Native American origin, even though it ends in *ash*. Instead, *calabash* derives ultimately from the Persian *kharbuz*, a compound made up of *khar*, meaning *large*, and *buza*, meaning *fragrant fruit*. This Persian word was adopted by Spanish as *calabaza*, which English adopted as *calabash* at the end of the sixteenth century.

steak tartar

See *tartar*.

steak

Although tigers may not seem to have anything in common with steaks, they do: tigers and steaks derive their names from a single, Indo-European source, one that also evolved into the words *stick* and *stigma*. This Indo-European source—pronounced something like *stei* and meaning *to pierce*—evolved into the Old Persian *tighri*, meaning *piercing weapon* or *arrow*, a name later transferred to the tiger because that feline is as swift as an arrow; the animal's Old Persian name then made its way, via Greek and Latin, into English where it appeared in the eleventh century as *tigre*, later respelt as *tiger*. The Indo-European *stei* also evolved into the Greek word *stigma*, the name of a wound caused by a piercing instrument; English adopted this word in the late sixteenth century, eventually using it metaphorically to mean *a mark of shame*. As well, *stei* evolved through Germanic into the Old English *sticca*, meaning *a stick*, sticks being used, like arrows, to pierce things; by the thirteenth century, *sticca* had acquired its more familiar spelling, *stick*. And finally, the Indo-European *stei* also evolved, again via Germanic, into the Old Norse *stik*, meaning *stick*; from this word, Old Norse derived *steik*, the name of a piece of meat impaled and cooked upon a stick, which appeared in English as *steak* in the fifteenth century.

stein

When beer is gulped from a stein, what the drinker holds in his hand is, from an etymological point of view, a stone, or at least an earthenware mug that is stone-like in its weight and texture. This German word for *stone* was adopted by English as a synonym for *beer mug* in the mid nineteenth century. Long before this, however, *stein* had become familiar to English speakers thanks to prominent German surnames such as *Steinmetz* and *Steinberg*, surnames that mean, respectively, *stone cutter* and *stone mountain*. The given name *Stanley* parallels these German surnames in so far as it derives from the Old English *stan* (a close cousin of *stein* and the immediate ancestor of *stone*) and *leah* (meaning *wood*).

stelk

See *bonny-clabber*.

stew

The word *stew* derives from the same source as the word *stove*, as do the non-culinary words *typhoid* and *stifle*. The ultimate source of these words is the Greek *tuphos*, meaning *smoke* or *steam*. In Vulgar Latin, this Greek word was apparently adopted as *tufus*, which was combined with the prefix *ex* to form the verb *extufare*, meaning *to take a steam bath*. When the Vulgar Latin *extufare* was adopted by Old High German, it was turned into a noun, *stuba*, meaning *a heated room*, which English adopted in the mid fifteenth century as *stove*. At first, the English word retained the same meaning as the Old High German word: that is, *stove* was used to refer to the kind of heated room we now call a sauna, a usage that explains why medieval medical treatises often extolled the benefits of sitting in a stove. *Stove* continued to be used to mean *sauna* until the middle of the eighteenth century, at which time the culinary sense of the word, which first emerged in the late sixteenth century, came to dominate. In French, the Vulgar Latin *extufare* developed rather differently than it did in German, becoming the verb *estuver*, which English adopted in the fourteenth century as *stew*. Here, too, the original meaning of the word was maintained, as *stew* continued to be used, even as late as the nineteenth century, to mean *sauna*. However, this sense of *stew* developed a pejorative connotation because such "hot houses" were employed as rendezvous for prostitutes and their clients; accordingly, *stew* often implied *brothel*, a usage that also survived until the nineteenth century. As the *sauna* and *brothel* senses of *stew* began to die away, the word developed its current culinary sense, *thick soup*, the connection being that stews of meat and vegetables are usually, like a sauna, smoking hot and steaming. Smoke and steam are also behind the previously mentioned relatives of *stew* and *stove*: the word *stifle*, which developed through French from the Vulgar Latin *extufare*, originally meant *to smother with smoke*. The word *typhoid*, which was adapted directly from the Greek *tuphos*, originally denoted any disease causing a delirious stupor similar to that induced by inhaling too much smoke.

stockfish

See *haddock*.

stove

See *stew*.

straw

See *strawberry*.

strawberry

In the Middle Ages, women stopped eating strawberries while they were pregnant because they feared that the berry would cause their child to be born with red birthmarks, a blemish still known as a strawberry mark. The word *strawberry*, however, is as innocuous as it sounds, deriving simply from *straw*—the hollow, dried stems of certain grains—and *berry*. This berry came to be associated with straw perhaps because gardeners have long spread chopped straw around the roots of the strawberry plant to protect them; alternatively, the long runners of the plant, after they die and dry out, may have been thought to resemble grain straw. A third possibility lies in the origin of *straw* itself: *straw* takes its name from being the part of the grain that gets *strewn* on the floor; likewise, the wandering runners of a strawberry plant appear to be strewn all over the garden, meaning that the strawberry might literally be a *strew-berry*. The English word *stray* derives from the same source as *strew* and *straw*, and so does the baking term *streusel*, the name of a crumb-like topping strewn onto the tops of cakes and pastries. Of these words, *streusel* is the most recent addition to English, having been adopted from German at the beginning of this century. Much older are *straw* and *strawberry*: both are first recorded in English about a thousand years ago, although *straw* did not acquire its sense of *a tube to drink through* until the mid nineteenth century. The verb *strew*, the oldest of these words, is first recorded in the late tenth century.

streusel

See *strawberry*.

strudel

Centuries ago, a German sailor would leap out of bed with his heart in his throat if someone on deck shouted these dreadful words: "Mein Gott! Der Strudel! Der Strudel!" The fear paralysing these sailors was evoked not by a chance encounter with the sweet and sticky pastry, but by the natural phenomenon it is named after—the whirlpool, which in German is called *strudel*. The pastry owes its name to being made by rolling dough around a filling, thus giving the final product a swirling appearance. The word *strudel* first appeared in English at the end of the nineteenth century.

subaltern's luncheon

In the British military a subaltern is an officer who ranks below a captain; as a result of his low status, a subaltern is often asked to work through the meal hour, leading to the phrase *subaltern's luncheon*, a meal the officer partakes of by drinking a glass of water and tightening his belt. The phrase was first recorded at the turn of this century, but a hundred years earlier the name *subaltern's butter* had also been applied to the avocado, this greasy fruit perhaps being the only edible oil product remaining by the time the subaltern finished his shift. The word *subaltern* derives from the Late Latin *subalternus*, meaning *subordinate*.

submarine sandwich

See *hoagie*.

succotash

See *squash*.

suet

The chopped up animal fat that my mother used to strew on snow banks for sparrows to eat is called *suet*, a product also added to steamed puddings and mincemeat (in the Middle Ages it was also rubbed on swords and iron hinges to keep them from rusting). The name of this multi-purpose animal-product derives, through French, from the Latin *sebum*, which is what the ancient Romans called animal fat. First recorded in English in the late fourteenth century, *suet* was joined in the eighteenth century by the word *sebum* itself, which was adopted as a name for the fatty secretion exuded by the human scalp, a secretion that lubricates one's hair. Slightly later in the eighteenth century, *sebum* also gave rise to *sebaceous*, a word meaning *unctuous, greasy, in dire need of shampoo*.

sugar

When Darius I, king of Persia, conquered parts of India around 510 B.C., one of the wonders he returned home with was described as "a reed that gives honey without the help of bees." The reed that so astonished Darius was of course the sugar cane, and the sweet crystals extracted from it were called—in Sanskrit, an ancient language of India—*sarkara*, a word meaning *grit* or *gravel*. This Sanskrit word entered Persian as *shakar* and Arabic as *sukkar* before being adopted by Medieval Latin as *succarum*. The Medieval Latin form developed into the French *sucre*, which was borrowed by English in the fourteenth century as *sugar*. The original Sanskrit word was also borrowed by Greek as *sakcharon*, which became, via Latin, the word *saccharin*, the name of a sugar substitute derived in 1880 from coal tar. Of the many different kinds of sugar, the most common—sucrose, the white, granulated sugar found in every kitchen—took its name in 1866 from the French *sucre*. This French word also gave rise in the mid fifteenth century to a confection called *succade*, made by preserving fruit in sugar. Over the centuries, succades were followed by hundreds of other sugar confections, making it less surprising that the average North American now consumes about 65 pounds of sugar each year. See also *caramel*.

sukiyaki

See *sushi*.

sumptuary laws

Beginning in the fourteenth century and continuing even till the eighteenth century, the British government enforced certain laws restricting what people could wear and eat. These laws were concerned not with rationing a scarce product (as was the case with sugar during the Second World War), as with trying to prevent the nation from degenerating into a moral maelstrom, a social chaos in which commoners dressed like lords, and lords squandered their family jewels on exquisite dainties, and dainties became so sumptuous that the very sight of them reduced the nation's citizens to blubbering idolatry. One of the first monarchs to address this pernicious threat was Edward III, who declared that no person could arrange a dinner of more than two courses, each course comprising no more than two dishes; sauces, also, were to be used modestly, and fish and fowl were not to be mixed. Later, in 1433, another Act of Parliament determined that anyone in Scotland below the rank of baron was forbidden to eat a pie or a baked meat, these dishes still being considered exotic novelties in that realm. By the seventeenth century, such laws had come to be known as *sumptuary laws*, a term that derives from the Latin *sumere*, meaning *to use up* or *to spend*, which is also the source of the word *consume*.

sunket

See *kickshaw*.

supper

See *soup*.

surf and turf

See *soufflé*.

sushi

Although *sushi* is perhaps the one word most recognized by speakers of English as being Japanese in origin, the name of this dish was not the first word, or even the first food word, borrowed from the Japanese language. The first Japanese word to enter English—apart from the name *Japan* itself—was *bonze*, meaning *Buddhist priest*, which appeared in 1588. After this, the first Japanese food word—*mochi*, denoting a rice cake—appeared in 1616, the year Shakespeare died. Then *sake* (a rice wine) appeared in 1687, followed by *soy* (a sauce) in 1696 and *miso* (a cooking paste) in 1727. *Sake*, incidentally, comes from *saka mizu*, meaning *prosperous waters*, and *soy* comes from *sho yu*, two words meaning *salted beans and oil*, a name that the Japanese themselves borrowed from Chinese. After these sporadic borrowings, the number of Japanese food words introduced into English dropped off for more than a century and a half. Then, in the late nineteenth century, between 1880 and 1900, the Victorians—who were suddenly crazy about things Japanese—started talking about, if not eating, all kinds of Japanese foods, including sushi (balls of rice garnished with fish), sashimi (raw, sliced fish served with radish or ginger), soba (buckwheat noodles), wasabi (a Japanese herb, somewhat like horseradish), tsukemono (pickled vegetables), tofu (a soya bean curd) and nori (thin layers of seaweed). The origin of some of these names is not known; *sushi*, however, derives from a phrase meaning *it is sour*, in reference to the fish being pickled or sometimes even fermented; *sashimi* derives from two words— *sashi*, meaning *pierce*, and *mi*, meaning *flesh*—in reference to the fish being thinly sliced; *tsukemono* also derives from two words, *tsukero*, meaning *to pickle*, and *mono*, meaning *a thing*, an etymology implying that everything on earth is potentially *tsukemono*; and *tofu* derives from *dou*, meaning *beans*, and *fu*, meaning *rotten* or *curdled*. In 1920, three more Japanese food words appeared for the first time in English in a Japanese advertising brochure: *udon*, a wheat flour noodle; *sukiyaki*, a dish of thinly sliced beef that takes its name from *suki*, meaning *slice*, and *yaki*, meaning *broil*; and *tempura*, a dish of battered fish and vegetables whose name the Japanese had taken from Portuguese missionaries in the seventeenth century. The Portuguese in turn had derived their word *tempero*, meaning *seasoning*, from the Latin word *temperare*, meaning *to blend*; this origin means that *tempura* is related to words such as *temperature* and *temperance*. The most recent infusion of Japanese culinary words into English occurred between 1960 and 1970 and includes *rumaki* (an appetizer of chicken liver, water chestnuts, and bacon); *dashi* (cooking stock— its name derives from *dashi-jiru*, meaning *to extract juice*); *shabu-shabu* (thin slices of beef cooked in soup—its name supposedly comes from the sound of beef slices swishing around in the broth); *oshibori* (a towel used to wash the hands before a meal—the initial *o* of the word means *honorable* and *shibori* means *that which has been wrung out*); *teriyaki* (meat marinated in soy sauce, then broiled—the *teri* part of the word means *glaze* while *yaki* means *broil*); *yakitori* (chicken broiled on a skewer—the *tori* part of the word means *fowl*); and *tepan-yaki* (a method of broiling food— its name derives from *tepan*, meaning *iron plate*). See also *hibachi*.

sweet

Unless it is utterly bland, a dish of food will either be sweet or savoury. Of these two terms, *sweet* is the oldest, dating back in English to the ninth century. Since then, not much has happened to the word *sweet* apart from its becoming a noun—a synonym for *candy*—about a hundred years ago. Before it entered English, however, the word *sweet*—or more precisely its ancient precursor—underwent some startling shifts in meaning, shifts that resulted in the emergence of the words *persuade*, *suave*, and *hedonism*, all relatives of *sweet*. These words trace their origin to a single Indo-European source, a word meaning *sweet* and pronounced something like *swad*. *Swad* evolved quite differently as it entered each of the various branches of the Indo-European family tree. In Greek, for example, it evolved into the word *hedone*, meaning *pleasure*, the connection being that pleasure, at least metaphorically, is sweet; the Greek *hedone* was then borrowed by English to create *hedonism*, a philosophy in which pure pleasure is the goal of human existence. In Latin, the same Indo-European source—*swad*—evolved into two words, *suavis*, meaning *agreeable* (sweet things are agreeable) and *suadere*, meaning *to advise* (good advice is sweet to hear); from these two Latin words, English derived *suave*, which describes someone who seems sweet and agreeable, as well as *persuade*, the act of advising someone to do something. Finally, in the Germanic language family, the Indo-European *swad* evolved into *swotja*, meaning *sweet*, which in turn developed into the German *süss*, the Dutch *zoot*, and the English *sweet*. As a result of these thousands of years of semantic and phonetic developments, it is possible to write this sentence— "Suave hedonists sweetly persuade"—made up entirely of words that derive from the same Indo-European source.

sweet potato

See *potato*.

sweetbread

The word *sweetbread*, the culinary name for the pancreas and thymus, is surely the result of an early and brilliant marketing ploy on the part of butchers everywhere. People, of course, will eat anything, but it may be easier to get them to buy and eat the pancreas and the thymus if you call it *sweetbread*, a delicious sounding name that blithely ignores the fact that those organs have nothing to do with bread and are no sweeter than any other part of the animal. This cunning strategy was clearly lost upon whoever gave headcheese its name, but was taken to heart by the makers of *Grape-nuts*, a cereal containing neither grapes nor nuts. The word *sweetbread* first appeared in the middle of the sixteenth century. See also *mincemeat*.

sweetmeat

See *mincemeat*.

sweller

Invented in the 1960s as the name of a can of food bulging at both ends because of an accumulation of gases caused by spoilage (therefore making the item eligible for a discount), the noun *sweller* ultimately derives from an Indo-European source that made its way into dozens of languages including—of course— Medieval Gothic where it appeared as *ufswalleins*, meaning *the state or condition of being puffed up*. The term *flipper*, incidentally, refers to a can of food bulging at only one end; the name derives from how the bulge, if pressed, will "flip" to the other end of the can.

Swiss chard

See *chard*.

swizzle stick

The little rod, now plastic but formerly wood, used to stir a mixed drink has been known as a *swizzle stick* since the late nineteenth century. The *swizzle* part of the name originated in the early nineteenth century as a generic name for any drink made from a mixture of intoxicating spirits. *Swizzle* may have derived from *switchel*—a drink of rum, molasses, and water, first referred to by name in the late eighteenth century—or it may have originated as a nonce word, that is, as a word whimsically invented by combining other words. If this is the case with *swizzle*, then perhaps it was formed from *swill* and *guzzle*, or *swallow* and *fizzle*, or *swig* and *sozzle* (*sozzle* means *to mix sloppily*). Rather similar to swizzle sticks are the little parasols placed in some cocktails, especially ones made with fruit juice. Whether these parasols originated as mere decoration or as a means of protecting cool drinks from a hot sun remains an open question. More certain is that these petite umbrellas have never acquired a name of their own. Accordingly, perhaps they could be given the name *ombrellino*, an Italian word originally denoting the small canopy extended over the elements of Communion when transporting them from one location to another. *Ombrellino*, like *umbrella*, derives from the Latin *umbra*, meaning *shade*.

syrup

See *sherbet*.

Tabasco

The hot chile peppers used to make Tabasco sauce derive their name from *Tabasco*, a city in Mexico where Edmund McIlhenny, the inventor of Tabasco sauce, acquired the seeds of the pepper plants that eventually grew into a fifty-million-bottle-a-year business. As a sauce, Tabasco has existed since 1868; as a city in Mexico, whose name in Nahuatl means *damp earth*, Tabasco has existed for centuries.

tabbouleh

Made from boiled, crushed wheat, tabbouleh derives its name— sometimes spelt *tabbouli*—from the Arabic *tabil*, meaning *seasoning*, a reference to the zesty herbs, onion, mint, tomato, and lemon used to flavour the dish. The dish was first referred to in English in the 1950s.

table

When the word *table* entered English sometime before the tenth century, it did not refer to an article of furniture found in a kitchen—or anywhere else for that matter—but rather to a wooden board or a flat slab of rock. Not surprisingly, therefore, when *table* did shift in meaning at the beginning of the fourteenth century, it first came to mean a compact surface made of stone,

Cupboard Love

wax, or other material and used for writing upon. It was not until late in the fourteenth century that *table* came to mean a flat surface with legs, upon which food is served. Nor was this the end of the word's expansion of meaning: in the late fifteenth century the plural *tables* came to mean the two sides of a backgammon board; an unlucky player would *turn the tables*—or in other words rotate the board—to try to change his fortune. The Latin *tabula* is the ultimate source of *table*, and from this Latin word English also gets *tablet*—literally meaning *little table*—and *tabloid*. The word *tabloid* was devised in 1884 by an American pharmaceutical company as the trademark name for a pill-sized tablet of concentrated medicine; however, by the beginning of the twentieth century, the *concentrated* sense of *tabloid* led to its being applied to the smaller, "condensed" newspapers we now know as *tabloids*. See also *tavern*.

table d'hôte

The table of the host is what the French phrase *table d'hôte* literally means. It was borrowed by the English early in the seventeenth century to refer to the large, communal table found in most inns where everyone, friends and strangers alike, sat to be served whatever meal the host and his servants had prepared for the day. In the late eighteenth century, after the French hit upon the idea of the restaurant—which differed from an inn because it served customers at individual tables and did not provide lodgings—the phrase *table d'hôte* came to mean any complete meal ordered at a set cost. Later on, the fact that the *table d'hôte* was served at a set cost prompted the French to invent a more sensible name, *prix fixe*, literally meaning *fixed price*, which the English borrowed in the late nineteenth century. Both these terms existed in contradistinction to *à la carte*, a French phrase meaning that the items of the meal are chosen by the diner one by one from the *carte* or menu. *Carte*, incidentally, derives from the Latin word *charta*, meaning *paper*, which in turn arose from the Greek *khartes*, meaning *a leaf of papyrus*. The Latin *charta* is not only the direct source of the French *carte* but also of the English *chart*;

in turn, the French *carte* developed into the English *card* and *carton*.

taco

The words *taco* and *lunch* are not related but they do have something in common: both originated as terms describing a small quantity of food: *lunch* derives from *lump*, while the Spanish word *taco* originally meant *wad*—both terms, in other words, originally described the amount of food needed to fill the average belly. In Spanish, *taco* is still used to mean *wad*, but in Mexican Spanish it was also bestowed upon a specific lunch item: a folded tortilla stuffed with various fillings. *Taco* first appeared in English about forty years ago. See also *lunch*.

tafelmusik

The German word *tafelmusik* literally means *table music* just as *tafelwein* is German for *table wine*. Tafelmusik was originally intended to be performed during a banquet or feast while the guests dined. Although a popular musical genre in the eighteenth century, the word is not recorded in English until the late nineteenth century. The word *tafelmusik* can also refer to sheet music that has one singer's part printed upside down so that two singers can sit across from one another at a table and read from the same page.

tahina

Made by crushing sesame seeds into a smooth paste, the Mediterranean sauce known as *tahina* or *tahini* derives its name from the Arabic *tahana*, meaning *to grind*. The word first appeared in English at the end of the nineteenth century but did not become well-known until the 1950s when Mediterranean cuisine came into vogue.

tamale

The Mexican dish made by placing spiced, chopped meat on a layer of corn meal and lard and then cooking it on the husk of a corn cob was named *tamalli* by the ancient Aztecs; the Spanish adopted the word as *tamal*, which was borrowed by English in the middle of the nineteenth century. Technically, *tamale* is an incorrect form of the word, since the singular of the Spanish name is *tamal* and the plural is *tamales*; nonetheless, almost everyone, including the learned waiters in Taco Bell restaurants, now refer to the item as a *tamale*.

tamarind

Although the tree that produces tamarind is native to Africa, the name of this spice actually means *date of India*. The name originated from the Arabic *tamar*, meaning *dried date*, and *hindi*, meaning *India*; the Arabs bestowed this name upon the tamarind tree because its pods resemble dates, and because India was their main source of the spice. Through Latin, the Arabic *tamar hindi* entered Spanish as *tamarindo*, which was then adopted by English as *tamarind* in the early sixteenth century.

tangerine

The tangerine was originally called the *tangerine orange*, because the fruit was first imported into western Europe through Tangier, a Moroccan seaport on the Strait of Gibraltar. By the mid nineteenth century, the name had been shortened to *tangerine*, and by the late nineteenth century the fruit was familiar enough that *tangerine* was also being used as the name of a colour, a reddish orange. Tangier has been a seaport for thousands of years, and may have derived its name from *tigris*, a Semitic word meaning *harbour*; traditionally, however, the city is said to have been named after Tingis, the daughter of Atlas, the giant who supported the heavens on his shoulders.

tapas

In Spain, glasses of wine are often served with hors d'oeuvres known as *tapas*, sometimes offered in such abundance that they take the place of a meal. Originally, these small snacks were simply slices of bread, garnished with some savoury item and placed on the top of the wine glass by the bartender. Setting the bread slice on the glass prevented wine from sloshing over the rim as the guests moved back into the social fray, and also allowed the guests to keep one hand free for hand-shaking and gesticulating until they reached a table where their drink and snack could be set down. Putting the bread on top of the glass prompted the name *tapas*, which is simply the plural of *tapa*, Spanish for *lid*. Eventually, as the Spanish became annoyed by the crumbs floating in their wine, the custom of using slices of bread as lids fell out of favour, but the word *tapas* continued to be used in Spanish to mean *hors d'oeuvre*, the sense it possessed when English adopted *tapas* in the 1950s.

tapioca

Tapioca is a starch derived from the root of the manioc, also known as the cassava, a plant indigenous to Brazil. Brazil is also where the word *tapioca* originated: in Tupi, a language spoken by one of the native peoples of Brazil, the name of the starch is *tipioca*, a compound formed from *tipi*, meaning *juice*, and *oc*, meaning *to squeeze out*. Literally, therefore, *tapioca* means *to squeeze out the juice*, an important reminder because the juice of the manioc plant contains hydrocyanic acid, a deadly poison; once this toxic juice is squeezed out, however, the remaining pulp may be safely cooked and eaten. In English, *tapioca* was first referred to in the mid seventeenth century.

tapster

See *bung*.

tarragon

The leaves of the tarragon plant were once thought to cure snakebites; this notion may have led to the herb's name, which derives from a Greek source meaning *little dragon*. The Greek name for the herb—*drakontion*, a diminutive of *drakon*, meaning *dragon*—was first adopted by Arabic as *tarkhun*. The Arabic *tarkhun* was then borrowed by Spanish as *taragona*, which in the early sixteenth century became the English name for the herb, *tarragon*. In the seventeenth century, tarragon was also sometimes called *serpentine* or *garden dragon*, which suggests that the fire-breathing origin of the word *tarragon* was well known. The history of *tarragon* also extends beyond its Greek origin: the Greek *drakon* developed from an Indo-European source meaning *to glance at*, thanks to the monster's ability to paralyse, if not kill, by simply looking at its victim.

tart

Imagine three families with the surnames *Saunders*, *Sanders*, and *Sander* all washing ashore on a desert island, and then trying— five centuries later—to sort out their family trees. That genealogical confusion would pale in comparison to the twisted etymological histories of the words *tart*, *tartine*, *torte*, *tourte*, *torteau*, *tourtière*, *tortilla*, *tortellini*, and *tortoni*. Each of these nine food words belongs to one of three distinct word families: the *tart* family, the *torte* family, and the *tortoni* family. Belonging to the first family is the word *tart*, meaning *small pastry*, which derives from the French name for the same dessert item, *tarte* (the adjective *tart*, meaning *sharp-tasting*, derives from an entirely different source). The earlier history of the French *tarte* is unknown: it was once thought to have derived from the Late Latin *torta panis*, a kind of bread, but linguists say it is unlikely that the *or* sound in *torta* could have shifted to the *ar* sound in *tarte*. From *tarte*, the French later derived *tartine*, the name of a slice of bread spread with butter or preserves, which English borrowed in the early nineteenth century. The second word family—the *torte* family—developed from the Late Latin *torta panis*, mentioned earlier as the name of a Roman bread. In French, *torta panis*—or rather its abbreviated form, *torta*—gave rise to *tourteau*, which English borrowed in the fifteenth century as the name for a large, round loaf; *torta* also evolved into the French *tourte*, which English borrowed in sixteenth century, spelling it *torte* and using it as a name for a bread-cake. Later on, in the early eighteenth century, English again borrowed the French *tourte*, this time retaining the French spelling, and using it to denote a pastry containing meat or fish. Still later, *tourte* inspired another word, *tourtière*, which means *meat pie* in French Canada but which English adopted in the 1950s as a fancy synonym for *pie-plate*. The Late Latin *torta* also evolved in languages other than French. In Spanish, it gave rise to *tortilla*, meaning *little cake*, which English adopted at the end of the seventeenth century; similarly, in Italian, *torta* gave rise to *tortellini*, also meaning *little cake*, which English adopted in 1937. The third word family contains only one member, *tortoni*, an ice-cream dessert named after the Italian café-owner who invented it in Paris during the 1890s. See also *tart* (below).

tart

The *tart* that means *sharp to the taste* neither derived from, nor gave rise to, the *tart* that means *filled pastry*; after all, tarts are not tart but savoury or sweet. In fact, the adjective form of this word—that is, the *tart* that means *sharp-tasting*—is first recorded in Old English about a thousand years ago, more than four centuries before the unrelated pastry *tart* appeared. Originally, however, the adjective *tart* did not mean *sharp* in the gustatory sense, but instead *sharp* in the punitive sense: a *tart* punishment was a severe one. This original meaning suggests that the adjective *tart* developed from the Old English word *teran*, meaning *to tear*, a word associated with pain and punishment. By the end of the fourteenth century, however, *tart* had widened to include its current meaning of *sharp to the taste*. See also *tart* (above).

tartar

The Tartars, a huge army of warriors led by Ghengis Khan in the thirteenth century, were renowned for being rather rambunctious, perhaps even boisterous. Since they passed most of their days pillaging, marauding, and wreaking havoc, they did not have much time to descant upon the gastronomic arts, and yet they did hit upon one culinary innovation, namely, the practice of placing a raw chunk of meat under a saddle so that after a long day's ride it would be tender and salty. During the Middle Ages, reports of this outlandish method of preparing meat reached Germany, prompting cooks to bestow the name *tartar* on a dish made by seasoning raw, minced meat with pepper, onion, and salt. In France, this dish became *steak à la tartare*, and a similarly-seasoned mayonnaise became known as *sauce tartare*. English adopted *sauce tartare* as *tartar sauce* in the mid nineteenth century, and borrowed the French name of the meat dish as *steak tartar* in the first decade of this century. Incidentally, the original form

Cupboard Love

of the Tartars' name was *Tatar*, but their anti-social behaviour caused their neighbours to associate them with Tartarus, the hell of ancient Greek mythology, and thus a second *r* was mistakenly added to their name. The tartar that dentists scrape off your teeth derives its name from a different source, specifically, from the Medieval Latin *tartarum*, the name of a crusty substance that forms on the inside surface of wine-casks. When purified, this by-product of wine becomes cream of tartar, used in baking.

tartine

See *tart*.

taste

Back in the thirteenth century, you tasted not with your tongue but with your fingers: the word *taste* originally meant *to touch* or *to feel*, and it did not completely lose this sense until the mid seventeenth century. At the same time, beginning in the late fourteenth century, the word *taste* slowly came to mean a special kind of "touching," the kind that "feels" the flavour of a food as it passes over the tongue. Given the original meaning of taste, etymologists have tried to relate it to *tangere*, a Latin word meaning *to touch*: for example, it has been suggested that *tangere* was combined with *gustare* to form *tastare*, an unrecorded Latin word that might have developed into the English *taste*. Alternatively, the source of *taste* may be the Latin *taxare*, meaning *to feel out* or *to assess*: according to this line of thinking, *taxare* gave rise to an unrecorded *taxitare*, which then developed into *taste*. If this latter explanation is the true one, then *taste* is a cousin of *tax*, a word that evolved directly from the Latin *taxare*. In the late fourteenth century, *taste* gave rise to *taster*, the name of a culinary officer whose job was to taste the food before it was served to the royal family to ensure that it contained no poison. Such tasters were also known as *gusters* and *forestallers*. See also *salver*.

tavern

The words *tavern*, *pub*, and *bar* designate establishments whose primary function is to serve liquor. Of these three words, *tavern* is by far the oldest; it was adopted at the end of the thirteenth century from French, which had derived it from the Latin *taberna*, meaning *a wooden hut*. The Latin *taberna* also developed the diminutive form *tabernaculum*, from which English gets the word *tabernacle*, the name of the tent covering the Ark of the Covenant; the holy *tabernacle* and the homely *tavern* are therefore closely related. *Bar* is the next word that came to mean a drinking place; when *bar* was adopted from French in the late fourteenth century, it referred only to any long, narrow piece of metal or wood. By the end of the sixteenth century, however, it had also come to signify the long, narrow counter in a tavern separating the customers from the servers, and by the early nineteenth century the name of this counter had also been extended to any establishment furnished with such a "bar." The word *pub* developed in the middle of the seventeenth century, but in the previous century the term *public house*—of which *pub* is an abbreviation—had been used more generally to refer to a place providing not only liquor but also food and lodging. Finally, there is also the word *cabaret*, which was adopted from French in the middle of the sixteenth century as a slightly more sophisticated name for drinking establishments; the word, whose ultimate origin is unknown, retained this sense until the early twentieth century when it came to mean a restaurant providing zany entertainment, and then—by extension—the entertainment itself. See also *bung*.

tavorsay
See *bouce Jane*.

tempura
See *sushi*.

teriyaki
See *sushi*.

thanks
See *wishbone*.

tharf-cake

The Old English word *tharf*, meaning *need* or *necessity*, is first recorded in the early eighth century, and last recorded in the early fourteenth century. Just as it was vanishing as an independent word, however, *tharf* became part of the compound *tharf-cake*, a name still in use until the end of the last century. As its "needy" origin suggests, tharf-cake was very plain fare: a simple but nourishing lump of unleavened bread, hardly the kind of thing that we would now call *cake*.

thermidor

This dish of cubed lobster mixed with cream, seasoned with mustard, and served in the halves of its shell acquired its name in 1894 when it was invented by a Parisian chef to honour the opening of a play by Victorien Sardou called *Thermidor*. In turn, the play borrowed its title from the name of the eleventh month in the calendar system implemented between 1793 and 1805 by proponents of the French Revolution. Thermidor was a summer month, and thus its Greek name literally means *gift of heat*. Other months in this calendar system also took their names from their seasonal attributes: *Fructidor* meaning *gift of fruit*; *Vendémiaire* meaning *vintage*; *Brumaire* meaning *fog*; *Frimaire* meaning *frost*; *Nivôse* meaning *snow*; *Pluviôse* meaning *rain*; *Ventôse* meaning *wind*; *Germinal* meaning *sprout*; *Floréal* meaning *flower*; *Prairial* meaning *meadow*; and *Messidor* meaning *gift of harvest*. The individual who actually invented the names of these months was the French poet Fabre d'Églantine.

thible

The rise of ready-made breakfast cereals in the last years of the nineteenth century marked the end of the tyranny of porridge, and with it the demise of the thible, a stick used to stir porridge. The thible is an excellent example of a device that people used for centuries before giving it a name: since ancient times people in England knew enough to stir their porridge while it cooked, but it was not until the end of the fifteenth century that it finally occurred to someone to call it a *thible*. Until then, they could only refer to the implement that prevented their breakfast from becoming a complete disaster as a *stick*. The origin of the word *thible* is completely unknown; the word *thibler*, meaning *one who wields a thible*, has never existed.

three-threads

At the end of the seventeenth century, a beverage called *three-threads* became a popular thirst quencher, its name deriving from its being made by mixing three different kinds—or "threads"—of beer. Soon after, some unknown tavern owner decided that, instead of mixing the three beers, it would be easier to brew a single beer that tasted like three-threads. When perfected, the resulting brew was called *entire* because its flavour extended across the entire range of the three beers that inspired it. In the early eighteenth century, entire also became known as *porter*, so named because porters—or luggage handlers—drank a lot of it; nonetheless, the original name, *entire*, continued to be used by brewers until the late nineteenth century. The word *thread*, incidentally, derives from an ancient Germanic source that meant *to twist*; the word *throw* derives from the same source, and that is why potters, as they sit hunched over their twisting pottery wheels, are said to be "throwing" pots.

thrive bit

The thrive bit, like the force piece, is what Mr. Manners gets to eat after a meal has ended. In other words, the thrive bit and the force piece are the last tid-bit of food left on the table, the food that only the greediest guest would deprive the mythical Mr. Manners of. This untouched piece of dinner is an important part of gastronomic etiquette because it attests to the host having provided enough food to ensure that the guests will "thrive." The irony is that the host may not, in fact, have provided enough food, but the still-hungry guests dare not satisfy themselves with the last piece that sits, enticingly, before them. The word *thrive* is first recorded in the thirteenth century, but since it derives from an Old Norse word, it must have been in use since the ninth or tenth century when the Vikings sailed to England to pillage and conquer its defenceless villagers. The Old Norse word that is the source of *thrive* was *thrifask*, meaning *to grasp for oneself*, the assumption being that grabbing and seizing are synonymous with thriving. The word *thrift*, which developed from the same source as *thrive*, acquired its sense of *frugality* in the sixteenth century as the emerging merchant class learned that penny-pinching helped a business thrive. The *force* in *force piece* derives from a Latin source, *fortis*, meaning *strong*. The word *force* was likely applied to the last tid-bit of the meal because many hosts, satisfied that their bounty was proven by the temporary presence of a thrive bit, would take this last morsel and force it upon some lucky dinner guest, who had to accept it after ritually protesting to be too full to eat another bite.

thyme

Although they were once spelt the same, *thyme* the herb and *time* the dimension are not related. Whereas *time* evolved from an Indo-European source meaning *to divide*, the aromatic herb acquired its name from the Greek *thumos*, meaning *breath* or *spirit*, because thyme was once burnt as a fragrant sacrifice to the gods (further back, the Greek *thumos* developed from the same Indo-European source as the English *fume* and *perfume*). The name of the herb appeared in English at the beginning of the fifteenth century as *thyme*, but was often respelt as *time* during the sixteenth and seventeenth centuries, thus allowing authors like Shakespeare to make puns on *wild time*. In the eighteenth century, the *time* spelling of the spice name again fell out of favour.

tid-bit

Since the mid seventeenth century, scrumptious morsels of food have been called *tid-bits*, a compound that derives from two words, one of them having an obvious origin, the other one not. The obvious one—*bit*—simply derives from the same source as the word *bite*: a bit is literally a piece bitten off (although the computer *bit*, the name of a tiny unit of information, derives from the first letter of *binary* and the last two letters of *digit*). The word *tid* has a more problematic origin. Until recently, it was thought to be an old dialect word meaning *nice* or *delicate*, the idea being that a tid-bit is a nice bit of food; the trouble with this explanation is that the word *tid* did not emerge until a hundred years after the appearance of the word *tid-bit*, suggesting that it was derived from *tid-bit* and not the other way around. Accordingly, a better explanation of *tid* is that it derives from *tide*. Before the fourteenth century, when it came to refer to the ebb and flow of the sea, the word *tide* simply meant *time*: in fact, *time* and *tide* derive from the same source, an Indo-European word meaning *to divide*. This *time* sense of *tide* persists in the archaic words *yuletide* and *Christmastide*, and was used throughout the Middle Ages in conjunction with religious holidays such as *Eastertide*, *Whitsuntide*, and *Shrovetide*. Because of the celebratory nature of such holidays, *tide* eventually came to be synonymous with *feast*, and any morsel of food remaining after a religious feast came to be known as a *tide-bit*, later corrupted to *tid-bit*. *Tid-bit* remains the usual spelling and pronunciation in North America, but in England *tit-bit* is more common, the change in form occurring as people confused the word *tid* with the word *tit*; the *tit* in question, however, is not the vulgar one that means *breast*, but rather the *tit* that means *small*, a word of Scandinavian origin. This *tit* occurs in compounds such as *titmouse*, the name of a creature that, despite its name, is not a small mouse but a variety of small bird. The titmouse has, of course, been a source of titillation for generations of British school boys, but only because the bearded tit—a small-billed marsh bird whose head-feathers resemble whiskers—is less familiar.

tierce

See *nipperkin*.

toad in the hole

See *spotted dick*.

toast

Although they now seem to be completely different things, the toast you eat for breakfast and the toast you drink to the bride and groom are actually one and the same. Since at least the early fifteenth century, it was common for revellers to toast slices of bread, spice them, and toss them into glasses of wine, apparently to improve the flavour of the beverage. Eventually, it also became fashionable for a man to announce, before drinking, that no spiced toast could improve the flavour of his wine as much as the name of his beloved. It was inevitable, therefore, that some witty fellow—early in the eighteenth century—started a fad by referring to his beloved as his *toast*, a metaphor suggestive of her supposed sweetness, and not intended to imply that she was sopping wet or crumbling to bits. In time, *toasting* came to mean the custom of verbally honouring any beloved guest before drinking, and continued to be known by this name even after wine ceased to be served with chunks of toast floating around in it. In origin, the word *toast* derives from the French *toster*, meaning *to grill*, which in turn evolved from the Latin *torrere*, meaning *to scorch*. *Torrere*, incidentally, is also the source of *torrid*, meaning *hot*, and even of *torrent*, meaning a furious river: a torrent, as it surges up and down, bubbling and frothing, almost appears to be boiling, and thus it acquired a name that suggests intense heat.

tofu

See *sushi*.

tomato

Although it is hard to imagine Italian cuisine without the tomato, that juicy, red fruit was not introduced to Italy until the sixteenth century; the tomato is, after all, a "New World" fruit, native to Peru and Central America where the Aztecs called it *tomatl*. When they returned to Europe with the fruit, Spanish explorers called it *tomate*, which is how the English spelt the name when they adopted it at the beginning of the seventeenth century; in the mid eighteenth century, however, the English started spelling the word *tomato*, the final *e* having been replaced by an *o* partly to make the word look more Spanish, and partly to make it more closely resemble *potato* (the resemblance to *potato* also caused the pronunciation to change, at least in North America, from *toe-mah-toe* to *toe-may-toe*). At first, the tomato was grown merely as a ornamental plant, due to the belief that the fruit was poisonous: the tomato belongs to the nightshade family, and its vines are indeed toxic. By the eighteenth century, however, Europeans had realized the culinary potential of the tomato, although North Americans remained leery of the plant until the early nineteenth century. Tomatoes are sometimes called *love apples* because of a linguistic mix-up: the Italians occasionally called the tomato *pomo dei Moro*, meaning *apple of the Moors*, because the fruit was first imported from Spain via Morocco; the Italians also sometimes called the tomato *pomo d'oro*, meaning *golden apple*, because one of the varieties introduced to them was yellow. One of these two Italian names—or perhaps both—was eventually mistaken for the phrase *pomme d'amour*, meaning *love apple*, which became the plant's English nickname in the sixteenth century.

torte

See *tart*.

tortellini

See *tart*.

tortière

See *tart*.

tortilla

See *tart*.

tortoni

See *tart*.

tournedos

A tournedos is the centre of a fillet of beef, grilled and served with any number of elaborate sauces or garnishes. The French name of this dish literally means *turn the back*, deriving from *tourner*, meaning *to turn* (as in *tourniquet*), and *dos*, meaning *back* (as in *dos-à-dos*, a square-dance call that tells the dancers to turn back to back). Many explanations have been offered for the origin of this name. The earliest, dating to 1877 when *tournedos* first appeared in English, suggests that the dish gets its name because it cooks so quickly that a chef does not have time to turn her back before it must be flipped. A more elaborate story tells of the composer Rossini asking a Parisian *maître d'hôtel* to prepare a newfangled beef dish; upon hearing Rossini's description of the dish, the *maître d'hôtel* announced he would be ashamed to bring such a strange, new dish to the table. In response, Rossini facetiously assured the *maître d'hôtel* that his guests would spare him any embarrassment by turning their backs to him as he brought them the dish. From then on, so the story goes, the dish was known as *tournedos à la Rossini*, or simply as *tournedos*.

tranch

See *carving*.

treacle

What North Americans call *molasses*, the British call *treacle*, a word that derives ultimately from a Greek word meaning *fierce or poisonous beast*. This Greek word—*therion*—gave rise to an adjective, *theriakos*, a form of which was used by the ancient Greeks in the phrase *antidotos theriake*, meaning *antidote for poisonous beasts*. From this phrase, the ancient Romans derived their name for such life-saving antidotes, *theriaca*, which made its way through Old French and appeared in English in the mid fourteenth century as *treacle*. *Antidote* remained the only meaning of *treacle* until the late seventeenth century when it was made the name of a syrup produced from unrefined sugar, a syrup whose sweetness made it a kind of "antidote" for bitter substances. Other words that derive from the same source as *treacle* include *fierce* and *feral*, both of which have stayed closer to the *wild beast* sense of their Greek ancestor. See also *molasses*.

treen

A thousand years ago, the typical English table setting consisted of a wooden bowl, a wooden plate, a wooden mug, and a wooden spoon; these utensils were made of wood not because it is an excellent source of fibre, but because other materials—such as glass, earthenware, and pewter—were either not invented yet or were too expensive to be used by the common people. The usual name for such wooden table utensils was *treen*, so called because they were made from trees (the *n* that appears at the end of *treen* is the same suffix that turns *gold* into *golden* or *wood* into *wooden*). Today, *treen* is a rather unfamiliar word because wooden utensils have been replaced by china and metal alloys; salad bowls, however, continue to be treen because the porous surface of the wood better retains the dressing, preventing it from pooling in the bottom of the bowl.

trifle

See *flummery*.

tripe

See *trollibags*.

trollibags

Most people consider the guts of an animal to be its least palatable component, but you would never guess this from the apparent delight that English speakers have taken in inventing or borrowing names for these edible parts of an animal's digestive system. These names include *tharm*, *guts*, *bowels*, and *entrails*; *inmeat*, *innards*, *intestines*, and *viscera*; *trillibub*, *trollibags*, *tripe*, and *mundungus*; *slumgullion*, *numbles*, *garbage*, and *giblets*. Each of these words originated in one of three ways. *Tharm* and *guts*, for example, arose as descriptions of what happens to food after it enters the alimentary canal: specifically, *tharm* derives from an Indo-European source meaning *to go through*, while *guts* derives from an Old English word meaning *to pour*. Some of the other words originated from the resemblance of the intestines to something else: *bowels*, for example, derives from the Latin *botellus*, meaning *small sausage*, while *viscera*, a Latin word, appears to have developed from an Indo-European source meaning *winding*. Still other words originated from the location of the organs they referred to: *entrails* and *intestines* both derive from Latin words meaning *within*, while *innards* derives from the native English *inwards*; similarly, *inmeat* arose as a name for the meat *in* the abdominal cavity. Many of the other words in the long list given above have such mysterious origins that little can be said about them. *Trollibags*, for instance, sounds like a British Barbie accessory, but in fact it is simply a variation of *trillibub*, whose origin is unknown. Likewise, *tripe*, despite being a familiar culinary term, derives from no known source; *mundungus* derives from *mondongo*, the Spanish word for *tripe*, but beyond that nothing is known about the word. All these words, incidentally, are still in use with the exception of *mundungus* and *tharm*. See also *garbage*, *giblets*, *slumgullion*, and *humble pie*.

tuna

As the name of a large fish (sometimes weighing over a thousand pounds), the word *tuna* did not appear in English until just over one hundred years ago when it appeared as a variant of the fish's older English name, *tunny*. Dating back to the early sixteenth century, *tunny* derived from the French *thon*, which in turn developed, via the Latin *thunnus*, from the Greek name for the fish, *thunnos*. As the name of a prickly pear, the word *tuna* appeared in the mid sixteenth century. This *tuna* derives from a West Indian source and entered English via Spanish.

turbot

See *halibut*.

turkey

Both the English and French names for the large fowl known as the *turkey* are the result of mistaken assumptions. The French name, *dinde*, literally means *from India*, because the Spanish conquistadors who returned from North America with the bird were under the impression that they were in India when they discovered and named it. Even worse, the English name, *turkey*, is the result of not one but two errors. First of all, in the mid sixteenth century the name *turkey* was bestowed on a bird that we would no longer consider a turkey at all: the African Guinea fowl. In England, this bird became known as *turkey* because it was imported to Europe by the Portuguese through Turkey, the country where many people wrongly assumed it originated. At about the same time, English explorers who were traipsing over what is now Virginia encountered a large, rather dimwitted bird that they mistook for some sort of "turkey," that is, for some sort of African Guinea fowl. Calling them *turkeys*, the explorers took a few of these North American birds back to England where they were successfully bred and became, along with the other so-called turkey, a popular dinner item. For about fifty years, until the beginning of the seventeenth century, the word *turkey* therefore referred to two different birds, the African Guinea fowl and the American turkey. Eventually, however, someone noticed that the two birds do not really look alike, and thus *turkey* ceased to be used for the African bird, the one that originally held claim to the name. Incidentally, the country Turkey, the source of the fowl's name, takes its name from a Persian word that probably means *powerful*; that country's name is also the source of *turquoise*, a precious stone first found within the Turkish dominions.

Turk's-head

Some cakes are so large that it is hard to bake their centres without burning their surfaces; accordingly, a round pan with a vertical cone in its middle is used to prevent the cake from even having a centre. In the late nineteenth century, the shape of this baking pan apparently reminded someone of a turban, a headgear of Middle Eastern origin, and thus it became known as the *Turk's-head*.

turnip

From the eighth to the sixteenth century in England, and even today in Scotland, turnips were called *neeps*, a word deriving from the Latin name of the vegetable, *napus*. In the sixteenth century, for some unknown reason, this name came to be seen as inadequate and therefore *neep* was compounded with another word to form *turnip*. This other word was likely either the English word *turn* or its French equivalent *tour*, the idea being that a turnip is so round it appears to have been turned on a lathe. The plant known since the fourteenth century as the *turnsole*—the berries of which produce a purple dye once used to colour jellies—likewise derives part of its name from the word *turn*, but for a different reason: throughout the day its flowers turn as they follow the sun across the sky.

tutti-frutti

The Italian phrase *tutti-frutti* means *all fruits*, a name that describes ice cream flavoured with a mixture of cherries, raisins, pistachios, and so on. The Italian *frutti* is obviously closely related to the English *fruit*, just as *tutti* derives from the same Latin source as the English *total*. That Latin source—*totus*, meaning *all*—also developed into the French *tout* as in *tout le monde*, meaning *everyone*. Another sort of ice cream also has a name that reflects its Italian origin: *Neapolitan*, the name of an ice cream made by alternating layers of vanilla, chocolate, and strawberry, means *in the style of Naples*, Naples being a port on the southwest coast of Italy. In turn, Naples has a name that is Greek in origin, deriving as it does from *nea polis*, meaning *new city*, so named when the Greeks founded it in the seventh century B.C. As the name of an ice cream, *Neapolitan* first appeared in English in the late nineteenth century, about fifty years after the appearance of *tutti-frutti*.

udon

See *sushi*.

ullage

When you buy a bottle of wine or a carton of milk, the ullage is the space near the top of the vessel containing no liquid. The term ultimately derives from the Latin *oculus*, meaning *eye*: thanks to the Gallic contempt for consonants, the Latin *oculus* evolved into *oeil*, an unpronounceable French word meaning *eye*; *oeil* then gave rise to the verb *ouiller*, meaning *to fill a wine-cask up to its eye*, the eye being the bung-hole into which new wine is poured. *Ouiller* in turn gave rise to the noun *ouillage*, signifying the space above the eye of the cask, which English adopted in the early fourteenth century as *ullage*. A word closely related to *ullage* is *inveigle*, meaning *to deceive*, which derives via French from the Latin *ab oculo*, meaning *away from the eye*.

umbles

See *humble pie*.

undertranch

See *carving*.

vanilla

One of the best kept secrets of ice-cream producers is that their most popular flavour, vanilla, derives its name from the Latin word *vagina*. For the ancient Romans, the word *vagina* meant *sheath* or *scabbard*, the protective casing from which a sword was drawn when danger threatened. This Latin *vagina* was adopted into Spanish as *vaina*, which subsequently developed a diminutive form, *vainilla*, meaning *little sheath*. The Spanish made this diminutive the name of the fragrant plant because its pods, from which vanilla flavouring is extracted, are indeed long and narrow like a miniature sheath. In the middle of the seventeenth century, English borrowed this word, *vainilla*, from Spanish, but changed the spelling to *vanilla*. At about the same time, English anatomists returned to the Latin they had learned as school boys and adopted the word *vagina* into English to refer to the "sheath" leading to a woman's uterus. The introduction of this learned term allowed the older word *cunt*, which had a long history as a bona fide medical term, to degenerate into mere profanity.

venison

Although *venison*, *venom*, and *Venus* may not seem to have much in common, they derive from the same Indo-European source, a word pronounced something like *wen* and meaning *to desire*. This Indo-European source developed into a cluster of Latin words, all beginning with *ven* and all somehow maintaining their ancestor's sense of *desire*. *Venari*, for example, emerged in Latin meaning *to hunt*, the connection being that when you hunt for something, you desire it. Via French, this word gave rise to the word *venison*, which—when it first appeared in English in the fourteenth century—referred to the meat of any animal that had been killed in a hunt; later on, in the eighteenth century, the word narrowed in meaning and came to refer specifically to the meat of a deer. Similarly, *Venus* emerged in Latin as the name of the Roman goddess of love because love was seen to be synonymous with desire; later on, the Romans named the second planet from the sun after Venus because they identified her with the Greek goddess, Aphrodite, who had previously had dibs on that lusty planet. Finally, the word *venenum* emerged in Latin as the name for a love potion, a drink designed to spark desire. In time, however, and probably for good reason, such potions came to be seen as little better than poison, which was the sense possessed by *venom*—the derivative of *venenum*—when it appeared in English in the thirteenth century. Incidentally, the Indo-European source of these Latin words also gave rise, after evolving through the Germanic family tree, to the word *win*, the connection being that you can win something only if you desire it. All these related words—*venison, venom, Venus,* and *win*—are of course well-established in English; however, considering deer meat is becoming an increasingly rare menu item, the word *venison* may, in a few generations, be as unfamiliar as *chevaline*. See also *chevaline*.

vermicelli

See *spaghetti*.

vermouth

Vermouth takes its name from one of the bitter herbs formerly used to flavour it, an herb known in Old German as *wermuota*. This German name was adopted by French as *vermout*, which in turn was borrowed by English as *vermouth* in the early nineteenth century. Further back in history, the Old German *wermuota*—and also the Old English name for the same herb, *wermod*—seems to have developed from a Germanic source meaning *man courage*, a compound formed from *wer*, meaning *man*, and *motham*, meaning *courage* (the first of these words is also represented in *werewolf*, meaning *man-wolf*, while the second evolved into the word *mood*). The plant probably earned this name, "man courage," because it was used as an aphrodisiac: it helped a man get his courage up. In English, the name of the herb shifted in the fifteenth century from *wermod* to *wormwood* perhaps because doctors, who used the herb to cure intestinal worms, mistakenly assumed that the word *wermod* must somehow be related to the word *worm*. Today, wormwood is used neither for curing worms nor making vermouth: in the early part of this century, it was discovered that the herb, ingested over a long period of time, is both poisonous and addictive. Accordingly, wormwood was either removed from alcoholic concoctions or, as in the case of absinthe, replaced with aniseed.

viand

See *vittles*.

victuals

See *vittles*.

vielliebchen

See *liebesknochen*.

vindaloo

Portuguese is the source not only of *tempura*, the name of a Japanese seafood dish, but also of *vindaloo*, the name of a hot curry dish originating in India. This Indian dish—made of meat in a sauce of wine and garlic—is called in Portuguese *vin d'alho*, deriving from *vinho*, meaning *wine*, and *alho*, meaning *garlic*. English colonists were introduced to the dish in India, and borrowed its name in the late nineteenth century.

vinegar

See *wine*.

vittles

Although *vittles* might seem to be a word only a hillbilly would use, it is actually more authentic than its highbrow variant, *victuals*. These two synonyms for *food* derive from the Late Latin *victualia*, meaning *nourishment*, which in turn developed from a Latin root that meant *life*. The Late Latin *victualia* entered Old French as *vituaille*, which became the English *vittle* (or *vittles*) in the early fourteenth century. In the sixteenth century, however, some people began to fear that English was becoming a barbaric language, and thus they attempted to bolster its classical heritage by respelling certain English words to resemble their distant Latin sources: *receit*, for example, became *receipt*, *dette* became *debt*, and *vittles* became *victuals*. These new Latinate spellings were not intended to change the pronunciation of the word in question, but sometimes they did, as was the case with *victuals*, which many people began to mispronounce as *vick-tyoo-uls*. *Vittles*, however, remains the original and more "English" spelling and pronunciation of the word. Closely related to *vittles* and *victuals* is the word *viand*, meaning *article of food*, a word that developed through French from the Latin *vivere*, meaning *to live*, which in turn evolved from the Latin root that meant *life*. The word *viand* appeared in English in the early fifteenth century, between the earlier *vittles* and the later *victuals*. Dozens of other words also derive from the same Latin root as *vittles* and *viand*, some of them obvious, like *vitamin*, and some of them surprising, like *viper*: the viper's name is apparently a contraction of the Latin *vivi-pera*, meaning *born living*, so called because the viper was thought to give birth not to eggs but to ready-made snakes.

voip

Foods that give no gastronomic delight, such as porridge or cream of celery soup, are *voip*; the word was invented in 1914 by Gellet Burgess, a humorist devoted to creating names for previously unnamed things. Burgess coined other food-related words as well: *fidgeltick* is food that requires tremendous effort to prepare, but gives little satisfaction—artichokes are a kind of fidgeltick, as are most fondues; *wog* is food that becomes stuck to a dinner guest's face, visible to everyone but the guest himself; *rowtch* refers to a person who demonstrates extreme fastidiousness when eating—someone who eats pizza with a knife and fork is a rowtch, as is someone who insists on crossing her knife and fork after finishing her meal. Burgess may have developed these words from real sources: *voip* suggests *void*, as in "void of pleasure"; *fidgeltick* suggests *fidgeting*, a repetitive action accomplishing nothing. As dandy as Burgess's words are, however, none of them have achieved currency with the exception of *blurb*, a quoted passage of fulsome praise found on book jackets. See also the book jacket.

wafer

In the Germanic language that English partly developed from, there existed a word pronounced something like *wab*. This word meant *honeycomb*, the patterned structure formed by bees to store honey, and it gave rise in English to words associated with other kinds of patterned structures: *web* and *weave*. These words in turn led to the surnames *Webster* and *Weaver*, bestowed long ago on people who wove fabrics for a living. The Germanic *wab* also developed in other directions. It entered German as *wafel*, the name of a light cake whose surface has a honeycomb pattern, which was then adopted into French as two words: Norman French took it as *waufre* and Central French took it as *gaufre*. (A similar splitting, incidentally, happened to the Germanic word *warnon*, meaning *to warn*, which became both *guarantee* and *warranty*.) The Norman French member of this pair, *waufre*, was adopted into English in the fourteenth century as *wafer*. Its Central French cousin, *gaufre*, entered English in the middle of the eighteenth century as *gofer*, yet another name for a thin batter-cake stamped with a honeycomb pattern by hot iron plates. More bizarrely, though, the Central French *gaufre* also became, in the early nineteenth century, the name given by French settlers in North America to a burrowing rodent that "honeycombs" the earth with its tunnels—the gopher. Finally, in the middle of the eighteenth century, Dutch immigrants to the United States introduced the word *wafel*, their name for a soft, hot cake served with butter; this word, which of course derived from the same Germanic source as *wafer*, was then respelt in English as *waffle*. Surprisingly, this *waffle* is not related to the verb *waffle* that means *to be wishy-washy* or *to be undecided*; instead, this verb form of *waffle* developed from the same source as the word *wave*.

waffle

See *wafer*.

walnut

Whereas we throw rice over a newly married couple to assure their fertility, it was once a custom in ancient Rome for the bride and groom to throw walnuts at children, not because the children were brawling and ruining the wedding party, but rather to represent the casting off of the newlyweds' childish natures. It was the Romans, too, who introduced the walnut to northern Europe and England, thus inspiring the Old English name for the nut: *wealhknutu*, literally meaning *foreign nut*. The *wealh* part of the name, in the Germanic language from which English partly developed, originally meant *Celtic*, the Celts being foreign as far as the northern Europeans were concerned; soon, however, the word also began to refer to any foreigner or foreign item, including those from southern Europe like the Romans. The *wealh* that became part of *walnut* also developed into the names *Wales* and *Welsh*, the Welsh, like the Romans, being foreigners as far as the Anglo-Saxon settlers of England were concerned; this Old English *wealh* is evident not only in *walnut* but also in *Cornwall*, a city on the southeastern tip of England whose name means *Welsh horn*, or in other words *foreign horn*, a horn being a promontory of land. Given that *Welsh* means *foreign*, the Welsh do not use that name to refer to themselves; rather, they call themselves *Cymry*, a Welsh word literally meaning *compatriots*.

wasabi

See *sushi*.

water

The ultimate source of *water* was an Indo-European word pronounced something like *wodor*, which gave rise to dozens of other words in other languages. In Greek, *wodor* became *hudor*, which gave rise in the thirteenth century to the English *hydro*, now used in words such as *hydro-electric*. In Latin, *wodor* became *unda*, meaning *wave*, which is the source of words such as *undulate*. In Russian, *wodor* became *voda*, the source of *vodka*, a diminutive meaning *little water* that entered English at the beginning of the nineteenth century. In Gaelic, *wodor* became the almost unrecognizable *uisge*, which was combined with another Gaelic word to form *uisge-beatha*, literally meaning *water of life*; later on, *uisge-beatha* evolved into *whiskybae*, which entered English as *whiskey* in the early eighteenth century. In German, *wodor* became *wasser*, the source of *vaseline*, a water-based lubricant. The word *water* is even related to some words that might seem further afield, including *otter*, an animal similar to the hydra (a mythical Greek monster) in that they are both water-beasts. Even the word *winter* may derive from the same source as *water*, winter being the season when water, albeit frozen, accumulates on the ground. See also *aquavit*.

watermelon

Before it acquired its current name in the early seventeenth century, the watermelon was known as *citrul* or *pasteque*. The older of these words was *citrul*, which originated in the fourteenth century and did not fade into oblivion until the mid eighteenth century; it derived, through French and Italian, from the Latin *citrus*, the connection being that the watermelon has a lime-coloured skin. *Pasteque*, on the other hand, originated in the late sixteenth century and was still in use in the nineteenth; it derived, through French, from the Arabic name for this watery fruit, *bittikha*. See also *melon*.

wedding cake

The customs surrounding wedding cakes are among the strangest that have ever developed. In the Vendée, a coastal region on the Bay of Biscay, the parents of the bridal couple traditionally purchase the largest wedding cake imaginable—sometimes weighing eighty pounds—and then have it borne into the banquet hall by attendants who fulfill their part of the tradition by dancing a little jig to demonstrate that the cake they are carrying, though heavy, is not too heavy; the custom seems to imply, "Yes, our cake is big, but it's not going to hurt you." Almost as strange is the North American ritual of the bride and groom both grabbing hold of the same knife—an action more plausibly associated with bar fights—so that they can pretend to cut the cake together. Such wedding-cake customs extend even further back in time than the term *wedding cake* itself, which is not recorded until the mid seventeenth century. Prior to that, wedding cakes were known as *bridecakes*, a term first recorded in the sixteenth century. More recently, probably within this century, the term *matrimonial cake* has also come into use. Of these three terms, it is *matrimonial cake* that has the strangest origin: the word *matrimonial* derived in the sixteenth century from the Latin *matrimonium*, which in turn developed from the Latin *mater*, meaning *mother*. Freud might argue that the origin of this word represents every son's oedipal urge to marry his mother, but it probably simply represents the fact that for women, for thousands of years, getting married was the same thing as becoming a mother: even today, the first thing people do after a marriage ceremony is throw rice, a talisman to ensure the bride's fertility. In contrast, the origin of the term *bridecake* is less sexist. The *bride* of *bridecake* simply developed from an ancient Germanic source that meant *woman getting married*. More interesting, perhaps, is that *bridal*—the adjective of *bride*—originated as an Old English compound of *bride* and *ealu*, meaning *ale*; a *bridal*, therefore, was originally a beer-drinking party held in honour of the bride. A more sober origin belongs to the *wedding* of *wedding cake*: it derives from an ancient Germanic source that meant *pledge*, a source that also gave rise to the words *wager* and *engage*. See also *infare cake*.

well-hung meat

When the term *well-hung* first appeared in English, it was applied to people with large, pendulous organs—men with big ears, for example. By the late nineteenth century, however, *well-hung* came to be applied to another kind of meat, that which is slaughtered and then hung for a time in a cool, dry room to improve its flavour. Today, a beef carcass is well-hung after being suspended for about five days at a temperature of about 2° Celsius. Formerly, however, meat was hung far longer, as a *haut-goût* flavour was once in vogue: in the eighteenth century, the famous gastronome Jean-Anthelme Brillat-Savarin recommended that a pheasant be hung—unplucked—until the meat of its breast turned green, or until its flesh was so near to falling off that the bird had to be tied together before being placed on a roasting-spit. To modern tastes, such meat would be over-hung.

Welsh rabbit

Welsh rabbit contains no rabbit and is not Welsh in origin; instead, it is a dish of melted cheese poured over toast, invented by the British and given its name to mock the Welsh, who were supposedly so gullible that they would accept such a dish as real rabbit. The dish was first referred to in the early eighteenth century, but within sixty years the humorous impulse behind its name had been largely forgotten; accordingly, the absurdity of referring to cheese toast as *rabbit* was accounted for by the suggestion that the name was actually *Welsh rare-bit*, as if it were a *rare bit* of food. This well-intentioned explanation caught on, promoted, no doubt, by the Welsh themselves and by restaurateurs who feared that a customer might order Welsh rabbit and actually expect to receive a rabbit. Other dishes, less well-known, have also acquired names intended to mock the inhabitants of some country or city. *Glasgow capon*, for instance, is the name of a dish made from herring, not poultry, which appeared at the beginning of the eighteenth century. At the end of that century, *German duck* appeared, the name of a sheep's head boiled with onions. Most recently, probably in the nineteenth century, *Cape Cod turkey* became the name of a baked codfish.

whet

A thousand years ago, you did not say your kitchen knives needed to be *sharpened*: you said they needed to be *whetted*. In fact, the word *sharpen* was not used to describe the act of giving a knife a better cutting edge until the sixteenth century. Once established, however, the word *sharpen* gradually overtook *whet*, so that nowadays *whet* is commonly used in only two places: in *whetstone*, the name of a fine-grained stone used to sharpen blades, and in *whet your appetite*, a phrase used since at least the sixteenth century to mean *to sharpen or stimulate your desire for food.* The familiarity of the expression *whet your appetite* has also beguiled many writers into wrongly using the word *whet* in the expression *whet your whistle*, meaning *to take a drink.* The original and more sensible form of this expression is *wet your whistle*, an idiom dating back to the fourteenth century (even Chaucer used it in *The Canterbury Tales*). The mistaken substitution of *whet your whistle* for *wet your whistle* was common throughout the seventeenth and eighteenth century but is less frequent now for the simple reason that *whet* has become a far less familiar word.

whisk

Cats have whiskers so they can gauge the size of hole they are tempted to slip through; chefs have whisks so that they can quickly beat an egg into a homogenous liquid. Both these tools take their name from a Germanic source meaning *twig*, because both whisks and whiskers resemble a small, pliable branch. Whisks, of course, are also used to sweep refuse from a table or counter, and thus in the early seventeenth century *whisk* became the name of a card game, so called because the discarded cards were "whisked away" after the hand was over; fifty years later, in the late seventeenth century, the name was corrupted to *whist*, which it has remained ever since. Another unlikely relative of *whisk* is *verge*, as in "I was on the verge of leaving." This *verge* derives from the Latin *virga*, a word that developed from the same Indo-European source as *whisk* and that also meant *twig*. When it first appeared in English in the early fifteenth century, *virga*— or rather *verge*—was used to mean *penis*, but by the end of the fifteenth century it was also being used as the name of an official staff brandished in public by the Lord High Steward (the propriety of bestowing a word originally meaning *twig* on either of these mighty sceptres is debatable). Eventually, this official staff—the verge—came to stand for the area of land under the authority of the Lord High Steward. A person travelling out of that area would be "on the verge" when she got to the border, and as a result *on the verge* came to mean *on the edge*.

white baker

In an early example of a trade guild trying to make its work seem more complex than it really is, bakers in thirteenth-century England divided themselves into The Company of White Bakers and The Company of Brown Bakers, the former devoted to the production of white bread, the latter to brown.

white meat

See *dark meat*.

wiener

See *hot dog*.

wiener schnitzel

See *schnitzel*.

windfall

Centuries ago, and probably still in some rural areas, the day after a storm was pie-day, the day on which all the apples and pears that had been blown down by the wind were gathered and turned into pies, pastries, and jams. Because it was the wind that sent them tumbling to earth, these apple and pears were called *windfall*, a word that eventually came to mean *unexpected blessing* because the fallen fruit, though slightly bruised, did not have to be painstakingly plucked from branches twenty feet in the air.

wine

The ancient Romans called fermented grape juice *vinum*, the source not only of the English *wine*—first recorded in the ninth century—but also of the German *wein*, the Dutch *wijn*, the French, Swedish, and Danish *vin*, the Italian, Spanish, and Russian *vino*, and even the Welsh *gwin*. The Latin word for *wine*—*vinum*—also gave rise to *vinea*, the Roman name for a vineyard; French adopted this word as *vigne* and used it to mean *trailing plant*, which is the sense it retained when it entered English as *vine* in the fourteenth century. The French *vigne* gave rise to another important word: *vignette*, a book illustration surrounded by a border of twisting vine; English borrowed this word in the mid eighteenth century, first as the name of an ornamental illustration, and later as the name of a written sketch of an interesting event. Another word arose from the practice of allowing wine to undergo a second fermentation until it became what the French called *vin egre*, meaning *sour wine*. The French *vin egre* became, of course, the English *vinegar*, first recorded in the fourteenth century. *Vinaigrette*, literally meaning *little vinegar*, appeared in English in the late seventeenth century but referred not to a salad dressing but to a small two-wheeled carriage similar to the carts once pulled through the streets of Paris by vinegar merchants. It was not until the late nineteenth century that *vinaigrette* acquired its current culinary sense. Incidentally, the *egre* part of the French *vin egre*—the part that means *sour*—derives from the Latin *acer*, meaning *sharp*, which is also the source of *eager*, meaning *to have a sharp or keen desire*.

winkle

The winkle is a small, edible snail, one usually poached and then eaten with bread and butter. Its name, first recorded in the mid sixteenth century, is short for *periwinkle*, which dates back another fifty years to the early sixteenth century. *Periwinkle* in turn derives from the Old English *pinewincle*, meaning *shellfish*, formed by combining the Latin *pina*, the name of a species of mussel, with the Old English *wincle*, meaning *winch*; the name was inspired by the resemblance of the snail's spiralling shell to a winch, a large spool used to reel in rope or chain. Also related to the Old English *wincle* is the word *wink*, the connection being that when you wink, your eyelid "curves" over your eye like an arc in a spiral. *Periwinkle*, incidentally, is also the name of a trailing plant better known as *myrtle*; this *periwinkle*, however, probably derives its name from the Latin *per vincire*, meaning *to bind thoroughly*, a name prompted by the plant's ability to extend itself over a large area and stubbornly resist removal.

wishbone

By the early seventeenth century, the archery and arm-wrestling competitions that once followed medieval feasts had evolved into another sort of mighty contest: the custom of boldly plunging one's ruffled arm into the chicken carcase, skilfully extricating—like Arthur pulling Excalibur from the stone—the furcula of the bird, and blithely challenging a fellow dinner guest to tug till it broke in two. Eventually it was noticed that this sport made poor drama—a tiny snap followed by each competitor examining his splinter of bone—and so mystery was added: the victor would be granted a wish so long as he never revealed it. The *u*-shaped bone at the centre of these contests was not, however, originally called a *wishbone*: it was called a *merry thought*, a gentle reminder that the contestants should use the power of the bone to wish for something good, not evil. In the mid nineteenth century, two hundred and fifty years after the name *merry thought* appeared, the synonym *wishbone* arose, as did the anatomical term, *furcula*. Of these three names, *furcula* is the most visually accurate as it derives from the Latin *furca*, meaning *fork*. *Wish* and *bone* derive from two Indo-European words meaning, not surprisingly, *wish* and *bone*. *Merry* and *thought* are more interesting: the Indo-European source of *merry* was a word meaning *short*, the idea being that a merry occasion made the time seem short; even more surprising is that the Indo-European source of *thought* was also the source of *thanks*—when you thank your hosts, you are literally giving them your thoughts. See also *fork*.

wog

See *voip*.

wok

The wok, a Chinese cooking utensil shaped like a huge contact lens, was first referred to in English in 1952, became a culinary craze in the late 1970s, and was relegated in the mid 1980s (by most people) to the top shelf of the cupboard along with the fondue pot, another victim of its own success. *Wok* derives from a Cantonese word meaning *pan*.

won ton

In Cantonese, *won ton* means *dumpling*, which is exactly what a won ton is, whether it is served in soup or as part of a side dish. In English, won tons were first referred to by name in the early 1930s.

Worcestershire sauce

Worcestershire sauce takes its name from the English county—or shire—of Worcestershire, the home of the condiment's inventor, Sir Marcus Sandys. With the assistance of the English grocers, Lea and Perrins, Sandys began selling his sauce in 1838, which by the 1860s had also come to be known as *Worcester sauce*, Worcester being the town that gave the county of Worcestershire its name. The town of Worcester derives its name from a compound formed from the Celtic *weogoran*, meaning *dwellers near the winding river*, and the Old English *ceaster*, meaning *Roman camp*, which in turn derives from the Latin *castra*, meaning *camp*. Accordingly, if *Worcestershire sauce* seems like a mouthful, be grateful that you do not have to ask your host to pass you *the-county-of-the-Roman-camp-near-the-dwellers-by-the-winding-river sauce*.

wormwood

See *vermouth*.

wow-wow

See *couscous*.

xanthan

Xanthan is a gummy substance produced by a bacterium that takes its full scientific name—*xanthomonas*, Greek for *yellow one*—from the colour of the mould it produces. Xanthan has two uses: in the food industry it is used to stabilize emulsions—that is, it stops certain beverages or ready-made sauces from separating into a thick part that sinks to the bottom and a thin part that rises to the top; in the oil-well industry it is used as a lubricant in drilling-muds—that is, it makes the sludge surrounding a drill bit more slippery, so that the bit turns more easily as it chews through the earth. Xanthan was first commercially produced in the 1960s.

xenia

Xenia, in ancient Greece and Rome, were table delicacies graciously presented to a tired stranger upon his or her arrival in the host's home. The word derives from the Greek word *xenos*, meaning *stranger*. In the Middle Ages, the custom of the xenia was co-opted by royalty, who turned it from a free act of kindness to a compulsory tribute that subjects bestowed on their prince when he travelled through their land.

xyster

Not wanting to waste any of a chicken or turkey, many cooks will scrape and pluck the remaining pieces of meat from a carcass before they throw the bones into the soup pot or trash can. Most often, the implement used to cut these scraps of meat from the bone is a simple kitchen knife, but an instrument specifically designed for this purpose also exists. It is called a *xyster*, a word that derives from a Greek source meaning *to scrape*. When the word first appeared in English in the late seventeenth century, it was used not in a culinary context, but in a surgical one.

yaffle

See *slurp*.

yakitori

See *sushi*.

yam

Although you might think that you ate yam with your turkey
last Thanksgiving, the odds are that you did not; instead, you
probably had sweet potato, a tuber that is often incorrectly
referred to as *yam*. In fact, despite resembling each other in size,
shape, and taste, the sweet potato and the yam are not related as
plants and are distinct in origin: the sweet potato, which has long
been cultivated and sold in North America, is indigenous to South
America, while the yam, which is rarely sold in North America,
is indigenous to Africa. The confusion of sweet potatoes and yams
dates back to the mid-seventeenth century when slaves taken from
West Africa to the United States transferred a name familiar to
them—*yam*—to the American sweet potato. The word *yam* had,
however, been in use in English before this time as a name for
the true, African tuber. This "proper" use of *yam* dates back to
the end of the sixteenth century, when English borrowed the
Spanish name for the African tuber—*igname*—and changed the

spelling and pronunciation to *yam*. The Spanish, in turn, had derived their word *igname* from one of several West African names for the tuber: perhaps the Hausa *nama*, which not only denoted the yam but also meant *flesh*, or the Swahili *nyama*, also meaning *meat*, or the Fulah *nyama*, also meaning *to eat*—all these West African words ultimately derive from the same source. The fact that *yam* derives from West African words meaning *flesh*, *meat*, and *to eat* suggests what an important food yams must have been in these cultures. Incidentally, the scientific name of the yam is *Dioscorea Batatas*, noteworthy because it is the only major vegetable to take its scientific name from a real person: Pedanius Dioscorides, a Greek physician who is considered to have founded the science of botany nearly two thousand years ago. See also *potato*.

yex

See *hiccup*.

yogurt

In the early part of the seventeenth century, an English travel writer reported that the people in Turkey were fond of a dish of sour milk called *yoghurd*. In the succeeding centuries, *yoghurd* was followed by many other attempts to render the original Turkish word into English, including *yaghourt*, *yooghort*, and *yohourth*. The matter has still not been settled, as *yogurt* is sometimes still challenged by *yoghurt* (the latter, in fact, is the better rendering of the Turkish source). The bacterium responsible for turning milk into yogurt is called *streptococcus thermophilus*, literally meaning *twisted-berry heat-lover*; biologists bestowed this name upon the berry-shaped bacteria because they need high temperatures to thrive and because they arrange themselves in twisted chains.

zabaglione

English has two names for the foamy dessert made by whisking together egg yolks, Marsala wine, and sugar: *zabaglione* and *sabayon*, both deriving from the same source but entering English via different routes. The common source of the words is probably the Latin *sabaia*, the name of a drink that originated along the eastern coast of the Adriatic Sea. In Italian, *sabaia* became *zabaglione*, the *ione* ending of the Italian word being an augmentative suffix that causes the word to mean *big sabaia*; English adopted this name of the dessert at the end of the nineteenth century. French, however, also adopted this Italian name, changing it to *sabayon* in the process; in the early twentieth century, English adopted this French name as well, and the two terms—*sabayon* and *zabaglione*—have existed side by side ever since.

zarf

When you visit an insurance agency, you don't bring a coffee mug with you, and your smiling insurance agents hardly want your lips on one of their pristine mugs, so you are usually served coffee in a paper cup placed in a little plastic holder with a handle. That plastic holder is called a *zarf*, an Arabic word meaning *sheath* and denoting a highly ornamented, metal vessel that holds—like its plastic counterpart—a smaller, plainer, hotter vessel. When the word *zarf* was adopted by English in the early nineteenth century, it referred only to this elaborate, Middle Eastern cup-holder; it was not until the 1970s that the term was adopted by manufacturers of plastic office products.

zucchini

What North Americans call a *zucchini*, the British call a *courgette*. Although they derive from different languages, these two words are alike in so far as they are both diminutives of words meaning *gourd*: the Italian *zucco* and the French *courge*. *Zucchini*, however, is not only a diminutive but also a plural form: accordingly, if you are purchasing just one of these vegetables you should—in order to be precise, pedantic, and puzzling all at once—refer to it as a *zucchino*. The words *zucchini* and *courgette* appeared in English in the late 1920s when the vegetable was introduced to British and North American markets.

zuppa inglese

Zuppa inglese literally means *English soup*, but this Italian dish is actually a rich dessert made by soaking a sponge cake in cherry brandy, filling it with custard, covering it with Italian meringue, and then browning it in an oven. The dish was invented in the nineteenth century by Italian ice-cream makers who called it *zuppa* because the sponge cake sat in a "soup" of brandy and custard, and *inglese* because they wanted to associate it with the English puddings fashionable across Europe at the time. Despite this indirect connection with the English, the name of the dessert did not appear in English until the early 1970s.